TOTAL
MATERIALS MANAGEMENT
The Frontier for
Maximizing Profit
in the 1990s

TOTAL
MATERIALS MANAGEMENT
The Frontier for
Maximizing Profit
in the 1990s

Eugene L. Magad
William Rainey Harper College

John M. Amos
Center for Applied Engineering
University of Missouri-Rolla

COMPETITIVE
Manufacturing
S E R I E S

VNR VAN NOSTRAND REINHOLD
New York

Printed in the United States of America

Van Nostrand Reinhold
115 Fifth Avenue
New York, New York 10003

Chapman & Hall
2-6 Boundary Row
London SE1 8HN, England

Thomas Nelson Australia
102 Dodds Street
South Melbourne, Victoria 3205, Australia

Nelson Canada
1120 Birchmount Road
Scarborough, Ontario M1K 5G4, Canada

16 15 14 13 12 11 10 9 8 7 6 5 4 3 2

Library of Congress Cataloging-in-Publication Data
Magad, Eugene L.
  Total materials management / Eugene L. Magad, John M. Amos.
     p. cm.
  Bibliography: p.
  Includes index.
  ISBN 0-442-20840-5
  1. Materials management.   I. Amos, John M.   II. Title.
TS 161M34 1989
  658.7—dc19   88-29161

—VNR COMPETITIVE MANUFACTURING SERIES—

Product and Process Design

PRACTICAL EXPERIMENT DESIGN by William J. Diamond
VALUE ANALYSIS IN DESIGN by Theodore C. Fowler
A PRIMER ON THE TAGUCHI METHOD by Ranjit Roy
MANAGING NEW-PRODUCT DEVELOPMENT by Geoff Vincent
ART AND SCIENCE OF INVENTING by Gilbert Kivenson
RELIABILITY ENGINEERING IN SYSTEMS DESIGN AND OPERATION by Balbir S. Dhillon
RELIABILITY AND MAINTAINABILITY MANAGEMENT by Balbir S. Dhillon and Hans Reiche
APPLIED RELIABILITY by Paul A. Tobias and David C. Trindad

Manufacturing (hard)

INDUSTRIAL ROBOT HANDBOOK: CASE HISTORIES OF EFFECTIVE ROBOT USE IN 70 INDUSTRIES by Richard K. Miller
ROBOTIC TECHNOLOGY: PRINCIPLES AND PRACTICE by Werner G. Holzbock
MACHINE VISION by Nello Zuech and Richard K. Miller
DESIGN OF AUTOMATIC MACHINERY by Kendrick W. Lentz, Jr.
TRANSDUCERS FOR AUTOMATION by Michael Hordeski
MICROPROCESSORS IN INDUSTRY by Michael Hordeski
DISTRIBUTED CONTROL SYSTEMS by Michael P. Lukas
BULK MATERIALS HANDLING HANDBOOK by Jacob Fruchtbaum
MICROCOMPUTER SOFTWARE FOR MECHANICAL ENGINEERS by Howard Falk

Manufacturing (soft)

WORKING TOWARDS JUST-IN-TIME by Anthony Dear
GROUP TECHNOLOGY: FOUNDATION FOR COMPETITIVE MANUFAC-TURING by Charles S. Snead
FROM IDEA TO PROFIT: MANAGING ADVANCED MANUFACTURING TECHNOLOGY by Jule A. Miller
COMPETITIVE MANUFACTURING by Stanley Miller
STRATEGIC PLANNING FOR THE INDUSTRIAL ENGINEERING FUNCTION by Jack Byrd and L. Ted Moore

SUCCESSFUL COST REDUCTION PROGRAMS FOR ENGINEERS AND MANAGERS by E. A. Criner

MATERIAL REQUIREMENTS OF MANUFACTURING by Donald P. Smolik

PRODUCTS LIABILITY by Warren Freedman

LABORATORY MANAGEMENT: PRINCIPLES & PRACTICE by Homer Black, Ronald Hart, Orrin Peterson

Materials Management

TOTAL MATERIALS MANAGEMENT: THE FRONTIER FOR MAXIMIZING PROFIT IN THE 1990s by Eugene L. Magad and John Amos

MATERIALS HANDLING: PRINCIPLES and PRACTICE by Theodore H. Allegri, Sr.

PRACTICAL STOCK AND INVENTORY TECHNIQUES THAT CUT COSTS AND IMPROVE PROFITS by C. Louis Hohenstein

Preface

Materials management has become an important activity in both manufacturing and service organizations. Rapid changes in the industrial environment, such as the introduction of automation and Just-In-Time, and demands for increased productivity and quality have increased the need for all personnel to be concerned with total control of materials. Clearly this trend will continue, and materials management will play an increasingly vital role in organizational success, especially for operations that are becoming automated. Materials management will be more critical in many service organizations where the materials group has received little attention in the past.

This book covers the basic materials management function and provides valuable insights into various other major functions related to it. We believe that each of these—manufacturing, marketing, finance, quality assurance, and engineering—is vitally involved in materials management, and any coverage of the subject that excludes these functions offers too narrow a perspective.

With increasing demand for materials managers, human resource requirements will be satisfied by individuals trained within the discipline and by personnel who have worked in other fields. The dimensions of materials management have grown so rapidly that many practicing managers are not aware that they are fulfilling material management functions. It is important that all individuals have the basic knowledge required to perform their roles in these organizations.

This book was written primarily for use in an advanced undergraduate college course or a graduate course, and for use by companies in internal development programs. We intend it also for individuals who read independently to improve their effectiveness in various areas of materials management.

The book deals largely with concepts, but includes many examples from various industries to clarify the concepts. Individuals already involved in materials management will discover that they are using some of these ideas intuitively. This book offers new systematic ways of looking at both familiar and unfamiliar concepts, relating them to other major functions. Our purpose has been to integrate these ideas into a body of knowledge, to help the reader gain insight and confidence, which are essential for anyone who wishes to become an effective materials manager.

The book is divided into four parts. Part I deals with the needs and activities of materials management in the organization and its relationship to other managerial functions. Part II discusses matters relating to the planning and controlling of materials management. The reader is introduced to various techniques of long-range planning, inventory control, production control, materials requirement planning, and distribution requirements planning. Part III discusses subfunctions closely related to materials procurement, movement, physical control, and distribution. Part IV covers some of the control and financial considerations future materials managers will experience in effectively implementing a total materials management program.

The authors are indebted to countless individuals who have helped us along our way. We are grateful to students who have helped by testing the product and to colleagues in our respective departments. Special appreciation is expressed to our colleagues in industry who have provided the motivation for our writing the book and have made many valuable comments and suggestions. Finally, we express our heartfelt thanks to our wives Janet Magad and Ruth Amos for their continued support and encouragement.

Eugene L. Magad
John M. Amos

Contents

Part 1

MATERIALS MANAGEMENT CONCEPT AND ORGANIZATION

1
Introduction to Total Materials Management

Materials management is an organizational philosophy that has evolved through application of the systems approach to management, an approach that provides for integration of all management functions.[1] A primary objective of this philosophy is to coordinate all business activities that are part of the materials cycle, from supplier through company operations and on to the customer. Materials management is an umbrella that integrates all the critical materials-related subfunctions, and, as such, is a major company function, among such others as engineering, finance, and manufacturing. (See Figure 1-1.)

According to Colton and Rohrs, materials management is "a wide spectrum of varied activities and is totally committed to providing a smooth flow from suppliers to production to finished goods inventory to customers."[2] Figure 1-2 represents a typical flow of materials from supplier to customer.

Total materials management can be defined as an organizational concept that fosters a total systems approach to plan, acquire, store, move, and control materials, in order to optimize all company resources and provide customer service consistent with company policy. The materials referred to in this definition are all materials that a company may control, including raw materials, supplies, work-in-process, and finished goods. Company resources include materials, people, money, and facilities.

HISTORY AND EVOLUTION OF MATERIALS MANAGEMENT

Since prehistoric times humans have been concerned with obtaining, moving, and controlling materials. Materials management is the result of a natural evolution; it did not develop quickly but grew as an obvious business solution to the need to achieve optimum effectiveness in the various materials functions.

Figure 1-1. Major company functions cooperating to achieve common objectives.

Early History

Frederick Winslow Taylor is known as the father of scientific management. Scientific management impacted the lower level of an organization's hierarchy—the shop floor, the foreman, the superintendent, and lower management.[3] During the late 1800s, Taylor made major contributions in time study, job design, personnel selection, and training. He recognized the need for functional specialists. Modern managers also recognize the need for functional specialists, such as buyers, inventory analysts, and master schedulers.

The term materials management, as well as the organizational philoso-

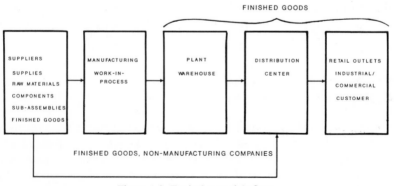

Figure 1-2. Typical materials flow.

phy, came into use after World War II. Beyond an enormously increased production capacity, the military requirements of the war demanded a means to reduce the time required to produce needed products. Through the 1950s and 1960s, fluctuations in national and international market requirements and economic conditions highlighted the need for total control of materials.

Total materials management began to spread as an organizational concept during the 1950s and 1960s, but not until the 1970s did U.S. industries come to increasingly adopt this organizational structure. The primary reason for this movement was a need to control costs and operations. During the 1970s, businesses were confronted with still other problems, among them scarcity of money, price controls, ecological concerns, energy shortages, and rapid increases in energy costs. There was a need to return to centralized control of the overall functional organization. Subfunctions such as purchasing, inventory control, production control, materials handling, and physical distribution might report to numerous executives within an organization. This fragmented organization of materials activities gave rise to many conflicts.

Consider a case in which the purchasing department is part of the controller or office manager's group. Here, the purchasing department typically will strive for large cost savings by buying materials at the lowest possible price. This may lead to increased inventory. Although procurement of materials at the lowest price might appear commendable, the net result could be increased costs. A company does not gain if it saves $1.00 per unit, but spends an additional $2.00 per unit on other expenses such as capital, transportation, storage, handling, and rework. In this case, the purchasing department is considered a "hero"—even though the company incurs increased costs. In an integrated materials management organization, purchasing professionals now speak in terms of total company costs, not just purchase price.

Similarly, the inventory control department may report to an operations executive. A prime objective of operations management is output; the operations executive is concerned with possible materials shortages that can result in downtime and loss of productivity. In these circumstances, there is an impetus to ensure an ample inventory. The operations executive will pressure the inventory control supervisor to maintain high inventory. The inventory control supervisor then has to forgo optimum inventory levels and resultant company benefits.

A similar situation confronts the physical distribution supervisor who reports to a marketing executive. Marketing executives are concerned with sales. To ensure customer satisfaction and high company sales, they want the physical distribution supervisor to maintain high levels of finished goods inventories.

These illustrations represent just a few of the internal organizational conflicts that have led many companies to a total materials management structure. The growing demand is illustrated by the classified advertisements in major newspapers (Figures 1-3 and 1-4).

Figure 1-3. Typical ads for managers of various materials management subfunctions.

Figure 1-4. Typical ads for materials managers.

Total Materials Management Concept

Neither the term materials management nor the concept of a totally integrated materials organization has been accepted by all businesses throughout the world. Some companies use other names, such as "physical distribution" or "logistics," for similar organizations. Others have embraced the title but not the full organizational philosophy. Despite numerous names however, the trend in recent years has been for companies to adopt the materials management title.

Business costs attributable to materials management are a significant portion of the total cost of goods and services. Increasingly, companies are recognizing the need to implement this type of organization to maximize profits, improve customer service, establish needed controls, and reduce costs. Such diverse organizations as hospitals, the military, manufacturers, railroads, food distributors, newspapers, universities, and insurance companies are creating materials management organizations.

Terminology

As indicated earlier, different terms are used to describe the materials function:

Physical Distribution. This term often refers to a phase of marketing management. Physical distribution controls the flow of finished goods from company to customer. In recent years this definition has been broadened to include movement of materials into the company.

Physical distribution may include incoming and outgoing traffic and transportation, order picking, materials handling, inventory control, warehousing, customer service, product packaging, and shipping—many which are identical to materials management functions. When not included in a materials organization, physical distribution is part of marketing, where it is concerned primarily with control and movement of finished products.

Logistics. Sometimes referred to as business logistics or logistics management, the logistics function originated in military organizations. Originally it included all activities required to provide equipment and supplies to widespread military operations during times of war and peace. Logistics originated in about 1670, when a new staff structure was proposed for the French army. The position of "Marechal General des Logis" was responsible for supply, transportation, selecting camps, and adjusting marches.[4]

The organizational concept of logistics has broadened beyond the scope of military operations in both the United States and Europe. Modern logistics has been defined as the movement of material or products from source to production, and from production to the market.[5]

The Council of Logistics Management (formerly The National Council of Physical Distribution Management) defines logistics as:

The process of planning, implementing, and controlling the efficient, cost effective flow and storage of raw materials, in-process inventory, finished goods, and related information from point of origin to point of consumption for the purpose of conforming to customer requirements.[6]

Misuse of Terms. Some companies have applied the title of materials management to a department or an individual without relating the term to a totally integrated systems function. They may consider it an up-to-date term and use it to be like other companies. Another problem relates to the term itself. In most companies, if an executive were asked if the company had a materials management organization, the answer probably would be yes. Every company has groups that "manage materials," but the company may not have what has come to be known as a total materials management group.

Sometimes supervisors of individual groups such as production control, purchasing, and transportation have convinced their companies to change their department titles to materials management without broadening their scope of responsibilities. These supervisors may intend to enlarge the scope of departmental activities, with the change in title being a first step toward accomplishing that goal.

The Changing Environment

The materials management evolution can be seen not only from the viewpoint of organization and systems; another consideration is the type of environment in which the group will function. Contemporary business and its environment are constantly changing, and the materials function must anticipate and react to change to maintain its effectiveness.

Factory and Distribution Center of the Future. Automation applications are increasing at a rapid pace in all industries. For years articles have been published on "the factory and distribution center of the future." Various groups have been active in developing equipment, software systems, facility designs, and so on, to turn such dreams into reality. Necessary ingredients of their success are the research and application efforts devoted to various technologies such as computer aided design (CAD), computer aided manufacturing (CAM), computer aided testing (CAT), robotics, material requirements planning (MRP), automated storage and retrieval systems (ASRS), and flexible manufacturing systems (FMS). However, a means to integrate all of these systems is needed.

Haphazard attempts to link stand-alone systems in different departments must be avoided. The factory or distribution center of the future will require a change in management style. Substantial savings will result if managers can increase their decision turnover, as they try to increase their inventory turnover. The speed and quality of communication must improve to correspond to the fast action of operations. As direct labor decreases, the need for mid-level professionals will increase. Various computer aided systems will make massive amounts of information available in easily digestible form with computer graphics and spread sheets. The real test will be for management to use the information, analyzing trends and understanding their implications.[7]

Achievement of a fully operational automated factory or distribution center with its large capital investment presents a series of challenges for materials management. Total materials management must eliminate downtime and preserve high capacity utilization. The materials group will require fully integrated software systems for all subfunction activities. Fewer personnel will be required, but individual members of the materials department will need a high degree of education and broad experience. Their responsibilities for company resources will increase greatly as their number decreases. The materials management team member will have to be very capable in order to meet the demands of increased automation.

Increasing Role of the Service Industries. The service sector in the United States is growing rapidly while manufacturing is decreasing. Consumer spending for services has greatly increased, with seven out of ten jobs now in service industries. Over the next few years, the service sector is expected to grow at a rate of 2.4 percent annually, compared to 2.1 percent in the manufacturing sector.[8]

Service industries include entertainment, finance, transportation, public utilities, hospitals, and educational institutions. They provide intangible functions for both business and consumer needs. Materials management responsibilities vary considerably in these industries. There is little concern for controlling raw material, work-in-process, and finished goods inventory in a movie studio as compared with a distribution or manufacturing company, but control of capital goods inventory is of the utmost importance. Scheduling (production control), purchasing, and materials handling are vital activities in a college. The total materials management function in service industry business often assumes a different organizational structure from the manufacturing type, including many nontraditional activities. A hospital example is illustrated in Chapter 2.

The materials group in a service company can profit from developments in the manufacturing and distribution industries. Material requirements planning (MRP), distribution requirements planning (DRP), cycle counting, and other techniques can be adapted. Materials management personnel should seek successful systems with application potential to increase productivity in service-oriented firms. For example, managers of a well-known New Orleans restaurant used MRP, ABC Analysis, and other materials management techniques to improve planning and control of labor and materials. They even were able to evaluate and update the restaurant's menu.[9]

Professional Societies

In the United States, Europe, and Japan, professional societies in the area of materials management are educating their members to new concepts and applications. Most U.S. professional societies concentrate on a particular portion or subfunction such as transportation, purchasing, production control, or inventory control; but in recent years there has been a trend for societies to broaden their interests. The expansion of technical activities has provided society members a valuable service. Listed below are some materials management professional societies that are active in the United States:

American Production and Inventory Control Society (A.P.I.C.S.)
American Society of Traffic and Logistics (A.S.T.L.)
Council of Logistics Management (C.L.M.)
Delta Nu Alpha (D.N.A.)
International Materials Management Society (I.M.M.S.)
National Association of Purchasing Management (N.A.P.M.)
Society of Logistics Engineers (S.L.E.)

MATERIALS MANAGEMENT SUBFUNCTIONS

Materials management depends upon the close cooperation and coordination of all its subfunctions. The International Material Management Society depicts this relationship as the planetary gear concept.[10] (See Figure 1-5.) The individual subfunctions are shown as gears, each of which must operate smoothly and with sufficient force to contribute to optimum operation of the drive element (materials management organization). If individual subfunctions fail or are ineffective, the effectiveness of the entire organization is reduced.

Dobler, Lee, and Burt have described materials management as three basic functions: planning and control, purchasing, and physical distribution. The planning and control functions include inventory control, production control, and scheduling. Purchasing functions consist of buying, subcontracting, value analysis, and expediting. Distribution functions encompass receiving, packaging, shipping, transportation, and warehousing.[11]

The following paragraphs discuss groups that may be included in a materials organization.

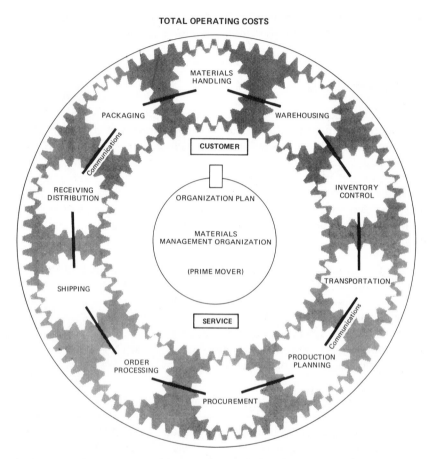

Figure 1-5. Planetary gear concept. (Source: *Materials Handling & Management Manual,* published by the Toronto chapter of the International Material Management Society.)

Planning

Short- and long-term planning are vital to every company. The primary objective is to maximize the use of company resources and provide for future customer demand. Major activities include

1. Translating the marketing department's sales forecast into long-term production requirements for periods that generally range from one to ten years.
2. Projecting requirements for materials, manpower, money, and facilities.

3. Providing basic control information for planning company budgets, personnel, cash flow, inventory, equipment, and so forth.
4. Performing strategic planning for materials operations to provide rational solutions for future "what if" questions.

Inventory Control

Inventory control includes activities and techniques required to maintain materials at desired levels. These materials generally include raw materials, work-in-process, and finished products. Major activities include

1. Determining how much material will be required to satisfy company operational demands.
2. Maintaining detailed records of all materials available, ordered, and consumed.
3. Determining optimum order quantities; issuing requisitions.
4. Providing appropriate reports to aid in decision making with regard to inventories.

Production Control

Production control is directing or regulating the movement of materials through the entire manufacturing cycle, from raw material through finished product. Major activities include:

1. Utilizing long-term plans and sales forecasts to develop short-term requirements.
2. Preparing schedules for producing parts, subassemblies, and products; considering manufacturing lead times, material and part availability, special orders, spare part requirements, and performance capabilities.
3. Dispatching orders to various departments to fulfill production requirements, and maintaining good communication with operations regarding schedule variations.
4. Expediting production orders, when required, to ensure on-time schedule completions, and preparing timely reports to evaluate the efficiency of production and the status of various orders.

Purchasing

Purchasing is responsible for procurement of materials from outside suppliers, in accordance with purchase requisition requirements. Major activities include:

1. Selecting acceptable suppliers, while negotiating to secure the lowest total acquisition costs.
2. Issuing purchase orders and expediting on-time receipt of materials, where required.
3. Acting as liaison between company departments and suppliers to solve problems involved with purchased materials.
4. Maintaining an ongoing knowledge of current market conditions, new materials, new processes, and other procurement factors that can affect company operations and costs.

Receiving and Stores

Receiving and stores is responsible for activities related to receiving, storing, handling, issuing, and controlling materials. Major activities include:

1. Receiving materials, which includes verification that the order was made and that the quantity received is correct, and preparation of a receiving report.
2. Storing received and inspected materials in accordance with efficient operating procedures that optimize use of space, equipment, personnel, and control of locations.
3. Issuing materials with authorized requisitions and accepting returned materials.
4. Maintaining control of physical counts to assure materials availability and performing periodic and annual physical inventories.

Materials Handling

Materials handling involves both design and physical movement. It is the function of developing and implementing appropriate manual, mechanized, and automated systems to provide movement of materials throughout the company. Major activities include:

1. Analyzing company operations to determine the need for improved materials handling.
2. Designing and justifying new materials handling systems that will provide increased production capacity, improved materials flow, reduced costs, improved working conditions, and reduced waste.
3. Providing user-oriented materials handling systems.
4. Transporting materials to and from storage areas and the point where they will be used.

Physical Distribution

Physical distribution encompasses all the operations involved in the movement and flow of finished products, from the time they are received to the time they are shipped to the customer. Major activities include:

1. Receiving finished goods from manufacturing departments or outside suppliers, verifying quantity, and identifying and moving materials to the warehouse. The warehouse could adjoin a manufacturing facility or be a separate building (distribution center).
2. Storing finished products in accordance with efficient warehousing procedures.
3. Performing order assembly/picking and packaging while using techniques that provide for high productivity, elimination of errors, and minimum damage.
4. Determining and arranging for the most economical method to transport incoming and outgoing materials and products.
5. Loading trucks, freight cars, and so on, for shipment to customers.

ROLE OF THE COMPUTER IN MATERIALS MANAGEMENT

The computer links all materials subfunctions and relates their activities to other company functions. The marriage between materials management and the computer began in the 1950s, when the computer was used primarily by large companies. Computer applications grew during the 1960s but were never fully implemented then for lack of adequate data processing facilities. In the 1970s materials groups in both large and small companies utilized the computer, as a result of progress in the development of large amounts of memory, terminals, data links, and software packages.

Computers provide materials personnel with a means to cope with information in an orderly and systematic manner. Data collection coupled with high-speed transmission allows information to flow speedily from points of origin, permitting the discovery and interpretation of significant trends or potential problems in the formative stage. The significant amounts of data needed to compile reports now can be collected, analyzed, and printed by a computer in minutes, instead of days or weeks. Computers have become a significant tool for providing fast, accurate decision-making information.

Matching the rapid development of computer equipment (hardware), data processing groups have provided an equally essential capability, directing the hardware through computer programs (software). The development of software is an important aspect of materials management. The types of computer programs available range from simple ones for performing the calculations of adding and subtracting, for maintaining inventory counts, to advanced analytical programs that use mathematical modeling to perform experimental analysis of alternative plans.

Many companies have benefited from successful computer applications. Those that do not have internal computer expertise have access to computer service firms. Terminals at the user location can feed data to and receive data from the computer service firm's equipment.

Computerized Purchasing

Information critical to purchasing activities can be computerized, so that it is available at the touch of a finger. This up-to-date information can include part/product name, supplier name, supplier history, projected delivery dates, price quotations, historical usage, and open orders. Computers can be used for follow-up, generating lists of items that require expediting and even letters to remind suppliers of promised delivery dates. Companies with multifacility operations can use the computer as a tool to review prices for comparable items and then advise individual facilities of price discrepancies. Computers can print purchase orders and acknowledgment cards for the supplier as well as copies of purchase orders for internal use. A scorecard indicating how effectively the purchasing department is operating also can be generated by computer. All these activities result in cost savings and better control of purchasing operations.

Automated Warehouse

Automated warehouses have helped to lower labor costs and reduce location errors. The fully automated warehouse places materials into storage and withdraws them on computer command. The computer maintains all pertinent information about the materials, such as part/product number, location, and quantity.

Computerized Production and Inventory Control

Production and inventory control devote a disproportionate amount of time to "fire fighting" and expediting. Any unexpected event, such as a machine breakdown or an absence of required parts/products, triggers a chain reaction. Emergency adjustments of schedule are made, often by individuals lacking necessary information. A compounding of problems results, which eventually causes an imbalance of facility capacity, waste of materials, and labor/equipment downtime. Through programs such as material requirements planning (MRP), the computer provides production and inventory control with a tool to minimize confusion. Note the word "minimize"; even with a computer system, problems still can occur. Computer systems allow for easy input of changes. The software program makes adjustments according to the many variables involved and produces revised schedules for immediate implementation. Anyone who has seen everyone from the company president on down expediting a particular order can appreciate the immediate benefits of computerized production and inventory control.

Application to Physical Distribution

From customer order processing to the point of delivery of material to the customer, computers have improved overall operations time and costs. Computer terminals have been used to process customer order information received by mail and/or telephone. In telephone contacts, the customer can be informed promptly of pertinent information such as product availability and current costs simply by touching buttons on the terminal keyboard and reading information displayed on a cathode ray tube (CRT) terminal. The computer reduces delays in order processing and invoice preparation. Another area that benefits from the computer is order picking and processing. Computers may print order picking labels that are properly sequenced for minimum walking time by the picker. These same labels then can be read optically, with a materials handling system directed to transport the products to the proper location for order accumulation and packing. Transportation of incoming and outgoing materials also benefits from computer applications.

Companies sometimes experience difficulty in implementing computer programs. A principal problem is inaccurate data, such as canceled orders that are not properly recorded, or materials that have been rejected by inspection but are still shown as inventory. Such inaccuracies undermine the credibility of a system, and encourage individual users to ignore it. One implementation mistake is to eliminate a company's manual system as soon as a new computer system is installed. There always must be a debugging period to eliminate problems in the computer system. If the manual system has been terminated, any problems with the new computer system probably will lead to chaos. The manual system should be maintained in parallel with the debugging of the computer system, and should be terminated only after management is assured that it is no longer needed.

Another problem experienced in computerizing operations is making the false assumption that a standard software package can be readily purchased and applied. This can be a costly error because of improper program operations and confusion among personnel. Tailoring software to company needs prevents this problem.

BENEFITS OF TOTAL
MATERIALS MANAGEMENT

Dobler, Lee, and Burt have reported increased numbers of companies establishing materials management programs. They refer to a *Business Week* management section report on materials management progress. Adoption of the concept is said to be proceeding rapidly. Vice presidents for materials of large, well-managed industrial firms, including the Gillette Company, Champion International, Rockwell International, Scott Paper Company, GTE Sylvania, and Xerox, report meeting the challenges of similar materials problems.[12]

Incorporation of current management techniques within the materials management program can prove very effective. For example, quality circles (QC) have been successfully introduced in companies such as Eastern Airlines and Dover Corporation. The QC concept was originated by an American, Dr. W. Edward Deming, and was adapted in Japan following World War II. Recently it has been applied in the United States as well. A quality circle consists of a small group of people, in the same department, who do the same or similar work. Groups of eight to ten members, who volunteer for participation, meet regularly to analyze and develop solutions to problems. Dover Elevator provides several examples of QC accomplishments. Shipping accuracy was improved by eliminating errors and reshipments, which resulted in $20,000 per month savings. Damage-free handling improvements cut scrap and rework totaling $5,269 a year.[13]

Maximum Company Profits

Like other major company functions, materials management is responsible for maximizing company profits. A common expression in industry, borrowed from accountants, is "the bottom line."[14] The bottom line that all companies seek is an increase in profits. Because the materials group controls company resources, it has significant potential for increasing company profits by reducing costs.

Cost reduction can be achieved by the following means:

1. Decreasing parts shortages (resulting in more efficient use of labor, machines, and materials).
2. Reducing inventory levels through improved controls.
3. Lowering transportation costs as a result of using minimum-cost shipping methods.

4. Reducing materials obsolescence through greater control of inventory and timely processing of engineering change orders.

5. Lowering purchase prices and total acquisition costs through the use of quantity buying and other techniques.

Improved Customer Service

Customer service can be defined as a customer-oriented company philosophy that integrates and manages all elements of customer relations within a predetermined optimum cost–service mix. Good customer service is crucial to company growth. Many companies rank customer service second in importance only to product quality. A common saying is that "the customer is king."

It is important that total materials management provide upper management with information about trade-off considerations inherent in decision making. Figure 1-6 shows typical examples of such trade-offs. As a company increases customer service levels, it will have to forgo minimum inventory levels. Maintaining safety stock, to assure satisfying higher than normal product demand, will conflict with management's desire for minimum inventory. A company's desire for no lost sales or minimum backlog of orders will require a relaxation of its attempt to obtain high inventory turnover (one way to compute inventory turnover is to divide the annual cost of sales by the average inventory level[15]).

The materials management philosophy is customer-service-oriented. There must be close coordination of the various subfunctions, all of which relate to customer service. Poor customer service is a symptom of a poor

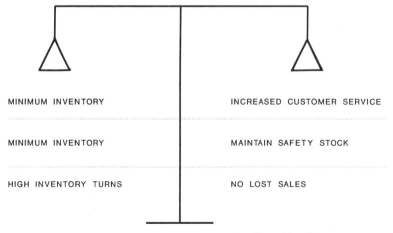

MINIMUM INVENTORY   INCREASED CUSTOMER SERVICE

MINIMUM INVENTORY   MAINTAIN SAFETY STOCK

HIGH INVENTORY TURNS   NO LOST SALES

Figure 1-6. Examples of business trade-off considerations.

materials organization. Factors pertinent to customer service in materials activities include:

1. Shortages of materials that can delay shipments.
2. Missed production dates due to poor scheduling.
3. Order processing errors.
4. Order assembly discrepancies.
5. Damage to products.
6. Incorrect shipments to customers.

Integration of Organization

A primary benefit of total materials management is the establishment of an integrated organization. All of the pertinent materials subfunctions are brought together under one umbrella. In many companies, these subfunctions are separate and often unequal. An umbrella organization tends to reduce conflict and encourage complementary groups to work together as a team. Figure 1-7 shows a typical fragmented group and how the same group would look as an integrated organization. Increased awareness and

FRAGMENTED MATERIALS ORGANIZATION:

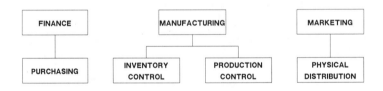

INTEGRATED MATERIALS ORGANIZATION:

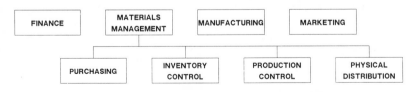

Figure 1-7. Fragmented materials organization and integrated materials organization.

improved communications are key benefits of this type of unified organization.

Leonard C. Cook, vice president materials management, Eaton Corporation, admits that materials management adds a layer of authority above subfunctions such as purchasing. He believes that it makes a buyer a more effective company team player and opens career opportunities. Purchasing managers are forced to consider other areas and broaden their perspective.[16]

The late President Harry Truman had a sign on his desk reading, "The buck stops here." He had final responsibility. Many hours of frustration have been spent in Monday morning meetings called to determine why something was not accomplished, or was not done on time. Note the cartoon treatment of an all too common situation (Figure 1-8).

Let us review a typical scenario in a company that has not consolidated all materials subfunctions under a single administrator. A meeting is called to determine why a customer's order was not shipped on Friday. The shipping supervisor denies responsibility, claiming that the order pickers did not pick the order on time. The finished goods warehouse supervisor says that it was not the order pickers' fault because production control did not produce the products on time. The production control supervisor places the blame on a shortage of parts. The meeting continues with each group indicating it was not at fault. After two or three hours of discussion, they all leave the meeting with a knotted stomach, secure in the feeling that it was not their fault. However, the fact remains that the customer did not receive the order on time! Meetings like this are being held in companies everywhere, all with fragmented materials management responsibilities. Buck-passing can be reduced through an integrated materials organization in which each subordinate supervisor assumes his or her proper share of

the small society   by Brickman

Figure 1-8. The small society, by Brickman. (Reprinted with special permission of King Features Syndicate, Inc.)

coordinated responsibility. Both management and the user department can look to one central individual for both answers and action.

Interaction of Individual Manager Objectives

Every manager is responsible for meeting the overall objectives of the company, but each manager recognizes that future success in the company is dependent upon the achievements of his or her own department. In a fragmented materials organization, individual supervisors concentrate on immediate objectives at the sacrifice of long-term goals; they fail to cooperate with other groups in order to achieve their own immediate objectives. Total materials management stimulates supervisors to accomplish individual departmental goals, while at the same time communicating and cooperating with other departments to achieve the short-term and long-term objectives of the entire company.

John J. Davin, vice president materials and facilities of GTE, discusses the problem of conflicting objectives as follows:

There is a natural tendency for functional departments — purchasing, production and inventory control, physical distribution — to look inward to accomplish their objectives. The purchasing manager prepares his budget, plans, and objectives each year and is held accountable for his accomplishments. Likewise, the inventory manager is expected to improve turns in order to make his profit contribution. Without coordination, these two managers may end up working against each other — one trying to bring materials into the plant on a volume basis, the other trying to prevent materials from accumulating ahead of production. Materials management is a natural solution to the dilemma. Instead of two managers reporting to different supervisors with dissimilar goals, a materials manager becomes the sole decision maker for materials as they flow through the organization. Here is where the potential is greater than if the functions remained separate. Being able to see the entire breadth of a situation, the materials manager will be able to place the correct emphasis in order to accomplish the objective.[17]

Improvement of Credibility

An important factor in the day-to-day operations of a company is the reliability and accuracy of each group's performance and activities. Company activities are similar to the relationships in a fine orchestra. Each individual and group within the company (or orchestra) must depend on others for correct timing and performance; if anyone falters, the overall performance is affected. In some respects, company activities are more complex than this. Individual departments begin to take safety precautions when they are forced to work with others who are less reliable than they. Days or even weeks are added to "cushion" projected requirement dates when they work with a group with a history of missed scheduled dates. Supervisors begin to hoard materials because they cannot rely on the stores group to maintain inventories. With a total materials management organization, various functions (marketing, manufacturing, etc.) get better, more reliable service. The materials management organization provides credibility of performance, which helps to reduce costs and lessen confusion. It also contributes to an atmosphere of mutual trust and cooperation.

Improvement of Resource Control

A goal of any organization, whether it is a profit-oriented company or a nonprofit organization, is control of the organization's resources. Through coordinated control of resources, materials managers successfully contribute to overall company objectives. Generally these resources are grouped into the four M's: materials, machines, manpower, and money (see Figure 1-9). All subfunction activities are related to the control of these four resources, both individually and in groups.

Materials. Control of materials resources is crucial for any organization with a materials management function, and this control relates to all areas. The purchasing group is responsible for procurement of materials to provide on-time deliveries, thus preventing costly disruptions in operations. Inventory control may be responsible for controlling thousands of items. The materials group tries to achieve optimum inventory turnover and minimum inventory levels while maintaining fully supplied company operations. Material lead times can be shortened with good communication among materials subfunctions. Greater control of materials will reduce obsolescence.

Companies with multiple divisions and/or facilities may have a variety of materials organizations. When this occurs, a company can compare diverse results. For example, in Motorola, Inc. some divisions have major product groups with similar products, customers, common problems, and identical management systems. Some have an integrated materials management organization, whereas others do not. With all other business evaluation factors being equal or better, inventory turnover is consistently at least 25 percent higher for the integrated materials management structure than for the other groups.

Machines (Facilities). Capacity requirements planning, for both the short term and the long term, will develop new facilities needs. Planning

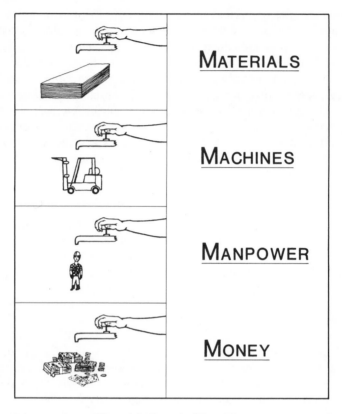

Figure 1-9. Control of four M's.

must be an ongoing activity to assure capacity availability when required. At the same time, every effort must be expended to provide optimum use of facilities by efficient production control techniques (i.e., efficient scheduling of machines, manpower, overtime hours, and improved facilities planning can contribute significantly to the maximum use of company capacity). The need for new buildings and equipment can be eliminated or minimized by effective control of operations.

Manpower. No company can grow and prosper without capable people. Usually with a fragmented materials management organization, individuals within each group have less chance for broad development; but as members of an integrated materials organization have a great opportunity to gain knowledge of the various areas. Personnel can be rotated and promoted between the subfunctions.

The materials organization can help to minimize operating department personnel requirements. Efficiency can be increased by reducing wasted hours due to materials-related problems such as excessive expediting, downtime due to lack of materials, and poor scheduling.

Money. Materials management provides a systems-oriented structure for minimizing monetary expenditures and controlling the management of money. Picture a typically frustrating situation for the controller or treasurer of a company. The busy executive tries to secure needed capital from a bank; later, upon walking through the company facility, the executive sees materials in a new light—not as different shapes and forms, but as money! "Why was I devoting so much time and effort to obtain money when it is sitting around everywhere in the facility?" the financial officer may ask. This may appear to be an oversimplification, but in many companies the materials management organization decreases monetary problems by minimizing inventories, reducing total costs of procurements, diminishing costs of materials handling and physical distribution, and instituting effective programs for measuring and controlling the various subfunction activities.

Reduction of Problems Associated with Production and Operations Complexity

Over the years, as society has progressed, industry has responded to its needs with products that provide an increased standard of living. Industrial functions have become more complicated as this has happened. For example, the Ford Motor Company originally made one model and one color of car, with no options. Today, a Ford customer has a seemingly endless number of cars from which to select. Have Ford's materials problems, associated with manufacturing so many types of cars, increased in scope? The answer is yes!

At the same time, many of the manufacturing processes used to make automobile parts and accessories have become more sophisticated and complex. As products and processes of various industries have become more complicated, problems associated with materials have increased for the manufacturing and distribution functions. One way to minimize these problems is to use total materials management.

Reduction of Duplicated Efforts

A fragmented materials organization has a natural duplication of activities built into it. All of the materials subfunctions are interrelated, and the overlap of activities inevitably contributes to repetition of efforts. Duplications are not unusual in records and data, in which each group maintains its own information. Also, duplication commonly occurs when many people in the company are expediting orders.

Duplication is reduced by using a total materials management organization. For example, a common data base may be used by all subfunctions. One report may take the place of several reports, at a great savings in clerical effort. Improved communication and structuring of individual subfunction responsibilities help to reduce duplication of employee efforts.

Improvement of Morale

Peters and Waterman reported in their study of successful American firms that excellent companies have a deeply ingrained philosophy that says, in effect, "respect the individual," "make people winners," "let them stand out," and "treat people as adults."[18] People usually enjoy working more when there is harmony in their work environment. A more recent phrase for this is "quality of work life." A fragmented materials organization can engender behaviors detrimental both to the accomplishment of company objectives and to good employee morale.

The total materials management organizational philosophy contributes to a winning team spirit, producing harmony and feelings of accomplishment. This type of structure also affords employees greater intracompany mobility. For example, with the fragmented organization approach personnel in such groups as shipping, receiving, and stores often are limited in specific career opportunities; but the identity and the importance of the individual are upgraded in an integrated organization. The increased mobility of personnel is an important factor in morale improvement in an integrated organization.

Enhancement of Communication

A total materials organization improves communication between the various materials subfunctions, as well as between materials management and other major company functions such as marketing, manufacturing, and engineering. The total materials concept provides a communication network that reacts quickly and facilitates improved rational action throughout the system. Combining the various fragmented groups enhances communication by shortening message channels, allowing common use of data, providing greater potential use of communication through data processing equipment, and encouraging the flow of information between people.

PITFALLS AND PROBLEMS OF MATERIALS MANAGEMENT

The following review of typical pitfalls and problems surrounding materials management programs can help managers to cope with such situations.

Lack of Qualified Managers

Capable managers with broad experience and knowledge of various materials subfunctions generally have not been available. Many managers have concentrated their work experience in one of the subfunctions such as purchasing, and believe that they have the qualifications to be a materials manager. Indeed, some could become effective managers, but many of them may fail because they lack broad experience. A new or continuing program's success depends upon having a qualified individual in charge. The materials manager's qualifications will be discussed further in Chapter 2.

Improved education and cross-training personnel within the materials organization have helped alleviate this problem. Some institutions of higher education have recognized the need for broad education in this area and have instituted college-level programs. Concurrently, astute materials managers are purposely building organizational capability by encouraging employees to improve their education and by transferring personnel among the various subfunctions.

Insufficient Upper Management Support

The success of a total materials management program is dependent upon upper management's understanding and continuous support. This is especially true in establishing a new organization. Management requires extensive education and understanding regarding the program's philosophy — what it is and what it is not. No one should presume that because a company has established a materials management program, all of upper management fully understands the principles and functions involved. Programs can achieve only mediocre success without executive level support.

Improper Planning and Implementation

Ineffective planning and implementation can destroy programs. Desire alone or the use of a new title for an unchanged organization will not ensure success. Management must understand the full requirements of instituting a total materials program. This is especially true of the time needed to successfully implement new functions. Failures have been traced to a desire for immediate results, which required and produced a shotgun approach. Disorganized management looked for immediate solutions at the expense of planned improvement followed by the innovations of new systems.

Lack of Credibility

The performance of the materials function might be criticized for two shortcomings: trouble avoidance and opportunism. The trouble avoidance context is the more familiar one: many people inside an organization are inconvenienced to varying degrees because the materials function, avoiding the effort required or providing inaccurate information does not meet minimum expectations.[19] Or the function will opportunistically satisfy only requests that can be resolved easily.

In such situations, marketing is repeatedly called by customers whose orders were not shipped on the date set by materials management. Production supervisors are unhappy because of frequent part shortages — machines and employees are idle because of poor scheduling. Finance and engineering complain about materials management not meeting commitments. The materials organization must establish a record of dependable performance; other groups within the company should be able to rely upon the information it provides.

Accusation of Empire Building

Finally, the accusation sometimes is made that the materials manager is building an empire. Skeptics complain, "They are only changing the organization to further their individual goals." If this is true, the resultant lack of achievement will doom the function.

The charge of empire building has been applied to other functions as well. When marketing was developing its present organization, the same claim was made. Then there were separate fragmented groups, such as sales and market research; but most companies now recognize the value of an integrated marketing organization. In the same way, materials management is becoming a valued entity within the organization.

SUMMARY

Business environments are becoming more complicated for both internal and external reasons. Companies are confronted with numerous problems related to materials, including rising costs, need for improved customer service, and increased product/operation complexities. An emerging solution to these and other problems is the organization of all materials-related activities, from supplier through company operations and on to the customer, into a total materials management function.

The ideal total materials management organization must be developed for individual companies. It may include all or most of the following subfunctions: planning, inventory control, production control, purchasing, receiving and stores, materials handling, and physical distribution. The efficiency and effectiveness of these subfunctions can be maximized by utilizing computer applications. This is especially true because systems groups, both within and outside the company, are available to provide all necessary software and hardware.

Many businesses, in such diverse industries as pharmaceuticals, electronics, transportation, hospitals, and distribution, have established integrated materials organizations in order to provide for company needs. Enumeration of the benefits derived from establishing a materials management group can help to justify an organizational change. These benefits include maximizing company profits, improving customer service, providing required credibility, improving resource control, improving employee morale, and enhancement of communication.

Any company contemplating implementation of a total materials function should be aware of difficulties that other firms have experienced. This knowledge can be valuable in achieving a successful program. Some of the problems include lack of qualified managers, insufficient support and understanding of the function by upper management, improper planning and implementation, lack of credibility, and the accusation that the materials manager is an empire builder.

NOTES

1. Bedeian, *Management*, p. 58.
2. Colton and Rohrs, *Industrial Purchasing and Effective Management*; p. 2.
3. Gaither, *Production and Operation Management*, p. 6.
4. Little, *The Military Staff, Its History and Development*, pp. 48–49.
5. *Logistics Decisions*, p. 3.
6. *What It's All About*, p. 2.
7. Savage, "Preparing for the Factory of the Future."
8. Boone and Kurtz, *Contemporary Business*, p. 39.
9. "Effective Planning and Cost Control for Restaurants Making Resource Requirements Planning Work," pp. 65–68.
10. *Materials Handling and Management Manual*, Chapter 16, p. 3.
11. Dobler, Lee, and Burt, *Purchasing and Materials Management*, p. 30.
12. Dobler, Lee, and Burt, *Purchasing and Material Management*, p. 29.
13. "Quality Circles—What it takes to make them work," pp. 45–47.
14. The bottom line refers to the last item in an income statement, which is net income or net loss.

15. Wallace, ed., *A.P.I.C.S. Dictionary*, p. 15.
16. Lipman, "Materials Management: A Blessing in Disguise," p. 49.
17. Farrell and Aljian, eds., *Algian's Purchasing Handbook*, p. 19-6.
18. Peters and Waterman, *In Search of Excellence*, p. 277.
19. Leenders, Fearon, and England, *Purchasing and Materials Management*, p. 10.

BIBLIOGRAPHY

Bedeian, Arthur. *Management*. Hinsdale, Illinois: The Dryden Press, 1986.

Boone, Louis E., and Kurtz, David L. *Contemporary Business*. Hinsdale, Illinois: The Dryden Press, 1985.

Carpe, R.H., and Carroll Jr., P.E. "Materials Management: Stretching The Household Budget." *Healthcare*, Nov. 1987.

Colton, Raymond R., and Rohrs, Walter F. *Industrial Purchasing and Effective Management*. Reston, Virginia: Reston Publishing Co., 1985.

Dobler, Donald W., Lee, Lamar, Jr., and Burt, David N. *Purchasing and Materials Management*. New York: McGraw-Hill Book Co., 1984.

"Effective Planning and Cost Control for Restaurants Making Resource Requirements Planning Work." *Production and Inventory Management*, First Quarter, 1985.

Farrell, P. V., and Aljian, G. W., eds. *Aljian's Purchasing Handbook*. New York: McGraw-Hill Book Co., 1982.

Gaither, Norman. *Production and Operation Management*. Hinsdale, Illinois: The Dryden Press, 1987.

Kress, M., "Donald Pais (Interview: General Motors Materials Management Vice President)." *Automotive News*, Mar. 1988.

Leenders, M., Fearon, H., and England, W. *Purchasing and Materials Management*. Homewood, Illinois: Richard D. Irwin, 1985.

Lipman, Rebecca. "Materials Management: A Blessing in Disguise." *Purchasing*, Oct. 23, 1980.

Little, J. D. *The Military Staff, Its History and Development*. Harrisburg, Pennsylvania: Stackpole Co., 1961.

Materials Handling and Management Manual. Toronto Chapter, International Materials Management Society, 1984.

Peters, Thomas J., and Waterman, Jr., Robert H. *In Search of Excellence*. New York: Warner Books, 1982.

"Quality Circles—What it takes to make them work." *Modern Materials Handling*, Nov. 19, 1982.

Schary, Philip B. *Logistics Decisions*. Hinsdale, Illinois: The Dryden Press, 1984.

Savage, Charles M. "Preparing for the Factory of the Future." *Modern Machine Shop*, 1983.

Wallace, Thomas F., ed. *A.P.I.C.S. Dictionary*. Falls Church, Virginia: American Production and Inventory Control Society, 1984.

What It's All About. Oak Brook, Illinois: Council of Logistics Management, 1985.

Wight, Oliver W. "Materials Management in Focus." *Modern Materials Handling*, 1983.

2
Organization of Total Materials Management

A primary contributor to a successful enterprise is an effective materials management organization. Managements that are poorly organized will not achieve their objectives and generally will operate below optimal profit levels.

Organization undergirds the entire company, so organizational design is vitally important to development and continued growth. As Peter Drucker has commented:

> Organizational design has to be grounded in an "ideal organization," that is, a conceptual framework. — Everybody knew of course that no ideal organization could be achieved in reality; reality always demands concessions, compromises, and exceptions. But one could hope to come close to the ideal — with exceptions truly "exceptional," that is, infrequent and confined to purely local situations.[1]

Individuals within an organization have different personalities, capabilities, and desires. The successful organization must recognize the importance of the individual as well as company objectives. Each person's strengths must be taken into account when management assigns responsibilities.

KEY ELEMENTS FOR MATERIALS MANAGEMENT ORGANIZATION

The primary objective of any materials management organization is to help maximize company profits. This is accomplished by optimizing total costs associated with materials, labor, money and facilities, while maintaining a high level of customer service. Although organizational structures and titles may vary from one company to another, their objectives remain the same. In seeking the ideal materials management organization, upper management must recognize the importance of both a good organizational structure and careful selection of people.

Inclusion of All Relevant Functions

In developing the materials management organizational structure, it is necessary to include all functions related to materials activities. A coordinated approach overcomes the shortcomings of the conventional organization, in which materials functions are organizationally splintered.[2] The motivation for establishing a total materials management organization is amplified when favorable reports are received from companies implementing fully integrated programs.

Effective control of total costs is facilitated by including all materials functions in one operating unit. Too often a cost savings in one department is offset by increased costs in another department, when organization planning is not coordinated. As an example, inventories can be considerably reduced, making it appear that inventory control is effective; but increased costs in production (downtime and delay) and in purchasing (order costs) may far outweigh the savings.

Status Considerations

One important consideration is the reporting level for the head of materials management. The materials activities in industries such as manufacturing, distribution, and service represent 40 to 90 percent of "product" cost. It is important that this function report to the top level of the organization. Unless materials management is accorded the status of a high position, it will be subordinate to other functions in the firm's decision making.

Motorola, Inc. has some materials managers (director level) who report directly to the division vice president/general manager, whereas others report to the vice president/director of manufacturing. Inventory turns have increased by at least 50 percent with the higher reporting relationship, with all other business evaluation factors equal or better.

In a corporate-wide restructuring at Eaton Corporation, the title of vice president of purchasing was superseded by vice president materials management. Purchasing benefited because it was part of strategic materials planning. Eaton benefited because it was able to meet the challenge of going into an economic downturn with better controlled inventories.[3]

Provision for Individual Company Requirements

It is essential that materials management organization meet specific requirements that best suit the needs of individual companies. For example, a business that does no manufacturing would not normally need a production control department within its materials management organization.

Sometimes politics within a company will affect the organization form.

This is a typical cause for differences in organization among individual companies. Usually, the reasons for variation from the ideal organization are not, as Peter Drucker indicates, "truly exceptional." Instead, they are often political. For example, in Company XYZ, the purchasing director was a strong, old-time employee. When a new materials management organization was formed, it did not include purchasing—the purchasing director was able to use his political clout to maintain his independence. Often in such cases the structure will change, consolidating purchasing into materials management, only when the purchasing executive leaves the company or a new president takes control.

Use of Guidelines for Good Organization

Materials management organizations must follow the same guidelines that have been found effective in management organizational design. These organizational golden rules provide for the assignment of duties and the coordination of personnel efforts to maximize company objectives.

Chain of Command. A clear chain of command must be established from the top down. Organization charts will aid in identifying the chain of command. For delegation to work effectively, members of the organization should know their position in the chain of command; otherwise, they could neither accept nor assign responsibility with any confidence. The scalar principle suggests that there must be a clear line of authority running from the highest to the lowest level of the organization. This clear line of authority will help materials group members to understand to whom they can delegate, who can delegate to them, and to whom they are accountable.[4]

Unity of Command. A basic tenet of organizational design is that each person must be accountable to only one other person (supervisor). At times, good organization will provide legitimate variations of this rule. For example, some larger companies have corporate materials management, as well as divisional and/or plant materials management organizations. In this case, an individual materials manager reports to a divisional general manager or plant manager for all normal supervisory functions. However, the corporate head of materials management is responsible for functional performance throughout the company, and would naturally review and coordinate divisional/plant materials management activities to be sure they conform to company policies and procedures. The head of corporate materials management is said to have staff or "dotted line" responsibility over divisional/plant materials management supervisory activities.

Span of Control. The number of people reporting to one supervisor is referred to as span of control. If managers have either too few or too many people reporting to them, the result will be ineffective operations. For example, materials managers who have too many people reporting to them cannot provide adequate time for guidance, training, and planning.

Companies fail to maximize the capabilities of managers who have too few people reporting to them. This also results in managers overcontrolling subordinates. Also, a small span of control will result in less effective communication between levels due to an increase in supervisory levels, and results in higher overhead costs for supervision and support services. V. A. Graicunas indicates that in selecting a span of control, managers should consider not only the direct one-to-one relationships with people they supervise but also the relationships with subordinates, in groups of two or more.[5] Figure 2-1 illustrates these relationships between managers and subordinates.

The number of individuals reporting to any one manager varies according to types of business activities. Variables include, but are not limited to, the following:

1. Predictability of work
2. Discretion allowed each individual
3. Job responsibility
4. Measurability of results
5. Task interdependence among subordinates
6. Knowledge/capability of people

Number of Subordinates	Number of Relationships	Number of Subordinates	Number of Relationships
1	1	10	5,210
2	6	11	11,374
3	18	12	24,708
4	44	•	•
5	100	•	•
6	222	15	245,970
7	490	•	•
8	1,080	•	•
9	2,376	18	2,359,602

Source: James A. F. Stoner, "Management", (Englewood Cliffs, N.J.: Prentice-Hall, 1978), P.250, Using V.A. Graicunas' formula. See footnote 5.

Figure 2-1. Relationships between managers and subordinates, related to span of control. (Source: James A. F. Stoner, *Management,* Englewood Cliffs, New Jersey: Prentice-Hall, 1978, p. 250, using V. A. Graicunas' formula. See footnote 5.)

7. Complexity of jobs
8. Proximity of jobs
9. Subordinate business experience

Authority and Suitable Responsibility

Subordinates cannot be given responsibility for a function without having the appropriate authority to properly perform that function. Productivity is substantially reduced by the difficulties inherent in diluted authority. A necessary part of delegation of responsibility and authority is that individuals must be accountable. Accepting delegated responsibility and authority creates an obligation (responsibility) on the part of a subordinate to perform his or her duties satisfactorily. Materials managers are held accountable for their own performance as well as the performance of their subordinates.

Supervisors at all levels must learn the importance of delegating responsibilities and authority to their subordinates. Increased delegation of tasks to subordinates will provide greater opportunity for the supervisor to seek and accept increased responsibilities from higher-level management. Also, it can improve task development and decisions. Allowing individuals who are closest to a situation and who possess a better overview of the facts to use their judgment generally results in improved morale and productivity.

TYPES OF ORGANIZATION FOR EFFECTIVE MATERIALS MANAGEMENT

The materials management organization design must provide for both immediate needs and future considerations. The structure, like many other critical aspects of the business, should not be set in concrete. However, it is poor management practice continually to change the organization because of individual circumstances. If sufficient thought and planning are invested in developing the type of structure required, minimal changes will be needed as growth occurs.

Growth of a Typical Company

A small business has no functional specialization. The owner is both a manager and an entrepreneur, responsible for providing both necessary capital and administrative capabilities. During the initial growth period, the owner will wear a rotating hat, performing various functions such as marketing, operations, finance, and materials management.

As the business continues to grow, the owner finds that various important tasks are not being accomplished. Lack of time and often insufficient expertise in specialized areas are problems. The work load gets heavier and heavier. Additional individuals with specialized knowledge must be brought into the business, to eliminate the bottleneck caused by the owner's inability to cope with increasing administrative demands. Beginning with the first new administrator, the owner must consider delegation of responsibilities to someone else. It is here that the need for organization arises.

An organization initially emerges when the owner delegates responsibilities and authority to another manager. At this point, materials management functions may be divided between the owner and the manager. Such subfunctions as planning, inventory control, and purchasing may be included in the responsibilities of the owner, along with marketing, finance, research and development, and engineering. All the other subfunctions such as receiving, shipping, purchasing (supplies only), scheduling, materials handling, and stores may be delegated to the manager (see Figure 2-2), along with responsibility for operations. This initial division of responsibility for total materials management functions introduces problems, which will grow as the company increases in size and as the materials activities are further divided among top executives.

As the company continues to grow, problems such as work load and communication difficulties increase in dimension, and the organization tends to become increasingly inadequate. Gradually additional manage-

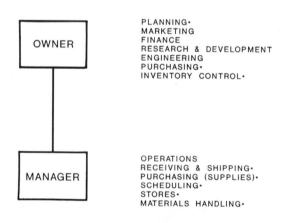

*Materials Management Functions

Figure 2-2. Divided responsibilities at first stage in the evolution of an organization.

ment specialists are brought into the organization to cope with these problems. An example of an organization in the second stage of evolution is shown in Figure 2-3. Division into functions varies considerably in this stage, depending upon the president and the management group. Functions included in the president's responsibilities would vary, depending upon individual capabilities and interests. Figure 2-3 indicates that the president's capabilities are product-development-oriented, but the president's responsibilities still would include planning. The operation manager's responsibilities would include operations, receiving, inventory control, production control, stores, and purchasing (supplies). However, two new positions now emerge: sales manager and office manager. The sales manager's materials management subfunctions include finished goods warehouse and shipping (including traffic). Purchasing responsibilities are included in the office manager's responsibilities.

Figure 2-3 reveals some common splits in materials management functions. Problems of fragmented organization emerge. The sales manager, responsible for the finished goods warehouse, will strive for high inventories to satisfy all customers. The office manager will control purchasing activities, often reducing purchase price at the sacrifice of total company costs. The operations manager will want high inventories to reduce downtime and productivity losses.

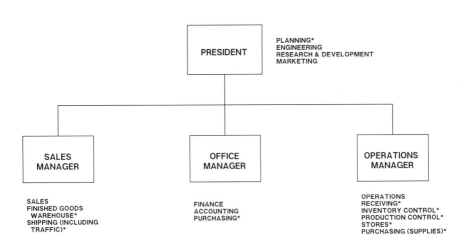

* Materials Management Functions

Figure 2-3. Divided responsibilities at the second stage in the evolution of an organization.

Ideal Materials Organization

Many companies must cope with increasing costs and control problems related to materials. Eventually it becomes clear that substantial advantages—through reduction of communication and coordination problems—can be obtained by bringing together again, under one responsible individual, all those functions that clearly are interrelated. This reintegration of interrelated materials functions is the basis of the materials management concept.

The rapid increase in the number of companies adopting materials management organization is typified by the manufacturing industries. In a 1979 survey, Miller and Gilmour[6] reported that "Nearly half the manufacturers responding to our survey now have materials managers playing important corporate and/or divisional roles, compared with a scant three percent reported in a 1966 survey." Those statistics indicated a dramatic rise in materials management organizations within little more than one decade.

An ideal organization is shown in Figure 2-4, reflecting the integrated format. The organization chart would be similar for both manufacturing and nonmanufacturing environments. Some activities may be deleted or changed, but the basic structure remains the same. The materials management executive reports to the president, as do other primary functions such as engineering, finance, and marketing. A systems design and computer applications group is not shown under the materials management organization in Figure 2-4. However, some companies are including this function in the organization to assure user-oriented outputs.

All the principal functions required to provide an integrated systems approach to total materials management are found in Figure 2-4. In the

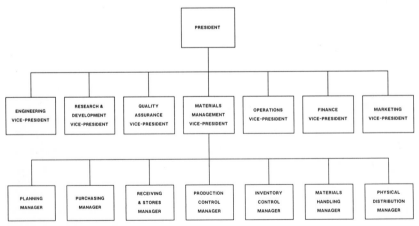

Figure 2-4. Desirable organization for a totally integrated materials management group.

Miller and Gilmour survey, respondents identified the person who reports to the head of materials management (Figure 2-5).[7] There is some ambiguity with such terms as production planning (which could include both production control and inventory control) and distribution (which could include finished goods stores, shipping, and transportation). Even considering the potential difficulty with terminology, the data show that key materials subfunctions report to the head of materials management.

Organizational Variations. A variety of functions may report to the head of materials management. One example is illustrated in Figure 2-6. The titles and functions of the purchasing manager, inventory control manager, and production planning and control manager are typically found in most companies. An example of title variation is the designation materials handling operations manager, indicating a group with a broad range of responsibilities—receiving, stores, physical movement of materials throughout the facility, and physical distribution.

The materials systems manager (see Figure 2-6) exemplifies the variety of organizational responsibilities sometimes included within the materials management group. The materials management organization is responsible for developing and implementing manufacturing systems related to materials management, whereas the corporate systems group develops and implements complete computer systems (both software and hardware) for these and other activities.

Other Basic Structures

Some companies are organized distinctively because of individual politics, management emphasis, and so on. These variances usually relate to the

	Percent
Purchasing	69%
Production Planning	77%
Distribution	39%*
Traffic	55%

*The distribution function existed as an identifiable entity in less than 50% of the companies in the sample. In most other cases, finished goods inventories, if any, were located in the factory, or distribution and traffic were synonymous.
Reprinted by permission of the Harvard Business Review. Exhibit from "Materials Managers: Who Needs Them?" by Jeffery Miller and Peter Gimour (July/August 1979). Copyright © 1979 by the President abd Fellows of Harvard College; all rights reserved.

Figure 2-5. Who reports to the materials manager. (Reprinted by permission of the *Harvard Business Review.* Exhibit from "Material Managers: Who Needs Them?" by Jeffry Miller and Peter Gilmour, July/Aug. 1979. Copyright © 1979 by the President and Fellows of Harvard College; all rights reserved.)

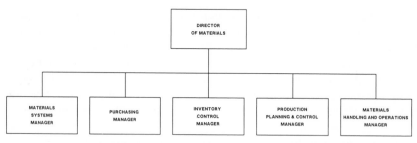

Figure 2-6. One variation of the materials management organization.

omission of one of the major subfunctions from materials management responsibilities.

Physical Distribution Separated. In this organization, all normal subfunctions other than physical distribution report to materials management (see Figure 2-7). Physical distribution is included in marketing. The argument for this type of organization usually is that "Physical distribution is an essential part of the marketing function."

An example of benefits gained by consolidating physical distribution into a total materials function was described by Steven Lazarus, senior vice president of Baxter Travenol Laboratories, Inc., a Deerfield, Illinois – based health care products manufacturer. Physical distribution was combined with warehousing, purchasing, production planning, inventory control, and logistics systems departments. All report to a vice president of materials management. Baxter Travenol's commitment to a total materials

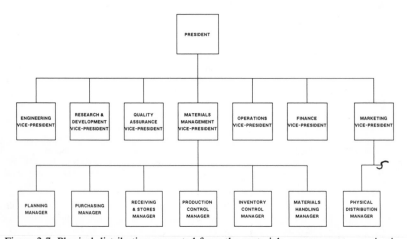

Figure 2-7. Physical distribution separated from the materials management organization.

management function has resulted in an inventory cut by $100 million, improved customer service, and reduced transportation costs. These improvements were made at the same time that sales increased at a 10 to 15 percent annual rate.[8]

The primary argument against separating physical distribution from the total materials management organization revolves around the importance of minimizing finished goods inventory. The materials organization that includes physical distribution can better coordinate various related subfunctions to control finished goods inventories and be responsive to customer requirements. If the marketing department controls physical distribution, there is a tendency to have higher finished goods inventory levels to "make sure customers get what they want." Also, the traffic group often concentrates on customer shipments. Traffic activities for both inbound and outbound shipments can be maximized under a materials management organization.

Manufacturing/Operations-Oriented. A common organizational structure for materials management is to have all or most subfunctions report to manufacturing/operations (see Figure 2-8). In many cases, this is the first step to achieving integration of all materials management subfunctions. The fact that they all may already report individually to manufacturing/operations makes it easier to reach agreement to group the subfunctions under a materials manager within the manufacturing/operations organization.

Materials management may report to manufacturing/operations for rea-

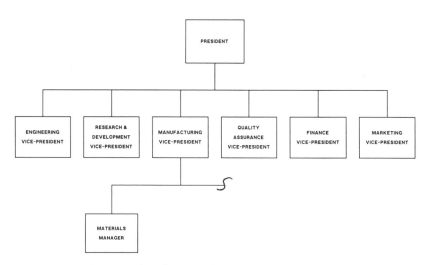

Figure 2-8. Manufacturing/operations-oriented materials organization.

sons other than ease of organization. One logical reason pertains to size of the company and span of control. If the president feels that his or her span of control would be too large by adding materials management to the top echelon, then it would remain under manufacturing/operations.

The primary reason not to include materials management under manufacturing/operations is that it provides a check and balance—a reason similar to that for excluding quality assurance from manufacturing. Keeping the materials organization separate from manufacturing/operations could help to minimize raw and work-in-process materials. Operations personnel interests are often allowed to dominate when materials management reports to manufacturing, a situation that results in reduced control of materials and overemphasis on end-of-month shipments.

Purchasing Separated. This organization is characterized by not including the purchasing function under materials management (see Figure 2-9). Purchasing reports directly to the finance department. A principal reason for this type of organization is that "Purchased materials represent a large percentage of financial outlays and therefore require close coordination with the finance department."

The primary argument for including purchasing in a materials management organization is that it minimizes total costs. A separate purchasing department may not closely coordinate its activities with other materials subfunctions such as inventory control and stores. This may result in lower prices but higher total costs.

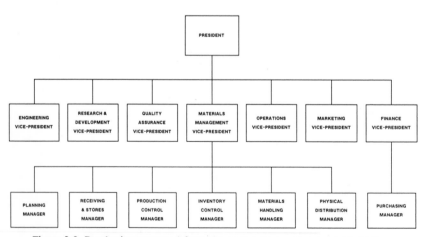

Figure 2-9. Purchasing separated from the materials management organization.

Centralized versus Decentralized

Figure 2-4 shows a centralized organization. This type of organization is normal for smaller companies or those with limited facilities. As a company grows by normal increase in business or by acquisition, there is a need to decentralize the organization. The concepts of centralized and decentralized refer to the extent to which authority has been retained at the top of the organization (centralized) or has been passed down to lower levels (decentralized). The primary question, which varies by company, involves the extent to which the organizational functions should be decentralized. Figure 2-10 is an example of a decentralized divisional materials management organization.

Decentralization has both advantages and disadvantages.

Advantages of Decentralization. Benefits of decentralization include the following:

- *Clear-cut accountability:* The performance of a division or plant can easily be measured in terms of the particular unit's profit and loss statement.
- *Coordinated functions:* All of the activities, skills, and expertise required to perform the function are grouped in one place, under a single materials manager. This eliminates delays and excuses such as, "It was not possible because plant purchasing does not report to me."

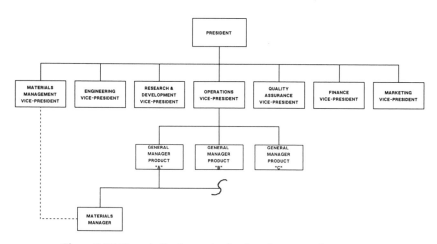

Figure 2-10. Decentralized organization based upon product groups.

- *Fast decisions and action:* The quality and speed of decision making are enhanced. Follow-up action can be directed at a local level, where managers are knowledgeable about specific details (i.e., products and people).
- *Management development:* This type of organization is conducive to the development of capable materials management personnel. Any organization that encourages the delegation of responsibility and authority will help to develop proficient personnel at various levels.

Disadvantages of Decentralization. Some problems of decentralization are:

- *Diluted interests:* The interests of an individual division or plant may be placed ahead of the objectives and needs of the entire organization. As an example, local managements that are subject to P and L (profit and loss statement) reviews, and included in a bonus program, may opt for short-term gains at the expense of long-term profitability.
- *Duplication of efforts:* Each division or plant wants to have staff members and specialists who perform all functions. Often this leads to duplication of efforts at the expense of the overall organization. For example, many companies experience added costs as various divisions or plants develop similar systems such as MRP (material requirements planning) programs.
- *Faulty communication:* Often totally decentralized materials operations lead to reduced communication between divisions and/or plants. There is no mechanism for or interest in communicating results of local successes, failures, and experiences, where they are pertinent to other divisions and/or plants.

Line and Staff Functions. Companies establish the centralized and decentralized relationships through line and staff functions. Line activities are those activities performed by personnel, typically working for a facility (i.e., plant or distribution center), where their work supports the everyday functions of the operating unit. Staff responsibilities consists of those activities performed to assist and/or support functions of the overall company or a division of the company. The central staff headed by a materials management executive (often referred to as corporate staff) reports to the president or executive vice-president (see Figure 2-10) and is responsible for the overall company materials management functions. This group has no direct responsibility for operating unit activities but has staff authority. The line materials manager reports to the head of an operating facility (i.e., general manager or plant manager).

Central staff materials groups develop policies and procedures that relate to all materials management functions, thus providing for uniform performance of various activities. The central staff executive is responsible for the functional performance of line materials management activities. This functional responsibility is referred to as dotted line authority. Central staff activities also eliminate much of the duplication of costs generated by various operating units. Some other activities normally performed by central staff personnel include:

- *Systems development:* An important activity is assisting in the design and development of systems (manual and computer) that will be beneficial to more than one operating facility. This responsibility sometimes includes implementation and debugging of the system.
- *Communication:* Central staff provide a clearinghouse for information that will be beneficial to various operating facilities. This may take the form of bulletins or informational papers containing specialized knowledge. The staff will communicate worthwhile experiences from one unit to another and information on savings related to individual materials management activities.
- *Centralized purchases:* The central staff can identify common materials that are purchased by different operating units. Negotiating contracts for consolidated purchases and shipments can provide significant cost savings.
- *Training:* Training is an essential and continuing central staff function. It can be performed by conducting seminars/meetings at central locations or in individual operating units.
- *Measurement:* The central staff should provide standard formulas/ratios that can be used by all groups to develop goals and objectives, measure performance, and identify areas requiring improvement. This information also can be useful to management for evaluating various operations. Measurement of all activities is critical to assessing and improving individual materials management group performances.
- *Consulting:* Consulting services similar to those available from management consulting firms can be provided by the central staff. One advantage of having internal personnel to perform this function is that they possess valuable knowledge of company products, policies, procedures, and personnel.

Hospital Organization

Figure 2-11 illustrates an organizational structure for a hospital. The organization chart for materials management varies from one hospital to another, and differs in many respects from that of its industrial counterpart. Usually some subfunctions are the same as in industry, such as purchasing,

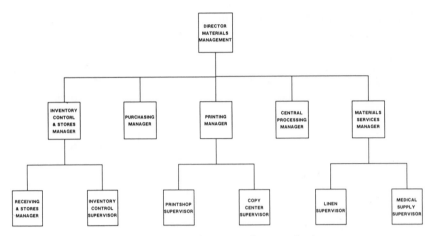

Figure 2-11. Example of a hospital organization.

receiving, stores, and inventory control. In addition, some departments perform functions similar to those in a manufacturing company. The linen department is responsible for distribution of clean linen throughout the hospital and collection and movement of soiled linen. Linen operations would be similar to materials handling in a manufacturing company, responsible for distribution of materials. In many respects the medical supply department is similar to the linen department in that it is responsible for distribution of various medical supplies throughout the hospital.

The central processing department, sometimes called central supply, is responsible for cleaning, sterilization, and decontamination of reusable medical supplies. It also issues and controls patient rental equipment. As such, this department performs some processing of materials, like a subfunction within a distribution center that prices and tags merchandise.

The printing facility (print shop and copy center) is not like any industrial materials management group. This department resembles a manufacturing department. Usually, the printing operation is a result of a decision to produce, rather than buy, printed items. The printing facility is part of materials management because of its relationship to purchasing and inventory control activities.

Some hospitals include additional, nontraditional activities within the function. These can include laundry, food service, pharmacy, property control, and patient transportation (not shown in Figure 2-11). Transporting patients is, in an objective sense, the same as distributing materials throughout a manufacturing plant or distribution center. Property control is similar to inventory control activities. The other activities (laundry, food service, and pharmacy) are included in materials management because there is no better logical association for them.

RELATIONSHIPS OF MATERIALS MANAGEMENT TO OTHER COMPANY FUNCTIONS

Materials management or, perhaps more correctly, the materials manager is perceived as effective when all assigned tasks are accomplished in a way that enables the entire operating unit (division, company, subsidiary, etc.) to meet its goals.[9]

The materials group must develop close cooperation and interrelationships with other functions of the company. Effective relationships are developed over a period of time, as functions are perceived as vital, credible partners. Each function must expect to give as well as receive. Materials management should expect to obtain full support from other company functions and provide similar support in return.

Two phases exist during the development of relationships with other company functions. In the critical initial phase, other functions are educated to fully understand the concepts and philosophy of materials management. Where fragmented groups have been merged into the organization, adverse reactions must be dispelled. Difficulties may exist with altered functions and with transferred individuals. Other management functions must be educated regarding the advantages of having a total materials management organization, in terms of improvements in materials flow, credibility of information, optimization of resources, and concentrated control of material costs. The entire organization, not only supervision, should be active in these educational efforts.

The second phase in developing relationships with other company functions is as important as the first. After the initial introductory phase, effort should be devoted to strengthening relationships. Channels of communication must be developed further to obtain the cooperation and information flow needed to achieve company objectives. Poor two-way communication is a common problem in most companies. A concentrated effort by all groups is needed to improve communication. Another essential activity during the second phase is developing and monitoring worthwhile, quantitative objectives or criteria for success.

Finance

The finance function is a central element of successful company operations. This group is responsible for maintaining cash flow, and it provides leadership in developing operating budgets. Materials management must relate to this function to achieve its objectives. Materials personnel should understand financial terms and theories. Chapter 14 has been included in this book to give the reader some exposure to basic aspects of finance.

Long-term capital decisions are required for new or revised facilities. Finance depends upon materials management, as well as other functions, for input regarding capacity requirements. This information is used to forecast and plan long-term monies necessary for buildings, equipment, and so on. Also, the materials group provides information pertaining to data processing systems requirements, which could be very expensive, and materials to be purchased beyond short-term considerations.

A common topic in the executive offices of companies, whether they be organized on a profit or a nonprofit basis, is cash flow. Materials management assists other functions in maintaining the company's cash flow by optimal control of expenditures. For example, a materials manager recently instituted a new inventory and production control system. After the system had been in effect for 18 months, the controller came to the materials manager's office and said enthusiastically: "Congratulations! This is the first time in five years that our company has been free of short term-debt. Your system was a major factor in this achievement."

The finance group constantly is besieged with requests for money, all for important, worthwhile projects. Although no one usually mentions it, all major functions of the company are competing for the monies available for new projects, and it is critical that materials management maintain a favorable competitive position by developing appropriate justifications. Managers must stay knowledgeable about all pertinent information used in justification procedures—for example, calculation of return on investment (R.O.I.), tax implications regarding leasing versus buying, and the need to service customers.

Marketing

The marketing function is responsible for monitoring current and future customer demand and projecting future product requirements, while materials management helps to provide good customer service. Close cooperation between the two groups can positively affect the availability and utilization of vital resources—that is, the company's money, manpower (labor), materials, and machines (facilities).

A major input of marketing to materials management is sales forecast data. These data represent the first step in development of planning requirements, and are a key factor in controlling company resources. The marketing function, with its customer contact and responsibility for market research, is the most logical source of sales forecasts. The forecast is often given in terms of product families or groups, and this information is then translated into specifics by planning and/or production control.

Marketing normally is responsible for establishing priorities for customer deliveries. In many cases, changes in priorities result in additional setups, turmoil, and/or delayed shipments. For example, if marketing insists that the assembly of blue elephants be stopped and changed to assemble two green elephants, a number of costs are incurred. First, setup cost is increased because the assembly line must be changed to make two green elephants, which could represent a high setup cost per unit. An additional set up then must be made from green elephants back to blue elephants. There is also a loss of capacity due to idle people and facilities during setups. Finally, other customer orders are delayed, and the risk of customer dissatisfaction due to late delivery is increased. Materials management must work closely with marketing to educate and inform the group of the various costs, loss of capacities, and customer order delays that result from arbitrary schedule changes. Marketing, aware of this information, should cooperate to reduce the number of hot orders.

Marketing depends upon credibility to keep customers satisfied. For example, assume that marketing asks if 5000 widgets are available for a customer order. Inventory control indicates that there is no problem, as there are 8000 widgets in stock. Marketing does not expect to be informed at a later date that a partial shipment was made because the finished goods inventory was incorrect. It depends upon materials management to provide accurate information and timely deliveries to customers.

The cost incurred when an item is out of stock is difficult to calculate, but a significant consideration. Both marketing and materials management must be conscious of this cost versus the cost of holding inventory.

Manufacturing

Materials management is an important service function that supports the manufacturing or operations group. In many companies, receiving and stores, inventory control, production control, and shipping were originally part of the manufacturing or operations areas, as a result of the need to control materials flow. This structure formed a foundation for the present close relationship between the two groups.

Manufacturing supervisors probably complain the most about frequent parts shortages. These shortages contribute to loss of capacity, interruption of operations, and delays in customer orders. Total materials management must provide manufacturing with the right part, at the right time, in the right quantity, and at the right place.

Generally most first-line supervisors in a manufacturing company are busy with many important matters such as training, personnel relations, and quality considerations. In some companies materials management abdicates its responsibilities for activities such as machine scheduling and expects the production supervisor to take care of them. As a result, scheduling is less efficient, and the production supervisor is burdened with additional duties that reduce the time available for primary activities. Materials management should make use of engineering standards to schedule machines efficiently and realistically. Production supervision must be responsible for conforming to the schedule, and problems should be reported to the materials group as soon as possible to facilitate their resolution.

Expediting is the activity responsible for following the progress of parts, subassemblies, products, or complete customer orders in order to accelerate project completion. In most companies expediters can be everyone from president to production worker. Expediting can be a source of confusion, duplication of efforts, and poor employee morale. Companies resort to excessive expediting because of a lack of good planning. Total materials management should provide proper planning systems and implement them so that expediting and its inherent high costs can be minimized.

Research and Design Engineering

Product development and materials management personnel must work together to provide products that satisfy customers and are profitable. Research and engineering personnel should utilize the expertise of materials subfunctions in developing and revising products.

Purchasing can assist the research and design engineering group by performing research pertaining to the availability of new materials and products. Many companies are now assigning the responsibility for this type of research to the purchasing department. With its knowledge of materials, products, and tolerances, purchasing can efficiently seek out sources that will benefit research and design engineering.

It is important that materials management and design engineering cooperate regarding engineering changes. Delayed processing of engineering change orders will cause many problems, including creation of obsolete parts, subassemblies, and products; additional rework of parts, subassemblies, and products; loss of capacity; and confusion. Phase-out or modification of products requires carefully organized planning to minimize obsolescence of materials. Product liability also is receiving increased attention, because of changes in the laws. Companies must be very careful during product transition periods to maintain control of product changes, as they can be sued over defective products. Complete records are required to identify product configurations.

A major goal of materials management is to standardize materials, as much as possible, while producing existing and new products. Standardization helps to reduce inventory levels, minimizes obsolescence, reduces storage space requirements, and decreases errors in product makeup. Not all materials can be standardized, but the research and design engineering department can decrease the use of new materials by educating its personnel in this area.

Industrial Engineering

The industrial engineering department can work with materials management to reduce labor, facilities, and materials costs. These groups can identify various problem areas and develop solutions that will help improve productivity and increase operational capacity. This team effort can be equally important in both manufacturing and nonmanufacturing environments.

Industrial engineering is usually responsible for plant layout within the company. Most companies also include material handling design within industrial engineering responsibilities. Materials management requires industrial engineering support to provide layout and material handling design and implementation for various functions, including packaging, unit loads, warehousing, materials flow, and materials handling systems. Industrial engineering should obtain input from materials personnel from the inception of a project and continue a close relationship through installation and follow-up. Such cooperation ensures that a new system will be user-oriented and successful. Input from the materials groups will be used by industrial engineering to select, justify, and plan projects. This information could relate to scheduling problems, storage problems, materials cost variations, and scrap problems.

Materials management depends upon industrial engineering to provide consistent, good work standards for use in scheduling operations, people, and equipment. The coverage should be very broad. In many companies industrial engineering standards are developed only for direct labor employees, but industrial engineering can develop work standards for all materials subfunctions. This is essential for measurement and control of materials management activities.

Industrial engineering can contribute information for capacity planning of both existing and new facilities. Identifying capacity bottleneck operations and solving these problems should be a team effort. Materials management is especially dependent upon industrial engineering for facilities information (i.e., machine capacity and routing) pertaining to new products and facilities. All materials subfunctions require this information to plan their operations. Industrial engineering can minimize the problems that normally result from new product introduction and new facilities debugging.

Quality Assurance

Quality assurance provides control of all product quality, for raw material, work-in-process, and finished goods. Communication between quality assurance and materials management must be effective, or bottlenecks defective products, and other problems will result.

Rejected materials present numerous problems. Such material must be isolated so that it does not, by mistake, mix with good-quality inventory. Also, in many companies rejected materials take up space sorely needed for other materials. Additional paperwork and follow-up time are required of materials management personnel to dispose of these materials. Quality assurance can reduce these problems by conducting accurate inspection procedures and by providing fast decisions and action to dispose of rejected materials (material review boards can be effective).

The quality assurance department must maintain good product quality throughout all operations, from receiving incoming materials to shipping finished products. If quality assurance fails at any point to provide good materials, many problems of materials management will result, among them scheduling difficulties, loss of capacity, and overtime premium payments.

Quality assurance and design engineering should work closely with purchasing personnel. They must provide sufficient quality specifications that suppliers will have all necessary information. Purchasing performs an essential role as an intermediary between suppliers, quality assurance, and design engineering, communicating problems and solutions between these groups.

Systems/Data Processing

The importance of systems/data processing in all functions of a company cannot be overstated. Materials management applications include mate-· rials requirement planning (MRP), distribution requirement planning (DRP), automated storage and retrieval systems (AS/RS), and purchasing systems. Computer systems provide a critical link between various materials subfunctions. This same link also connects the group and other company functions. Systems/data processing must provide all necessary support to the materials function regarding systems analysis, software development, and hardware capacity. Sometimes it is difficult to obtain sufficient support to implement required programs because of limited personnel and equipment, as well as the higher priorities of other department projects. Then materials management projects suffer. Some companies solve this problem by assigning systems/data processing personnel to the materials group, as illustrated in Figure 2-6.

The systems/data processing group analyzes various operations to develop a logical, efficient plan for organizing each operation in relationship with other operations or functions. The flow charts and other data developed by systems/data processing form a foundation for software development. Materials personnel should be involved in this development process, from the beginning, to assure user-oriented systems.

Computers are programmed in different languages including FORTRAN, COBOL, APL, and BASIC. Skilled systems analysts and programmers can provide effective programs, limit development costs, and reduce development time. However, software development is a very costly and time-consuming process. In many instances, it may be more economical and expeditious to buy software and modify it to individual company requirements rather than to develop it.

There are basically two kinds of hardware. The first type is the central processing unit (CPU), which is the primary computer device for controlling the sequence and pacing of all operations. The second is peripheral support devices, required to provide input, storage, and output. Systems/data processing should cooperate with materials management to provide proper hardware and sufficient capacity to perform required functions. Otherwise, materials-related costs will be excessive, and customer service will suffer.

REQUIREMENTS OF THE MATERIALS MANAGER

The materials manager must be an experienced professional—someone who is an expert not only in the technical aspects of the job and knowledge of the company, but also in the use of the principles, concepts, and practices of good management.

John J. Davin, vice-president materials and facilities, GTE, Stanford, Connecticut, describes the materials manager role as follows:

The overall concept of materials management is the organizational grouping of purchasing, production, inventory control, and physical distribution – transportation functions under a single manager. . . . The emphasis is on the integration of materials functions. While purchasing, production, and physical distribution managers are concerned with the specific requirements of their activities, the materials manager is a generalist concerned with all the functions simultaneously. He is a planner, organizer, integrator, and motivator. The job spans functional barriers and represents a unified input to top management for materials.[10]

Primary Responsibilities

Success of the materials function depends on the success of the materials manager. The manager's functions cover a broad spectrum of responsibilities, which must be coordinated to achieve total materials management.

Concepts are mental models and ideas that establish a framework for thought; they are essential to an understanding of a complex subject. Still, mere conceptualization of materials management is not enough to provide techniques for dealing with the subject; it is necessary to articulate the concepts in a highly developed structure.[11] The materials manager must establish an ideal organization for the company; then the important task remains of providing capable personnel.

Objectives related to those of the overall company must be developed for the materials group. These objectives should be worthwhile and achievable, and should help motivate all personnel. Objectives, goals, and standards are important means of control of the individual subfunctions, as well as of the overall function.

Policies provide all personnel with broad guidelines that lead to effective action. Their broadness allow some latitude to individuals in fulfilling their job responsibilities. Procedures are much more definitive than policies; they show step-by-step actions. Policies and procedures should be developed for all materials activities, as they facilitate uniform, efficient operations and are useful for training personnel.

Sales forecasts must be translated into long-term plans. This responsibility includes providing for all necessary resources, as well as controlling or minimizing these resources. The materials manager contributes to long-term planning of all vital resources. All materials subfunctions can assist in providing valuable information for long-term planning.

The productivity, accomplishment, and morale of the materials group hinge on its having a capable leader. A competent materials manager will mold the group into a successful team, but this responsibility can be accomplished only by devoting significant time and monies to the development, motivation, and training of materials management personnel. In recent years there has been increased emphasis on implementing innovative motivation techniques, including industrial democracy, quality circles, and Theory Z.[12] There are many motivation theories, some that have been in existence for many years and others of relatively recent origin. Materials managers should not be anxious to find "the" theory and apply it to every situation they encounter.[13]

The materials manager is responsible for providing stimulation and for directing innovation. Today, major emphasis is channeled to developing integrated systems for materials management activities, including both manual and computer systems. The reduced costs and ready availability of computer software and hardware have led to increased applications of integrated systems.

The materials manager is responsible for utilizing budgets to control operations, expressing the plans, objectives, and programs of the organization in numerical terms. Monthly budgets must be developed, implemented, and periodically reviewed and reconciled for any major variations. Budgets are just one of the planning and controlling techniques used by the manager to control various activities; Chapter 13 covers this subject in greater depth.

The bottom line of a company's profit and loss (income) statement will be considerably improved by the materials manager's success in implementing an effective cost reduction program. Program objectives will be achieved and enhanced by delegation of responsibilities to individual subfunction supervision and coordination of these activities. Effective materials cost reduction programs and higher company profits are the benefits of such coordination.

Authority

Authority is delegated to materials managers by upper management. In many ways the ultimate success of the materials group depends upon the manager's status. Optimally that status is achieved by the manager's reporting to the highest level of the company. A survey of manufacturing companies made by Miller and Gilmour (see Figure 2-12) indicates that 22 percent report to the general manager or president, 43 percent report to a manufacturing manager, 4 percent report to control or finance, and 31 percent report to other managers.[14] This 1979 survey, in comparison to

Position	Percent
General Manager or President	22%
Manufacturing Manager	43%
Control or Finance	4%
Other*	31%

*Various positions such as executive vice president, vice president of administration, etc.
Reprinted by permission of the *Harvard Business Review.* Exhibit from "Materials managers: Who Needs Them?" by Jeffery Miller and Peter Gilmour (July/August 1979). Copyright © 1979 by the President and Fellows of Harvard College; all rights reserved.

Figure 2-12. To whom the materials manager reports. (Reprinted by permission of the *Harvard Business Review.* Exhibit from "Materials Managers: Who Needs Them?" by Jeffry Miller and Peter Gilmour, July/Aug. 1979. Copyright © 1979 by the President and Fellows of Harvard College; all rights reserved.)

1960s data, shows an increase in heads of materials management reporting to top management, including the president, executive vice president, and division general manager. Nonmanufacturing companies would probably reflect similar or higher percentages.

Types of authority vary by management position. Materials management executives who are part of a central organization possess line authority, as indicated in Figure 2-6. In a corporate staff position, the materials executive would have line authority over those personnel who report directly and functional staff authority over materials personnel in various divisions or groups, as illustrated in Figure 2-10.

Qualifications

Selection of a capable materials manager is a critical step in developing the total materials management organization. That manager must be able to guide the entire group to achieve company goals. Without a proficient manager, the organization will be like a sailboat without a rudder.

One challenging aspect of selecting an individual to perform this job is its broad requirements; the ideal person should have a very extensive background. A review of the qualifications of the ideal materials manager can help companies to develop people for future positions, and can serve as a guide to individuals interested in this satisfying career path.

A broad formal education is a primary requirement. Business administration and engineering curricula give a desirable base of knowledge. College courses covering each of the materials subfunctions provide specific knowledge. Continuing education courses and seminars offered by colleges can contribute significantly to the materials manager's education, as they provide expertise in specific areas of knowledge. Professional societies are another source of education, in training practitioners to achieve certification and in teaching current techniques.

Experience in the various materials subfunctions would provide the broad knowledge necessary to administer a total materials management program. Companies sometimes have difficulty finding qualified individuals with broad backgrounds for materials management. This problem will be reduced as more companies implement cross-training programs, which allow individuals to gain experience in various positions and subfunctions.

An essential factor in the manager's background is successful experience as a supervisor. Someone may be technically capable, but it does not follow that he or she is qualified to be a supervisor. The materials manager must have proven capability in planning, organizing, controlling, motivating, developing innovative programs, and making decisions. Experience with the successful application of sound project management techniques and a supervisory background in implementation of a multifunctional materials management system would be valuable.

The materials manager position is very demanding. It requires someone with multifaceted personal qualifications. The individual must be determined, loyal, and intelligent, and possessed of initiative, self-motivation, and a willingness to accept responsibility. The proper person for this position will be able to apply the scientific process to systems analysis and improvement. He or she must successfully sell these concepts to upper management and others within the company. Many valuable, innovative systems have been buried in desk drawers because of a manager's inability to justify and sell concepts. The manager also would have to be honest, articulate, and empathetic, in working with people in various levels throughout the organization.

The materials manager must enjoy performing a broad array of activities. The reason why many managers work as hard as they do is that they like their work; they enjoy the act of accomplishment. The work itself provides their reward.[15]

Activities outside the workplace can contribute greatly to personal development and capability. One important resource is professional societies (see Chapter 1). These groups provide meetings, conferences, and seminars that contribute to state-of-the-art knowledge. They also provide good contacts for specific information and sharing of experiences. Other outside activities that could enhance one's experience and knowledge base include churches, civic organizations, and school boards.

SUMMARY

Company organization is critical to the success of any business. The total materials management structure within any firm must satisfy individual company requirements while providing optimization of materials group objectives. Major objectives of the group would include an integrated materials organization and adherence to basic guidelines to provide good structural relationships.

The ideal materials organization would contain all of the subfunctions, including planning, inventory control, production control, purchasing, receiving and stores, materials handling, and physical distribution. Arguments can be given for separating physical distribution and purchasing from the total group, and for having materials management report to the head of manufacturing.

Advantages and disadvantages of concentrating both personnel and authority in centralized and decentralized groups must be weighed in determining the best organization. Alternative configurations to consider include hospital organizations.

Initial and ongoing relationships should be developed among major company functions in order to fulfill overall business objectives. Materials management can attain success by achieving credibility and developing two-way communication with finance, marketing, research and development, industrial engineering, quality assurance, and systems/data processing. The executive in charge of the materials management organization must have broad ability to integrate all subfunctions and effectuate group objectives and goals. This executive optimally should report to the highest company level. Selection of a capable individual would include consideration of his or her education, experience, personal traits, and outside professional activities.

NOTES

1. Drucker, *Management: Tasks, Responsibilities, Practices,* pp. 599–600.
2. Leenders, Fearon, and England, *Purchasing and Materials Management,* p. 42.
3. Lipman, "Materials Management: A Blessing in Disguise," p. 49.
4. Stoner and Wankel, *Management,* p. 307.
5. V. A. Graicunas, "Relationship in Organization," *Bulletin of the International Management Institute,* Vol. 7 (March, 1933), pp. 39–42, reprinted in Luther H. Gulick and Lyndall F. Urwick, eds., *Papers on the Science of Administration* (New York: Institute of Public Administration, Colulmbia University, 1937), pp. 182–187.
6. Miller and Gilmour, "Materials Managers: Who Needs Them?" pp. 143–144.
7. Ibid.
8. Lazarus, "This Commitment Pays Dividends," p. 33.
9. Johnson, "Operating Controls—The Key to Effective Materials Management," p. 461.
10. Farrell and Aljian (eds.), *Aljian's Purchasing Handbook,* p. 19–3.
11. Terseine and Campbell, *Modern Materials Management,* p. 5.
12. A discussion of these and other techniques can be found in most current management texts.
13. Jauch, Coltrin, Bedeian, and Glueck, *The Management Experience: Cases, Exercises and Readings,* p. 77.
14. Miller and Gilmour, "Materials Managers: Who Needs Them?" p. 151.
15. McAfee and Poffenberger, *Productivity Strategies,* p. 159.

BIBLIOGRAPHY

Drucker, Peter F. *Management: Tasks, Responsibilities, Practices.* New York: Harper and Row, 1974.
Farrell, P. V., and Aljian, G. W., eds. *Aljian's Purchasing Handbook.* New York: McGraw-Hill Book Co., 1982.
Greisler, David S., and Aggarwal, Sumer C. "Hospital Materials Management: Potential for Improvement." *Journal of Purchasing and Materials Management,* Spring 1985.
Heyel, Carl, and Menkus, Belden. *Handbook of Management for the Growing Business.* New York: Van Nostrand Reinhold Co., 1986.
Jauch, L., Coltrin, S., Bedeian, A., and Glueck, W. *The Management Experience: Cases, Exercises and Readings.* Hinsdale, Illinois: The Dryden Press, 1983.
Johnson, Ernest A. "Operating Controls—The Key to Effective Materials Management."

1982 Conference Proceedings, American Production and Inventory Control Society, p. 461.

Lazarus, Steven. "This Commitment Pays Dividends." *Traffic Management,* Jan. 1983.

Leenders, Michael, Fearon, Harold, and England, Wilbur. *Purchasing and Materials Management.* Homewood, Illinois: Richard D. Irwin, 1985.

Lipman, Rebecca. "Materials Management: A Blessing in Disguise." *Purchasing,* Oct. 23, 1980.

McAfee, R. Bruce, and Poffenberger, William. *Productivity Strategies.* Englewood Cliffs, New Jersey: Prentice-Hall, 1982.

Miller, Jeffrey A., and Gilmour, Peter. "Materials Managers: Who Needs Them?" *Harvard Business Review,* July–Aug. 1979.

Przybyla, Kenneth. "Organizing for Successful Materials Management." *A.P.I.C.S. Annual International Conference Proceedings,* American Production and Inventory Control Society, 1985.

Rowbottom, R. "Cutting Out Management Overlap," Nov. 1987.

Stern, Joel M., and Chew, Donald H. *The Revolution in Corporate Finance.* New York: Basil Blackwell, 1986.

Stoner, James A. F., and Wankel, Charles. *Management.* Englewood Cliffs, New Jersey: Prentice-Hall, 1986.

Terseine, Richard, and Campbell, John. *Modern Materials Management.* New York: Elsevier North-Holland, 1977.

Vincent, D. R. "Understanding Organizational Power." *Journal of Business Strategy,* Mar.–Apr. 1988.

Part 2

PLANNING AND CONTROL OF MATERIALS MANAGEMENT

3
Materials Management Planning

After World War II, there was an increased emphasis on planning by management at all levels. This change affected management of both manufacturing and service operations, and resulted from a need to improve customer service and operating efficiency. The tendency to pay greater attention to planning has continued, and has spurred the growth of materials management and the need for planning at the materials management level.

The increased emphasis on planning has been accompanied by a formalized approach, as a constant methodology is needed to determine the labor, capital, equipment, and materials required by materials management and other functions to produce a desired output (Figure 3-1). The output can be a product in a manufacturing, distribution, warehousing, or retail environment; but in industries such as hospitals, universities, government, and civic organizations, the end product is not a physical product, but a service. Regardless of the nature of the output, and whether the organizations are public or private, profit or nonprofit, materials management must have formal plans.

THE NATURE OF PLANNING IN MATERIALS MANAGEMENT

In today's competitive environment survival depends on anticipating and meeting customer requirements; but, unfortunately, customers are not always predictable. This uncertainty is counteracted through effective planning by materials management and other groups dealing with change. The planning process provides an effective framework from which materials management can direct its future activities, establish priorities, and handle changes in priorities. As a foundation for future action, planning, by its very nature, must be based on current and historical data.

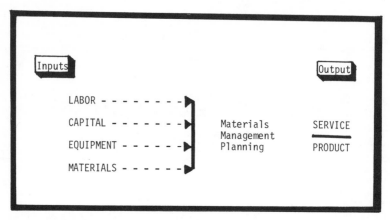

Figure 3-1. Materials management recognizes that planning is necessary to produce a desired output from given inputs.

Materials Management Planning

The planning process is a mechanism for setting overall operating levels.[1] It utilizes various strategies to decrease materials handling, eliminate bottlenecks, and change operating capacities. Inherent in the process is the analysis of labor, facilities, and equipment, as a basis for ascertaining future requirements based on an organization's overall goal and objectives. Units of measure may be units, pounds, gallons, labor hours, machine hours, and so on.

The plan must be a formal written document that considers capacities and priorities, and complements the fulfillment of corporate objectives. The materials management plan is information provided to management, together with plans from marketing, manufacturing, engineering, quality assurance, and finance.

Terminology. As the philosophy of formal planning has evolved, it has become necessary to establish a common vocabulary—in many instances, words, or terms, that have been used before. The same terms often have had different meanings, depending on the company, or division, in which they were used. However, the increased mobility and communications of materials management professionals have made it necessary to standardize terminology. This is being accomplished with the aid of professional societies and formal educational institutions.[2] The following terms and definitions are related to materials management:

- *Materials management plan:* A statement of projections, costs, and requirements, based on overall company plans. A materials management plan is usually stated in terms of units or some physical volumes, and should agree with the operating/production plan.

- *Master schedule:* A statement of selected items that a company expects to build (in a manufacturing environment) or purchase (in a nonmanufacturing environment).
- *Detailed capacity planning (capacity requirements planning, CRP):* The process of determining the operating/manufacturing load and timing of labor and machine hours required to meet the master schedule; both released and unreleased orders are included.
- *Material planning:* Establishment of the quantity, timing, and locations of materials required to satisfy the master schedule.
- *Operating/production plan:* An agreed-upon strategy that results from setting the overall level of output needed to achieve management's objectives in terms of:
  (a) changes in customer service levels (or backlog), and
  (b) maintaining a stable work force.

- *Operating/production schedules:* A plan that authorizes and sequences jobs in a department, and specifies the quantities, items, and priorities of those jobs.
- *Resource requirements planning (RRP):* An analysis of the impact of an operating/production plan or a master schedule on key resources. This technique is used to ascertain the reality of a production plan or a master schedule prior to its implementation.

Planning Span. For materials management, a variety of planning needs should be satisfied, as different levels of information are required. Materials management is involved in long-range planning, but it also is directly concerned with what is going to be produced today and tomorrow, and is responsible for planning the movement of materials to meet production schedules. The net result is the development of strategic/long-range planning, tactical/medium-range planning, and operational/short-range planning (Figure 3-2).

Strategic/Long-Range Materials Management Plans. The time horizon for strategic planning is generally one to ten years; however, this depends on the company and the uniqueness of its product. For example, materials management planning for an Automated Storage/Retrieval System ASRS is significantly longer than that for a forklift truck or hand truck. This is so because the lead time needed to plan, design, and construct a useful life for the ASRS facility is much longer than that needed for the forklift truck.

Inherent in a materials management long-range plan is the setting of

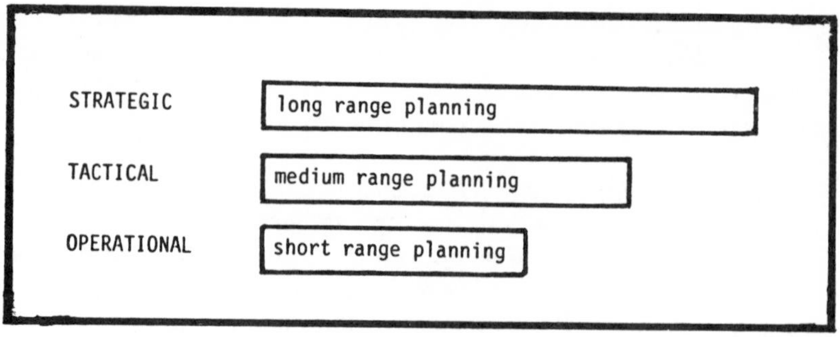

Figure 3-2. Levels of planning.

corporate objectives, which determines the future direction of the company. Typical long-range company objectives are market share, growth rate, return on investment, social responsibilities, and profit maximization, all of which have a direct impact on materials management plans.

In conjunction with setting corporate objectives, it is necessary to forecast the future external environment. Such a forecast provides a guideline for the character of social and economic trends in the marketplace. The corporate objectives, combined with a forecast of future market conditions, provide a basis for long-term planning for materials management. The accuracy of the resulting plan is inversely proportional to the time span it covers. Sales can be more readily predicted for tomorrow than for a month, a year, or even five years from now. Consequently, definitive measures such as pieces, labor hours, and machine hours are not used. In lieu of these specific terms, long-range plans are expressed in sales, and other broad terms are used.

Successful strategic planning involves constant monitoring and commitment by management at all levels and recognition that modifications are constantly necessary, which fortunately improve the accuracy of plans. In most cases, reasons for these changes will result from external conditions, not from changes in corporate objectives.

Tactical/Medium-Range Materials Management Plans. Medium-range plans, which are more specific than long-range plans and are achieved in one to three years, may include installing conveyors for materials handling and increasing materials handling productivity of employees through training programs. These plans are courses of action, in that they will serve as effective ways to achieve long-range plans.

Medium-range plans are much more explicit than long-range plans, and are framed in more definite terms to fit the particular company; they can be described so that materials management can form a clear image of them. These plans complement one another, and each one helps to further long-range plans. Although relatively permanent, even these plans are not so concrete as to be unaltered by the changing environment. This is especially true when plans of other units change, for either the company or the plant.

Operational/Short-Range Materials Management Plans. These plans will be achieved in the near future, or in less than one to two years. Often short-range plans are made without reference to long-range and medium-range plans, but many problems arise if planners fail to consider the effect short-range plans have on long- and medium-range plans. The importance of integrating the types can hardly be overemphasized; no short-run plan should be made unless it contributes to achievement of the overall materials management plans.

When short-range plans fail to contribute to medium-range plans, they actually impede or require changes in them. For example, if materials management acquires special materials handling equipment without considering its effect on production capacity or long- and medium-range materials management plans, it probably will hamper future plans for orderly expansion. A complex reorientation of plans will be required, or the urgency of obtaining the materials handling equipment may be so haphazardly expressed as to thwart the plans for a new automated materials handling facility.

Material managers must continually scrutinize short-range plans to see whether they contribute to long- and medium-range plans. It is also necessary that subordinate managers in materials management, production, inventory control, and so forth, be briefed regularly on these plans so they will make consistent short-term plans. Otherwise, the inconsistencies in short-range plans can set precedents for further errors.

Types of Materials Management Plans

The breadth of planning varies with each individual's position and the management policies of the particular organization, but all managers have some degree of planning responsibility. Materials management plans are critical to other departments and widely applicable in the organization; so materials management must obtain information from many other departments in order to develop their plans.

Failure to recognize the plans of other departments has often skewed the effectiveness of the planning process. A plan is needed to operate a manufacturing plant, but materials management must be included as part of the plan. The operating plan must provide for an effective materials handling system. The materials management plan involves courses of action, including a purpose (or mission), objectives, strategies, policies, rules, procedures, programs, and budgets (Figure 3-3).

A clear definition of the materials management plan is necessary because various managers and subordinates may have difficulty in formulating plans or in developing meaningful ways for accomplishing them. In addition, the other managerial functions (organizing, staffing, leading, and controlling) are designed to support the accomplishment of an overall plan; therefore, planning logically precedes the execution of managerial functions. In practice, the materials manager will have different projects at different stages of development, involving all of the managerial functions at the same time.

A plan is unique in that it establishes all future actions and efforts. It is concerned with what must be done to accomplish objectives, the kinds of organizational relationships and people required, what subordinates are to do, and controls to be applied. Because unplanned actions cannot be managed, any attempt to manage without a plan is meaningless; then there is no way to direct people, determine what resources are needed, identify required relationships, or establish needed controls.

Objectives. Objectives are the ends toward which activity is directed and resources are aimed. All levels of an organization will have objectives. Naturally, the objectives of each unit should contribute to the attainment of the firm's overall objectives. For example, the firm's objective might be to make a given level of profit for the coming five years by producing a

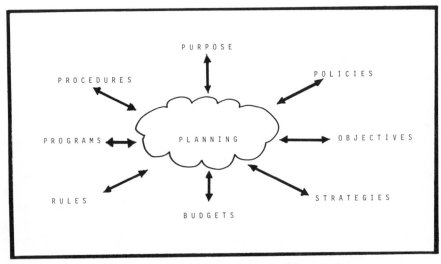

Figure 3-3. A plan involves any course of future action.

complete product line. The objective of materials management is to move materials in the most efficient manner possible, and on time, so that the production line will not experience delays in receiving materials. Although these objectives are consistent, they differ in that the materials management unit alone cannot assure that the firm's objectives are accomplished.

Objectives are the bases for a firm's strategies, policies, procedures, and rules. An objective for materials handling cannot be a guess, or a wished-for result. Instead, it must be determined in the light of an established purpose and existing circumstances. In addition, the plan to accomplish a specific materials management objective must include, for example, the required resources, as well as any requirements from other units.

Strategies. Most often strategies are denoted as a general program of action, including the necessary resources, that will allow attainment of established objectives. Decisions must be made about resources needed to attain goals, and policies necessary to acquire and use these resources. In other words, strategies are basic plans for long-term objectives: courses of action to follow and resources necessary to carry them through to fruition.

The purpose of strategies is to determine and communicate major objectives to various units and activities. Strategies show how materials management can help accomplish these objectives, as well as providing a unified direction and special emphasis. Strategies are not detailed programs, but are guides to each unit's actions. Therefore, they are both useful in practice and important in the planning process. The strategies for materials management are not independent or separate from others, but are actually a combination of projected actions involving other activities and units.

Policies. A policy is a part of a plan, in that it provides a general understanding that guides management in making decisions. Unfortunately, many practices of the materials manager soon may be interpreted as policies by subordinates. Policies set limits and assure that decisions are consistent with planned objectives. Through policies, materials management is assured of unified types of actions and avoids repeated analysis; thus materials managers can delegate authority, and decisions can be made as set forth by the established policies.

Because policies are guides to decision making, some discretion must be exercised in setting them. When policies are established with no discretion, they often are really rules. Some policies are quite broad, whereas others are very narrow. For example, a policy stating that all materials are to be moved in a safe manner is a rule not a policy. Policies should be formulated as a means of encouraging some discretion by the materials managers using them. The amount of discretion needed will depend mainly on their position and authority within the organization. Certainly, the president will have greater discretion and initiative to interpret policy than the vice president of materials management in the same firm. The materials manager at plant level abides by the president's basic policy, plus any interpretations made by the vice president of materials management and the plant manager that may result in a narrower scope of derivations.

Making policies that facilitate achievement of the firm's objectives is difficult for materials management. Objectives change, whereas policies are rarely updated. Also, policies are seldom written down; so there are problems in interpretation—and when many people interpret policies, widespread variations result.

Procedures. Procedures are exact methods to be used by all personnel in materials management in order to accomplish certain operations. A procedure is a guide to action, an established sequence of required actions. Although procedures exist throughout an organization, they are more specific and numerous at lower levels of the organization than at higher echelons. Procedures concerning the operation of materials handling equipment will be more specific in nature at this level; detailed actions should be defined because very careful control is needed here. The best way to obtain this control and ensure efficiency in routine activities and operations is to define required actions thoroughly.

For materials management and related operations, typically a manual outlines procedures. These procedures frequently cut across departmental lines so that the manufacturing department may almost encompass materials management along with many other departments. The same occurs with materials management, which also cuts across these lines.

Rules. Rules, the simplest type of plan, frequently are confused with policies and procedures. A rule is a specific, definite action for a given situation. Although related to procedures, rules differ from them because rules guide actions without any specific time sequences. Rules allow no deviations from stated courses of action, and they do not interfere with procedures. An example of a rule is: "All in-coming shipments must be counted or weighed and compared with invoices." This rule reflects management's decision that action must be taken, without exception.

Rules differ from policies in that rules serve as guides that permit no discretion, whereas policies are guides to thinking and serve as boundaries for decision making. Rules, as well as procedures, are established to direct actions, thus preventing people from using their own discretion. Rules should be used as absolute guides; if materials management desires that choices be made, then policies should be developed, rather than rules, so that decision making will not be restricted.

Programs. Programs document steps to be taken (with consideration given to needed human and capital resources) to carry out specific courses of action. Consequently, they combine objectives, policies, procedures, and rules. A program may be a major undertaking with many related programs and subprograms, or it may be a minor activity involving only a department with several workers. For example, a program to install new materials handling equipment must have subprograms involving equipment maintenance and spare parts, special training programs, and maintenance of facilities. If its use will reduce labor, some workers must be relocated and retrained for other jobs. The program must be developed in such a manner that installation of the equipment will result in only minimum interruptions in the flow of materials. In any program, proper timing is a very important factor. A program that is rushed and is accomplished too soon may create as many problems as a program that is accomplished too late.

STEPS IN THE MATERIALS MANAGEMENT PLANNING PROCESS

The steps in planning presented here refer to a materials management program for an organization. These same steps essentially are followed in any thorough planning process.[3] Small projects are relatively simple; consequently, some of the steps can be more easily accomplished by the materials manager in smaller projects than in major ones. In any situation, these steps are practical and of general application (these steps are shown in Figure 3-4). In most cases managers (all of them, not just materials manager) fail to devote sufficient time to making planning decisions, even when thousands of dollars are involved in the project.[4]

Planning must play a basic role in the management of a firm's activities, as a necessary first step in the management process. Through effective planning, the materials manager offsets the uncertainty of change, focuses on objectives, improves productivity, and facilitates control. These effects make planning a necessity for managers at all levels, especially for the materials managers.

A materials manager does not plan for future decisions, but for the future impact of today's decisions. A plan implies that decisions have been or will be made. When making decisions, a materials manager must consider inputs from many information sources. Otherwise, both the planning and any decisions made will be incomplete.

Planning Period. In some cases, a planning period will be for only a week or the planning period may last a number of years. At any given time, the materials manager will be planning a variety of activities, for different

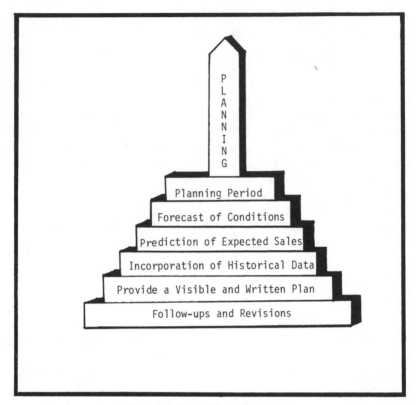

Figure 3-4. Foundations of planning.

planning periods. Planning must encompass a period of time during which management can foresee the fulfillment of its current decisions; the materials manager must plan far enough ahead to anticipate a recovery of his or her decision. The "recovery of the decision" may involve costs, product costs, or capital equipment. Because of the various lengths of time required for assessing each of these variables, one cannot say that a planning period should last one year, five years, or even ten years; it depends on the characteristics of the activity concerned.

There is no uniform length of time for which a company should plan. A new AGVS for a manufacturing plant, for example, will require a plan stretching many years into the future, with time allowed for conception, design, engineering, and development, plus time for systems operations. This would be especially true for the type of specialized equipment that requires technical training and operational changes in the plant layout.

If the planning period appears to be longer than the materials manager can foresee with reasonable certainty, and if it is not feasible to incorporate enough flexibility into the plans, at reasonable cost, then the materials manager may arbitrarily reduce the length of the planning period. This may be accomplished by recovering costs over a shorter period, particularly those involving capital expenditures where the investment factor can be written off. Other alternatives may be leasing capital facilities, rather than purchasing them, or constructing materials handling facilities designed to handle a wide variety of products so that when the company's product line changes (for example, for the production of larger units), the facilities will be able to handle different products.

To be effective, the materials manager must continually monitor progress and design new plans to meet any changes that have occurred. The manager should recognize changes, and should be prepared to use them to advantage, to keep moving toward the department's objectives and to provide some operational flexibility. This is especially important when the manager is involved with long planning periods and large capital outlays. Almost invariably, however, any built-in flexibility is costly; so the manager may have no practical alternative but to plan for long periods of time. Companies such as oil companies that are required to have long planning periods for pipelines because of inflexible conditions have developed excellent long-range plans.[5]

Forecasting.   An essential ingredient of any level of the planning process is a forecast that describes the future. Planning and forecasting are very distinct managerial functions and are not identical, although many managers treat them the same way. Forecasting is determining what will happen in the future, and includes anticipated business conditions, sales volumes, the political environment, and so on. Planning involves deciding how to cope with these expectations. A forecast furnishes premises on which to develop a plan; thus, the forecast is a prerequisite of planning.

In a forecast, attention is given to economic and demographic factors of the environment, as well as technological, social, political, and other factors that might affect the operation. Forecasting is concerned with very specific information, such as the kinds of markets, the quantity of sales, price ranges, new technological development, anticipated wage rates, new tax rates and policies, and many other important factors. All are needed to develop a realistic plan. Because materials management is anticipating the environment in which it will operate, the forecast must include those elements that affect operations. The materials manager must do more than just respond to changes as they occur; he or she must forecast changes and take appropriate actions. A materials manager who foresees the critical changes that will affect given plans has a far better chance of being successful than one who does not.

Certainly, if the future could be forecast with accuracy, planning would be relatively simple. The materials manager would only need to take opportunities into account, determine the resources required, and then decide what to accomplish. Naturally, a high degree of success would be assured. In practice, unfortunately, forecasting the future is not so simple; it is a very difficult task for all managers. Thus, the need for reliable forecasts is especially important and critical. The key role it plays in the planning function compels managers to give high priority to this phase of planning.

The composition of the materials manager's forecast often is affected by both old and new plans of other functions, but the materials manager's plans eventually become the major forecast for the materials handling unit. Different forecasts, used by different managers, can lead to uncoordinated plans. Thus, it is the major responsibility of top management to assure that subordinates such as the materials manager understand the forecasts and plan upon which they are expected to act.

Considering Alternatives.   Materials management constantly must be aware of all future opportunities and must consider them in light of the unit's strengths and weaknesses. This requires the manager to visualize every possible opportunity clearly and completely, and to analyze its consequences, problems, and expected gains. Developing objectives depends on a mental awareness of opportunities.

Establishing Management Objectives.   There is always the danger that the objectives chosen for materials management will be inconsistent with those of other units or the organization. For example, the objective of always having materials available for production might contradict the objective of achieving lower costs for the organization. The organization, as a whole, is a unit; objectives must be interconnected and mutually supportive. If not, managers will tend to pursue paths that may seem appropriate for their individual operations, but which could be detrimental to the overall organization.

Mutually supportive objectives are not always easy to identify because they require planning as "a network." Top management must work with materials management in developing objectives and plans that support that network or system of organization. This demands that top management carefully disseminate company forecasts, work with materials management and other units in setting up objectives and plans, and review the final objectives and plans.

Developing Plans.   Materials management objectives and plans can be developed from a company's objectives. Such a plan specifies the results expected from the action taken; where major emphasis will be placed; what will be accomplished; and the strategies, policies, procedures, rules, budgets, and programs that must be implemented by the materials manager to produce the desired results. A company's objectives give direction to its overall plan, which should reflect the objectives of each major units. These, in turn, become the plans for the units.

In developing objectives and plans for materials management, the materials manager must understand the company's objectives and any implied plans, in order to formulate a valid materials management plan. The materials manager also must be aware of established company policies, plans, and critical planning information.

Written Plans. Forecasts and plans eventually must be put in writing to include both qualitative and quantitative information. Materials managers may think that well-developed plans and forecasts are achieved in day-long meetings, and thus communicated adequately to all. Although such meetings are useful and important in obtaining inputs from all levels of materials management, their results must be written down, reviewed, and revised in order for materials management to translate, communicate, and implement them. Otherwise, in a few weeks most people will have forgotten, or misinterpreted, what was actually agreed upon at their meetings.

Materials management plans are not necessarily completely separate; considerable interaction is required for interdepartmental exchanges of information on such matters as capital investment major programs. Consequently, preparation of a written plan is a requirement, and the larger the firm, the more necessary it is that such a plan be formalized.

For the materials manager, plans should be formally prepared with maximum participation from subordinates and inputs from other units. In that way, they will feel that they had a part in developing the plan and will be more likely to work to assure its accomplishment in the future. Participation helps subordinates to formulate and coordinate plans, focus on future alternatives, and recognize the purposes for planning. These plans are approved by their supervisors, who in most cases will have some suggestions, especially if participation was limited in developing them. Active participation in the planning process is necessary so that materials management can have the benefit of employee ideas and thinking. Often, however, it is preferred that materials management develop plans without outside influence, biases, and prejudices, with input provided only after a tentative plan has been developed.

Follow-up and Revisions. All forecasts are subject to some degree of error; the best analysis cannot guarantee complete accuracy. However, even though guesswork never can be omitted from forecasts, it must be reduced to a minimum. The more experience a company has in making forecasts and plans, the more quickly it will develop a consistent record of accuracy.

Because of their inaccuracies, short-term and long-term forecasts and plans must be revised quarterly and yearly, respectively. These revisions often prove to be essential because each revised forecast will include a wide variety of current data (i.e., sales, prices, production rates, costs, plus many other factors). Through constant updating of forecasts and plans, valuable experience is gained, so that plans are used more effectively. Materials management often fails to examine the underlying assumptions of a forecast—whether it is supported by facts, reasonable estimates, or reflection of policies and plans. The same applies to a forecast or plan that is out-of-date because new information is available. Plans must be continually reviewed to ensure that they include the latest information.

FORECASTING METHODS

One of the major planning elements for the materials manager is the company's sales forecast. To a considerable extent, it provides a basis for materials management programs. The sales forecast provides the foundation on which internal plans can be developed by all the groups in the company.

The sales forecast is a prediction of expected sales of a firm, by both products and prices, for a specified number of months, or years. By using the forecasts for a certain period of time, with a degree of confidence, management can forecast and plan the various activities of the organization to achieve the predicted sales. With a valid sales outlook, management can decide what must be produced, what materials must be handled, and what funds are available for operations and for capital improvements. Because these expenses are under management's control, forecasts of expenses normally are more accurate than are forecasts of sales revenues. A forecast of sales is possibly the most difficult variable to predict, and management appears to have the least control over it.

The company must make every effort to develop the most accurate forecast possible. In practice, however, there are many reasons given for not developing a forecast; these may include a large sales backlog, the small size of the firm, a lack of information, unique product lines, inability to devote the time and resources required for an accurate forecast, and so forth. Unfortunately, these all are poor excuses for failing to develop the most accurate forecast possible. Making regular forecasts increases the validity of the forecasts. The ability to forecast sales is essential for any successful operation, especially in any highly competitive industry. Interestingly, more formal methods are being used today than the guesses and managerial hunches that characterized the past.

Forecasting Information. Very reliable economic forecasts are prepared regularly for the nation's employment, productivity, income, and gross national product, by the President's Council of Economic Advisors, the Federal Reserve System, the Conference Board Form, banks, and other economic groups. These national-level forecasts have a record of being highly accurate over time. Most economic forecasts are derived from a combination of the gross national product (GNP), productivity indexes, unemployment percentages, and average hours per work week. Data are readily available for all of them. However, problems may occur in forecasting various components of the gross national product such as personal consumption expenditures, capital investment and inventories, residential construction, and other segments of the GNP.

These national forecasts can be used to forecast a specific industry and then used for the company. This approach is based on the logic that most companies' sales are part of the total national economy, and, as it changes, so do company sales. Actually, many companies have found that their sales are related to or parallel to the national economy, which either lags or leads them. For example, a company's sales might correlate with national consumers' disposable expenditures, but then lags them by two months. By using this information, a very useful, short-term forecast can be made.

A tremendous amount of information is available about individual industries. This information, along with national forecasts, is invaluable in making a company's sales forecast. Forecasts and historical studies are available for industries through government trade associations, and most federal agencies prepare economic data that can be used for forecasting. All information published by federal agencies now can be obtained through the National Technology Information Service, in the Department of Commerce, or through the individual federal agency. A company's trade association generally provides a wide variety of statistical data that are useful in forecasting. In addition, trade publications, private research organizations, and banks generally have excellent information available that is a "must" in forecasting. Management's major problem is not a lack of information, but deciding what information to use.

Forecasting Techniques. Formal forecasts rely extensively upon the utilization of various techniques and methods. As techniques have improved with wider use of computers, making formal forecasts has become common practice. Forecasting often consists of three different forecasts: one from the sales force, another on how the economy is likely to affect the company's sales, and another of statistical projections from past trends. Management reviews all three of these to formulate the company's forecast.

Sales force forecasts generally are developed by sales estimates from each salesperson. These are then consolidated for district, regional, and national levels. Test marketing may yield further data on sales of certain items. These dollar sales forecasts are converted into unit demand forecasts, which are necessary for operations and materials management.

Economic projections range from econometric models to a panel of economists to computer projections based on mathematical models for broad economy groups. Mathematical models include a wide variety of data from all possible sources to make projected forecasts.

Historical projection methods extend past trends into the future. Common projection methods generally used are means, trends, seasonal moving average, exponential smoothing, leading indicators, correlation, and simulation.

The use of trend and cycle analysis involves summarizing an applicable series of data that reflect sales, or are basic indicators of sales volume. From these data, sales forecasts are projected by extrapolation, or the projection of past trends. This analysis is based on the assumption that past conditions will continue unless something major happens. These forecasts must be carefully analyzed to determine whether or not something will happen that will significantly alter projections.

The most commonly used statistical technique is correlation analysis, which measures the relationships between sales and other factors (Figure 3-5). In correlation analysis, management is trying to obtain a close relationship (correlation) between sales and some index (the national or industrial) on which to base sales forecasts. Although it may be necessary to lag or to lead by a time period in order to obtain a close correlation, this type of analysis provides a highly reliable basis for forecasting. Many companies have found that sales have a close relationship to some index, thus giving an accurate correlation. Therefore, management must analyze many relationships, using leads and lags, in order to find the most reliable indicators of a company's sales.

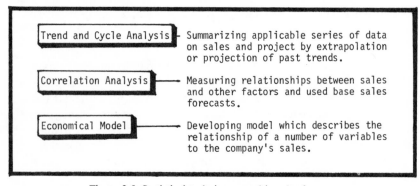

Figure 3-5. Statistical techniques used in sales forecasts.

Another forecasting technique is the development of an economic model that describes the relationships of a number of variables to the company's sales.[6] An economic model that accurately describes these relationships is a very useful forecasting device. When using these techniques, materials management must realize that it is impossible always to have reliable trends, correlations, or relationships, and that major changes will occur that will not be reflected in these statistics. Each company's management will have specific procedures and guides for making forecasts that fit the various characteristics of its industry and organization.[7] Any general approach to forecasting will be modified to meet management's desires.

The first step in preparing a company's forecast is to develop predictions of what general business conditions will be in the future (Figure 3-6). These are derived by considering forecasts of the gross national product, disposable income, price indexes, and other basic economic conditions. Forecasts for most of these economic series can be obtained from government agencies, banks, and various economic groups. Predictions are made about industry volume from these forecasts. Before forecasts are final, however, meetings are held with company personnel to make sure that all factors have been properly considered. Outside input can be obtained to verify national and industry forecasts.

At the same time, initial forecasts are made by the sales organization for each territory and by-product line, which must be modified by management to compensate for either optimism or pessimism of certain groups. These forecasts are carefully evaluated, on the basis of economic and market statistics in combination with historical series and judgment of future conditions as they may affect company sales. In addition, consideration is given to both external and internal factors that have a bearing upon sales, such as price changes, production capacities, markets, technological changes, and promotions. Using the industry forecasts, conferences are

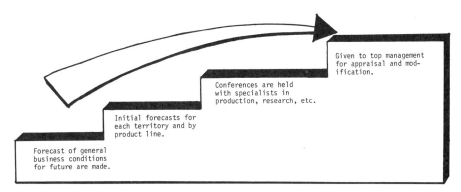

Figure 3-6. Steps in making a forecast.

held with representatives of materials management, production, marketing, research, finance, and others to arrive at the company forecast. The forecast may be changed and modified by top management. The resulting forecast becomes the guide for all departments.

Many failures occur in planning, usually because of poor forecasts. Special alterations must be made in this phase because of difficulty in identifying all factors that affect the company's future operating environment. Even when these variables have been identified, it is still quite difficult to determine the degree to which they will affect operations. The objective is to develop a consistent and meaningful forecast for use in planning.

The materials manager must be concerned with several sources of forecast information. Long-range forecasts are a basis for the outlay of large amounts of capital for fixed resources. Short-term forecasts for the firm's products are the key information for how much labor, inventory, and supplies will be involved in the plant. From this information will come input to master scheduling, for planning the priority-order and timing of particular products and services and the production/capacity plan.

Updating Forecasts. Any forecast, regardless of its type—whether short-term or long-term special, or otherwise—needs to be constantly updated and revised. Because of rapidly changing environmental conditions, management must frequently pay special attention to its forecasts.[8] The impact of factors arising from the external environment (namely, economic, technological, political, social demand, raw materials, and other resources) is usually quite difficult to assess and to update. These factors can have a significant influence on a company's forecasts. Moreover, these factors are not completely separable, and interactions between them complicate the problems. Also, internal changes must be considered—major equipment changes, strategies, labor demands, deaths of key individuals, and other elements that influence forecasts.

Applications of Forecasts. To use forecasts effectively, materials management must actively participate in the entire forecasting process. Materials managers at all levels must respond, react, and manage within their own environment. They must be alert to changes and realize the importance of taking them into account when making decisions. A materials manager cannot just react but must plan for contingencies in the decision-making process. Forecasts of the future environments in which plans are expected to operate are essential. Many prejudices and attitudes must be acknowledged. Also, materials management may have made earlier commitments that do not fit new or evolving situations. These problems must be reconciled.

It is not enough to be responsive to the present situation; one must anticipate the future in which plans will operate. A materials manager who foresees critical changes that will affect materials management plans has a better chance of success than one who does not. Also, the effective materials manager must be aware of the decisions and plans of other departments. The decision by sales and production managers to add a product line, for example, gives rise to many materials management requirements, and the need to develop plans for them.

The forecasting function has four important objectives: (1) to cope with uncertainty and changes, (2) to focus attention on plans, (3) to facilitate the planning process, and (4) to increase efficiency. When forecasts indicate changes, planning difficulties may occur; but if forecasts show wide variability, planning is even more difficult. Materials managers, especially those at lower levels, do not appreciate the significance of forecasts and changes. Consequently, they generally are not ready for changes when they occur.

Broad, well-prepared forecasts cause materials management (typically immersed in day-to-day problems) to consider the future, develop overall plans, unify departmental activities, and revise and extend existing plans. It is impossible to plan without well-prepared forecasts, just as there is no way to operate effectively without utilizing plans based on these forecasts.

Forecasts generally lead to increased efficiency because of their emphasis on planning, which, in turn, provides for a coordinated, directed effort, an even flow of activities, and deliberate decisions rather than snap judgments. Forecasts provide the basis for smooth operation. The efficiency of forecasting can be plainly seen at all materials management levels. The forecast permits materials management to plan for the movement of parts and subassemblies and determine exactly when they must be made available. After forecasts are made, it is necessary to lay out plans so that materials management will know how to contribute to the job at hand, but, unfortunately, this step sometimes is left to chance and to the discretion of individuals.

IMPLEMENTING PLANS

In spite of all the effort that goes into planning, plans often are not well implemented, and the failure to follow through is a major cause of many problems. Failure to implement plans can be related to materials management in many ways. Unfortunately, similar instances can be found in all kinds of organizations, government agencies, universities, churches, and companies.

Means-End Staircase

A very important part of planning is implementation. In developing a plan, various goals, objectives, and plans for the organization are established. One effective method for presenting them for action is known as the means-end staircase.[9] In this method, the three types of goals—long-range, intermediate, and short-term—are depicted as resting on the steps of a staircase.

Long-range and intermediate goals are relatively permanent; for example, the long-range goals of a company include resource planning, whereas the intermediate goals are the master production scheduling (MPS) goals, which are somewhat more imminent and more specific than the long-range goals. The third type of goal on the means-end staircase includes a series of necessary shorter-range goals, such as materials requirements planning (MRP).

The means-end staircase concept can be viewed as a set of steps showing the relationships of a company's lesser goals. Statements are arranged on these steps so that each serves as a means of attaining the goal on the step just above while being supported by the goal on the step just below. One can visualize the step beyond short-term goals as one or more of the intermediate goals. The goal on the intermediate steps is to make a decision, to choose the most effective means for achieving one or more of the intermediate goals. As each of these decisions is made, it is viewed as a means to achieve a larger goal, but thereafter it also becomes a goal, requiring that a means must be found for realizing it. As each decision is made, it is placed on the step just below the goal it will help achieve. Each new decision, in turn, becomes a goal, and so on down the staircase. (Figure 3-7 helps make this concept clear. Notice that the intermediate and ultimate goals are also shown as part of the staircase.)

This concept may be utilized in other planning. For example, for an operation where the production plan goals contain intermediate goals to help in achieving the MPS, there must be a means to achieve them. The means, in this case, would be to develop an MRP, which is needed within the system. Accomplishing this latter action, then, becomes a short-range goal. Again, to achieve this goal, a means is needed; one of the means could be to schedule production. The production schedule would then become a goal, as well as being the means for achieving the goal of developing an MRP.

As this group of plans is developed, it can become a goal for another set of "staircases" that might proceed along technical lines. For example, the means for achieving a specific goal might involve budgeting sufficient funds and allocating the required resources to find a product that would satisfy these needs. This, then, becomes a goal (i.e., securing enough cus-

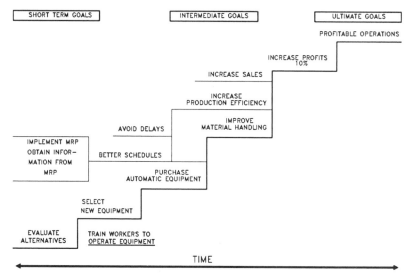

Figure 3-7. A partial means-end staircase for materials handling.

tomers to support the effort). This, in turn, requires a means for securing the needed funds, and, when it is achieved, the goal for developing the project will require the assignment of qualified personnel to carry out the work. The provision of appropriate personnel becomes a means of doing this, and it, in turn, must be a goal, of hiring and allocating sufficient personnel. These means ultimately become part of the implementation process.

This form of thinking about plans cannot readily be reduced to charts or writing. Instead, it becomes a thought process whereby a determination is made of the various steps needed to achieve the goals or objectives that have been set. The speed of this thought process will most likely increase dramatically as one becomes accustomed to this approach. It has certain other advantages in that it helps identify the steps that are missing in the total process and thus establishes the subordinate "staircases" needed to achieve these short-range goals.

Success in achieving goals or objectives depends on finding the most effective means that materials management can employ. In a clearly framed means-end staircase, each step is an action that meets the following tests:

- It is the means available for achieving the goal on the step above it.
- It is a cause that is powerful enough to produce the goal on the step above it.

- It serves as a goal for selecting an effective means to be placed on the step below it.
- It is a decision that has not yet been carried out.

Customarily, several means-end staircases are used simultaneously to attain intermediate goals. These may be considered the subsystem. Certain steps contained in one staircase may serve as a means of furthering steps on other staircases.

The means-end staircase is a way of viewing decisions already made but not yet put into effect — in other words, plans that have not yet been implemented. By using this technique, a materials manager is able to reappraise earlier decisions and be sure that each decision is the most effective means available for achieving the goal just above it. Many times the materials manager may find that some decisions were weak or inadequate, and may conclude that some did not produce good results, that a better alternative is now available, or that an earlier decision has had some spurious effects. For example, a piece of equipment may have been ordered that, in turn, required hiring new people, who, perhaps, were not adequately trained; and as a result, an inferior product was produced. The materials manager rushed to purchase the equipment. Using a means-end staircase approach in formulating goals and means would have prevented these undesirable results.

Gaining Acceptance of Plans

Converting plans to reality requires that materials management establish systems and procedures for execution, comparing planned activities to objectives, determining the availability of facilities, and revising any or all plans, if necessary. After a plan has been developed, it must be implemented and a sequence of events determined — the order in which different work activities will be processed. Implementation of a plan requires setting up operations to conform to a planned pattern, reporting on operating results, and then revising the plan as required. The procedures involved are similar for a materials management operation in a testing laboratory, a grocery chain, or a service organization.

A materials management plan from which others stem must be company-wide and have the continuing support of top management. This is the single most important aspect of planning. Materials management's counseling and rigorous reviews of subordinates' programs will stimulate planning interest throughout the organization.

The support of subordinates for their specific activities is essential. Certainly upper management must review and approve plans if an effective program is to be implemented throughout the organization. Materials management needs to make decisions and guide planning, but often time does not permit the development of knowledge, or assistance from subordinates, to implement the plans. This situation can be overcome if top materials management follows these steps:

- *Organize the planning activities through appropriate and clear delegation.* Materials managers must be held responsible for planning within their areas of authority. They must be directly involved in the planning process so that all of them understand the individual plans, the forecast, and the commitment required.
- *Provide communication among and between levels in the organization.* Ensure that materials managers have clear objectives, plans, and policies, which are being communicated to individuals who must follow them.
- *Give materials managers an opportunity to contribute to plans that affect their areas of responsibility.* An effective way to ensure knowledge and loyalty among subordinates is to have as many people as possible participate in planning. Enthusiasm and intelligent action are more likely in such an environment.
- *Assure that subordinate activities' short-range plans support management's long-range plans.* Middle- and first-line materials managers focus their attention on short-range plans and regard long-range plans as someone else's concern. Top materials management's responsibility is to ensure that subordinate activities support their plans. Successful implementation is not possible when subordinates' actions are not in accord with top materials management's plans.

Even though changes are necessary for any system of plans, there is always some resistance to them because plans must be revised. Changes are likely to be acceptable in any organization when:

- They are understood.
- They do not threaten the security of the enterprise.
- Those affected helped create the changes.
- They result from the application of previously established impersonal principles, instead of being dictated by personal order.
- They follow a series of successful changes, rather than a series of failures.
- They are inaugurated after prior changes have been assimilated, and not during the confusion of other major change.
- They have been planned, and are not experimental.
- People are new on the job.
- People share in the benefits of those changes.
- The organization has been trained to accept change.

To implement plans successfully, all materials managers must be involved in developing them and must participate in making decisions. In practice, better decisions can be made by a responsible materials manager if he or she has a clear picture of the forecast and related information on which the plans are based.

Typical Problems

Many problems are associated with planning the materials management operations of a company, which must coincide with production, inventory control, and other functions; events do not always turn out as expected. The most critical problems in planning are summarized below.[10]

Lack of Commitment. Despite extensive interest in planning, often there is no commitment to planning by materials managers involved. It is especially critical if top materials management has this attitude, causing first-level materials managers to feel the same way. Then attention is given to present problems rather than to planning. Most materials managers feel more useful when they are involved in today's problems, rather than in planning for the distant future. Making decisions where they can see immediate results gives them a sense of importance. Successful planning requires an environment created by top materials management that forces materials managers to plan for the future.

Top management must establish company-wide objectives to rigorously review materials management plans and goals of other units. This activity naturally stimulates planning interest throughout the company; it requires materials management at all levels to establish objectives and develop well-reasoned plans to present to management. Top managers do not have the time, or the knowledge, to develop detailed materials management plans; they need materials management to present plans for their approval and guidance.

Inaccurate Forecasting. A common complaint concerns the difficulty of formulating accurate forecasts for sales and, in turn, for manufacturing. Because the future cannot be known with accuracy, forecasting is subject to errors. This problem can be reduced by using contemporary forecasting techniques; and as forecasting skills are acquired, the accuracy of these forecasts will improve. True planning involves alternative forecasts and alternative plans so that unexpected circumstances can be reflected in immediate actions. With continuous forecasting and planning, events generally can be forecast, and known alternatives can be implemented by materials management.

There are many ways to plan for the unexpected, such as maintaining excess inventory, safety stocks of raw materials, excess capacity, and so on. Planners should recognize the consequences of forecast errors and their cost; mistakes can result in overestimating demand (where excess production and inventory lead to another set of problems) or understating demand (where insufficient inventories cause stockouts and lost customers).

Another problem in forecasting is the timing of the expected demand, as opposed to the quantity of demand. When orders are large, relative to demand in a given period, then requirements are large for short periods of time. Thus, when the demand occurs—or timing—is an important consideration.

Rapidly changing industries present another forecasting problem. Successions of changes often are magnified and complicated to make forecasting difficult. Some changes, which are exceptionally complex and affect rapidly changing products, are almost beyond comprehension. Although all companies are subject to changes, the degree of instability and complexity varies considerably from industry to industry, and even with firms within an industry. Fortunately, many changes that cause problems are of a recurring nature, involving similar elements. For example, the utilization of a plant and equipment have common elements, despite differences in products. These common elements must be identified to simplify the planning and forecasting done during a change.

Lack of Use. After forecasts have been carefully developed and approved, there is always the matter of ensuring their use by materials managers. This is especially true of revised forecasts that may affect current operating plans. Taking action is difficult, especially if some forecasts are regarded as confidential. One technique is to analyze various materials managers' "needs" and make sure that important forecasts are made available to them. Certainly, there is a risk of leaking confidential information, but this alternative is better than having uninformed people implement plans without adequate information. Their competitors often know their strategies, forecasts, and programs fairly well anyway; it is unfortunate if the company's own subordinates, who are responsible for implementing plans, do not have needed information.

After forecasts are developed, an effective practice is to disseminate them to those who need them. Then, as current conditions change, supplemental forecasts are developed and distributed to the managers concerned. These are needed whenever requests, such as budget proposals or program recommendations, are made. Materials managers must understand that forecasts are constantly changing and that their plans need to be updated to coincide with the forecasts, even after they have been approved.

Inadequate Leadership. Many forecasting and planning problems occur because of a lack of administration, or poor management of that function. Typical problems involve:

- *Policy inflexibility:* Once established, a policy becomes ingrained in the company, and changing it becomes difficult for anyone.
- *Labor organization:* The existence of strong unions tends to restrict freedom in planning, because of employee work rules, wage policies, and so forth.
- *Government:* Every company is faced with the inflexibilities of government in areas that are affected by local, state, and national government activities. These include taxes, antitrust legislation, and fair-trade policies, all of which may cause conflicts.
- *Employee attitudes:* Both materials managers and employees develop patterns of thought and behavior that cause frustration in instituting new plans, simply because of the unwillingness, or inability, of employees to accept changes.
- *Lack of communication:* A major problem area involves materials managers' lack of understanding of company objectives and forecasts.
- *Lack of employee participation:* Plans are best accepted when employees and materials management are given opportunities to contribute to plans affecting their areas of concern.

EVALUATING THE PLANNING PROCESS

A primary purpose of planning is to establish controls and measures by which performance can be evaluated. This requires formal reporting of actual performance and comparison of results with plans. Differences must be analyzed, causes determined, and plans changed accordingly, and revised plans implemented.

Multi-function Involvement

Many functions and activities are involved in accomplishing the objectives of established plans for materials management. Unfortunately, any group can diminish the chances of accomplishing these objectives, or affect these plans. When this occurs, corrective actions must be taken and schedules revised. After these changes are ascertained, corrections are made in the MRP, which provides materials management with the information required to change plans.

If the MRP cannot be rectified, then the MPS must be revised, based on priorities of orders, availability of materials and capacity, and the need for utilizing capacity. Materials management traces products through the production process to reschedule appropriate activities. Any changes in priority of the components required for fabricating MPS items will allow components to be rescheduled, as needed. This process is especially applicable in the short-range, when the MRP has been developed and implemented.

Measurements

Measurement of performance should reflect damage in handling products, efficiency, and utilization. If materials management has planned capacity for 200 standard hours per period, but performance reveals an average of 168 standard hours, it makes little sense to plan for 200. The MPS should reflect the actual capacity of the materials handling equipment, and corrective action should be taken to improve the output. Other measures used are delivered performance, capacity utilization, investment, and back orders. Measures utilized will differ by facility and product lines, and separate evaluations for each plan may vary appropriately.

Because customer service has become an important objective for the entire company, it can be a primary criterion for evaluating performance. There are an infinite number of ways for measuring service, each with its own value. Some of the most common measures are

- Orders handled on schedule.
- Total items handled on schedule.
- Dollar volume handled on schedule.
- Days operating items not out of stock.
- Time without stock shortages.

The same measures used in the plan also must be used in the actual measures. In addition, these same measures must be utilized in each time period so that consistent comparisons can be made, trends developed, and the information used in the decision-making process.

Management Support

One method for determining if management supports the materials management planning system is to answer the following questions:

- Is planning the rule rather than the exception?
- Are continued development, refinement, and application of plans taking place?
- Are plans prerequisites for decisions?
- Is the planning process occurring continuously?

Plans must be implemented and their results evaluated. Planning is a continuous activity. Refinement of forecasts and detailed planning are required for preparing short-range production schedules that may take place over the entire time period.

A supportive management will establish a climate that involves:

• Planning that starts with top management.
• Planning that is well organized.
• Removing obstacles to planning.
• Communicating objectives, policies, and strategies.
• Extensive participation in planning.
• Integration of plans.

Planning will be recognized and supported, and facilities will be made available so that materials managers can effectively undertake all phases of planning. If adequate plans are made well in advance, materials managers seldom will be forced to make quick decisions, in a crisis situation, or to handle immediate problems.

INFORMATION SOURCES FOR PLANNING MATERIALS MANAGEMENT

Materials management plans grow out of "other" plans. If production management makes large investments in robotics, or its production line, these become important decisions affecting the plans for materials management. Planned changes in production require that materials management generate new plans for handling materials based on revised projections of both quantities and qualities of materials. Therefore, planning for materials management is directly affected by and based on production plans.

The production plan is aggregate planning that establishes overall output and inventories by broad product groups, by quarter, covering at least a year. It is a plan for such factors as the size of the labor force, aggregate inventory level, resource requirements, and customer demand. The objective of production plan is to provide sufficient finished products to meet a marketing plan objective, while staying within financial and production capacity constraints. A production plan should cover at least 12 months and be stated in the broadest terms possible.

As demand changes, from period to period, the production plan and inventory levels must be adjusted so that planned production of all products does not exceed demand and available resource requirements. Implementation of a production plan also is necessary. As the production period approaches, planning becomes better refined and developed—a vital stage for materials management planning (Figure 3-8). (Materials resource planning is discussed in greater detail in Chapter 6.) The MPS (master produc-

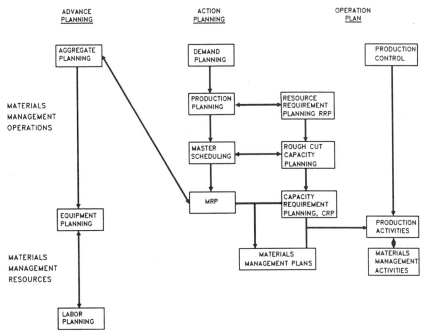

Figure 3-8. Major planning elements of materials management operations.

tion schedule) is a statement of all anticipated production, by time period. For some organizations, a production plan is developed in greater detail as a medium-range plan, which alter may be refined into an MPS.

For the materials manager, a practical approach to getting the job done is to utilize RRP (resource requirement planning), a computer-assisted method of simulating MPS alternatives in order to project loads on capacity.

Production Plans

The objective of master scheduling is to formulate a plan for meeting demands. Orders and/or forecasts for specific items are needed as a basis for establishing a master schedule. In master scheduling, a major concern is the availability of capacity. The two main sources for planning demands are actual customer demand and forecasted demand. Actual customer demand refers to booked orders, whereas forecasts are estimates of demand anticipated for periods beyond those that actual customer orders account for.

A master schedule is used to plan basic units or major subassemblies, and no attempt is made to maintain separate parts number classifications for each of the many options, as such detail is unnecessary. Common groupings are frequently used for planning purposes at this level. These commonalities—style, color, options, and so forth—are assigned during the final week of production.

Rough-cut capacity planning (RCP) is used in materials management planning, and is considered an early warning of difficult scheduling problems. Calculation of the feasibility of an RCP requires the availability of a load profile for product groups. This is multiplied by the scheduled quantity to determine a capacity requirement. Summing up the requirements for all product groups gives the required capacity. The RCP required to implement the MPS must be compared to the available capacity.

A load profile, composed of the capacity requirements of all components that comprise the product group, is developed from routing file data. From this analysis, work centers, including materials handling, that have either excess capacity or constraints can be looked at to see if shifts may be possible between the centers. It is the job of the scheduler to determine how to make changes and resolve these problems. RCP is concerned with areas where problems exist, and not with areas where capacity is ample. RCP does not consider the sequence of operations, or the specific periods in which production will occur in a work center.

The next step in the sequence that concerns materials management is to develop an MPS for an anticipated quantity of specific items selected for manufacturing per planning period. At this time, marketing and manufacturing should agree to meet a specific demand requirement with available resources. The master schedule is established within the broad policy limits established by the production plan and from rough-cut capacity planning.

Basic steps in the development of an MPS are as follows:

- Select items and levels to be represented by the schedule.
- Make revisions that are necessary to obtain consistency between orders and the MPS.
- Organize the MPS by product groups.
- Establish a time period to be covered by the MPS.
- Obtain the necessary information.
- Prepare an initial draft of the MPS.
- Calculate the rough-cut capacity requirements plan (RCP).
- If necessary, revise the initial draft of the MPS to obtain a feasible schedule.

An MPS is a plan for covering, or meeting, customer demands for end products. The MPS is actually a schedule for producing a product mix of major components, assemblies, or complete products. It is a statement of the anticipated manufacturing schedule for these items, by quantity, per planning period (usually per week). The MPS is used for short-range planning and control in areas of detail scheduling, hiring, training, budgeting, financial planning, accounting, inventory control, purchasing, and materials handling.

Master schedules of forecasts and orders are combined with the MPS, a bill of materials, and inventory to formulate an MRP. An MPS determines what components are required and when they must be ordered, either from an outside vendor or in-house. It establishes basic requirements. When materials, equipment, and personnel are adequate, an order can be released and the workload assigned. If either materials or capacity is inadequate, the MPS must be revised until an acceptable schedule is developed. Therefore, it is usually necessary to make simulated runs to determine if the proposed master production schedule can be satisfied, or met, by the system.

Materials Resource Planning is a technique for projecting the quantity and timing for dependent demand items, and for rescheduling orders to adjust to changing requirements. The MRP establishes materials requirements, in a time-phased format, so that orders are released with sufficient lead time to ensure receipt of materials for production. Inventory is scheduled over given time frames, as needed, and the right components are identified, in the right quantities, for use at the right times. This plan minimizes unnecessary materials management work.

The MRP system identifies needed materials and keeps priorities up-to-date. Materials are ordered in accordance with specified due dates, which are kept valid. Rescheduling is required when changes occur due to delays in delivery from a supplier. The use of an MRP loads key work centers. If anticipated materials requirements are generated for sufficiently long time spans, materials handling an labor requirements can be accommodated.

The MRP brings together the MPS and the detailed inventories and orders needed to satisfy the MPS. This coordination must be ongoing to create either new or revised schedules as changes occur. The MRP uses demand information—what components go into a finished product, the time it takes to produce a component, current inventory status, and the timing of purchases.

An MRP involves defining the components required for each individual product and the sequence of relationships for these components. This requires a given schedule, for a given time period, and consideration of inventories of each component. These requirements should be obtained for all components, by time period.

The MRP provides materials management information for:

- An MPS, by identifying changes in order due dates for use in rescheduling predicted shortages and delays on the MPS; thus orders can be rescheduled.

- A CRP's order information, so that loading can be established for work centers.
- Purchasing and in-house production units, as a basis for changes in priorities.
- Performance measurements for management.

When planned production is within established capacity constraints, no major disparity should be encountered in implementing plans. However, unexpected changes may occur in the manufacturing capacity of a unit, even during a short-range planning period. In addition, seemingly small changes in quantity, timing, or type of product can affect the required and available capacity for different products in specific work centers. In fact, key suppliers' plants can alter the actual available capacity.

The primary objective of CRP is to assure continuing high-level utilization of overall capacity. The CRP establishes the capacity required (by time period) to produce a given output in each work center. A valid CRP involves the following steps:

- Obtaining data concerning each required item (from final assembly to materials handling) for each work center, as well as the lead time required with supplier capacity. These data are usually available in the routing file, work center file, and purchase file.
- Scheduling each product requirement on the basis of an MRP.
- Planning work centers in accordance with the scheduled MRP, without considering capacity constraints.
- Comparing capacity requirements with available capacity.
- If capacity is sufficient, accepting the MRP. If capacity is insufficient, the capacity is increased, or the MRP schedule is revised.

A rough-cut capacity requirement plan and a resource requirements plan can provide for capacity planning in the long- and medium-range planning periods. In the short-range period, actual available capacity and capacity requirements must be determined to ensure on-time production.

For capacity requirement planning (CRP) the following information is needed:

- Shifts to be worked during the planned period.
- Number and types of machines available during shifts.
- Labor to be available during each shift.
- Past performance records, in order to establish standards for unit production.
- Productivity for the actual capacity utilized, in order to schedule labor hours.

From analysis of the above information, the actual detailed capacity can be determined.

Manufacturing Plans

A manufacturing plan determines the specific capacity required to produce products and identifies which work center and machines will be utilized in the process. The plan involves:

* Scheduling input and output by time period, for each work center.
* Determining the difference between scheduled and actual capacity.
* Determining variations and appropriate corrective actions.
* Balancing production within established constraints and alternatives.

The manufacturing plan is not committed until the latest possible time. Conditions change, and premature revisions of the manufacturing plan will likely be followed by other revisions, as updated information concerning order priorities, projected work centers, and managerial status is available. The manufacturing plan sets the stage for execution and establishes plans that are achievable and coordinated. The right products are scheduled for production at the right times. All situations are considered, using the required information on tooling and capacity. The most efficient usage of available resources is planned.

The manufacturing plan closes the planning and control loop. It coordinates the many variables involved in products, production processes, facility layout, production facility, materials handling operations, and workforce personnel. The manufacturing plan converts other plans into action by implementing them, reporting the results achieved, revising these plans to reflect current situations, and requiring actions to achieve desired results. This necessitates appropriate prior master planning for materials, capacity requirements, and adequate personnel. Each operation requires a different plan, information, and organizational resources.

The scheduling of production orders is designed to ensure that orders are initiated at the proper times, and that capacity is adequate and appropriately utilized. The key information for a production schedule is obtained from MRP and a CRP; it begins with the releasing of orders from the MRP to production. Control over all orders is the responsibility of production, with each other having an established priority. The priority dates are used to sequence the flow of work orders through the production process.

A CRP may be used to monitor planned versus actual production at the various work centers. A common procedure is to use weekly input/output reports. When planned and actual production differ substantially, adjustments in the plan are required to bring them into closer agreement. Both the MRP and the CRP must be monitored constantly if production is to remain on schedule and progress efficiently. An MPS is the primary input under the short-range planning process; requirements stated in it go into the materials requirements plan (MRP), which establishes time-phased requirements for both components and materials. The MPS and the resulting MRP provide for determination of priority planning objectives.

An RRP fulfills requirements of the capacity planning function in the long- and intermediate-range planning periods. Therefore, the primary function of the MRP procedure is to formulate a time-phased schedule of requirements for raw materials and work in processing inventories used in manufacturing. An MRP is used to plan and control all manufacturing resources—inventory, capacity facilities, and capital equipment. This MRP can be used to derive an MRP subsystem within the organization, such as materials handling.

Interestingly, these planning principles are applicable to planning in any setting, including service organizations. Measures of inputs, processes, lead times, and output may differ, but the concepts and procedures remain essentially the same. They may require some minor adjustments to fit the particular organization or unit.

RELATIONSHIPS WITH OTHER COMPANY FUNCTIONS

Objectives require considerable planning, so they are often thought of as the end points of the planning process. The most significant objective of most firms is to operate at a profit, which requires expending the minimum amount of available human and material resources in achieving planned activities. The profit is the surplus of revenues received over expenses incurred in the sale of products and services desired by consumers.

The materials managers in integrated operations will not have "profit responsibility" in a strict sense, but materials managers and all persons in charge of operations must have a clear understanding of the profit objective, as well as other major objectives. A common practice has been to state objectives in broad terms, which are actually meaningless and virtually impossible for lower-level managers to implement. A common objective, for example, is "to improve the firm's profitability during the next five years." This objective is relatively meaningless because subordinates have no way of knowing what their input must be. It is management's task to state objectives meaningfully to subordinates.

Objectives are general in nature and need commitments of from one to five years, or more. A major coordinating role of materials management is to make its objectives meaningful and complementary to those of other units that materials management interacts with (Figure 3-9). An under-

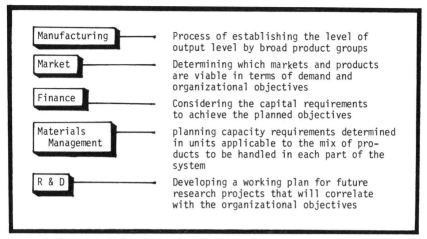

Figure 3-9. Major activities related to materials management planning.

standing of materials management planning may be enhanced by a discussion of the major activities that it impacts: manufacturing, marketing, finance, materials management, and R & D (the first three of which are covered in the following paragraphs). A complete materials management plan cannot be achieved until final preparations have been completed for these groups.

Manufacturing

Manufacturing planning establishes the level of output by broad product groups, for each quarter of the year, with monthly levels projected for at least two to three months. These plans also include such factors as the size of the work force, the facility, and other requirements.

A manufacturing plan generally reflects data requirements in physical terms (tons, pounds, barrels, units, and standard man-hours of production). Product line requirements depend on the nature of the product and the manufacturing equipment required. In manufacturing varied products, differentiation must be made between type, model, and so on, all of which require different manufacturing equipment.

The purpose of a manufacturing plan is to provide finished products in a given period to meet projected requirements, while staying within the firm's financial and manufacturing capacity constraints.[11] When demand varies from period to period, the manufacturing plan must take this variability into account by producing for inventory, which requires additional financial resources or reduced production. The manufacturer's plan encompasses all products, and determines resource requirements for varied divisions or plants within a firm. As the manufacturing period approaches, planning becomes more refined, and a master production schedule (MPS) is developed. An MPS depicts all the anticipated manufacturing for a specific planning period.[12] A manufacturing plan may be developed in great detail and later refined into an MPS, or the manufacturing plan may be incorporated directly into the MPS. Materials management is a vital link to the manufacturing plan. It cannot be finalized until materials management plans are developed.

Marketing

A market plan determines which markets and products are viable in terms of demand and organizational objectives. Any market plan involves a market forecast predicting the forthcoming environment, including political, social, economic, technological, and competitive situations.

The market plan starts with an analysis of objectives, a forecast, and product life cycles. This analysis considers the life spans of products, demand stages for each product line, consumer acceptances, social and economic conditions, rates of development of competitive technology, and technological innovations. Such evaluation may lead to recommendations for phasing out present products and developing new product lines. The market plan involves products that will be manufactured and distributed, markets that will be served, and levels of demand for each product line, all critical to materials management planning.

Finance

A financial plan considers capital requirements for achieving planned objectives. Increased manufacturing activity requires additional working capital for raw materials and labor. Distribution industry firms require funds for finished goods inventory. Capital often is unavailable when required, so financial planning is crucial to success.

Determination of the funds required for a project is the cornerstone of effective financial planning. Materials management must identify capital requirements and assess the financial commitment needed; then finance can plan for the required funds. Materials management usually figures the initial capital expenditures and the capital needed to operate the equipment or project. Because of cost overruns, it is necessary to include a contingency financial plan as part of the initial capital requirements of the prospective project.

Materials management estimates of capital requirements must be supported by an assessment of the proposed project. The project or equipment must be specifically defined, and then a projection for capital funds can be prepared in the financial plan. All too often optimistic projections and estimates are made, resulting in undercapitalization. Too often the financial planning is left to the finance department although materials management should have an important role in preparing any financial plan.

SUMMARY

The importance of planning for materials management cannot be overemphasized. Without planning, there can be no direction, no objectives. The planning process provides materials management with an effective way to direct future activities, establish priorities, and produce desired results. Planning is divided into: the development of strategies/long-range planning, tactical/medium-range planning, and operational/short-range planning. A plan involves courses of action, which may include a purpose, objectives, strategies, policies, rules, procedures, and programs. Planning must be a function of every materials manager; all have some degree of planning responsibility.

New activities, in particular, require major changes in materials management. These changes may involve storage of raw materials, parts, and semiprocessed or finished products that may require special handling, such as packaging and cleaning. The necessary input for materials management plans is found in these basic operations:

- Long-range operational plans
- Manufacturing processes for different products and service groups
- Work center plans
- Marketing plans
- Waste materials

Changes in any operation, such as installing robots, usually necessitate additional materials handling facilities; so planning for materials handling must be coordinated with production, inventory control, and so on.

Capacity requirements must be determined in appropriate units that are applicable to the mix of products handled by the system. The units of measure may be pieces, gallons, tons, standard work hours, feet, and so forth. In many cases, the materials to be moved first must be measured, before plans can be formulated. This may be accomplished by observing and recording operations over a typical period. Activities recorded over a four- or five-week period may be sufficiently representative to provide a valid estimate of actual weekly capacity, but before using such data, management must make sure that materials handled during the period typify the difficulty of handling, materials demands, storage, size, shape, weight, and so on. Certainly, observations over a longer period would increase the accuracy of data, as would information collected at random intervals.

An essential part of any planning process is forecasting the future. Planning and forecasting are very distinct functions: forecasting is determining what will happen in the future, anticipated business conditions, sales volumes, and the political environment; whereas planning is deciding on how to cope with expectations. A forecast furnishes premises on which to develop a plan, and thus is a prerequisite to planning.

The planning steps for materials management involve being aware of opportunities, establishing objectives, forecasting, developing formal materials management plans, and follow-up and revisions of plans. The planning process is enhanced by resources requirements planning, capacity requirement planning, master production scheduling, and materials requirement planning. Developing materials management plans and effectively implementing these plans are very important tasks. An effective method for implementing plans is the means-end staircase technique, which is a way of viewing decisions already made that have not yet been implemented by materials management.

Common problems in planning are lack of commitment by top management, inaccurate forecasting, and inadequate administration, which includes employee attitudes, lack of communication, lack of employee participation, government policies, and policy inflexibility. Overcoming these problems requires a comparison of actual results in which plans and differences are analyzed and causes determined, so that future plans can be revised. Materials management plans must be coordinated and must complement company plans.

NOTES

1. Koontz, O'Donnell, and Weihrich, *Management*, p. 79.
2. Ibid.
3. Koontz, O'Donnell, and Weihrich, *Management*, pp. 217–226.
4. Fogarty and Hoffman, *Production and Inventory Management*, pp. 2–10.
5. Koontz, O'Donnell, and Weihrich, *Management*, p. 216.
6. Wheelwright and Mahridahis, *Forecasting Methods for Management*, Chapter 3.
7. Armstrong, *Long-Range Forecasting*. Chapter 1
8. Koontz, O'Donnell, and Weihrich, *Management*, pp. 217–218.
9. Amos and Sarchet, *Management for Engineers*, pp. 63–66.
10. Visagie, "Production Control in a Flow Production Plan," p. 19.
11. Adam and Ebert, *Production and Operations Management Concepts, Models and Behavior*, pp. 94–95.
12. Schonberger, *Operations Management Planning and Control of Operations and Operating Resources*, pp. 107–114.

BIBLIOGRAPHY

Adam, Everett E., Jr. and Ebert, Ronald J. *Production and Operations Management Concepts, Models and Behavior,* 2nd ed. Englewood Cliffs, New Jersey: Prentice-Hall, 1982.

Amos, John M., and Sarchet, Bernard R. *Management for Engineers.* Englewood Cliffs, New Jersey: Prentice-Hall, 1981.

Armstrong, J. Scott. *Long-Range Forecasting.* New York: John Wiley and Sons, 1978.

Del Mar, Donald. *Operations and Industrial Management Designing and Managing for Productivity.* New York: McGraw-Hill Book Co., 1985.

Fogarty, Donald W., and Hoffman, Thomas R. *Production and Inventory Management.* Cincinnati, Ohio: South-Western Publishing Co., 1982.

Hellriegel, Don, and Slocum, John W., Jr. *Management,* 4th ed. Reading, Massachusetts: Wesley Publishing Co., 1986.

Koontz, Harold, O'Donnell, Cyril, and Weihrich, Heinz. *Management,* 7th ed. New York: McGraw-Hill Book Co., 1980.

Plossl, George W. *Production and Inventory Control Applications.* Atlanta, Georgia: George Plossl Educational Service, 1983.

Plossl, G.W. *Production and Inventory Control: Principles and Techniques.* Englewood Cliffs, New Jersey: Prentice-Hall, 1985.

Reichling, John. Interview.

Schonberger, Richard J. *Operations Management Planning and Control of Operations and Operating Resources.* Plano, Texas: Business Publications, 1981.

Tersine, Richard J. *Principles of Inventory and Materials Management,* 2nd ed. New York: North Holland, 1982.

Wheelwright, Steven C., and Mahridahis, Spryos. *Forecasting Methods for Management.* New York: John Wiley and Sons, 1977.

Visagie, Martin S. "Production Control in a Flow Production Plan," Roneyn Everdell Master Production Scheduling. Washington, D.C.: American Productivity and Inventory Control Society, *A.P.I.C.S. Conference Proceedings,* 1976.

Wight, Oliver W. *Production and Inventory Management in the Computer Age.* Boston: Cahners Books, 1974.

4
The Integration of Inventory Control in Materials Management

Inventories provide a rational approach to operations by aiding smooth flow, effective utilization of facilities, and efficient materials management, all to better serve customers.[1] The various operations of both manufacturing and nonmanufacturing businesses are connected—from raw materials to finished goods—through the inventory control process. This allows each unit enough independence to operate efficiently. With adequate inventories, supplies can be ordered and shipped, and production runs can be made without excessive costs for setups and ordering. This allows more efficient handling of optimum-quantity lots. Various Japanese techniques of inventory control, such as the Just-In-Time and others, try to achieve these benefits without maintaining large inventories.

Inventories play an important role in any type of organization; thus they directly affect materials management. The inventory system can even, to a certain extent, determine the type of materials management operation a company requires. It is not uncommon for companies to have from 10 percent to as high as 55 percent of their total invested capital in inventories; so inventory control is vital to all segments of the company.

INFLUENCE OF INVENTORY CONTROL OBJECTIVES

Primary objectives of inventory control are: (1) to improve customer services, (2) to maximize return on investment, (3) to increase production efficiency, (4) to minimize inventory investment, and (5) to improve management.[2] (See Figure 4-1.) These objectives in turn support those of the company. In all industries, including manufacturing, wholesale, retail, health care, and educational organizations, inventories serve an important role in achieving the company's objectives.

Inventories may include raw materials, work-in-process, semifinished

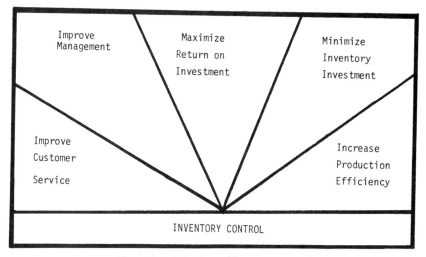

Figure 4-1. Objectives of inventory control.

parts, and/or finished products. A service organization has similar inventories to those of a manufacturing company. For example, a restaurant has the capacity for providing meals, but demand for meals (finished product inventory) requires that inventories be created from raw materials and supplies.

Improving Customer Service Through Protection Against Stockout

Inventories provide protection against stockout (lack of inventories) due to demand variability in the marketplace. If forecasts of demand are reliable, inventory levels can meet the estimates with relative accuracy, and can be kept fairly low. The customer service ratio (Table 4-1) ideally will approach unity.

Exposure to stockout occurs when inventories are low and in danger of running out. It may occur when there are raw materials shortages. Sole-source suppliers with production problems also have an increased risk of inadequate supplies. Although a stockout may have little effect, normally the lack of a particular product could shut down an assembly line, or cause customers to go to competitors. The degree of consequence depends on product cost. If the cost is very high, a company cannot always afford to invest in excess inventory, if it is low, the inventory can be obtained inexpensively, and high inventory levels can be maintained. High obsolescence, another important consideration, is similar to high product costs.

Table 4-1. Customer Service Ratio.

I. Make-to-Stock Companies (Mfg & Nonmfg)

$$\text{Customer service ratio} = \frac{\text{Number of orders shipped complete}}{\text{Total number of orders}}$$

or

$$\text{Customer service ratio} = \frac{\text{Number of line items shipped complete}}{\text{Total number of line items}}$$

II. Make-to-Order Companies (Mfg.)

$$\text{Customer service ratio} = \frac{\text{Number of jobs shipped on time}}{\text{Number of jobs shipped}}$$

Another factor is the space required; because bulkier items require more space, fewer bulky items can be maintained in inventory, and the space cost per item necessarily greater.

The consequences of a stockout, including the potential for losing business and customer goodwill, are intangible; and management is often unwilling to reduce its inventories to minimum levels in the face of uncertain demand and the long lead times sometimes required to obtain new supplies. The effect of this uncertainty is to increase inventories, thereby decreasing the frequency of exposure to stockout. Quantities ordered, demand, lead time, inventory levels, and times to order independently influence the risk of stockouts. Minimum inventories require closer scheduling for materials management than high inventory levels.

Maximizing Return on Investment

Investment in inventories is a major cost, so a major management objective is to maintain minimum inventories. Because there are many different processes and activities, there is no standard inventory level that applies to all companies. Different investment levels are required for different product lines within the same company; so the establishment of inventory levels must be a joint decision of production, materials management, marketing, and financial management, and must reflect cash flow, customer service, and management objectives. Various factors influence the inventory levels of a company, including the following:[3]

- Use of manufactured or purchased components
- Type of product (stock or made to order)
- Distance from suppliers and customers
- Warehousing availability

- Production cycle time
- Consignment stocking policies

Inventory management requires the establishment of procedures, policies, rules, and guides for various inventory situations, which, in turn, requires management to explicitly analyze different situations during the production, materials management, warehousing, and marketing phases. Inventory must be carefully analyzed to detect short-term seasonal fluctuations, identify long-term trends as early as possible, and avoid the end-of-year inventory situations that perennially cause problems for many companies. The analysis also should involve evaluations of finished goods, work-in-process, and raw materials. Inventory levels can be compared to budgeted inventory levels to determine whether differences are due to changes in volume, scrap rate, labor costs, lead time, and so on. These analyses are the basis for corrective actions that are made to meet cash flow and other financial objectives, and to determine whether inventory costs are within the company's objectives. If not, then management has the option of revising production, marketing, and materials management plans to bring inventories within the desired boundaries.

Increasing Production Efficiency

Maintaining an inventory allows for efficient materials management, with the inventory serving as a buffer between production and demand. Inventories allow operations to use the most efficient methods available. When production must be increased, materials management must hire and train new employees, and must add new equipment, increasing costs. In addition, new employees usually require more supervision and they are generally less productive than more experienced personnel, thereby increasing costs. Even scheduling overtime, which avoids many indirect costs, tends to decrease productivity, especially when overtime becomes excessive. Conversely, decreasing the materials management work force also is expensive: unemployment claims must be paid, morale declines, and employees tend to look for more permanent positions elsewhere. Anticipating such changes, workers often will decrease their productivity to make their work last as long as possible. Reduction also affects materials requirements, losing quantity price advantage and volume transportation savings. All these changes will decrease efficiency. Proper inventories allow normal, steady production that fully utilizes facilities.

An operation with changing rates of production requires greater materials management facilities to meet higher rates during certain periods. If an increase in production rate occurs when a firm is operating at less than normal capacity, an increase in volume can reduce unit costs and increase aggregate productivity. Efficient utilization of facilities depends on many factors, and a steady state is an important contributor to minimizing unit costs of materials management.

Minimizing Inventory Investment

In an organization with inventories of many types, the aggregate inventory investment may be large; therefore, all inventories are forecast for different time periods in the planning periods to minimize inventory investment. To achieve this objective, periodic inventory evaluations combined with cycle counting programs enable management to spot short-term seasonal fluctuations, discern long-term trends early, and avoid end-of-year inventory surprises. This requires a system with the capability of measuring finished goods, work-in-process, and raw materials inventories.

Determination of the total dollars invested in inventories constitutes an absolute measurement of inventory investment. This can be used for comparisons and to obtain relative measures of investment. Actual levels can be compared to budgeted levels, and variances can be analyzed, providing a basis for corrective action.

Projected inventory investments by period are necessary for cash flow analysis and to determine whether the inventory investment will be within the financial strategy of the organization. To minimize inventory investment, materials management must ascertain that these levels are within guidelines, thus assuring an efficient operation. Then materials management has the information needed to revise its operation to meet the firm's objectives.

Improving Management

One benefit of good inventory control is improved managerial performance in all areas—financial, marketing, materials management, and manufacturing. This improvement can occur in many ways. For example, marketing will improve sales through better service to customers; there will be fewer stockouts, less obsolescence, more accurate customer service, and more accurate pricing of products. These improvements in inventory management result in more efficient materials management.

ROLE OF INVENTORIES IN MATERIALS MANAGEMENT

Both manufacturing and service organizations expend great effort to increase the efficiency of handling various inventories used in serving customers. These inventories may include raw materials, work-in-process, components, and/or finished goods (Figure 4-2). Inventory flows in the company are a dominant part of the materials management process, and critical to its operation. In fact, it is not uncommon for inventories to absorb over half of a company's total expenditures because of the thousands of items that must be managed and handled during the production process.[4]

Because of fluctuations in demand and uncertainty in obtaining materials from suppliers, a buffer of safety stock must be carried in a raw materials inventory. In addition, raw materials often are purchased in large volume to lower purchase prices, freight rates, and materials handling costs. When these quantities are received, a raw materials inventory is created, and production uses the materials over a period of time.

Work-in-Process

Because the output rates of successive operators are different, work-in-process inventories must be maintained during production. Even with each operation producing equal quantities during and eight-hour work period, there are work-in-process inventories; for example, one operation may produce sufficient quantities for the eight-hour operation in only four hours, resulting in work-in-process inventories. In very unusual operations, an assembly line of sequence operations will have equal output rates for each operation, requiring all machines to produce at the same rate; but without work-in-process inventories, when one operation breaks down, or runs out of materials, the entire line is stopped until corrections are made. To overcome this, work-in-process inventories are maintained; and they also provide the flexibility of scheduling different products. Thus, some operations will continue even if one unit is idle because of mechanical breakdown or materials shortages.

Typically there are work-in-process inventories between production operations that are relatively independent of all other operations. This

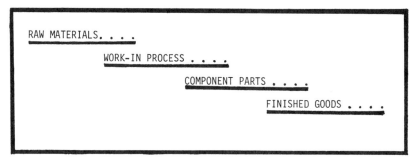

Figure 4-2. Classes of inventories.

same situation applies where one plant uses the output from another plant. Use of work-in-process inventories between plants allows two plants to operate relatively independent of each other.

Use of work-in-process inventories requires that materials management integrate them between operations, transporting the inventories between plants, for example. Thus materials management plays an important part in the effective use of these inventories.

Components

In both manufacturing and service companies, products and services may involve many component parts. Planning to have component parts available at the right time and place involves not only arranging orders for parts in a proper sequence; materials management must schedule the handling of these component parts. Component inventories are maintained because of changes in lead time, difficulty in obtaining parts, unreliable supplies, and variable utilization rates.

Because they are used to make finished products, component parts require special inventory control attention. The lack of any component part can directly cause production delays. Therefore, these parts may need special care from materials management during the production cycle (such as individual handling for small quantities); they are very critical to operations.

Finished Goods

Exact demand cannot be determined for each time period, so it is difficult to schedule production or purchase of products exactly. Therefore, forecasting is needed for inventory control. Uncertainty or demand also necessitates the maintenance of finished goods inventories, as unscheduled production can delay production runs, increase costs, and cause other problems.

Finished goods inventories result when production levels are constant, but demand patterns are seasonal. Uniform production rates are required for effective use of facilities, raw materials, and labor, which all will operate efficiently at a stable level of output. Uniform production allows stabilized employment levels, thus avoiding "hire, train, and layoff worker" cycles, which lower morale. Constant rates of delivery and overtime can be maintained; excessive use of production facilities is avoided, as peak production periods are unnecessary. This economic stability optimizes the production process. When demand is less than production, the finished goods inventory increases, and when demand is greater than production, the inventory declines; the inventory costs incurred are offset by the decreasing costs associated with nonuniform production.

In a production operation that yields many products, facilities must be changed for each product. The cost of the change overs, such as learning curves for workers, machine adjustments, and production downtime, may be exorbitant if not spread out over many units. Long production runs make the average cost per unit, including setup and fixed costs, low. With extended periods of production of one product, at rates greater than demand rates, finished goods inventories increase. These inventories allow for the changing of facilities to another product. With this type of production, finished goods inventories can rise and fall as production changes from product to product, enhancing flexibility.

With level production outputs, materials management can schedule more efficient operations but still must contend with fluctuating finished goods inventories. Such finished goods inventories seem to be a necessity if customer satisfaction and competitive costs are to be achieved.

INVENTORY COSTS INFORMATION FOR MATERIALS MANAGEMENT

Successful inventory control requires adequate accounting information, which is achieved through inventory records, inventory evaluation, costing systems, and inventory status reports.[5] From purchasing through final distribution, materials managers should rely heavily on accurate accounting. If the information is inaccurate, materials management can anticipate unmet schedules or late deliveries to the operating units.

Inventory Accounting Systems

There are two methods of accounting for inventories: perpetual inventory and periodic inventory.

A perpetual inventory system consists of recording each inventory transaction as soon as it occurs to provide an up-to-date account of the current number of: units on order, units in inventory, units allocated to production, and units in inventory not committed to production. The perpetual inventory system is required by materials requirement plan (MRP) systems in a manufacturing company, and is used extensively with present computer systems. With computers, perpetual inventory systems are maintained hourly for both manufacturing and service organizations, even those at widely separated locations.

A periodic inventory system involves a count, or measure of inventory, at fixed intervals. Future orders are based on units in inventory and expected demand; units in inventory will equal the sum of the forecasted demand plus expected demand during shipments and safety stocks. The characteristics of many items in inventory preclude continuous review, making a perpetual inventory inappropriate. Some items, especially dependent-demand items, are best controlled by a perpetual system, whereas others are controlled more effectively by periodic review. Characteristics of a periodic inventory system are as follows:

- Demand generally is an independent variable.
- Recording withdrawals is difficult, and continuous recording is expensive.
- Groups of items are combined into one order for a common supplier to greatly reduce ordering costs.
- The shelf life of items is limited.
- Economic advantages exist in generating lot shipments and maintaining maximum capacity of facilities.

The periodic inventory system is used in managing finished goods, raw materials, and work-in-process. Although there are many different ways of using and modifying the periodic inventory systems to meet various managerial requirements, the most common method is to combine the company's ordering procedure with its periodic inventory system or the optional replenishment system with a periodic inventory.

Inventory Costs

Costs are the basis for making inventory management decisions on the quantity of inventories being maintained at all operational levels. Although different costs occur in different situations and at different magnitudes, there still are common costs applicable to inventory decisions. When considering inventory costs, one must be concerned with all relevant costs, such as the cost of carrying sufficient inventory to cover demand versus the loss in profits incurred by lack of inventory.[6] (See Figure 4-3.)

Inventory involves accounting for all costs and assigning them to operational outputs; all costs incurred are assigned to individual units. To make decisions, materials managers must understand these costs and their roles in the inventory decision-making process.

Fixed Inventory Costs. Fixed inventory costs do not vary with output level. In the short run, inventory decisions are not concerned with fixed inventory costs, but are based primarily on variable inventory costs. Generally, the time horizon and the magnitude of the costs determine which costs are fixed, and which are variable.[7]

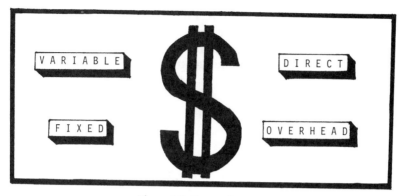

Figure 4-3. Types of costs.

Another way of viewing fixed costs is to identify those costs that remain constant even though the sales volume changes, assuming a relevant sales volume range and a short-run time period. Examples of fixed inventory costs include the annual warehousing facilities costs such as warehouse labor, utilities, repairs on buildings, and depreciation of equipment.

Variable Inventory Costs. Costs that vary with output provide useful information for short-run decision making because they can be closely identified with specific operations. When changes in production occur (increases or decreases), variable costs change (increase or decrease). Variable inventory costs indicate the extent to which facilities are being utilized. Fixed inventory costs are not identified with production, but are related to capacity over a given time period, whether or not production occurs.[8]

Variable inventory costs may be seen as the part of total costs that varies in direct proportion to changes in production volume, assuming a relevant production volume range. As production volume changes, per unit variable inventory costs may be either constant, decreased, or increased. At unusually high and low production volume levels, variable inventory costs are likely to vary considerably. An extremely high level of production volume, for example, means additional inventory requirements, which will create additional materials handling. More workers and delays due to crowded conditions, all of which cause inefficiencies, result in higher per unit costs.

Direct Inventory Costs. Those costs related to inventories that can be directly related to an order, lot of parts produced, or product are called direct costs. Inventory labor is considered a direct inventory cost because the cost is clearly identifiable and can be directly traced. Even the inventory depreciation may be considered direct, if based on volume. Supplies used in various operations are not classified as direct costs because specific volumes or amounts are not traceable to finished products. Other direct costs include labor that is directly identifiable with the finished product, such as workers who convert material into finished products and operate machines; but salaries of foremen and engineers are considered indirect costs.

Overhead Costs. All costs that are not directly traceable to a finished product are overhead costs. This generally includes all costs other than those for direct materials and direct labor. Overhead costs are synonymous with indirect costs. Examples of overhead costs are supplies, depreciation, power used in production, taxes, insurance, repairs, and maintenance on equipment and buildings.[9]

Other Inventory Costs. Determining the cost of less-than-adequate inventories versus the cost of more-than-adequate inventories is a complex problem because of the numerous relevant costs. Lack of inventories can result in the costs of production delays, lost orders, or even lost customers; however, more-than-adequate inventories result in excessive expenditures to support inventories and inefficiencies. Some major costs associated with inventories are:

- *Order cost:* This includes costs of negotiating purchases, placing orders, expediting delivery, inspecting the shipment, and moving it into storage. Ordering costs have a fixed component, so the cost per unit decreases as larger volumes are ordered.
- *Carrying cost:* This includes the interest on invested capital, handling and storage costs, insurance, taxes, obsolescence and spoilage, and any systems costs such as computer processing costs.
- *Capacity-associated cost:* When capacity is increased to provide for fluctuations in demand, costs are increased for direct labor, supervisors, and equipment investment, and there are increased costs due to inefficiency resulting from production rate changes.
- *Stockout cost:* Stockout costs occur when insufficient stock exists to fill an order. Customers are willing to wait to receive back order items, but costs result from maintaining paperwork related to the back order and the possible loss of future sales due to customer inconvenience. The cost of a lost sale is the loss of profit on the item plus loss of the item's contribution to overhead costs plus possible additional losses due to future orders being placed with competitors. Stockout generates loss of goodwill and loss of sales. Unfortunately, stockout costs are virtually impossible to calculate in a straightforward, explicit manner, but this makes them all the more important.

- *Transportation (pipeline) cost:* Transportation requires additional inventory units, which represent increased investments, damaged product, and possible lost units. The resulting costs are commonly referred to as transportation (pipeline) costs.
- *Hedge cost:* This is the cost due to the additional purchases sometimes added to inventory for the express purpose of avoiding price fluctuations, especially price increases.

Costing Systems

Costing systems include actual costs and standard costs. Actual costs are incurred from expenditures. Standard costs are a predetermined norm based on efficient operation. Actual costs are seldom equal to standard costs but oscillate around them. Standard and actual costs are developed for inventories, production, materials management, and so on.

Actual Cost System. Expenditures incurred as a result of past transactions are actual costs, and are the basis for an actual cost system. Such costs are available after products have been produced, or a project has been completed. Carefully compiled costs, which are *promptly* available, are necessary and useful, but there are limitations to the usefulness of actual costs, particularly for managerial decision making. Actual costs are not an adequate basis for measuring efficiency because only limited information about efficiency can be determined by analyzing actual costs. Unit costs for the past period can be compared with average unit costs for the last six-month period, but if there were changes in wage rates, materials, prices, volume changes, or new equipment, then differences in unit costs will not be a reliable indication of the efficiency of operations. In short, few valid conclusions about efficiency can be made based on last-period operations if significant changes were made. In these situations greater validity results from comparing production with the last period's or last year's average cost. In this instance, average costs, not actual costs, are the most relevant.

Standard Cost System. In this system, unit costs are developed before operations occur and are compared with actual costs to provide current decision-making information. These predetermined costs provide a guide to costs expectations for the coming period.

The degree of difficulty experienced in developing standard costs is influenced by many factors, mainly the size, complexity, and stability of operations. Developing standard costs involves a detailed analysis of all materials, labor, and overhead. Specifications as to the kinds, grades, quantities, and expected prices of materials are needed to determine materials costs. All steps in both manufacturing and nonmanufacturing processes are studied to determine the amounts and kinds of direct labor utilized and wage rates that will prevail, as well as a cost for overhead. Through careful study and analysis, these predetermined costs for overhead can have considerable validity.

Standard costs are short-run cost targets. These costs represent short-run goals that provide a basis for efficiency measurements. Like any other short-term goal, standard costs must be continually revised; otherwise, they will become a mere comparison of actual costs of past years. The use of a standard cost system requires constant updating.

Even when great care is taken in computing predetermined costs, it is likely that actual costs will deviate from standard costs. These deviations, or differences, are referred to as variances. When actual costs exceed standard costs, the variance is unfavorable; but when actual costs are below standard costs, the variance is favorable. Variances serve as signals to management to determine the reasons for deviations and to initiate immediate remedial action, if necessary. This feedback, comparing actual costs with standard costs, helps managers to determine whether the firm is meeting its objectives. Improved decision making is a result of such analysis of past experience.

Variable and Absorption Costs. Absorption costing is used for the preparation of financial statements for investors, creditors, and others outside the company. Absorption costing includes all the costs associated with the finished products—direct materials, direct labor, and the fixed factory overhead used in production. Under variable costing, fixed overhead costs are immediately treated as a period expense, whereas fixed overhead costs show up in the assets associated with the work-in-process and finished goods inventories under absorption costing. The differences between absorption and variable costing are illustrated in Table 4-2.

With variable costing, costs are closely identified with specific units. If costs increase or decrease, variable costs tend to follow the unit, indicating the volume of business or utilization of facilities. Although fixed overhead costs are not readily identified with the unit of production or volume, they are related to volume over a given time period. Variable costs occur because of activity, but fixed overhead major costs occur over time whether or not there is activity. As shown in Table 4-2, absorption costing can distort inventory, cost, net income, and assets, hindering decision making. However, variable costing excludes fixed overhead costs from product cost, work-in-process, and finished goods. Inventories are understated and misleading in pricing decisions.

Inventory Valuation

Two common techniques are used to compute inventory valuation: LIFO and FIFO. The LIFO (last in – first out) method of inventory evaluation is based on the assumption that the most recently received (last in) is the first

Table 4-2. Effects of Absorption and Variable Costing on Inventory Income and Assets.

	ABSORPTION		VARIABLE	
	AMOUNT	PER UNIT	AMOUNT	PER UNIT
Direct material	$10,000	$10.00	$10,000	$10.00
Direct labor	15,000	$15.00	15,000	15.00
Variable overhead	12,500	12.50	12,500	12.50
Fixed overhead	7,500	7.50	—	—
Total costs	$45,000	$45.00	$37,500	$37.50
End inventory (200 units)				
200 × $45	$ 9,000			
200 × $37.50			$ 7,500	
Expenses				
Cost of goods sold (400 units)				
800 × $45.00	$36,000			
800 × $37.50			30,000	
Fixed overhead				
(period expense)			7,500	
	$45,000		$45,000	
Effect on:				
Income statement	$ 1,500 higher		$ 1,500 lower	
Assets and retained earnings	1,500 higher		1,500 lower	

to be used or sold. The FIFO (first in – first out) method of inventory evaluation is based on the assumption that the oldest inventory (first in) is the first to be used (first out).

The effects of FIFO and LIFO inventory valuation are compared in Table 4-3. As shown, during periods of rising price levels, use of LIFO results in expenses that are closer to current replacement costs. However, the balance sheet is carrying historical costs, not current costs. Similarly, using FIFO the expenses on the income statement are understated, and the balance sheet valuation of inventories is closer to current costs.

EFFECTS OF INVENTORY MANAGEMENT TECHNIQUES ON MATERIALS MANAGEMENT

An enormous variety of inventory management techniques exist, directly affecting materials management in arranging its operations. Each technique is especially designed for controlling a given inventory situation, considering such variable factors as the degree of uncertainty of demand for and supply of materials, cost of developing and maintaining the system,

Table 4-3. Effects of FIFO and LIFO Inventory. The Examples Reflect Purchasing Two Batches of 100 Units, the First Batch at $1.00/Unit and the Second Batch at $1.50/Unit.

	(FIFO)		(LIFO)
Income statement:			
Sales (100 @ 5)	$500		$500
Inv. used $100		$150	
Other costs $300		$300	
Total costs	$400		$450
Net income	$100		$ 50
Balance sheet:			
Inv. on hand	$150		$100
Other assets	850		$850
Total assets	$1,000		$950
Return on assets	10%		5.3%

and inventory accuracy requirements. Manufacturing organizations probably have the most complex inventory management problems, as they require finished goods inventories for expected demand; this involves forecasting customer demands, ordering the right amounts of products to replenish inventories on a timely basis, and building flexibility into the system to respond quickly to changing customer demands. Inventory management techniques for service, retailing, warehouses, and other systems parallel those used in manufacturing organizations.

Ordering Systems

Work-in-process inventories generally occur between production processes because of different output rates of operations. They are required for continuous and efficient production operations. Work-in-process management is concerned with how much inventory to carry before and after each production step. Running out of materials needed to support operations is as serious as having poor-quality materials; both cause confusion for materials management and increased costs. Inventory management is complex; various techniques must be used to manage the many different inventories.[10] Good inventory management involves providing the level of inventory service necessary for operations to meet objectives or minimize costs.

Inventory managers are concerned with when and how many to order. Appropriate ordering depends on the given item, service level objective, and costs. Successful materials managers must understand each inventory well, as there are various factors involved in choosing the correct ordering system.

Two-Bin System. The two-bin ordering system has the advantage of being a practical and simple application of inventory control, where each material has two bins that physically hold it. In this system, material is utilized and withdrawn from the larger of two bins (the pick bin) until the bin is empty. At the bottom of this bin, or attached to it, is a prepared purchase requisition for another order of material. At this time, the requisition is sent to the purchasing department. Material is subsequently drawn out of the smaller (reserve) bin, which contains enough material to last until the new order arrives. The smaller bin contains both the expected demand during the order lead time and required safety stock. When the new order is received, both bins are filled, and a purchase requisition is again placed in the bottom of, or attached to, the larger bin.

Control problems can result from using the two-bin system. Order pickers may select parts from the reserve bin instead of the pick bin; this results in insufficient stock during the replenishment cycle and a stockout. Also, purchase requisitions may be lost or misplaced, causing the inactivity related to placing a purchase order and eventually having a stockout.

Fixed-Order-Quantity System. In the fixed-order-quantity system of inventory management, orders are placed for the same quantity of material for each inventory cycle. This is often referred to as the reorder point (ROP) system. This technique allows inventories to be used until a critical inventory level is reached. The quantity ordered is constant, but the time interval between orders is allowed to vary.

Figure 4-4 illustrates the fixed-order-quantity system. (This graph is commonly called a "saw tooth" curve.) Demand is satisfied until the order point is reached. At this point an order is placed for a specific, predetermined quantity of material. The order quantity can be developed by making an arbitrary judgment or by calculating an economic order quantity (EOQ). The order point is based upon how long it takes to obtain a new supply of material (lead time), which includes materials management requirements.

The EOQ is calculated by the following equation, which can be illustrated in graphic form (see Figure 4-5):

$$EOQ = \sqrt{\frac{2UO}{MC}}$$

where:

EOQ = Economic order quantity
U = Annual usage (units)
O = order cost (\$/order)
M = Material cost (\$/unit)
C = Carrying costs (% in decimal form)

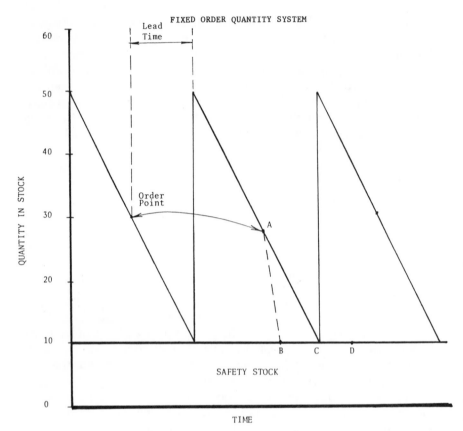

Figure 4-4. Fixed-order-quantity system.

The safety stock provides insurance against a shortage of materials due to unexpected events. For example, if demand is greater than normal ($A-B$ in Figure 4-4), there will be a stockout during time period $B-C$. Also, if a late shipment occurs, and material is not received until D, then there will be a stockout during the time period $C-D$. Having safety stock protects against stockouts.

Fixed-Order-Period System. A fixed-order-period system provides for reviews of inventory levels at fixed intervals, at which time new orders are placed for enough materials to bring the inventory levels back to some predetermined levels. Orders are placed at equal intervals, with the amounts ordered each time being based on inventory levels at the time of review, the desired inventory levels (including safety stocks), and expected demand during the lead time.

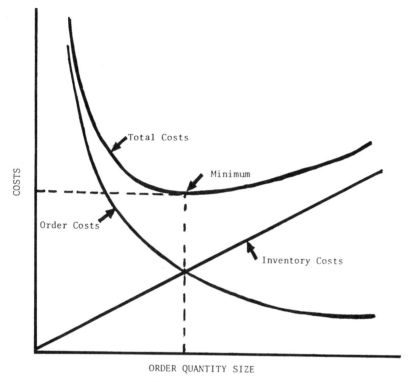

Figure 4-5. EOQ costs curves.

In this inventory ordering system, the quantities are unequal, but the intervals of time, when orders are placed, are uniform. Between reviews, the uncertainties of demand and lead time requirements make this system more subject to stockout than the fixed-order-quantity system. The fixed order period is based on estimates of demand during the entire period between each review. This system usually requires more safety stock than other methods need, to accommodate the increased risk of stockouts, which in time gives materials management greater flexibility. The fixed order period is ideal for inventories where it is desirable to physically count inventory on a regular basis. Perpetual inventory counting is not feasible.

Minimum-Maximum System.   Upper and lower inventory limits are established, through policy, to eliminate overloading of production, to avoid exceeding order-handling capacity with a large number of small orders, and to prevent production of quantities greater than required. These limits may be stated in physical terms, such as no fewer than 25 units and no more than 785 units, or in terms of requirements, such as no less than 15 working day and no more than 30 working days. Thus, the quantities ordered are determined on these minimum–maximum levels.

Material Requirements Planning (MRP). In most cases MRP is considered a scheduling inventory control technique. MRP is accomplished by a computer system that coordinates the production schedule with requirements for raw materials, parts, subassemblies, and assemblies used during each time period to support the proposed production schedule. For example, MRP schedules periodic changes in raw materials and work-in-process requirements in response to changes in either the production schedule or the supply conditions of materials. Therefore, MRP drastically affects raw materials and work-in-process inventories. Inventory management is incomplete unless and MRP system is included as an integral part of inventory management.[11]

MRP can be used systematically to plan the timing of inflows of materials, which are closely matched to production requirements and can quickly be adapted to meet changing demand, production, and supplier needs. With this system requirements for large raw materials and work-in-process inventories are drastically reduced; and better control exists over quantities and timing of deliveries of raw materials, parts, subassemblies, and assemblies to production. In essence, materials management must assure that the right materials are delivered at the right time; and, if necessary, incoming materials can be increased or decreased in response to changes in the production schedule. These controls help to reduce labor, inventories, and overhead costs.

Just-In-Time System. The objective of the Just-In-Time system is to have the right material at the right place at the right time.[12] Achieving this objective requires an efficient materials management operation, along with all others the system works best in certain types of production environments. The product line needs to be relatively limited, with most of the parts repetitively manufactured. Vendors supplying parts need to be located physically close to the manufacturer. Production schedules are frozen for a fixed period (usually a month), and when changes in production are required, they are made only in small, incremental steps.

The Just-In-Time system can be used as: (a) a production control, materials-movement system and (b) a productivity improvement system.

The system is illustrated in Figure 4-6. Each work center has a raw materials inventory that is processed through the work center with the output becoming finished goods inventory; but the parts in the raw materials inventory of work center #2 are identical to the parts in the finished goods inventory from work center #1. This relationship can be applied to work centers in a plant, or to work centers in a vendor's plant. Inventory is

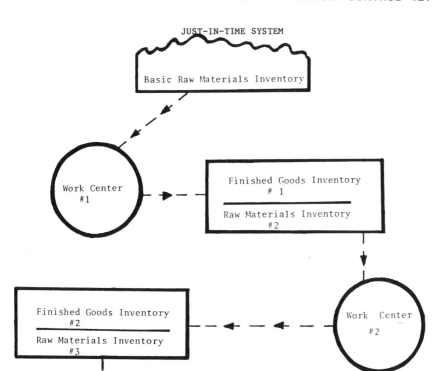

Figure 4-6. Just-In-Time system.

stored in standard containers that also are used to convey the materials. Only one container is used at a time through the production process. The goal is to have the fewest parts possible in each container, and to continue reducing the number of parts per container until the goal of one-piece production and movement is reached.

The Just-In-Time approach requires that daily production of each product be firmly established over a period of time. Then the various production departments and vendors are informed of the established production schedule, but they are not given detailed orders or schedules authorizing them to produce parts. This scheduling is done not for the sake of efficiency, but to have a smooth, constant flow of materials through the work centers. Just-In-Time breaks the production rates of all products down to their lowest common denominators when the detailed assembly schedules are established. The objective is to run the smallest quantity of each product possible, while maintaining the ratio between the production rates of the various products. This approach results in an even flow of work for each work center. Just-In-Time serves as a very effective inventory control system.

Kanban System. This is Toyota's approach to Just-In-Time.[13] In Japanese, the word "Kanban" means card. In this system, each container holds a card (Kanban) in addition to the parts. When the assembly department takes a container with finished goods from a feeding work center to the assembly line, the Kanban is removed from the container and is sent back to the proper work center. This Kanban becomes a work authorization for the work center to make one container of parts. When this container of parts is completed, the Kanban card is put into the container and moved into the finished goods area. The Kanban card is essentially a production work order that circulates between the finished goods inventory and a work center, but work is performed only when there is a Kanban card.

When a work center is authorized to produce a container of finished goods, it withdraws a container from raw materials inventory. In this container is another Kanban card, which now gives the work center authorization to move a container of its finished goods to the assembly department as well as authorization to produce one container of finished goods to replace the one that is to be moved out. This same process is repeated with the other work centers.

The sequence in which the Kanban card arrives at a particular work center determines the detailed production schedule of the work center. If it is producing parts *D*, *G*, and *M*, the work center may receive cards in irregular sequence, such as *G*, *B*, *D*, *M*, *M M*, and *D*, but production is always done in the same sequence in which the Kanban is received. Thus, the sequence of Kanban cards is the detailed production schedule and must be followed exactly. This requires materials management to follow a tight schedule.

Lot Sizing System

Lot sizing refers to the order-quantity, lot-size, or batch-size decision. Lot-size alternatives arise for stocked items and not for one-time purchases. Lot-sizing methods usually focus on controlling the costs of carrying inventory and processing orders.

With each order, there is a "cost," which involves all the costs of placing and receiving the order including materials management handling. Lot sizing involves a consideration of how much to order and the trade-off of ordering costs and holding costs. Various lot-sizing policies are possible. For economic reasons, quantities that are larger than the period's requirements are frequently ordered so that holding and ordering costs will be equal.

If production scheduling is certain, demand will be known, but this situation is very unusual. However, lead times also vary. These variations require buffer stocks that necessitate balancing the holding, ordering, and stockout costs, all of which complicate establishment of the lot size. A very important consideration is the economics of these decisions. In ordering, one must specify a certain lot size to be purchased or produced. Table 4-4 summarizes the most commonly used methods of lot sizing. There are two basic techniques, those that generate fixed order quantities of the same size and those that vary with order quantity.[14] Each has specific uses and is effective for various applications, as indicated in Table 4-4.

Inventory Priorities

Monitoring inventory levels is a key function of inventory management. Also inventory priorities are of great concern to materials management as they indicate what type of system must be used for a particular line. A number of techniques are used to establish priorities and monitor inventory control operations, including ABC analysis, inventory turnover ratio, and critical ratio.

ABC Analysis. This method provides inventory items with the degree of attention they deserve. It is based on a general, widely applicable concept — the Pareto principle, named after Vilfredo Pareto (1848 – 1923), who was educated as an engineer and renowned as an economist, sociologist, and political scientist. Pareto noted that many situations are dominated by a relatively few vital elements; for example, 90 percent of wealth is in the hands of 10 percent of the population.[15]

The ABC principle involves classifying inventory according to the Pareto principle of relative importance and establishing different management controls for different classifications, with control being proportional to the importance of each classification. The letters A, B, and C represent different classifications of descending importance. These classifications reflect the difficulty of controlling an item and the importance of costs and profitability.

Table 4-4. Lot Sizing Methods.

- Fixed order quantity: Order of specified amount.
- Lot for lot (LFL): Exact orders for net amounts of each period.
- Least unit cost: Orders for periods that give the lowest unit cost.
- Fixed period requirements: Order for a given number of periods.
- Period order quantity: Dividing EOQ into the annual demand, orders per year.
- Economic order quantity (EOQ): Orders for EOQ amount.
- Least total cost: Quantity order that minimized the total setup and carrying costs.

Table 4-5. ABC Technique.

TYPE	% OF TOTAL ITEMS	% TOTAL YEARLY $ COST
A	10	70
B	20	20
C	70	10

ABC analysis usually is based on annual dollar volume, as in Table 4-5. In practice, many other criteria may affect the classification of items in an ABC analysis, including the following:

• Annual dollar volume
• Unit costs
• Costs of stockout
• Storage requirements
• Risk of items in stock
• Critical requirements

The procedure used to classify an item requires examining these factors to determine the most critical (highest-priority) ones, then ranking the various inventory items in descending order of importance, and determining the appropriate ABC classification. Examples of different controls used for the various classifications are as follows:

• A items: High value, tightest control, most accurate records, highest priority, careful order quantity determination, and close evaluation of forecasts.
• B items: Normal control, normal processing, and use of EOQ.
• C items: Basically simple control, few or no records, lowest priority, large order quantities, and items counted infrequently.

Inventory Turnover Ratio. One of the techniques used to monitor the effectiveness of an inventory control system is the inventory turnover ratio, calculated as follows:

$$\text{Inventory turnover} = \frac{\text{Cost of goods sold (12 months)}}{\text{Average Inventory}}$$

Inventory turnover ratios can be very useful in measuring the effects of changing inventory management strategy. The ratio is often computed by considering not only averages for all inventory but also various meaningful material classifications. For example, in monitoring a retail hardware business, the cost of all goods sold and the average for total inventory would be computed, to give the total inventory turnover ratio. However, inventory turnover ratios also would be determined for individual groups such as paint, small appliances, and lighting. Optimum turns for small appliances would not be the same as for paint. Using individual inventory classifications improves the effectiveness of this tool.

The ratio may be computed on the basis of either annual sales or annual cost of goods sold (see Table 4-6). However, the computation can be deceiving when the average sales figure is used. Because total sales includes profits, and profits vary with products, use of sales data can skew the conclusions. For example, Table 4-6 assumes that all of the sales for Part A

Table 4-6. Examples of Inventory Turnover Ratio for a Group of Items Based on Annual Sales and Costs of Goods Sold (COGS).

(a)

	ANNUAL SALES $	ANNUAL COGS $	AVERAGE MONTHLY INV. $
Part A	$1000	$ 200	$ 50
Part B	1500	1200	400
Part C	500	300	100
Part D	2000	1800	450
	$5000	$3500	$1000

$$\text{Inventory turns (sales)} = \frac{5000}{1000} = 5.0$$

$$\text{Inventory turns (COGS)} = \frac{3500}{1000} = 3.5$$

(b)   Assuming all part A's sales are shifted to part D:

	ANNUAL SALES $	ANNUAL COGS $	AVERAGE MONTHLY INV. $
Part B	$1500	$1200	$ 400
Part C	500	300	100
Part D	3000	2700	625
	5000	4200	1125

$$\text{Inventory turns (sales)} = \frac{5000}{1125} = 4.4$$

$$\text{Inventory turns (COGS)} = \frac{4200}{1125} = 3.7$$

are shifted to Part D. Inventory turns computed using sales drastically decrease from 5.0 to 4.4, even though no changes in inventory occur. Unfortunately, no standard inventory turnover ratio can be used to compare all product lines, as each organization has different requirements.

Inventory turnover ratio objectives also must consider cash flow requirements, customer service objectives, and characteristics of the company. For most companies, the objective is based on customer service, process cycle time, purchased and fabricated parts ratios, and stocking policies.

Like many other management tools, the inventory turnover ratio has its shortcomings. High turnover negatively affects customer service and manufacturing efficiency, while increasing order cost and receiving cost. Too low turnover can cause poor cash flow, high inventories, and material obsolescence. Even with these deficiencies, it is a worthwhile technique for materials management to use to measure and monitor, and to minimize lag in reflecting changes.

Critical Ratio. This ratio is an index of the relative priority of an item. It compares the rate at which inventory for an item is being depleted to the rate at which operational lead time is being reduced (see Figure 4-7). The critical ratio is either an order point or a time-phased requirement system. The critical ratio (CR) is computed as follows for an inventory item:

$$CR = \frac{\text{Demand time}}{\text{Supply time}}$$

Examples of the critical ratio for three different situations are as follows:

Item # 1 —
Good

$$\frac{A}{B} = \frac{0.5}{0.5} = 1.0$$

Item # 2 —
Expedite

$$\frac{A}{B} = \frac{0.1}{0.5} = 0.2$$

Item # 3 —
Slack

$$\frac{A}{B} = \frac{0.9}{0.1} = 9.0$$

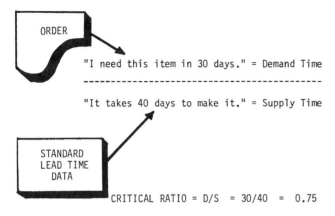

CRITICAL RATIO = D/S = 30/40 = 0.75

This order must be processed through all operations in 3/4 the normal time. It should take priority over all items which have a higher Critical Ratio.

Figure 4-7. What is critical ratio?

The critical ratios for these three different situations show that Item #1 is on schedule and Item #3 has slack time, but Item #2 needs immediate attention.

Records Maintenance

Successful inventory management requires adequate records maintenance, including both physical and financial control. The records provide managerial control, together with inventory evaluation methods, storekeeping, and security. The inventory records include such data as:

• Part numbers and names
• Brief descriptions
• Storage locations
• Lead times
• Safety stock
• Suppliers' names and addresses
• Cost
• Yield
• Group parts and assemblies used
• Substitutes if any

This information may vary because of engineering, manufacturing, or inventory management changes. The following information also may be included:

- Quantities ordered, dates, and order numbers.
- Quantities received, dates, and order numbers.
- Inventory on hand.
- Quantities issued to production, or shipped, and order numbers and previous allocation.
- Available balance.

Sound inventory management requires accurate record keeping, as inaccurate records may cause:

- Excessive inventory of some items.
- Inaccurate reporting of financial data because of under- or over-inventory.
- Excessive inventory that may result in obsolescence.
- Stockout, resulting in downtime, increased overtime, extra setup, and increased expediting.

Accurate inventory records maintenance requires:

- Responsible persons to ensure records accuracy.
- Adequate management support.
- Development of an adequate system.
- Adequate training.
- Audits of records and correction of inaccuracies.
- Adequate rewards for performance.
- Positive attitude of personnel, to maintain accuracy.

Management must demand data integrity, for personnel are more likely to perform well when their supervisors insist upon accuracy. To maintain data integrity, counting and identification of materials must occur at various places in the operation. Individuals performing these tasks should be trained to realize that the operations require accuracy, and all personnel (receiving, shipping, stores, etc.) must count and identify materials with this in mind. All information must be accurate, including storage locations. Manufacturing operators must accurately record the quantities of acceptable production and scrap for each operation, a practice that facilitates materials management. Maintenance of accurate records may require a variety of equipment, such as containers used to hold designated quantities, electronic counting scales, hand counters, and storage facilities, which aid materials handling. Data on issues, receipts, shipments, completion of operations, scrap, and allocations should be processed through the information system regularly. With electronic processing equipment, this requirement is relatively simple; thus many organizations have such information on a timely basis.

Performance Measurement by Cycle Counting

ABC is universally accepted and can be applied to select items to be counted on several different bases. Dollar value (projected usage) is the most common, but one can also use customer order line frequency (number of transactions), common component frequency (MRP gross requirements), or lead times (stockout insurance).

From the viewpoint of financial assets, dollar value is most important. Accounting usually wants to count all high-value items (regardless of "fast vs. slow" movement), but for the purpose of cycle counting items, projected usage, or throughput, is the only proper basis for measuring accuracy. Table 4-7 illustrates the point.

To further establish the point, assume that the count was taken immediately after receipt of a replenishment quantity of 90 pieces of Item A, as illustrated in Table 4-8.

Error % based upon usage is stable, but error % based upon on-hand balance of record may vary wildly. If the record showed one piece, but two were counted, the error would be 100 percent. After shipment of one more piece, the record would show zero, with a count of one. Mathematically, percent error would approach infinity.

Therefore, the percent error based upon balance of record is useful only when applied to the total inventory, that is, annual physical inventory. When items are counted during the year, the balance of record varies with the replenishment cycle. Projected usage, or throughput, provides the stability required for performance measurement. When items selected for cycle counts are based upon dollar value of projected usage, management

Table 4-7. Effects of Errors on Performance Measurement.

	ITEM A	ITEM B	REMARKS
$ per unit	$50	$50	At cost
Usage per year	1000	10	Forecast
Inventory	10	50	Record
Cycle count	9	49	Actual
Discrepancy	−1	−1	Piece
Basis % error			
On hand	−10.0%	−2%	
Usage	−0.1%	−10%	

Table 4-8. Effects of Change in Inventory on Performance Measurement.

ITEM A	BEFORE	AFTER
Usage per year	1000	1000
Inventory	10	100
Cycle count	9	99
Discrepancy	−1	−1
Basis % error		
On hand	−10.0%	−1.0%
Usage	− 0.1%	−0.1%

has closed the loop by applying the ABC principle for both selection and performance measurement.

EFFECTS OF POOR INVENTORY MANAGEMENT ON MATERIALS MANAGEMENT

All inventory systems are subject to problems in two major areas: maintaining adequate control over each inventory item and maintaining accurate records of stock on hand. If problems occur here, materials management will have difficulty in maintaining efficient operations because of inaccurate information. Symptoms of these problems are many, varying in degree from operation to operation.

Inaccurate Inventory Records

Inaccurate records are a good indication of poor inventory management. When inaccuracies occur, actual physical counts may differ from those recorded; and if these differences are always beyond specified tolerances, the problem can be attributed to poor inventory management. Another indication of poor record keeping is that management seems to be more concerned about C items in the typical ABC classification than A items. Management's selection of items for counting frequently lacks any criteria. A lack of regularly planned audits of inventory records, including actual physical counting of the quantities of each item in inventory to verify inventory records, is also a symptom of inaccurate, or careless, record keeping.

Poor Customer Service

The most obvious sign of poor service is late deliveries, resulting in unfilled orders. In such situations, customers must be willing to wait for receipt of items, or they will cancel the orders. Other indications include the existence of few, if any, customer service objectives; lack of concern about measuring performance; idle time in a facility such as materials handling due to materials and/or component shortages; and stockouts of inexpensive items.

High Inventory Levels

Large inventories are required when there are demand and supply time variations due to poor service, high ordering costs, stockout avoidance, and excessive production disruptions. These large inventories require excessive expenditure of funds and increase the possibility of obsolescence. Good inventory management has the objective of determining a rational approach for balancing these two-sided risks. High inventory levels indicate inadequate attention to the application of inventory management techniques; management has taken the easy way out by having excess inventory.

Excessive Expediting

Excessive expediting to satisfy customers indicates poor inventory management. Increased inventory investment and decreased customer service may result if a system is overburdened, physically or administratively. Such stress to the system may produce some or all of the following problems: material lots are lost; materials handling throughout the company is inefficient; setups create scheduling difficulties; the information system is unable to handle the volume; the storage capacity is exceeded, resulting in damaged material lots; material lots are misplaced because of inability to use normal storage locations. All of these circumstances lead to excessive expediting.

Manufacturing Problems

In manufacturing, poor inventory management has the same consequences as poor customer service. When a stockout occurs during production, the operation must be either stopped or changed to another product line that does not require the stockout material. As a result, scheduled shipping dates are not met, and back orders occur.

When poor inventory management prevails in manufacturing, many problems may arise in order preparation. For example, there may be a lack of, or deficiencies in, the following: specifications, recording orders, order follow-up, processing of invoices or plant reports, orders for internal fabrication of items, required setup, and financial arrangements. All of these problems produce delays and increase production costs. Cost variances occur when actual costs are higher than standard costs.

Personnel Problems

Inventory problems are responsible for many personnel problems throughout the organization. These problems usually are attributed to poor planning, organizing, directing, and controlling of both physical and human resources. Most of the problems can be alleviated by adequate training, both formal and on the job; but they can have a serious effect on materials management.

RELATIONSHIPS WITH OTHER MATERIALS MANAGEMENT SUBFUNCTIONS

Inventory control must be compatible with other materials management groups within the organization, and vice versa. The integration of inventory control within total materials management is vital. Materials management executives must be familiar with and understand inventory control techniques and their relationships to other activities—production control, purchasing, materials handling, and receiving and stores. Companies may have different names for the various activities, and some may even combine two or more of them, but every company has major activities that are equivalent to these.

Production Control

The production control group is responsible for such activities as establishing production and shipping schedules. A direct, functional relationship between production control and inventory control is necessary to ensure an even flow of materials. Materials management must keep abreast of production and shipping schedules so that labor, materials, and equipment are scheduled and available at the right times and places.

Production control must be informed of any changes in scheduled shipments of inventories. This also applies to changes in inventory policies. Lack of inventories will cause many problems for production control, including disruption of schedules, loss of production, and overtime schedules. Conversely, an uninterrupted flow of materials will allow production control to operate efficiently.

Organizations now try to minimize inventories by having vendors supply products on a tight schedule using Kanban and Just-In-Time systems. There must be effective inventory and production control groups within the company. Constant harmonious relationships must exist between these two functions to optimize performance and costs.

Coordination of production and inventories must begin in the planning stages of a new production operation or a new product. If either the production control or the inventory control function varies from planned operations, the other function must be informed of the specific details, and its inputs must be considered in any decisions. Changes in any operation should not be made without close consultation between inventory and production control managements.

Purchasing

Purchasing has direct contact with vendors who supply goods and services to the company. Inventory management must work closely with purchasing to ensure that all company policies and requirements are achieved; otherwise, inventory control activities will be ineffective. Managers of inventory control purchasing and material management must work together in the following areas:

- Monitoring vendors' shipping practices to include shipping schedules, carriers, packaging, and loading procedures.
- Assuring vendors of product specifications. Defective materials that are received cannot be included in usable inventories.
- Acquiring new equipment and disposing of surplus equipment. This can affect inventory control's ability to order desired quantities of materials.
- Informing both groups of vendors' violations of shipping schedules so that purchasing can take corrective action against the vendors and inventory control can adjust strategies and plans.
- Ensuring that purchasing will consider inventory policies when special-quantity purchases are made, and that inventory control will keep purchasing advised of its ability to accommodate such special quantities.

Materials Handling

The layout, locations, and arrangements of facilities have a great influence on the cost and efficiency of materials handling and inventory control policies. A close relationship should exist between materials handling and inventory control so that they can plan together in developing new facilities and rearranging existing ones.

The design of new facilities provides special opportunities to reduce handling costs and inventories, as some operations may become more efficient through design. The most effective methods and kinds of equipment needed to optimize costs can be developed; so materials handling facilities are now among the principal considerations in inventory policy. Savings in handling costs have proved the value of this concept, but it must be applied by professional personnel. For development of inventory policies, the adaptability, dependability, and capacity of equipment must be known. Materials management should provide sufficient information to inventory control to achieve these savings, such as optimum order quantities related to storage and handling capacities, as well as the storage capacities needed.

Receiving and Stores

Receiving and stores and inventory control activities are naturally related. Receiving plays a critical role, as shipments from suppliers arrive and must be accurately recorded to include date of arrival, supplier, items, and quantity. Items must be inspected, as required, and controlled until they reach their proper locations. Receiving must confirm that items are labeled properly, and that they correspond to those listed on the purchase order. It must then distribute them to their proper locations. A decision must be made as to whether materials management should move items directly to work centers or to given storage locations. Movement in the wrong location could result in production delays and lost items. Inventory control depends upon receiving and stores to maintain appropriate data integrity to optimize inventory objectives.

Inventory management should provide lists of critical items to be expedited by receiving, as appropriate. Receiving should inform inventory management of partial shipments, quantities that exceed the overshipped tolerances, and items that do not meet inspection requirements. Special instructions are needed about which items should be returned, reworked, accepted, or sorted.

Inventory policies, such as Just-In-Time, which requires suppliers to deliver parts once or twice daily and then have them moved directly to the production line, need special consideration; prior instruction is necessary on the exact handling procedures to use.

Receiving and stores must interact with the materials handling system because characteristics of materials received, inventory policies, and availability of facilities frequently influence the selection of storage facilities. For example, in the receipt of high-volume inventories, the advantages offered by a mechanized system make a receiving or storage operational change worthwhile. Also, a particular container may be suitable for high stacking, palletization, or unitization; this can result in reduced labor for handling and cost savings in storage and transportation. Thus inventory control and receiving and stores must maintain constant communication.

RELATIONSHIPS WITH OTHER COMPANY FUNCTIONS

Marketing, manufacturing, engineering, quality assurance, and finance are some major areas in which inventory management has a direct role.

Marketing

A company's marketing program is directly influenced by its inventory control policies and practices. Sales forecasts are a critical contributor to the inventory control planning process for raw materials, work-in-process materials, and finished goods. Accurate market forecasts have a direct correlation with inventory management's success in achieving minimum inventories. Inventories can be designed to be sales and marketing tools; for example, inventory management should support marketing to achieve special promotions. It is foolish to advertise and then not be able to deliver for lack of inventory.

Sales policies with customers can dictate shipping load configuration and the use of pallets, slipsheets, or other unitizing equipment. The type of carriers (both owned by customers and common carriers) and delivery schedule requirements also will dictate plant and dock load and handling methods, and the degree of mechanization used. Inventory management should coordinate activities with production control, materials management, and physical distribution to achieve the benefits of these marketing programs.

Manufacturing

During the manufacturing process, the primary role of inventory management is to support production operations by providing raw material inventories to the proper production locations as required. Work-in-process inventories at the workplace and processed finished good inventories are also integral parts of this support function. Inventories occur in almost every department of a typical production facility. Inventory control policies and the effectiveness of the group's activities are directly related to the achievement of efficient manufacturing activities.

The manufacturing operation creates additions to work-in-process inventories. It is not uncommon for an item to change part numbers and become a different inventory unit as many as 50 times during a product's manufacturing cycle. These may be single items or items that are combined with others and then moved to another operation, but each time they become some type of work-in-process inventory. The work-in-process inventories between operations are a very important part of the production function.

Work-in-process inventories at various workplaces are costly. They are the least controlled of all inventories in a manufacturing company. It is critical that inventory control, production control, materials handling, and manufacturing cooperate to minimize these inventories. The inventories needed for manual feeding of single items to machines and disposing of finished items represent a major portion of any operation. During this time, an operator is either handling inventory items or preparing to handle them. As the items move through the manufacturing process, there may be opportunity to improve the use of inventories.

Engineering

The knowledgeable engineer must be able to understand inventory problems that exist when systems are designed, and should treat them as inventory problems, not as production, marketing, or other problems.

Design engineering, which is concerned mainly with product design, has a direct impact on the amount and type of inventories required to produce various products. Product design must consider the relative inventory requirements of the design stages, and it may influence inventory control practices. For example, if the design engineer includes existing parts in a new design, that will reduce inventory problems and costs.

Process or industrial engineering determines and specifies the types of operations and processes needed to convert raw materials into products. In most cases, an engineer will design process specifications only to the point at which materials are fed into the operations and at the point of removal. The engineering function should cooperate with inventory control management to plan for all materials and their input and output points in terms of optimum lot sizes, and to include these requirements in engineering specifications. This information is needed for accurate determination and calculation of inventory requirements. Another engineering function is to select and design machines, tools, and fixtures in relation to the inventory size required to make a product by established processes. All these elements directly affect inventory policies and practices.

Quality Assurance

To assure the quality of its products and services, a company develops policies, procedures, and guidelines to establish and maintain quality standards. Quality assurance includes all factors that significantly affect quality, both external and internal. A quality assurance program begins with management's formulation of objectives that reflect customers' priorities and the company's production capability. Customers are vital for the business so their inputs are valued. Production capability depends upon the engineering design, adequate-quality inventories, and the technical ability to produce a product or service that can perform according to specifications, meet delivery schedules, and be reliable and cost-competitive.

Quality specifications are formulated as part of the overall product specifications, which include inventories. From these specifications, standards are established to control raw materials, work-in-process, and finished products. The quality group also considers servicing of products after delivery to the customer.

Specific procedures are used to assure quality: measurement feedback, comparison with standards, and corrections when necessary. Without these steps, it is impossible to determine whether a product meets the established quality standards. The critical part of this process is to have quantifiable standards, which often arise from design specifications or service objectives. When measurable characteristics are developed and compared with qualified standards, then a logical basis for evaluation is established from which consistent decisions can be made with respect to acceptance, rejection, or correction of a product or service.

The responsibility for controlling quality must involve everyone who has anything to do with a product or service, including inventory control managers. The quality measurement generally is performed by a specific quality control group or quality assurance, which is responsible for coordinating quality assurance activities. Recently, some companies, especially in Japan, have shifted inspection to the production workers themselves. Self-inspection fosters pride in workmanship.

Quality assurance activities take place during input, transformation, and output phases of a process, their use depending somewhat on where the activities can most effectively and economically be implemented. Quality assurance in production involves the measurement of material characteristics, physical dimensions and properties, design, and product reliability for products in various classes of inventories. In the service industries quality assurance may consist of monitoring service time and quality of output, which are measurable.

Finance

Inventories add to the cost and investment of a company, whether in manufacturing, warehousing, transportation, or distribution. The investment and cost are substantial in many instances, so investment in inventories must be considered when there are any changes or cost-reduction programs. A firm that minimizes these costs and investments, or one that generates the greatest benefits from small inventories, will have a competitive edge in the industry and market it serves. At times, it may be necessary to increase the investment in order to reduce overall costs.

Accounting practices sometimes mask the role of various inventory activities by making them a part of indirect costs. Inventory control should strive to identify pertinent costs by segregating them from other costs. Inventory costs may be identified as:

- Direct inventory costs, which can be directly identified with inventory activities.
- Combined activities costs, which are inventory costs combined with those for other activities, such as costs for moving items to quality control inspection stations.
- Distribution-related activities costs, which are commonly considered distribution costs. These include transportation costs within, to, and from the plant. Inventory costs may be identified in similar categories related to inventory control.

Inventory management must have a thorough understanding of costs, and knowledge of the financial group's policies and procedures is essential when management is considering inventory policy changes. There must be an economic evaluation of the cost-effectiveness of proposed policies, as related to company objectives. Criteria for justifying a policy may vary from company to company. Payback period, return on investment, discounted cash flow, and MAPI (Machinery and Allied Product Institute) are commonly accepted methods of economic evaluation.

Inventory management must be able to justify investments; it must prepare appropriate cost analyses for desired systems. Much effort must be devoted to collecting and evaluating data, comparing alternative approaches, developing solutions, identifying equipment needs, and establishing the financial justification.

SUMMARY

Inventories provide a rational approach to operations by facilitating the smooth flow of processes, utilization of facilities, and materials management. Supplies can be ordered and shipped and production runs made without excessive costs for setups and ordering, and each unit has sufficient independence to operate efficiently. It is necessary to understand inventory control and its relationship to materials management before choosing a particular inventory system, if inventories are to serve their objectives.

The primary objectives of inventory are to improve customer service, maximize return on investment, increase production efficiency, minimize inventory investment, and improve management. The availability of inventories supports these objectives. Inventory control decreases stockouts and obsolescence and improves equipment utilization. Effective materials management complements these inventory activities.

Inventory management is concerned with accounting for raw materials, work-in-process, components, and finished goods inventories. Two methods of accounting used for inventory control are the perpetual and the periodic methods. To control inventories, a variety of inventory techniques exist such as two-bin systems, the fixed-order-quantity system, and the fixed-order-period system. Lot size considerations, inventory parameters, and priorities all enter inventory control decisions.

This variety of techniques is especially designed for controlling an inventory situation by considering such factors as the degree of uncertainty of demand, the supply of materials, the cost of developing and maintaining the system, and inventory accuracy requirements.

Monitoring inventory levels is a crucial function. A number of techniques are used to establish priorities and monitor inventory control operations, including ABC analysis, inventory turnover ratio, and critical ratio.

There are many indications of poor inventory management, including poor customer service, inaccurate inventory records, high inventory levels, excessive expediting, and others. unfortunately, these problems usually occur simultaneously and directly affect materials management.

Inventory control complements the materials management subfunctions—materials handling, purchasing, and receiving and stores. In addition, inventory control relationships are directly involved in marketing, manufacturing, engineering, quality assurance, and finance.

NOTES

1. Buffa, *Modern Production Management*, p. 371.
2. Plossl and Wight, *Production and Inventory Control: Principles and Techniques*, pp. 174–177.
3. Schonberger, *Operations Management Planning and Control of Operations and Operating Resources*, p. 124.
4. Fogarty and Hoffman, *Production and Inventory Management*, pp. 175–177.
5. Johnson and Gentry, *Firney and Miller's Principles of Accounting*, pp. 203–215.
6. Buffa, *Modern Production Management*, p. 372.
7. Johnson and Gentry, *Principles of Accounting*, p. 424.
8. Johnson and Gentry, *Principles of Accounting*, p. 425.
9. Johnson and Gentry, *Principles of Accounting*, 423–436.
10. Fogarty and Hoffman, *Production and Inventory Management*, pp. 207–223.
11. Cook and Russell, *Contemporary Operations Management*, pp. 384–391.
12. Fox, "OPI—An Answer for America, Part III."
13. Ibid.
14. Schonberger, *Operations Management Planning and Control of Operations and Operating Resources*, pp. 167–177.
15. Monks, *Operations Management/Theory and Problems*. pp. 551–552.

BIBLIOGRAPHY

Brown, R. G. "Inventory Control," in *Handbook of Operations Research—Models and Applications.* New York: Van Nostrand Reinhold Co., 1978.

Buffa, Elwood S. *Modern Production Management,* 5th ed. New York: John Wiley and Sons, 1977.

Cook, Thomas M., and Russell, Robert A. *Contemporary Operations Management,* 2nd ed. Englewood Cliffs, New Jersey: Prentice-Hall, 1984.

Elmaghraby, S. E. "The Economic Lab Scheduling Problem (ELSP): Review and Extensions." *Management Science,* Vol. 24, No. 6 (Feb. 1978), pp. 587–598.

Fogarty, Donald W., and Hoffman, Thomas R. *Production and Inventory Management.* Cincinnati, Ohio: South-Western Publishing Co., 1983.

Fox, Bob. "OPI—An Answer for America, Part III." *Inventories and Production,* Vol. 3, No. 1 (Jan./Feb., 1983), reprint.

Fuchs, Jerome H. *Computerized Inventory Control Systems.* Englewood Cliffs, New Jersey: Prentice-Hall, 1976.

Greene, James H. *Production and Inventory Control Handbook.* ISBN: 0-935406–35-2/LC: 83-73021. Falls Church, Virginia: APICS, 1983.

Hax, Arnaldo C., and Candea, Dan. *Production and Inventory Management.* Englewood Cliffs, NJ: Prentice-Hall, 1984.

"Inventory/Management: An Introduction." ISBN: 0-935406–35-2/LC:83-73021. Falls Church, Virginia: APICS, 1983.

Johnson, Glen L., and Gentry, James A., Jr. *Firney and Miller's Principles of Accounting,* 7th ed. Englewood Cliffs, New Jersey: Prentice-Hall, 1970.

Monks, Joseph G. *Operations Management/Theory and Problems,* 2nd ed. New York: McGraw-Hill Book Co., 1982.

Plossl, George W., and Welch, W. Evert. *The Role of Top Management in the Control of Inventory.* Reston, Virginia: Reston Publishing Co., 1979.

Plossl, G. W., and Wight, O. W. *Production and Inventory Control: Principles and Techniques.* Englewood Cliffs, New Jersey: Prentice-Hall, 1967.

Schonberger, Richard J. *Operations Management Planning and Control of Operations and Operating Resources,* Plano, Texas: Business Publications, 1981.

Wight, Oliver W. *Production and Inventory Management in the Computer Age.* Boston: Cahners Books, 1974.

5
Roles of Production Control in Materials Management

Production control is a service-oriented activity that balances the needs of manufacturing, materials management marketing, finance, engineering, and other departments. Many principles and techniques are used by the various departmental managers to control operations, but production control focuses on procedures that contribute to total materials management — it is responsible for the planning and control of manufacturing resources, including facilities, personnel, and materials.

Planning (discussed in Chapter 3) begins with forecasting demand and continues with estimates of production rate, capacity level, labor and inventories requirements, and equipment usage. Product schedules are developed from item demand projections and production/capacity plans, and they are followed by inventory planning, which determines the demand for components used to assemble end products. The next requirement is the scheduling of operations and parts order control determinations. Engineering provides for product design, methods used, time frames, and quality control specifications; materials management assures deliveries of resources at the right times and places. From these scheduled activities, measurements of output and resources utilization are compared with plans and standards; corrective actions are taken when there are variances.

Production control cannot be considered as self-contained blocks of activities on an organization chart; it depends on many other functions. Production control is involved with the entire range of organizational activities.

PRODUCTION CONTROL OBJECTIVES

Production control is difficult to attain for many reasons. Particularly problematic to materials managers are uncertainties that directly affect day-to-day operations. A productive system must be dynamic and adaptive; it must be concerned with the coordination of materials, labor, and equipment. The achievement of production control depends upon defining

141

objectives. Together, the objectives constitute a formal system that provides an integrated, unified approach to resource utilization. Some major objectives of production control are discussed below.[1]

Optimizing the Use of Production Resources

Optimizing the utilization of a company's production resources is an important objective, but achieving optimal solutions is rarely possible because all possible alternatives must be evaluated. Considering all relevant data is practically impossible because resources and costs are time-dependent; an optimum at one point in time is not necessarily optimum subsequently because conditions change rapidly in most businesses. With such limitations, most managers do not optimize, but instead attempt to achieve satisfactory results that can be deemed feasible in terms of time and effort. In this regard, "optimal" denotes the balancing of objectives.[2] To achieve optimization of production resources, comparisons can be made to establish standards and goals. This approach overcomes the imperfections and incompleteness of data as well as the complexity of calculations required to achieve optimum performance. Differences between production standards and actual measures must be evaluated periodically to determine whether corrective actions are required.

Development of Contemporary Production Standards

The establishment of timely standards for manufacturing includes engineering specifications for each product—the minimum and the maximum. These specifications are standards that can be used in developing schedules. They provide production control with timely information about the characteristics of each component of the product to ensure proper handling, efficient production, and effective functioning of the operation. They facilitate the assembly and manufacture of the final product.

All groups (including materials management subfunctions) involved in producing the firm's products and services require timely information from production control. Standards must be described to ensure conformity to the intended function in terms of timeliness, cost, and quality. This information must be both broad and general, including all products; and it must be precise providing specifications for only one product.

Accurate Production Cost Controls

The cost control objective is to provide orderly data for production control through interpretation of various information, so that production control can determine causes of deviation and initiate corrective action. Because it uses cost control information regularly, production control must be given accurate information and be informed of anticipated changes.[3]

Production control must work with the company's accounting department to ensure the use of proper forms, and it should be aware of any changes in accounting procedures so that reports are interpreted properly. Production control also must know how the cost control system works and how management function operations relate to the cost of other operations especially materials management. A production cost control system involves establishing cost standards for all of the company's products and operations. Production control then uses the cost standards (or budget) to develop a cost control system; this step requires the use of actual and estimated costs of materials and personnel in all labor classifications needed for production. The projected overhead for each department is determined, and is included in the department's unit standard costs.

The accounting department's standard costs are combined with the actual costs of operations to form a performance report, which the production control group uses to identify problem areas. Production control is then able to determine how it is performing, although a detailed analysis generally is required before it can reach conclusions.

Production control must analyze direct labor and materials together with overhead expenses. Overhead expenses include both fixed and variable types; variable overhead expenses rise and fall in relation to the amount of direct labor or materials used in the process, whereas fixed expenses occur independently of the amount of activity. Some overhead expenses can be both fixed and variable, such as repairs, maintenance, supervision, utilities, and so on. Parts of each of these expenses are fixed, but other parts vary with the amount of activity.

Monthly, weekly, or biweekly reports, together with a budget report for units/departments, allow production control to identify potential problems. In the example illustrated in Table 5-1, the expenses for labor costs and variable overhead are considerably more than standard. Production control must study these expenses to determine why they are so high and to initiate corrective action.

A large amount of detailed information is available to back up the reports, which can be broken down even further into various operations. The objective of obtaining such details is to provide production control with immediate indications of out-of-control conditions. Knowledge of cost control systems allows production control to utilize various accounting reports intelligently, to discover potential problem areas in the company's operations before small problems become large ones. Cost control systems can reflect all facets of organizational performance, and production control management should be involved, to understand what will be

Table 5-1. Basic cost control report/departmental performance report.

July
Plant Summary

DEPT	STANDARD	ACTUAL	VARIANCE
	$(000)	$(00)	$(000)
Production Dept A	$684.5	$693.2	$ 8.7
Production Dept B	$255.4	$282.7	$27.3
Production Dept C	$538.0	$539.9	$ 1.9
Administrative Dept	$ 19.2	$ 18.5	$ (.7)

July
Production Dept B
Monthly Performance Report

Direct Labor			
Framing	54.4	49.2	(5.2)
Machinery	44.8	63.6	18.8
Packaging	15.2	14.2	(1.0)
Total	114.4	127.0	12.6
Materials			
Material 1	19.5	17.8	(1.7)
Material 2	28.6	30.0	1.4
Total	48.1	47.8	(.3)
Variable O.H.			
Supervision	10.5	12.5	2.0
Inspection	2.1	4.1	2.0
Material handling	5.9	7.8	1.9
Overtime	3.1	7.2	4.1
Payroll Taxes & Benefits	7.9	9.6	1.7
Repairs	11.2	15.5	4.3
Total	40.7	56.7	16.0
Fixed O.H.	52.2	51.2	(1.0)
Total	255.4	282.7	27.3

expected of it and to have some input in developing the systems. Such items as employee morale, delayed shipments, and product quality are not reflected in cost and budget reports; but if these factors present problems, action must be taken to solve them.

Maximizing Production Capacity

Long-range plans must be developed to provide enough personnel, materials, and production capacity during each time period to generate the overall output needed to satisfy customer demands. This involves planning, scheduling, facility capacity development, and inventories for the operation.

Sufficient volumes of product are needed to meet expected demand from customers during each time period without excess production, with its increased warehousing costs and loss of products through damage and obsolescence. Constant observation of production and demand is necessary to maintain a satisfactory balance between the two.

Optimizing Customer Service

Even with ample production capacity allocated for the various products and services, customer satisfaction is an important aspect of production control. This objective is achieved by efficiently scheduling the finished product. Thus a major objective of production control is to optimize the quality of service as well as of products, stemming from the realization that the level of service is an important element in the overall efficiency of an operation and other functions of the company. Severe production control problems may result when the quality of service is not carefully monitored.

Maintenance of high-quality services by production control and other functions benefits a company in several ways:

- Customers continue to buy the products.
- Satisfied customers influence others.
- Increased sales generally can reduce unit costs.
- Quality services reduce wastes and rework, as well as increasing efficiency, thus causing lower per unit costs.[4]

Production control managers should strive to obtain the benefits of high-quality customer services and to avoid the consequences of substandard services. Unwanted consequences of substandard performance may include dissatisfied customers, a reputation for unresponsiveness, shrinking markets, product recalls, or product liability suits. Of course, the customer service objectives of production control will be determined by the nature of each particular product and service. Thus, optimized customer service should be concerned with maintaining certain physical and chemical aspects of products, performance, tolerances, specifications, packaging adequate to protect the products during shipment and handling, prompt deliveries, and an attractive product appearance. Management should strive to provide courteous and accurate service that will please the customer.

Customer service objectives should be defined before any product or service is furnished. Production control management should ensure that input is handled in an acceptable manner so that products meet appropriate specifications (i.e., strength, size, color, finish, appearance, content, and weight). Personnel providing services should be qualified by completing training programs, obtaining certification, or providing evidence of skills, knowledge, and personal characteristics.

Production control's objectives involve the materials, employees, and equipment required to maximize customer service (see Table 5-2). Inputs to any production system are handled through various processing steps whereby they are sequentially converted into outputs. Production control is concerned with having all units arrive on time, undamaged, and in proper quantities for processing. Monitoring serves to alert the manager that corrective action is required before poor-quality service causes delays.

In summary, the objectives of production control are to have all operations conform to plans, report on operating results, and alter plans as required to obtain desired goals. These objectives have broad applicability because production control is necessarily involved in all phases of manufacturing including engineering, design, materials management, testing, research, and so on. An effective production control system should be capable of providing:

- Current production status—what orders are presently in process, materials requirements, manufacturing, and process location.
- Future production operations—information on scheduled start and completion time of individual operations.

Table 5-2. Examples of products and services, with corresponding production control quality concerns.

PRODUCT/SERVICE	OBJECTIVES
Hospital	Schedule operations to achieve maximum capacity and minimum patient waiting. Supplies arrive at correct times. Patient-handling equipment operates with precision.
Job machine shop	Projects are scheduled to utilize equipment at maximum capacity.
Aircraft manufacture	Production schedules are controlled. Assemblies are completed when required.
Chemical manufacture	The proper amount of each chemical enters the process. Moisture and other chemicals are not absorbed during processing.

- Schedules of quantities of materials, location requirements, and time frames.
- Relative priorities of the production schedule.
- Monitoring and control of lead-time requirements, work center queues, and work-in-process.
- Reports of efficiency, personnel attendance, operator times, and other quantity counts for planning, payroll, unit efficiency, and labor distribution reports.

Achieving each objective is a major task in itself. Together these objectives constitute a formal objective that integrates and coordinates human and equipment resources with a company's materials management and other operations. Production control objectives are heavily dependent upon coordination with materials management and other functions such as manufacturing. The production control manager or director delegates responsibility to the department managers for coordinating activities, maintaining schedules, and so forth, to achieve these objectives.

TYPICAL PRODUCTION CONTROL ACTIVITIES

Production control is concerned with how, when, and where products and services are provided; it essentially bridges the gap between material and capacity plans and the finished product, with materials management having a critical role. Production control activities are directly involved in assuring that materials, labor, and equipment are properly coordinated in the production process. These activities include delineating data requirements, dispatching, scheduling, feedback, and corrective actions.

Manufacturing Order Control

Well-organized data files are essential for an effective production control system, especially implementing or using material requirements planning (MRP). For manufacturing, this usually consists of defining the specifications of the operations required to manufacture a product; these specifications are set forth in the routing schedule, which shows what work centers each component-part order goes through and how long it takes in each work center. This information is contained in a routing file, which is a record for each part. The file includes the total manufacturing lead time based on a typical lot size, a list of the required processing operations identified by ascending order of work center number, a brief description, the setup time required, and the run time per unit (see Table 5-3).

This information, together with assembly drawings, completely specifies how a product is to be manufactured and determines the product's lead

Table 5-3. Routing file data for a cylinder housing.

| PART NO. | 203PX | | | | | |
| LEAD TIME | 28 DAYS | | | LOT SIZE | | 50 UNITS |
WORK CENTER	MACHINE NUMBER	OPERATION NUMBER	DESCRIPTION	SETUP TIME (MINUTES)	RUN TIME/PART (MINUTES)
2	180	20	Turn	3	7
4	015	50	Mill	4	4
5	045	70	Turn	30	10
7	115	90	Heat treat	5	15
9	118	110	Grinding	3	8

time. The routing file provides vital information to materials management. Complete routing files are necessary to support an efficient production control system. The production order master file, which contains information on each production or shop order, is prepared using data from the routing file. This file maintains a summary record describing each order or job, generally consisting of the following information:

- Order numbers assigned to identify each order, or job; these should reflect the product, type or model, and time period.
- Quantities to be produced, reflected in pounds, gallons, models, and so on.
- Completed quantities or units reported through all operations and inspections.
- Scrapped quantities or number of units scrapped at the production process centers of the order, with separate records of scrapped quantities during setup.
- Disbursed materials or quantities of each material and/or component parts used for each order.
- Dates on which orders are scheduled for completion, or if rescheduled, the new completion dates.
- The priority of each order relative to all other orders.
- Balances due or quantities ordered minus the sum of the quantities completed and scrapped.[5]

A production-order detail file contains a record for each operation necessary to process that order, and consists of the following:

- Operation number, which identifies the operation.
- Description of the operation.
- Reported time for setting up equipment for the operation per order.
- Reported run time for performing the operation per order.

- Completed quantity reported, which meets quality requirements for the operation.
- Scrapped quantity reported, during and upon completion of the operation.
- Due date, showing when the order is scheduled for completion or showing the revised due date, if rescheduled.[6]

The control files are especially useful for monitoring production because there is a record of each active order. This information is valuable in recalculating priorities to keep them valid, and for use in conjunction with the planning files. The latter include the work center file, containing a record for each work center of the number of shifts per planning period, machine hours per shift, number of machines available for each shift, labor hours per shift and hours available per shift, the efficiency ratio, and other related data; and the routing file for each manufactured part, which includes the lead time, required processing operation, and possible alternative routing.

Scheduling

Scheduling techniques used for production control depend upon the type of industry, organization, product, operation, and information needed (such as materials management data). The many techniques available can be grouped into three types: charts and boards, other scheduling approaches, and mathematical programming methods. The techniques are not mutually exclusive; most production control groups use some combination of them. These techniques are applicable to materials management scheduling.

The objective of scheduling is to assign jobs to the available work centers to:

- Meet required delivery dates for all jobs.
- Minimize work-in-process inventories.
- Maximize the use of workers and machines.

The schedules deal with work center loading problems, including input control of work released to bottleneck work centers, input/output control over work center loads, priority control of operation in work centers, and expediting urgent jobs when all else fails.[7]

Most scheduling pertains to finished products in production control, but it also involves scheduling materials and parts needed before the finished products are produced. Three questions must be answered in scheduling a given order: When *can* the job be completed? Based on standard times, when *should* the job be completed? Based on the customer's need, when *will* the job be completed at present production rates?

To prepare a schedule, the production control department must know:

- What to make.
- When to make it.
- Where to make it.
- How to make it.
- How much time is required to make it.
- What to make it of.

The required data are usually found in the sales forecast (what customers want, and when it is required), the bill-of-materials (what is needed to make an item), and the process sheet (how to make it and how much time is required).

Scheduling provides the timetable for product deliveries and for determining materials and component requirements compared with available productivity capacity; thus specific jobs may be assigned to specific work centers on a weekly, daily, or hourly basis. This involves assigning start dates and completion dates to the individual components and designating the work centers where work is to be performed. The scheduling problem is complicated because hundreds or thousands of individual jobs may be competing for time in a limited number of work centers. Further complicating scheduling are many unforeseen interruptions and delays—in raw materials deliveries, breakdowns of machinery, changes in job priority, and absenteeism of workers.

If production time, setup time, or inspection time exceeds scheduled standard times, the schedule must be adjusted. Scheduling should be based on standard times developed through considerable analysis, but an accurate lead time usually is very elusive. Accurate lead time estimates and accurate schedules are possible only when work centers are not congested, and orders can be processed to meet scheduled times. A prime objective of scheduling is to keep work centers uncongested so that orders can be completed without unnecessary delays.

Scheduling personnel should provide enough work assignments to keep work centers operating near their capacity. Generally, however, operations required to produce certain parts or products are not spread evenly over all work centers; some centers tend to be overloaded while others are underloaded. To complicate scheduling for production control, the order mix often changes quickly, causing the pattern of overloading and underloading to change accordingly. Scheduling seems an impossible task—arranging for a sufficient volume to keep operations at capacity, yet knowing that delays will occur that will make existing schedules unrealistic. It is extremely difficult to forecast delays due to the changes that generally occur in an order mix. The task is compounded when several operations or work centers are involved.

To overcome these complex problems, an organizational schedule is developed, based on aggregate planning, routing, and sequencing (setting priorities) for the entire process. By using aggregate schedules, individual schedules also can be established; beginning and ending dates are determined by using estimates of the processing duration and due dates for all orders. These schedules then provide a basis for dispatching individual orders to production. Schedules for specific dates are developed according to the orders, labor, and materials observed at each work center; but a detailed schedule usually is not completed until dispatching (setting priorities) has been accomplished. After priorities have been assigned, waiting orders can be processed.

Charts and Boards. Various charts and boards may be used for scheduling manufacturing operations. The Gantt chart, developed by Henry L. Gantt, is widely used for schedules.[8] In its basic form, the Gantt chart has time divisions on the horizontal axis with rows representing the operations or resources to be scheduled (see Figure 5-1).

Lines, bars, brackets, shading, and other such devices are used to mark the start, duration, and end of each scheduled event or operation. The schedules for a variety of operations may be displayed on a single chart. The objectives of a Gantt chart are to illustrate, improve the understanding of, and focus attention on the main items. It is useful for many production applications, including project planning, scheduling operations, and machine loading.

The Gantt chart is usable if:

- There are a limited number of operations work centers. When a large number of operation work centers are displayed, the schedule tends to be confusing, and keeping the chart up-to-date becomes all but impossible.
- Cycle times are relatively long or similar. It is impractical to use the Gantt chart when hours, days, and weeks all are involved on the same chart.
- Work routing is short. When a single product may pass through many operations work centers incurring unpredictable delays, the Gantt chart is impractical.[9]

Numerous other mechanical and magnetic charts and boards are available to facilitate control. A Boardmaster uses cards that snap into small grooves along the horizontal line scale. Other systems make use of mag-

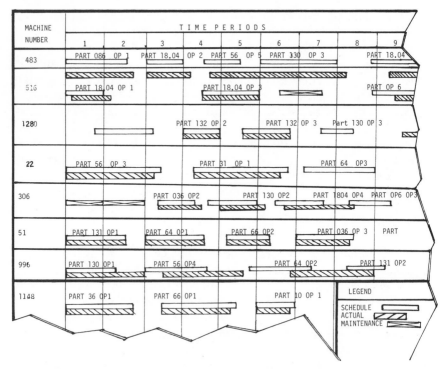

Figure 5-1. Gantt chart used for machine loading.

netic card folders and revolving discs. However, the use of these physical methods of control is decreasing in favor of up-to-date reports that can be supplied by computers.

Other Scheduling Approaches. Two common general scheduling approaches are block scheduling and operational scheduling. Block scheduling is detailed scheduling in which each operation involves a fairly long period or block of time, at least a week or more. For operations of less than a week, operational scheduling is the actual assignment of target starting and/or completion dates for operations (or groups of operations) to show when they must be done if the order is to be completed on time. Every part, subassembly, and assembly is a separately planned order. The orders are scheduled as jobs, lots, batches, or repetitive production news.

Two other approaches to scheduling are forward scheduling and backward scheduling (see Figure 5-2). Forward scheduling starts as soon as requirements are known and often results in completion of the part before the required due date. The time phasing must be done by forward scheduling, which is by period. For example, in companies such as steel mills where orders are manufactured to certain specifications and rapid delivery is required, time phasing is done by forward scheduling (by period). However, this results in more work-in-process inventory and higher inventory carrying costs.

Backward scheduling is used when parts are produced for an assembled product. After the required schedule date is determined for the assembly, the required schedule date is calculated for each part. Production and lead times are used to work backward to determine the proper release date for each part order. Parts are delivered when needed rather than as soon as possible.

Some firms combine both approaches by starting in period one with plans to finish when due. This creates slack time in the production cycle to give flexibility during emergencies and changes. When work centers are unavailable for an operation, the operation is moved ahead in the schedule.

PERT/CPM.   For planning and control over large projects, PERT (program evaluation and review techniques) or CPM (the critical path method) is used. These methods are based on a task sequence chart known as a network (see Figure 5-3, an abbreviated network). Actually PERT/CPM may be more than a planning and control technique; it can be a complete management system. The managing of large projects would involve a computer-based PERT/CPM system, which would help in coping with:

• Project planning and sequencing

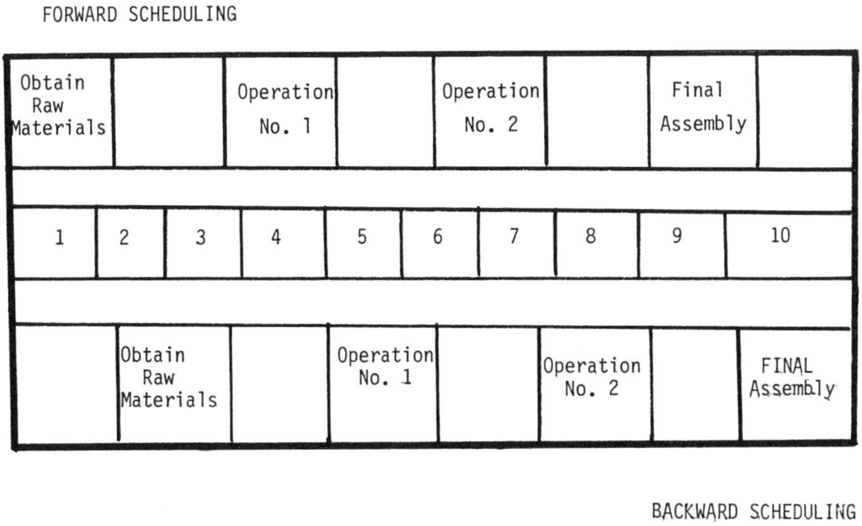

FORWARD SCHEDULING

Obtain Raw Materials		Operation No. 1		Operation No. 2		Final Assembly	

1	2	3	4	5	6	7	8	9	10

	Obtain Raw Materials		Operation No. 1		Operation No. 2		FINAL Assembly

BACKWARD SCHEDULING

Figure 5-2. Forward and backward scheduling.

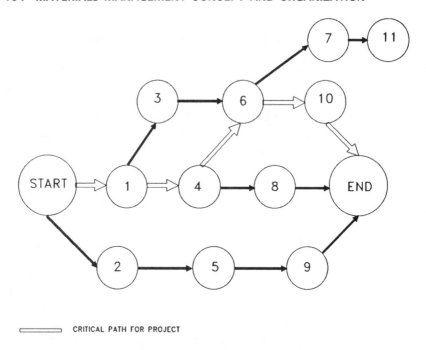

CRITICAL PATH FOR PROJECT

Figure 5-3. A PERT/CPM network.

- Time estimating and path analysis
- Project scheduling subsystems
- Reporting and updating

This information would permit intensive control using the management-by-exception principle.

Mathematical Programming Methods. Other scheduling techniques include linear programming, simulations, and dynamics programming. These methods are all difficult to implement and manage unless computer programs are employed. They can be effective when scheduling involves many different orders, a large number of machines, many different operations, and a variety of available resources. Internal operations can be integrated in these programs with other materials activities such as procurement, materials management, and warehousing. An integrated computer-based scheduling and control system is necessary for management to maintain control over operations and coordinate diverse activities in very large organizations. The most common of these systems is MRP (discussed in Chapter 6).

Priority Control

Through priority control, first-line supervision is informed of the priority of available tasks and the sequence in which orders are to be processed. A dispatch list is prepared for each work center with updating depending on the cyclic processing time. For example, if orders take a day or less to produce and process, then the dispatch is prepared on a daily basis. If production processing takes several days, the dispatch is prepared weekly with midweek revisions. For a continuous production process, a list is prepared indicating which orders are to be started by the production line (a production line can be viewed as a single work center).

The priority list identifies the date, the plant, the work center, and the work center capacity, together with lists of orders, quantities, capacity requirements, and priorities. Orders generally are listed in descending priority. A final list ranking orders should be based on multiple criteria, including a formal priority order, scheduled starting date, input control of work centers, availability of tooling, status of parts, requirements in other work centers, and various other priority criteria.

Priority Criteria. Priority criteria are guidelines for determining the sequence in which orders will be processed. Some firms use these criteria in place of priority planning, such as in material requirements planning systems, but others use the criteria in conjunction with these planning systems. Priority criteria are often single heuristics, which are relatively easy to use and still effective if they are carefully selected and the results are used within the limitations. Where a more complex mathematical method is used, additional information is required to optimize the priority. The most common of these methods is linear and dynamic programming.

An efficient priority control system should reflect real needs and rank these needs in order of their importance. Also, the system should update priorities as due dates or quantities change. Although manual systems can perform these functions on a limited scale, large production operations depend heavily on systematized inputs for priority control. A dispatch list is probably the most widely utilized tool for priority control because it lists all available orders for each work center and ranks them according to relative priority. Specific priorities for orders are established as scheduling becomes a reality, and they are implemented via the dispatch list. Through a dispatch list, work responsibility is assigned to appropriate departments; consequently, this information is vital to materials management. A dispatch list normally will contain two to three days' worth of work, which gives production control limited flexibility in setting schedules.

Criteria that minimize flow time do not necessarily yield low process costs or high machine utilization. These criteria use only one factor in determining priority: first come, first served. This method appears fair, but a customer who urgently needs a particular product and requires fast service will not be adequately served by it. Some of the methods with the lowest average flow times result in low process costs, but they undoubtedly leave some customers with long processing times.

Clearly no single rule is best for all situations, but some of the most popular priority criteria used extensively by management are:

- Shortest processing time
- Longest processing time
- Preferred customer order
- Earliest due date
- First come, first served[10]

Heuristic Criteria. These criteria establish limits on the maximum amounts of waiting time for orders. One common method uses the shortest expected processing time as a base and then utilizes other rules. This approach could involve assigning priority to orders that may experience bottlenecks or to specific orders with the longest remaining processing time. Beginning an assignment on the basis of the shortest operating time puts equipment into operation at the start of the scheduled period. Special attention can then be given to bottlenecks, and other jobs may be scheduled to keep production moving as steadily as possible. On the other hand, with longest processing time, the longest jobs can be scheduled first, and shorter ones can be set later in the scheduling period. Using either the shortest or longest processing time appears effective. The longest processing time approach keeps critical equipment in operation once jobs have started, and uses individual rules simultaneously in developing priorities.

Critical Ratio. The critical ratio is a priority criterion that develops a priority index ratio expressed in terms of time remaining to do work (see Chapter 4 for specific details). This is a dynamic criterion, in that it is constantly updated to provide close and timely control as a basis for advanced scheduling. The critical ratio is designed to give priority to those orders that most urgently need work.

As an order gets further behind schedule, the critical ratio decreases; an order with a ratio of less than 1.0 is behind schedule, whereas an order with a ratio that is equal to 1.0 is on schedule. If a ratio is greater than 1.0, the order has slack time.

Lead Time. Lead time is the interval between the time an item is ordered and the time it becomes available for shipment (see Figure 5-4). To a great degree, lead time is the work-in-process and consists of the following:

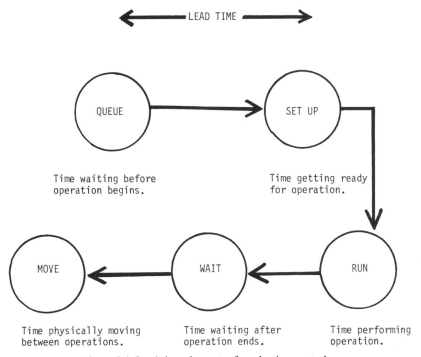

Figure 5-4. Lead-time elements of production control.

- Time the job is in backlog waiting to be processed (queue).
- Time required to retool or set up for the job.
- Time required to process the job.
- Time the job waits to be moved.
- Time involved in materials handling.

Lead time consists of both workload and capacity. Workload is the amount of work or backlog at the work center, whereas capacity is the rate at which work flows through the work center. For most work centers, the capacity is relatively fixed. The question becomes, how fast should orders be released to a work center? If this rate is faster than the output rate, the work-in-process and the lead time increase. Uncontrolled lead times may result in an excessive number of orders in process, causing a shortage of space, delays in materials handling, and other problems. Work centers with poorly managed lead times frequently fall behind schedule and are unable to make scheduled delivery dates, so that the center loses control over priorities and must resort to rescheduling orders. Both of these situations result in poor quality and low productivity.

Production control is often pressured to quote lead times in order to accommodate a sales representative's promises. Lead times should accurately reflect all elements. If sales considerations require a shorter lead time for a customer than expected, then management must be willing to substitute the scheduled capacity of another customer's order to meet this demand; otherwise the firm may have made a commitment that cannot be met. Overloading a production system inevitably causes a loss of the firm's credibility and, in turn, its ability to earn a profit. Therefore, the most important factor in controlling lead time is to control the rate at which orders are released to work centers.

Line of Balance. A line of balance is a simple and inexpensive technique for controlling production of a repetitive nature, limited-quantity production, or large-scale products. The graphic simplicity of this technique makes it effective, and it is a comparatively easy way to update charts and contrast the line of balance for each period. A line of balance is future-oriented, as discrepancies indicate potential problems, which will result if action is not taken to get production back on schedule (see example in Figure 5-5). This technique is similar in concept to an MRP (with respect to time phasing of subassembly and part requirements), although it does not offer the flexibility or quick responsiveness of an MRP.

There are four major steps in calculating line of balance:

1. A graphic time-phased, cumulative delivery schedule is prepared to schedule products over a period of months.

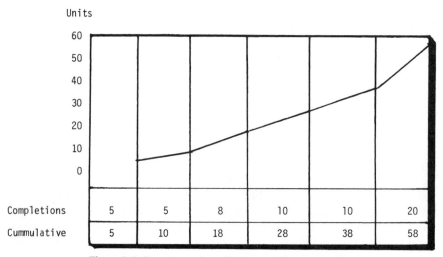

Figure 5-5. Cumulative line of balance delivery schedule.

2. A process plan is developed to show total production sequence in the form of control points on a lead-time chart. All required parts and subassembly components are charted on a production plan that identifies lead times required to attain the delivery schedule. These lead times reflect the quantities of items needed for inventory and/or work-in-process at weekly/monthly intervals to meet shipping schedules.
3. Progress is plotted for each period on a bar chart to compare each control point against the time-phased, cumulative delivery schedule.
4. A line of balance is calculated for each reporting period to show the cumulative quantities required to meet future delivery schedules. The line of balance is plotted on top of the bars on a progress chart, which shows the physical number of components and parts on hand at a given time period. Discrepancies are then studied to determine how to meet schedules.

Shop Floor Control

Shop floor control refers to a system of monitoring the status of production activity in the plant and reporting the status to production control. A reporting and status feedback system provides information concerning orders that are being processed and completed, or reasons why they are not being processed on time. The overall process is illustrated in Figure 5-6. In any manufacturing organization, an almost unbelievable array of problems can cause delays. For many organizations, schedule changes are the order of the day for a variety of reasons, both internal and external.

External problems may include customers changing specifications, quantities, or delivery dates, or even canceling orders. Suppliers' parts may fail quality control inspection or be late in arriving at the plant. Internal problems also are numerous, such as specifying incorrect routing, producing the wrong lot sizes, or not finding defects until products are made.[11]

Materials management requires reporting systems that summarize difficulties and deviations in both materials and labor (see Figure 5-7). It is important to identify current problems and take corrective action to lessen future difficulties. Without accurate information on the current status of production, there can be no feedback, and necessary corrections cannot be made.

Operations do not always go as planned, but any nonconforming activity should be the exception, and management should use feedback to deal with it. For corrective action to take place, plans must be fed forward and measured results fed backward — a cyclic process. The information that is fed back is analyzed, and new plans are developed and fed forward. The scope of contact can be quite extensive; the control system measures and

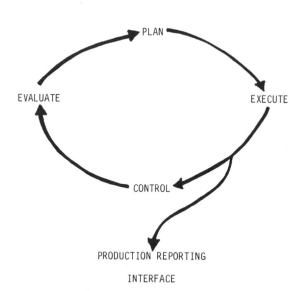

MANAGEMENT CYCLE

PLAN

EVALUATE

EXECUTE

CONTROL

PRODUCTION REPORTING

INTERFACE

Figure 5-6. Production reporting and status control objective management cycle.

reports the results of management's activities. The periodic reports indicate the effectiveness of planning, as well as ways in which it can be refined and improved.

Materials management is concerned mainly with output and input measurements. Control of operations is achieved by comparing measurements of quality output and performance output to materials management controls. Over time, the actual costs of inputs (resources) may be compared with standard costs. Such a report relates outputs to inputs and results in cost-variances. Detailed analyses of utilization and the efficient uses of various inputs will generally show causes for cost-variances.

Cost-Variance Reporting. Cost-variance reports are concerned with (1) variances from budget and (2) variances from standard costs.[12] The variances from standard costs are more relevant to production control, and in turn to materials management, than variances from budget. Standard costs may be established for any product or service that includes expenditures for standard labor, materials, direct costs of utilities, tools, equipment, and space. Because these costs are difficult to relate precisely to a given product or service, they are totaled over a particular time period and allocated to individual activities and products. Over time, the effects of overestimating

Figure 5-7. Production reporting and status control reports.

allocations tend to balance the effects of underestimates. The accumulated standard costs for all items produced over the time period are then compared with the actual costs of accumulated labor and materials and with estimated costs for tools, equipment, and space.

Actual resource-usage data are needed in order to calculate resource costs for labor, material, and other direct usage requirements. The differences between standard costs and actual costs are cost variances. From these variances, other reports can be used to pinpoint specific areas that may need corrective action.

Resource-Usage Reporting. Resource-usage information is collected to prepare efficient production reports or materials management reports and to further pinpoint the direct causes for any variances. The utilization rate is expressed as the percentage of the available resources that is actually used:

$$\frac{\text{Materials management resources used}}{\text{Materials management available resources}} = \text{Percentage utilization}$$

This general formula can be applied to materials handling equipment usage by determining time of usage from equipment recording meters. Space usage is often expressed as a percentage of the total available space. A resource-usage report is often broken down by the types of space or by the types of use.

There are many other kinds of detailed measures of the effectiveness of shop floor control systems (see Figure 5-8). Measures of materials might be concerned with damage, theft, deterioration, movement delays, and misplacement, all of which tend to decrease productive materials use. Absences and tardiness due to illness, jury duty, labor union activities, and so on, are included in the measures of labor utilization. Resource utilization reports must be used discriminately, however, and generally should be used with other materials management controls and practices. It should be

```
┌─────────────────────────────────────────┐
│ ┌─────────────────────────────────────┐ │
│ │           W.I.P. LEVEL              │ │
│ ├─────────────────────────────────────┤ │
│ │           W.I.P. TURNS              │ │
│ ├─────────────────────────────────────┤ │
│ │    ACCURACY OF W.I.P. INVENTORY     │ │
│ ├─────────────────────────────────────┤ │
│ │        DELIVERY PERFORMANCE         │ │
│ ├─────────────────────────────────────┤ │
│ │        LEVEL OF EXPEDITING          │ │
│ ├─────────────────────────────────────┤ │
│ │       EQUIPMENT UTILIZATION         │ │
│ ├─────────────────────────────────────┤ │
│ │       ABILITY TO LOCATE JOBS        │ │
│ └─────────────────────────────────────┘ │
└─────────────────────────────────────────┘
```

Figure 5-8. Common measures of shop floor control effectiveness.

noted that 100 percent utilization is not necessarily ideal. Equipment that is utilized 100 percent of the time will have such high usage that long backlogs and delays in getting work completed will be almost inevitable. The utilization rate generally is used as an indication rather than as a true measure of efficiency.

Labor utilization rates are measured through work sampling methods. A sampling technique generally is used because continuous observation is costly, and self-reporting cannot always be depended on to be accurate or truthful. Sampling also may be used to measure equipment utilization when other means are not available.

Labor is the only resource whose efficiency can be measured with any relevancy because equipment, for example, cannot operate at any speed other than normal. Generally, labor efficiency is determined by the following formula:[13]

$$\text{Efficiency} = \frac{\text{Actual output}}{\text{Standard output}}$$

This is a measure of actual speed, pace, and effort against standards. Labor efficiency information has been collected for outputs, and standard outputs have been developed.

The measuring of output in large-scale operations generally involves counting the units handled that meet quality standards. Units may be expressed in square yards, pounds, tons, or client visits; and they may be measured in units per day, week, or some other time unit. Counts may vary from the scheduled output, and are then expressed as deficiencies in actual output as compared with scheduled (standard) output.

Processing of job lots must go through multiple work centers, with output measurement taking place at each station. This involves a unit count of parts successfully produced and the time required for their completion, so that priorities can be determined for materials and upcoming work centers. A report may summarize parts moved out compared with raw materials moved into each work center; this is vital information for materials management. Another measure of success is whether due dates are met by one work center or all work centers together. Percent of completion is a suitable measure for work centers with long processing times.

Input/Output Control. The input/output control technique values scheduling for work centers through an input/output control report that shows which work centers are failing to meet planned outputs, and whether the work centers are at fault for forwarding less than the planned inputs to the next work centers. This input/output control helps to manage capacity by revealing which work center outputs are inadequate, and which inputs are inadequate or excessive.[14]

The input/output report indicates each work center's performance as compared to a planned schedule for a given number of work periods. This planned schedule input is the average of the capacity requirement plans (CRP) for a given number of time periods (see Figure 5-9). An average CRP is used in the input/output control analysis because of the erratic rate that is projected in the CRP and the variances in events occurring in the work centers.

At the bottom of the report, actual output is shown; this can be compared with planned output. The analysis of an input/output report, as illustrated in Table 5-4, shows a drop in actual output that results in a buildup of work-in-process. This buildup may cause work centers to have delays at a future date because of inadequate output from the previous work centers.

Comparing planned input with actual input in Table 5-4 shows a lack of work coming to the work center. This indicates that previous work centers are bottlenecks and need attention. An analysis of the input/output control reports for all work centers may identify bottlenecks so that materials managers can then determine how such performance affects them. Materials management must constantly be aware of how production strategies can be changed to overcome these problems, by such means as authorizing

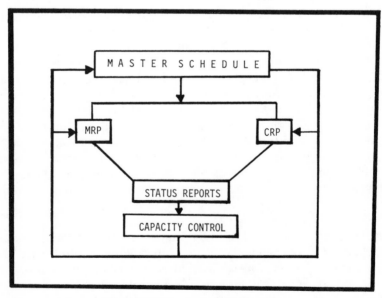

Figure 5-9. Flow chart of status reports.

Table 5-4. Input/output control analysis report for a work center.

	WORK PERIOD NUMBER		
CONTROL FACTORS	4	5	6
Planned input	130	130	130
Actual input	100	90	110
Cumulative deviation	−30	−70	90
Planned output	130	130	130
Actual output	125	105	95
Cumulative deviation	−5	−30	65

overtime, improving timing of work, improving layout, or using different equipment. If actual output cannot be increased to planned output, then the master schedule must be changed.

The information required to develop an input/output analysis report generally is available from other data sources such as input control. The schedule uses input control to release shop orders, which may consist of orders due for release in the next few days, those due for release immediately, and some new rush orders. In addition, there may be orders that were due for release on a previous day but were held back because certain work centers were overloaded.[15] The purpose of input control is to determine a mix of shop orders that neither overloads nor underloads any one work center. At the beginning of the production process, the manager determines the work centers that are critical; and when these work centers are identified, an order may be scheduled earlier than actually needed in order to get it into the critical work center in a slack period. The goal is to release a mixture of shop orders, including some with high priorities, to balance their impact on bottleneck work centers. The actual input and output are simply a count of work produced, and the planned output is the same as the planned input.

An input/output analysis report is concerned with work center capacity control. Priority control at each work center is essential because any given work center generally has waiting (queue) time. In priority control, ordered jobs are selected in sequence, by using up-to-date information on the urgency of the operation. Priority can be based on current operations or on characteristics of the whole order. (See previous discussions on priority.) Priority control is only one of the essential parts of any production control system.

Expediting. Expediting is disruptive, expensive, and not always successful; companies use it as a last resort. When all other methods fail, the expediting procedure is used to search quickly for needed parts for an urgent order. This method can involve preparing rush shop orders and purchase orders, hand-carrying paperwork, making special trips to freight terminals to meet incoming orders, making phone calls to search for parts or orders in transit, or pushing an order ahead of others. For some companies, expediters are an important part of the production control department; however, materials management expediting causes serious scheduling interruptions.[16]

INFLUENCE OF PRODUCTION CONTROL SYSTEMS

Once the production process has started, managers of all units (i.e., materials management) must keep operations on a steady course toward company goals. From these production control systems, information is provided to materials management to adjust for changing activities so that overall performance stays in tune with objectives.

Traditional Production Control Process

Control processes have been developed conceptually, theoretically, and mathematically during the past decades. Some of these techniques are difficult to transfer directly to actual operations because complex and different conditions may exist that theoretical systems have ignored. Even with these limitations, however, the traditional basic control theories provide production control with a theoretical basis for designing a system to control operations. Therefore, materials management needs to be acquainted with how these control systems were developed. The purpose of a control process is to help an operation achieve its production objectives. Production control is not an end itself, but a means of achieving production objectives. Conceptually, a control system includes inputs, outputs, measurement comparisons, and actions.

A production control system is concerned with inputs being converted into a desired output, with outputs being measured during the process. These measurements are used to detect discrepancies by comparing the measured output to preestablished standards and alerting management to deviations between standards and measured outputs. Corrective actions are usually initiated when indicated discrepancies are outside established tolerances. After modification of the operation, they are measured again, and the control process is repeated. Because feedback is vital, information flows are essential in the control system design.

Production Control Systems That Impact Materials Management. The two basic kinds of control systems are the open and the closed types. An open system utilizes some of the elements within the system as well as other control elements that may not be an integral part of the system. With a closed system, all the control elements are contained within the system.[17]

The two types of feedback systems are negative and positive. Negative feedback systems eliminate or correct deviations from goals whenever the deviations are outside established specifications. When such deviations occur, the feedback is an opposing action. A positive feedback system, however, does not seek a constant status the way a negative feedback system does. Instead, the positive system seeks constant improvement or growth, where each instance of feedback reinforces the process. Thus, as the system becomes more accurate, its efficiency increases.

Attributes of Production Control Systems Related to Materials Management. Three attributes of control systems are stability, sensitivity, and responsiveness.[18] The stability of a control system depends on the regularity and intensity of disturbances, the types of control response, and the system's sensitivity and responsiveness. Determining the stability of a control system is important to management because corrective actions made to an unstable control system can sometimes result in deviations greater than those created by the initial problem. Responses may lead to unstable oscillations for a period of time before a steady behavior occurs. The objective of any control system is to process outputs with steady state stability. If such stability is impossible, then knowing how the control system will react to any corrective action is essential.

The sensitivity of a control system indicates the amount of measured error needed before control actions are initiated. The degree of sensitivity is reflected in a predetermined tolerance range that is designed and built into the control system. Highly sensitive control systems may cause frequent control actions of a small magnitude; insensitive control systems cause infrequent but extreme control actions. Managers should give careful consideration to the sensitivity required of a control system while it is still in the developmental stages.

The responsiveness of a control system is a measure of how quickly the control response is evoked after an error has been detected. Generally, corrective action is taken immediately, but some factors in the system may prohibit immediate action. Taking action may require time and planning, during which the status may change again. The timing of control actions thus must be properly phased by managers; severe consequences may result if premature corrective actions are taken, possibly causing serious detrimental oscillation of the system. Corrective actions should avoid amplifying problems. This safeguard may be accomplished by lengthening or reducing response delays. Determining the responsiveness of a control system is a complicated problem.

EFFECTS OF MATERIALS MANAGEMENT IN DESIGNING PRODUCTION CONTROL SYSTEMS

Production control and materials management are interrelated functions, and in designing a production control system, their interactions must be considered. Production control systems must be designed to achieve established goals, which may be formal or informal, open or closed. Most production control systems are so complex that the control processes are continuously interwoven throughout the system.[19]

Materials Management Function

The materials management function is a major variable in the design of production control systems. Almost all units in both production and service organizations are highly dependent upon materials management operations. This is true even for continuous manufacturing processes and automated units within a system; although these systems depend extensively on capital and technology, and their operations are relatively routine, materials management is an important link to their control.

Performance standards often state system goals in relatively vague terms, and performance may vary substantially from time to time; many of its aspects cannot be quantified, and evaluations and measurements tend to be subjective. However, for materials management, inputs and outputs need to be measured precisely.

For manufacturing processes that are continuously producing standardized units of output, the control system becomes substantially different from that of a job shop. By using an information network, inputs and outputs can be more easily measured than they are in a system that is dominated by people. Generally, people-oriented industries use a closed-control process, whereas capital-oriented industries utilize a more complex control system. There are exceptions, however, and infinite combinations are used, in which systems are designed to consider a variety of characteristics.

Materials Management Factors

Certain materials management factors relate to the broad, overall design of a system and its structure. These elements are directed toward reviewing, evaluating, and revising relationships between materials management and the various systems to maintain coordination and balance. Certain other controls primarily deal with day-to-day evaluations and adjustments of inputs and outputs. Because these two aspects of control are interrelated, the design of the control system should involve both. The control system should also ensure that activities conform to preconceived plans by using measurement, feedback, comparison, and corrective action.

Decisions about which factors to control generally are based on either conscience or expediency. Characteristics that are readily visible and measurable are selected, rather than others that may be more directly related to goals and plans. The system should be designed so that:

- Appropriate characteristics can be controlled by it.
- Characteristics are defined to relate directly to strategic plans.

Measurement problems often exist when output depends on human creativity, or when employee–machine interactions are difficult to evaluate because explicit bases do not exist. Some techniques do permit subjective evaluations in the seeking of information, which do aid in providing precise measurements.

Information Requirements of Materials Management

Lack of information inhibits effective control because feedback is often delayed, distorted, or unclear. Therefore, a production control system should be designed to ensure that information is both accurate and timely. In practice, many refinements of production control, including procedures and techniques, have been made possible by the use of computers. Not only are reports updated daily or weekly, but complicated schedules now can be routinely prepared. Functions such as materials management can receive timely information from other departments, and other departments can have information regarding materials management—all through the use of computers. In the past, such information could not be provided in such a timely manner. With current data readily available, information can be obtained immediately on the progress of orders, bottleneck operations, reasons for interruptions, and delays due to equipment or improper operator performance, as a basis for control of operations; typical computer applications are illustrated in Figure 5-10. Decisions on estimating delivery dates to customers, shifting workloads or equipment among materials management units,. and obtaining additional resources may be made more quickly and with greater accuracy by using computers.

Computers have changed the design of production control systems for many activities. For example, a large number of shop recorders were sold to manufacturing firms for plant use, to record output and input data, which included the labor and materials charged to a given job and the quantities of units produced. Foremen and workers entered the data each day (or more often) so that new schedules and priorities could be devel-

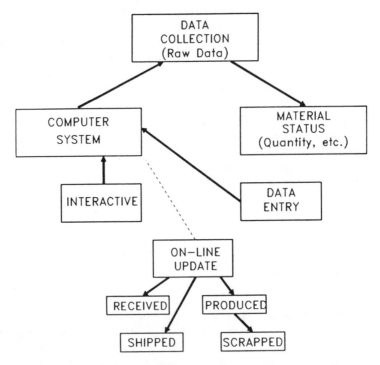

Figure 5-10. Production reporting and control using data processing.

oped. It was too easy to enter false data, however, so many of these recorders ended up on the shelf. Now that computers are available, shop recorders are enjoying increased use, and they are effective now because they are linked to terminals, which, in turn, are linked to a mainframe computer to form a computer network. The terminals are programmed to perform data checks. For example, one check is made to compare the production quantity entered by an operator with the quantity entered by the preceding work center operator. If there is a difference between the two values, the system will not accept the data. With on-line shop recorders, firms are able to have high-priority, up-to-date information virtually instantly. This makes continuous calculations of priorities possible and results in shorter lead times, making the system more responsive to customer requirements.

Were it not for computers and their ability to manipulate massive amounts of data, companies would be unable to utilize many of the techniques available today, such as MRP. With inexpensive minicomputers and microprocessors, nearly all manufacturing and service firms can have this control information.[20]

A computerized production control system requires formality and discipline in an organization and offers predictable results that lend themselves to improvement over a period of time. Thus, firms can avoid the kind of informal control that results in material shortages due to delays, overdue shipments, higher costs, and "buck passing," all of which undermine confidence in the system.

The computer keeps totals of current inventory levels and issues ordering instructions and information for materials management. With relatively direct access to computer files, materials management finds it advantageous to maintain information on a time-phased basis, incorporating data on what items are requested.

Many firms have hundreds of items that require some form of materials handling. Present-day usage calculations and record keeping would be impossible if it were not for computers and their unique information storage and retrieval capabilities. Materials management is ideally suited to computerization, which can be integrated into a total computerized management information system for the organization. Although computerization of materials management does not automatically solve problems, a computer keeps records of such items as quantities, time requirements, and usages, and then makes calculations of demand patterns, variances, and lead time. In other words, it essentially does busywork and routine calculations.

Time-phased systems, such as materials requirements planning (MRP), are not only used as control systems, but scheduling systems as well. The MRP system coordinates inventories with scheduling activities to provide an effective control system. In fact, the MRP system is the heart of today's computerized inventory systems, as well as materials management systems.

The time period between the detection of problems and the initiation of corrective actions is critical in control systems for materials management. Information is often distorted through transmission, interpretation, and handling throughout the production control system; and small deviations may, in reality, become major problems for materials management if there are undue delays in transmitting the information. Production control design should ensure:

- Frequency of information transmission, which will help maintain control.
- Intermittent or continuous transmission of information, to assure an effective system.

Costs Control Requirements for Materials Management

As the variety of products and conversion processes increases, so does the complexity of materials management. When there are only a few activities, a relatively simple yet effective control system can be designed. If the production process and variety are large, the control system must be broad-based; but with a wide variety of processes and products, it is all but impossible to design a system that can objectively measure all possible conditions. In the face of such diversity, the design should include ways of decreasing the variety or complexity of the system by combining activities or by some other means.

To obtain maximum benefits from a control system, the cost control required by materials management must be included in its design; accounting techniques play a vital role here, as in any operation. Although the materials management process is designed to handle output at a desired volume, selling prices are generally determined in the marketplace, based on factors that are beyond management's control. Therefore, materials management and other production costs are the only variables that management can directly control; so operation costs are the primary target for many cost control systems.

Operational cost goals are reflected in the budgets of most operating units, and actual costs usually are periodically monitored and compared against standards. When deviations occur that are beyond an allowable range, corrective action should be initiated. Cost control information also can provide a basis for many other necessary actions.

A control system may include cost centers in materials management in its design and assign responsibility for performance; but such a cost center may actually be a work group, a machine, or a department. In any event, scheduling for a cost center should provide for efficient utilization of resources.

Materials Management Control Standards

A control system should include standards for comparison so that materials managers can know when control actions are required. For example, standard costs can be developed, such as costs for direct labor, overhead, and so on. These standards may be established by using the methods presented in various accounting textbooks.

Periodically, records from each cost center should be updated. By comparing actual costs to cost standards, areas can be detected where improvement is required, or where standards should be changed. This periodic review should be provided for by the system design. In designing a control system, there may be a tendency to ignore relationships, such as the relationship of materials management to the production system. However, decisions that result in desirable materials management performance may cause disturbances in other subsystems. Thus, the stability of an overall control system is generally sensitive to, and dependent on, actions in various subsystems. A key to effective materials management is having an accurate information system that can provide materials requirements, materials availabilities, and appropriate timing for materials procurement. Schedules and plans are also crucial in assuring effective control of materials management activities.

It is reasonable to assume that a perfect control system seldom exists in actual materials management situations, as all major characteristics must be integral parts of the control system. In designing and updating the production control system, the major characteristics of materials management must be emphasized.

CRP AND CAPACITY CONTROL MEASURES

Material requirements planning (MRP) is a technique for determining the quantity and timing of demand-dependent items and rescheduling orders to adjust to changing requirements. Although MRP ensures that materials will be available at appropriate times, that is of little value unless sufficient capacity is available. Capacity requirement planning (CRP) determines what personnel and equipment resources are needed, including materials handling, to meet the production objectives set forth in the MRP.[21] Material requirements planning and capacity requirement planning logically lead to capacity control of the operation (see Figure 5-11). An MRP is generated on the basis of the master schedule (see Chapter 6), whereas a CRP determines the capacity and time required for each work center to produce a given output.

Figure 5-11. Materials and capacity control flow chart.

Capacity Requirement Planning

For materials management, capacity decisions are intended to ensure that capacities are being utilized according to a capacity requirement plan (CRP). This entails: measurement of the rate of labor and facilities usage, plus feedback of this information into the system data base; comparisons with standards established by the CRP; and corrective actions when actual output differs from planned output. Corrective action can involve shifting workers to different work centers, authorizing overtime, changing production within the plant, or working with customers to revise delivery schedules. Status reports are among the most common control techniques.

Capacity Control

Capacity control is concerned with ensuring that the amount of actual labor and machine capacity or other alternatives are in agreement with the MRP and CRP; if not, various actions may be taken (see Figure 5-12). This requires accurate measurement of actual output, feedback, comparison with the MRP and CRP, and corrective action.

The most commonly used status reports include shortage reports, rework reports, scrap reports, order status reports, and delay reports. Other reports utilized for capacity control are those concerning labor and materials usage, production progress, derivative activity utilization, and completions. These status reports should be used to communicate to materials management, and should include reports from purchasing and inventory control personnel to production supervisors.

ALTERNATIVE 1: REALLOCATE WORK FORCE

ALTERNATIVE 2: CHANGE AND/OR ALTERNATIVE ROUTINGS

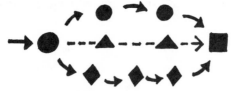

ALTERNATIVE 3: SUBCONTRACT

ALTERNATIVE 4: INCREASE AND/OR UPDATE EQUIPMENT

ALTERNATIVE 5: PRODUCE RATHER THAN PURCHASE INTERMEDIARY PRODUCTS

Figure 5-12. Correcting capacity control to capacity requirement planning.

Capacity is a measure of the productive capability of materials management facilities, and may be expressed as design capacity, system capacity, or output capacity. Capacity typically is measured in common denominators of units such as tons, pieces, or work time available.

For capacity control purposes, capacity refers to demonstrated capacity as measured from the average of past work center reports:[22]

$$\begin{matrix} \text{Demonstrated} \\ \text{capacity} \end{matrix} = \begin{pmatrix} \text{Number of} \\ \text{machines} \end{pmatrix} \begin{pmatrix} \text{Machine} \\ \text{hours} \end{pmatrix} \begin{pmatrix} \text{Percentage} \\ \text{of utilization} \end{pmatrix} \begin{pmatrix} \text{System} \\ \text{efficiency} \end{pmatrix}$$

The three types of capacity factors are: demonstrated, required, and maximum. Demonstrated capacity should be equal to required capacity. There is no maximum capacity, as additional capacity can be obtained by adding shifts, obtaining new facilities, and manipulating controllable factors, including labor facilities, machines, loading, shifts worked/day, days worked/week, overtime, subcontracting, alternative routing of work, preventive maintenance, and number of setups. Other less controllable factors are absenteeism, labor performance, machine breakdowns, materials shortages, scrap and rework, and unusual tool requirements.

Many capacity problems occur, in both manufacturing and service industries. These are evident in the long lead time needed for many products and in the queues at service facilities at retail stores, banks, and other sites. Under-utilization of facilities also indicates capacity problems.

It is important that managers recognize capacity problems because, in the long term, management is concerned with maintaining a planned level of capacity to demand. This requires assessing the market, competition, technological trends, and external economic variables, in addition to an internal balance among production units and work centers. Constant attention is necessary to keep expected levels of required and available capacity in balance.

CRP takes material requirements from the MRP system and converts them into labor and machine load requirements for each work center. In CRP, the objective is to develop work center loads that are in balance with work center capacities. When required and available capacities are unbalanced, changes must be made in capacity or in the requirements imposed by the MRP system. Capacity control measures the rate of utilization for labor and equipment. Feedback of this information for comparison with standard hours established by the CRP and corrective action when output differs significantly from planned output ensures that capacities are utilized according to the CRP.[23] Achieving this balance in the short range may include using overtime, shifting some workers to different jobs, and subcontracting.

JUST-IN-TIME PRODUCTION

Japanese managers have demonstrated the ability to manage production systems effectively. Some credit of this success has been attributed to their Just-In-Time approach to production and inventory control, which directly affects the way materials management operates. Implementing a Just-In-Time system is not a quick and easy process with guaranteed results. The entire materials management function must be analyzed, and a consistent and methodical approach to the control of materials must be developed. Clearly, the role of materials management is crucial; it forms the foundation for an integrated approach to Just-In-Time. The implementation and the operation of a Just-In-Time system have a massive impact on the materials management function, and the likelihood of success is directly affected by the ability of the firm to forge new relationships.

The Just-In-Time System

The terms Just-In-Time and Kanban are not synonymous. Kanban is a subsystem that facilitates a clear and direct flow of information and thus allows the Just-In-Time concept to function. The Just-In-Time approach embodies a wider perspective than Kanban, extending from the control of raw materials through the processing operations to the control of finished goods. It requires integration of the design elements of the materials management/production system for the efficient flow of materials.[24]

Kanban means "signboard" or "ticket" in Japanese. Tickets control the flow of materials through the system. The goal of Kanban usage is to have each materials item arrive just in time for the production operation. With a Kanban, achieving this goal depends on the characteristics of the production environment.

In a Kanban system, the flow of materials is associated with the relationship between two work centers; the consuming work center is dependent on the producing department, which may be a vendor for its necessary components. This effort is accomplished through the movement of Kanban tickets, which identify the product, routing, and order quantity information.

Several types of Kanbans are used, including the conveyance Kanban and the production Kanban. All activities dealing with materials flow and conversion are associated with a Kanban, as no activity is permitted without an attached Kanban card. The quantity of materials is controlled by the number of Kanbans in the system. Material flows from a work station through an intermediate storage area to another work station. All material is moved in standardized containers, with each container holding a portion of the day's production requirements. Each container has a production

Kanban card attached and cannot be taken for use until a materials handler arrives with a conveyance Kanban card. When the container is taken, the production Kanban is detached and returned to the producing department, thereby authorizing replacement of the material removed. The conveyance Kanban is now attached to the container, which moves to the consuming department. The conveyance Kanban cannot be used until the material within the container is actually used. In this way, the total amount of inventory is controlled by the Kanban cards, as the production of additional inventory is delayed until current inventory is used.

Effective use of a Kanban system requires a smoothed daily production rate. The aggregate production schedule and the master production schedule must be adjusted on a daily basis because the production lot size (a standardized container) for a Kanban system is smaller than the lot size used in an MRP system, which is a weekly lot size.

Kanban usage requires frequent production setups; so minimizing the setup time becomes a major goal for production management. Materials management supports this uninterrupted flow of materials and parts through the manufacturing system. Group technology, which groups parts with common processing characteristics, is important to the Kanban system. A Kanban strategy is to have a limited number of products or items manufactured under the responsibility of a single profit center or cost center. This is important in reducing the complexity involved in planning and controlling production and materials handling activities.

Just-In-Time Materials Management

The main objective of a Just-In-Time production system is to minimize raw materials and work-in-process inventories by providing each work center with only necessary parts or materials at the time they are required. The goal of the Just-In-Time system is to have one unit or lot of output produced as it is needed at each succeeding work center.

Operating a Just-In-Time system requires active coordination with materials management; in fact, that is the starting point for the materials flow cycle. Just-In-Time materials management is very similar to a Just-In-Time production system. Under Just-In-Time materials management, parts or materials must be delivered in small quantities to the work center as they are required. This can involve many deliveries of parts or materials during an eight-hour shift.

Just-In-Time materials management involves:

• Frequent and reliable deliveries.
• Reduced materials handling times.
• Reduced lot/unit quantities.
• High-quality materials handling.

Just-In-Time materials management is not a drastic departure from conventional materials management. Materials management always has been concerned about the length of time required for materials handling, and Just-In-Time materials management attempts to reduce the time by utilizing smaller quantities to increase efficiency. If properly implemented and operated, Just-In-Time materials management is in harmony with conventional materials management. The important feature is that Just-In-Time materials management considers all factors as variables, even those that have been regarded as uncontrollable, with major emphasis on attempts to reduce handling time and lot sizes.

Reducing Lot Size and Handling Times

In Just-In-Time, great emphasis is placed on reducing setup costs through the reduction of setup time, which is achieved mainly by studying and analyzing the setup process. A similar analysis must be undertaken for the materials handling associated with handling each lot. The main materials management considerations in handling a lot are: size of lot, distance moved, route of movement, rate of demand, time involved, and whether to use storage or go directly to another process. With Just-In-Time systems, such practices as group technology, smoothed daily production, and limiting the number of products or items manufactured in a factory eliminate the many problems of materials management. The significantly reduced lot size is of concern to materials management, but small lots can usually be managed at less cost.

Benefits of Just-In-Time materials management are numerous. First, Just-In-Time materials management practices reduce handling time because the system requires only small volumes of materials that are needed immediately and are used evenly over the production period. In addition, inventory levels are reduced to the point that raw materials or component parts do not have to be placed in and removed from storage. This permits materials management to fully utilize equipment and materials management employees, thereby increasing its productivity and efficiency.

Second, Just-In-Time materials management requires a significantly shorter delivery time, so that reliability is greatly improved. The increased reliability contributes significantly to system efficiency.

Third, improved quality levels occur when quantities are small, even in materials management activities. Sources of quality problems are quickly identifiable and can be corrected immediately. As an added benefit, the quality-consciousness of materials management employers also tends to improve, producing an improvement in quality in materials management services.

Fourth, reductions in lead times and setup times increase materials management flexibility, as do the smaller lot sizes.

Changes Required for Just-In-Time Materials Management

The fundamental objective of the materials management function is to provide the company with quality service in a reliable manner using optimal methods. To achieve this objective, materials managers have emphasized such techniques as on-time movement of materials, and the like. Utilization of Just-In-Time materials management does not alter the fundamental objective of the materials management function. However, the basic approach used in achieving the objective is different, for Just-In-Time materials management emphasizes long-term relationships. This requires enduring cooperation between materials management and other units in which both benefit, or a mutual effort to reduce costs and a sharing of the resultant saving. In most firms, this calls for a reexamination of the philosophy underlying line and staff relationships.

RELATIONSHIPS WITH OTHER MATERIALS MANAGEMENT SUBFUNCTIONS

Production control has a close relationship with inventory control, purchasing, physical distribution, receiving and stores, and materials handling. Effective communication between these vital activities is required for an efficient production control system. Ineffective activities by any group result in a wide variety of problems for production control.

Inventory Control

Inventories of materials, supplies, and finished products are important resources in production operations. They are vital assets whose maintenance frequently requires a large amount of working capital. Because working capital is a scarce resource, it must be conserved through the use of an effective inventory control system. Inventory control provides critical inputs for production control and operational decisions. Poor inventory control practices, such as allowing changing inventory levels or inaccurate inventory accounting, result in a wide variety of problems for production control.

Many individuals in an organization make decisions concerning inventory control; consequently, the effects of these decisions on production control vary widely in scope and significance. The establishment of inventory control policies has a broad and significant impact on production control. In inventory control, managers should determine the boundaries, magnitude, and composition of aggregate inventory control and production control. This should be done to ensure that decisions are rational in terms of organizational objectives. Unfortunately, there are many factors, such as demand, lead time, delivery requirements, handling requirements, and cost factors, that influence the inventory control system and the appropriateness of production control systems.

Inventory is a buffer or shock absorber between customer demand and the production system, between finished assembly requirements and component availability, between the input materials required for operations and the output of preceding operations, and between the production process and suppliers. Production control strategies are an important part of inventory buffering, as inventory separates demand from immediate dependence on supply sources. These facets of inventory have special significance in any production control system.

Purchasing

The purchasing function involves obtaining the materials and services needed by production. Effective purchasing requires extensive control prior to receiving an order and upon actual receipt of the material purchased. The purchasing department is responsible for providing an uninterrupted flow of material, to allow production to meet its schedules. Purchasing must coordinate its activities with production.

Purchasing exercises control over purchase orders, purchase commitments, and vendor performance, all of which affect production control performance. The purchase order determines the status of each order, order price, quantity, product specifications, shipping procedure, and supplier, with all necessary information for production control. Purchase commitments begin with the MRP and planned purchase orders; the resulting decisions affect production control activities.

The active cooperation of purchasing, materials management, and quality control is required for proper control of supplier quality. Quality control starts with the supplier selection process, which is initiated by purchasing. It is important that suppliers be able to meet quality requirements; otherwise, materials will be rejected and returned to the supplier. A lack of materials can result in production downtime and increase the work load for materials management. Purchasing then will have added responsibilities for obtaining replacements, even to the point of reordering from another supplier. At these times, production will have many problems in trying to balance various resources to compensate for lack of material during the interim period.

Physical Distribution

Because time and place are valuable, the objective of physical distribution is to have products at the right place, at the right time, at a minimum cost.

Physical distribution activities are important to production control because distribution system policies and strategies must encompass all functional areas. These areas are systematically related: decisions in one often affect the other and in turn production control. For products to be finished and orders to be filled for shipping from the factory to customers, effective production control is needed, to prevent delays and encourage production to remain on schedule.

Some distribution services may be purchased, especially when sales volumes are low in a particular area, but often distribution centers and warehouses are necessary on a limited basis. A distribution center can perform a wide variety of services for production in given areas, including packaging and the special alternatives necessary for automated production.

The nature of a product, distance, cost, and time requirements, as well as modes of transportation, determine the distribution system and control required. Distribution problems frequently encountered by management that are of concern to production control are:

• Warehouse allocation.
• Inventory levels.
• Locations of distribution centers.
• Modes of transportation.
• Services to be provided at distribution facilities.
• Control systems needed.

These problems are directly related to the company's production control systems.

Receiving and Stores

The receiving and stores (warehousing) departments are closely related by their activities to production control. Shipments arrive at receiving, and the date of arrival, supplier, items, and quantities are recorded. The shipments are then forwarded to the proper locations and inspected. These activities are essential for production control.

The physical activities of receiving and stores involve preventing misplaced items, unrecorded issues, and pilferage, and require that all materials movement that is authorized and recorded be essential for production control. Some shipments may go directly to production areas; those shipments, as well as materials moving from receiving to production lines at regular intervals during production, must be coordinated with production control. In all cases, clearly defined communication must be established between receiving and production control for each raw material and component part moving between them, and this requires proper inventory records. In any situation, storekeepers and materials handlers must consult and work closely with each other. Lax practices can lead to many problems, delays, and slowdowns in production. Successful production control requires that receiving/stores provide adequate support to the production control function.

Materials Handling

Production processes are not always physically adjacent, and components are frequently manufactured in one area and then moved to another location. The emphasis that a company places upon materials handling depends upon the types of operations and the importance of materials handling to the success of those operations. When material costs are a high percentage of product costs, there is a need for highly refined materials handling systems. Production control depends upon the timely movement of the correct material to the correct production location. Anything less than this results in manufacturing problems.

Establishing controls for materials handling is complex because materials handling activities span many facets of the organization. An excess of materials in the manufacturing area causes problems for production control, just as a shortage of materials causes production delays. Accordingly, materials handling does much to facilitate production and the production control process. Without a good handling control system, materials are easily lost or damaged, and unnecessary movements may take place. Production controls are most effective when the flow of materials has been carefully planned, and the materials handling function has been considered.

RELATIONSHIPS WITH OTHER COMPANY FUNCTIONS

The relationship of production control with other company functions involves maintaining a balance within the company through reviewing, evaluating, and revising relationships among the various activities and departments. This includes day-to-day evaluation and adjustment of inputs and outputs to achieve the short-range objectives of the company. Production controls are interrelated with these objectives, and the involvement of operational with organizational control is essential.

Manufacturing

Production control is a service group for support of manufacturing. The design and implementation of a production control system represent a major effort, which should consider the various types of assemblies, subassemblies, fabricated components, equipment, and production technology found in the manufacturing department. For example, the initiation of group technology in manufacturing affects equipment layout, which is a key factor in performing production control activities. Under the group technology concept, the entire production setup is changed, as each location performs different functional operations. Special tooling, materials handling, and equipment require completely different production control techniques.

For products and services that must be flexible to handle specialized customer orders, a rigid continuous flow must be replaced by a more flexible and responsive conversion process. This can be a job shop that processes to order, emphasizing the need for flexibility. This job shop is characterized by longer processing times, frequent setups, and in-process inventories of materials, parts, and components. Complex production control operations are needed for this arrangement.

Manufacturing management must understand the characteristics and objectives of the production control system because production control and manufacturing are closely interrelated. The two functions must cooperate and communicate with each other. For example, the manufacturing process needs to be considered when production control capabilities are adapted to manufacturing.

Marketing

Marketing's role is to define and evaluate the kind and magnitude of a company's need and to disseminate this information to all concerned in the company. In response, specific products and services can be developed. Accordingly, the marketing function is the primary link between the organization and the firm's customers. Therefore, production control's ability to provide timely customer shipments is of direct concern to the marketing function, and marketing partially determines or influences many parts of the production control system. The different criteria employed to evaluate the marketing and production functions often result in conflicts about the design and utilization of the production control system. This situation may be made more complex by a lack of integrated functional policies geared to achieving organizational objectives.

Marketing is concerned about customer complaints, delivery schedules, and delays—all of which are results of the firm's production control system. Marketing wants corrective actions to be taken immediately by production control to correct these and other problems. Harmony between marketing and production control frequently depends on a reliable and efficient information system, so that control report indicators can be put into action and problems corrected immediately, to maximize customer satisfaction.

Finance

A firm's activities generally depend on the availability of financial resources; the financial function is concerned with the evaluation of present and proposed control activities to determine the most efficient use of funds. Production control must be justified as a worthwhile activity that is essential to the achievement of company objectives; production control managers must present facts about costs and benefits.

The financial function includes the maintenance of accounting records. Accounting provides information on cost, work center productivity, and other types of control information that will assist production control managers. However, these managers must define in detail the type of information required for the established control system, in terms of units, time periods covered, when required, format, and so on. If this is not done properly, the information received will be inappropriate for control purposes and can contribute to excessive accounting costs.

Quality Assurance

Quality assurance is concerned with quality planning and control, and it includes inspection, a broad-based function. Production control has an important role in assuring that products and services meet specified quality levels. The combined efforts of production control and other staff units are required to achieve optimum levels of quality.

Preventing product defects is largely a matter of providing the right operating resources: good-quality material, well-trained work force, and well-designed and well-maintained equipment. Because of increased concern with improving the quality of goods and services, quality assurance is more than inspection; it also involves preventing defects. Quality assurance must work closely with production control to satisfy this requirement.

Engineering

The engineering function is concerned with designing products and services, and perhaps production methods. In many cases, engineering must assume the function of monitoring various operations in cooperation with production control, especially during the early stages of new product planning and equipment changes. Engineering plays a key role in developing and providing the specifications used by production control.

Engineering is involved in planning the company's line of goods and services along with marketing, finance, production control, and other groups. Production control is interested in ensuring that materials are available, existing capacity is utilized, and production targets are attainable — all of which involves engineering in various degrees. Engineering is involved in all phases of the production function. Engineering determines product technology and materials, which in turn determine the performance characteristics of manufacturing. Because of the engineering role in manufacturing, engineering decisions are of extreme importance and require production control input. However, engineering is only one component of production control decisions, and must be integrated within the management of production control.

SUMMARY

Production control depends on many other functions, especially materials management; and it must be dynamic and adaptive to meet numerous demands. Achieving production control objectives requires management of production control activities to coordinate their efforts with the many related functions. Production control is concerned with how, when, and where products and services are provided. It essentially bridges the gap between materials and capacity plans and finished products, with materials management having a critical role. Production control activities are directly involved in assuring that materials, labor, and equipment are properly coordinated in the production process. These activities involve delineating data requirements, dispatching, scheduling, feedback, and corrective actions.

Typically, production control involves a wide variety of techniques, including mathematical programming and priority control using critical ratios, lead time, line balance, and priority criteria. In addition, shop floor control utilizes input–output control, expediting, cost-variance reporting, and resource-usage reporting. Design of the production control system must include extensive analysis concerned with controlling people, information requirements, cost control, and control standards.

Production control and materials management need to work within, and interact within, each other's functions, and both must consider their interactions. Because of the complexity of production control systems, these processes are continuously interrelated throughout the system.

Material requirements planning (MRP) determines the quantity and timing of demand-dependent items, and reschedules orders to adjust to changing requirements. Capacity requirement planning (CRP) determines what personnel and equipment resources are required, including materials management, to meet the production control objectives in the MRP. An

MRP is generated on the basis of the master schedule, whereas a CRP determines the capacity and time required for each work center to produce a given output. Just-In-Time is an approach to production and inventory control that directly affects the way materials management operates. Implementing a Just-In-Time system is not a quick and easy process; therefore, the materials management function must be analyzed, and a consistent and methodical approach must be developed. The role of materials management forms the foundation for an integrated approach to Just-In-Time production, with close relationships among the materials management subfunctions of physical distribution, receiving and stores, and materials handling. In addition relationships with other company functions must be maintained among the various activities and departments. Through these groups, production control completes the manufacturing loop.

NOTES

1. Ebert, *Production and Operations Management, Concepts, Models, and Behavior In Engineering*, p. 32.
2. Chase and Aquilano, *Production and Operations Management*, p. 10.
3. Gaither, *Production and Operations Management: A Problem-Solving and Decision-Making Approach*, p. 362.
4. Blanks and Salarzana, "Using Quality Cost Analysis for Management Improvement," pp. 40–55.
5. ——— "Shop Floor Controls." APICS Training Aid, Milwaukee APICS Chapter, p 1–3.
6. ——— "Shop Floor Controls," p. 3–4.
7. Schonberger, *Operation Management-Planning and Control*, pp. 221–222.
8. George, *The History of Management Thought*, Chapter 1, pp. 4–10.
9. Schonberger, *Operations Management-Planning and Control*, pp. 215–216.
10. Conway, "Priority Dispatching Rules and Job Lateness in a Job Shop," p. 23.
11. Schonberger, *Operations Management-Planning and Control*, pp. 108–109.
12. Schonberger, *Operations Management-Planning and Control*, p. 233.
13. Schonberger, *Operations Management-Planning and Control*, p. 236.
14. Schonberger, *Operations Management-Planning and Control*, pp. 221–224.
15. Schonberger, *Operations Management-Planning and Control*, p. 221.
16. Wight, *Production and Inventory Management in the Computer Age*, p. 119.
17. Monks, *Operations Management/Theory and Problems*, pp. 17–18.
18. Ebert, "Aggregate Planning With Learning Curve Productivity," pp. 171–182.
19. Holstein, "Production Planning and Control Integrated," pp. 121–129.
20. Wight, *Production and Inventory Management in the Computer Age*, pp. 23–24.
21. Orlicky, *Materials Requirements Planning*, pp. 239–255.
22. Fogarty and Hoffman, *Production and Inventory Management*, pp. 86–87.
23. Fogarty and Hoffman, *Production and Inventory Management*, p. 85.
24. Fox, "OPT—An Answer for America." *Inventories and Production*, Vol. 3, No. 1 (Jan./Feb. 1983), reprint.

BIBLIOGRAPHY

Adam, Everett E., Jr. and Ebert, Ronald J. *Production and Operations Management, Concepts, Models, and Behavior in Engineering.* Illinois: Prentice-Hall, 1982.

Ammer, Dean S. *Materials Management and Purchasing,* 4th ed. Homewood, Illinois: Richard D. Irwin, 1980.

Bailey, Peter, and Farmer, David. *Managing Materials in Industry.* London: Gower Press, 1972.

Blanks, Lee, and Salarzana, Jorge. "Using Quality Cost Analysis for Management Improvement." *Industrial Engineer,* Vol. 10, No. 2 (Feb. 1976), pp. 40–55.

Chase, Richard B., and Aquilano, Nicholas J. *Production and Operations Management — A Life Cycle Approach,* 3rd ed. Homewood, Illinois: Richard D. Irwin, 1981.

Conway, Richard W. "Priority Dispatching Rules and Job Lateness in a Job Shop." *Journal of Industrial Engineering,* Vol. 16, No. 6 (July–Aug. 1965), p. 23.

Ebert, R. J. "Aggregate Planning with Learning Curve Productivity." *Management Science,* Vol. 23, No. 2 (Oct. 1976), pp. 171–182.

Ericsson, Dag. *Materials Administration.* London: McGraw-Hill Book Co., English translation, 1974, Swedish edition, 1971.

Fogarty, Donald W., and Hoffman, Thomas R. *Production and Inventory Management.* Cincinnati, Ohio: South-Western Publishing Co., 1983.

Fox, Bob. "OPT — An Answer for America," *Inventories and Production,* Vol. 3, No. 1 (Jan./Feb. 1983), reprint.

Gaither, Norman. *Production and Operations Management: A Problem-Solving and Decision-Making Approach.* Hinsdale, Illinois: The Dryden Press, 1987.

George, Claude S., Jr. *The History of Management Thought.* Englewood Cliffs, New Jersey: Prentice-Hall, 1968.

Holstein, W. K. "Production Planning and Control Integrated." *Harvard Business Review,* Vol. 46 (May–June 1968), pp. 121–129.

Laufer, Arthur C. *Production and Operations Management,* 3rd ed. Cincinnati, Ohio: South-Western Publishing Co., 1984.

Leenders, Michiel R., Fearon, Harold E., and England, Wilber B. *Purchasing and Materials Management,* 7th ed. Homewood, Illinois: Richard D. Irwin, 1980.

McElhinnery, Paul T., and Cook, R. I. *The Logistics of Materials Management: Readings in Modern Purchasing.* Boston: Houghton Mifflin Co., 1969.

Monks, Joseph G. *Operations Management/Theory and Problems,* 2nd ed. New York: McGraw-Hill Book Co., 1982.

Orlicky, Joseph. *Materials Requirements Planning.* New York: McGraw-Hill Book Co., 1975.

Schonberger, Richard J. *Operations Management-Planning and Control of Operations and Operating Resources.* Plano, Texas: Business Publications, 1981.

Shinner, W. *Manufacturing in the Corporate Strategy.* New York: John Wiley and Sons, 1978.

"Shop Floor Controls." *APICS Training Aid.* Milwaukee A.P.I.C.S. Chapter.

Wight, Oliver W. *Production and Inventory Management in the Computer Age.* Bosline, Massachusetts: CBI Publishing Co., 1974.

Zenz, Gray V. *Purchasing and the Management of Materials,* 5th ed. New York: John Wiley and Sons, 1981.

6
The Impact of Material Requirements Planning and Distribution Requirements Planning on Materials Management

Material requirements planning (MRP) and distribution requirements planning (DRP) have been two of the most significant developments in production control and materials management for the past several decades. Other scheduling and control concepts and methods now being developed are based on these systems.

The wide use of MRP has fostered a reexamination of master production schedule (MPS) aggregate planning, production activity control, and other concepts, because the essence of MRP is a master production schedule (MPS). Material requirements planning (MRP) schedules the materials required to meet production goals for each time period in the planning horizon. Working with the given production schedule, MRP determines the quantity of raw materials, parts, subassemblies, and assemblies needed in each time period to produce the quantity of finished products desired. MRP is able to respond periodically to required changes in production schedules or the supply of materials.[1]

Distribution requirements planning (DRP) has evolved to schedule the distribution operation and integrate production and distribution activities. DRP optimizes the planning for distribution of products by determining the aggregate time-phased net distribution requirements at the same point in the materials flow as in the master production schedule of the MRP.

Both MRP and DRP are necessary tools for materials management even though they are generally considered inventory control techniques. They provide the logical tie between materials management, production, and distribution, and are designed to do this on an ongoing basis.

MATERIAL REQUIREMENTS PLANNING (MRP) RELATED TO MATERIALS MANAGEMENT

MRP is a formal, computerized information system that integrates the scheduling and control of materials. Through a set of logically related records, procedures, and rules for decision making, MRP translates a master production schedule (MPS) into time-phased net requirements for each inventory item needed to implement the schedule and spells out the plan for covering these requirements.[2] The system specifies materials to be procured and the actions to be taken, and determines when they are needed during the planning period.

MRP Objectives

MRP is necessary because of the volume of materials, supplies, and components involved in producing a company's product line and the speed with which management needs to react to the constant dynamic changes of the economy. An MRP system has the following objectives:[3]

- Improve customer service, thereby increasing sales and lowering prices.
- Reduce inventories.
- Provide a change-sensitive, reactive manufacturing system.
- Improve efficiency through:
  - Reduced idle time.
  - Reduced setup costs.
  - Avoidance of unplanned delays.
  - Fewer canceled orders and changes in order quantities.
  - Information for schedule planning before actual release of orders.
  - Aiding in capacity planning.

Improved customer service involves more than just having products on hand when orders are received; it includes meeting promised delivery dates and decreasing delivery times.

An effective MRP system provides materials management with the necessary information to make intelligent materials handling decisions. When schedules are based on adequate information, they are generally realistic and can usually be met. Better control of raw materials and components eliminates delays and decreases production times, resulting in better service. The use of MRP permits decisions on the timing of materials input to production, requirements for materials from suppliers, and production levels necessary to meet customers' needs, thus eliminating large work-in-process and raw materials inventories. It helps managers control the quantity and frequency of raw material deliveries to production operations, assuring the delivery of the right materials at the right times.

Although MRP is primarily aimed at manufacturing operations, firms that mix components, materials, and package items also can benefit from MRP through reduced labor, materials, and overhead costs.[4] They can:

- Increase production capacities through decreased idle times.
- Increase materials handling efficiency, thus reducing delays.
- Reduce stockouts and materials delays, so that production output is increased even though the same sources are used.
- Reduce reworks caused by using incorrect materials.

MRP Assumptions

MRP is effective in manufacturing operations of either the mass production or the job shop type. However, it generally is most effective for companies with the following production characteristics:[5]

- Products are produced by using a defined sequence of materials (components, parts, and subassemblies).
- A dependent demand exists.
- Demand for components is variable and/or discontinuous in nature.

A dependent demand exists for an item when the item is directly related to the demand for other items or end products, as when requirements for subassemblies and component parts depend on demand for the final product. Once the demand for the final product is known, dependent demand for items used in the manufacturing process can be determined. Independent demand for an item exists when demand is unrelated to another item. Independent demand is usually determined through forecasting techniques. Generally, there is independent demand for items such as final products sold to customers, service parts, and parts required for destructive testing.

When an MRP is properly utilized, the demand for component parts is discontinuous and fluctuates, even when the demand for the final product is constant. This can occur when a fixed-order-quantity or an order-point system is used to control the final product inventory, as periodic reordering creates a discontinuous and variable demand for the parts required to make the final product. An adequate MRP can respond to these complex requirements for materials and component parts.

Proper use of an MRP is based on the following assumptions and prerequisites:[6,7]

- The final product consists of component parts that are uniquely identified.
- A master production schedule exists, and is stated in bill-of-materials terms.
- A computerized bill-of-materials exists at planning time.
- Inventory records provide data on the status of every item.
- Lead times are known for individual items.
- File data are accurate and up-to-date.
- All components go into and out of inventory stock.
- Discrete disbursement and usage of component material is required.
- Component parts for the final product are needed at the time of assembly order release.
- Independent processing of manufactured items is done.

The above requirements are critical for setting up an MRP. Implementing an MRP requires that MRP data files, shop floor control, and data integrity be well established. In addition, the bill-of-materials file must be computerized—which is itself a major task.

Purpose of an MRP

The main purpose of an MRP is to control the inventory levels, priorities, and capacity of the system.[8] Controlling inventory means ordering the right part at the right quantity and time. Controlling priorities entails assigning the right due date and maintaining an accurate load. Capacity planning means proper scheduling for a maximum load with adequate time to view future loads. Thus an MRP assures that the right materials are at the right place at the right time, and that the materials required by the production schedule are in place, but only when needed. Having materials on hand before they are required puts a restriction on finances and uses extra space. Excess material may obstruct efficient production, and increase the complexity of canceling orders. Some common terms used in MRP are defined in Table 6-1.

MRP versus Order-Point

MRP uses many of the traditional concepts of inventory management. Before the development of MRP, manufacturing companies typically managed their inventories with order-point systems. However, an order-point system does not perform well for managing inventories that have dependent demand.

The differences between order-point and MRP are illustrated in Table 6-2. MRP uses a requirement philosophy, whereas order-point uses replen-

Table 6-1. Terms often used in materials requirements planning.

1. *Bill-of-Materials File*—Also called product structure file. A major input to the MRP computer program that breaks all products or end items into their assemblies, sub-assemblies, parts, and raw materials. These components are identified, their relationships defined, and the quantity of each component required to produce one finished end item is specified.

2. *Capacity Requirements Planning*—Computerized techniques that reconcile master production schedules to production capacities.

3. *Changes to Planned Orders*—A primary output of MRP. These reports show how planned order schedules for a material should be changed. Orders are delivered earlier, later, or cancelled altogether, or quantities are changed as required to adapt to modified master production schedules.

4. *Dependent Demand*—Demand from production departments for raw materials, assemblies, parts, and other components required to produce end items.

5. *End Item*—A product, service part, or any other output that has an independent demand from customers, distributors, or other departments.

6. *Gross Requirements*—The quantity of a material needed in each time period to meet either inventory deficiencies or direct customer or production department demand. These quantities directly result from the explosion of end items from the master production schedule into their components.

7. *Inventory Status File*—A major input to the MRP computer program. It documents the status of each material held in inventory—material on hand, planned orders, orders released, materials allocated, and so on. Additionally, planned information is included—lot sizes, safety stock levels, lead times, and so on.

8. *Master Production Schedule (MPS)*—A schedule of the quantity of all products or end items planned to be produced in each production department in each time period over the planning horizon.

9. *Material Requirements Planning (MRP)*—A Production & Operations Management computer information system that dynamically develops a schedule of planned orders of materials in each time period of the planning horizon. MRP determines how much of each material should be ordered in each future time period to support the master production schedule.

10. *MRP Computer Program*—A computer program that is the central processor of MRP information. It receives inputs from the master production schedule, inventory status file, and bill-of-materials file. The MRP logic transforms inputs into its primary outputs—planned order schedule, order releases, and changes to planned orders. The MRP computer program also modifies the inventory status file and supplies operations managers with other secondary reports.

11. *Net Requirements*—The difference between the gross requirements for a material and the quantity available.

12. *Order Releases*—Those future planned orders for a material that are authorized to be actually placed with suppliers or production departments. Orders for a material are released only a short time into the planning horizon of the planned order schedule.

13. *Planned Order Schedule*—A planning schedule of the quantity of each material to be ordered in each time period in the planning horizon.

14. *Planned Receipts*—The quantity of each material to be received in each time period of the planning horizon.

15. *Planned Releases*—The quantity of each material to be ordered in each time period of the planning horizon. This schedule is deduced by offsetting the planned receipts to allow for lead time. The composite of all planned releases is the planned orders schedule.

Source: From *Production and Operations Management* by Norman Gaither, Copyright © 1980 by The Dryden Press, CBS College Publishing. Reprinted by permission of CBS College Publishing.

Table 6-2. Differences between order-point and MRP.

	ORDER-POINT	MRP
Demand	Independent	Dependent
Order Philosophy	Replenishment	Requirement
Forecast	Use past demand	Uses MS
Control	ABC	All items
Objectives	Manufacturing	Customers
Lot Sizing	EOQ	Discrete
Types of Inventory	Finished goods & components	WIP & RM
Demand Pattern	Random	Predictable

Source: Roger G. Schroeder, *Operations Management—Decision Making in Operation Functions*, Copyright 1981, McGraw-Hill Book Company. Reproduced with the permission of McGraw-Hill.

ishment. With replenishment, materials are replaced when they run low; in MRP, the requirement philosophy means ordering only when a need exists as directed by the master schedule. In MRP, if there are no manufacturing requirements for a particular component, orders will not be initiated even if inventory levels are low. MRP is tailored for manufacturing where demand for components is uneven. When production is scheduled, the components are ordered, but when no production is scheduled, no orders are made because demand is zero. When order-point systems are used in uneven demand patterns, components are carried even during periods of zero demand.

Forecasts for order-point systems are based on past demands for replenishing stock levels. For MRP, future orders are based on requirements generated from the master schedule, which is derived from higher-level demand forecasts; the past demand is unimportant.

Neither ABC nor EOQ inventory control methods can be used in MRP systems. In manufacturing a product, all components are important, whether they are A or C; so it is necessary to control all parts. Also, the use of the EOQ assumption is not allowed because of the lumpy demand patterns of components; the lot sizing for MRP is based on discrete requirements. With EOQ, orders would be calculated without regard to requirements and end up with inventory, causing unnecessary carrying costs.

Statistical inventory control techniques are appropriate for managing final products for which there is independent demand, whereas an MRP is appropriate for dependent demand situations. With independent demand, the objective of the order-point system is to provide high customer service; with dependent demand, the objective of MRP is to support the master production schedule.

In almost every important aspect MRP differs from order-point systems. Each has its own specific purpose. MRP is designed especially for manufacturing operations involving raw materials and work-in-process inventories. Using an order-point system in such an operation can result in excessive inventory levels, late deliveries, and lack of components.

MATERIALS MANAGEMENT PLANNING WITH THE MRP SYSTEM

MRP follows a specific sequence (see Figure 6-1):[9]

- Based on orders, prepare a master production schedule, stating the number of each product to be produced for each time period.
- From the bill-of-materials file, specify the quantities of each material required for each product.
- From the inventory control status file, obtain the number of units on hand from the previous time period.

Using these data, the MRP program prepares planned order schedules, order release requirements, and reschedules as required.

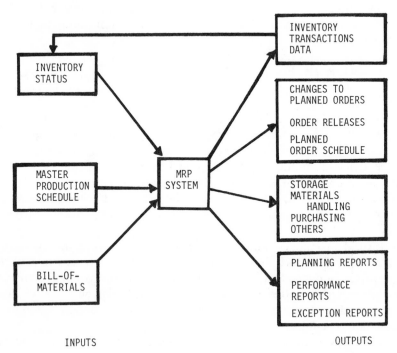

INPUTS   OUTPUTS

Figure 6-1. The MRP system.

Product Demand

The demand for a company's products is determined by regular customer orders, which normally are received during a given time period and have promised delivery dates. This type of order generally varies in amount from season to season, and may require adjustments due to unforeseen circumstances. Other orders for stock items are predicted based on forecasts; this independent demand is further analyzed to determine the safety stock, order points, and order quantities required and to attain the desired level of customer service.

These two types of demand (regular and independent) for final products are the inputs for the master production schedule. In addition, there is a demand from customers for specific parts and components for service and repairs. These customer orders are not treated as part of the demand schedule; they are usually added to the MRP as part of the gross requirements for parts and components.

Master Production Schedule (MPS)

The master production schedule establishes the types of products that will be required during specific time periods. It is assumed that the schedule is feasible and that adequate capacity such as materials handling is available to meet the requirements. The master production schedule is the most important input into the MRP system. Resource limitations can be taken into account by comparing the master production schedule to a rough-cut capacity plan. A rough-cut capacity plan serves as an early warning of scheduling problems; it measures capacity requirements across broad groups of similar resources and identifies potential work center bottlenecks (i.e., in materials management). The master production schedule may be modified to coincide more closely with available capacity, ensuring that a production schedule is feasible.

Bill-of-Materials

A bill-of-materials file, or product structure file, lists the items required to manufacture the product and the quantity of each item used per product unit. It also defines the sequence in which the product is assembled. The purpose of a bill-of-materials in an MRP is to determine the demands for parts and materials required to produce the end products scheduled in the master production schedule, which provides materials management with its requirements.

The bill-of-materials must have the following characteristics:[10]

- It must lend itself to forecasting optional product features necessary for MRP.
- It should allow the master production schedule to have a manageable number of end items, stated in terms of bill-of-materials numbers.
- It should allow the planning of subassembly priorities.
- It should employ the same numbering system used in customer orders.
- It must be usable for final assembly scheduling.
- It must be usable as the basis for product costing.
- It must lend itself to efficient computer programming.

If the present bill-of-materials does not meet these requirements, it must be modified for the purpose of MRP while still serving its primary purpose of providing product specifications. Bill-of-materials requirements vary from company to company, depending on product complexity. For the purpose of MRP and materials management, the bill-of-materials must uniquely identify raw materials and subassemblies of the product. Subassembly numbers cannot be arbitrary, but must reflect the manufacturing process; that is, the assembled part number dictates the subassembly numbers. If assembled components are forwarded as a completed task to storage or to another assembly operation, they must be given subassembly numbers. The MRP system generates orders for such subassemblies and plans their priorities, but it only can do so for items with individual identities. If these subassemblies were to have the same numbers as the finished product, the MRP would not distinguish between them.

The identifying number of each item must define that item's content. The same subassembly number is not used to define two or more different sets of components. In addition, the MRP assumes that the bill-of-materials accurately reflects the way materials are handled and flow through the operation, which includes the state of completion at each subassembly.

The bill-of-materials for MRP must specify the:

- Composition of a product.
- Process stages in manufacturing.
- Product structure in so-called levels of manufacturing, which represent steps in the completion of the product.

The schematic representation of the product structure defines the relationship among the items that make up the product in terms of levels. These levels are vital for MRP because they determine the precise timing of requirements and order releases, and set priorities for the system necessary for materials management. Although the typical production process requires many components, these components may include multiples of a single item or many sets of items with specific relationships. Figure 6-2

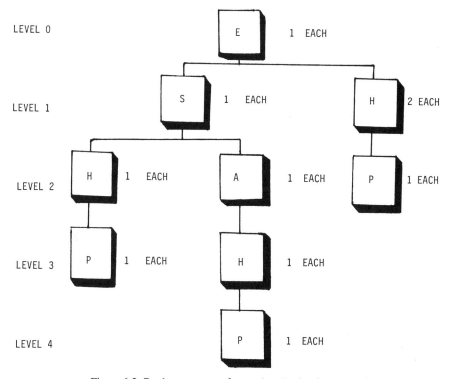

Figure 6-2. Product structure for product E with four levels.

illustrates the levels of a typical product structure. The end product is level 0, and its components and subassemblies are levels 1 through 4. Each successively lower level represents additional fundamental components for the product, whether purchased parts or subassemblies.

To illustrate how the logic of MRP works, Figure 6-2 shows the product structure of product E, which is made of one part S and two parts H. Part S is made of one each of H and A. By computation, if 100 units of E are required, the requirements for components are:

Part H: $2 \times 100 = 200$
Part H: $1 \times 100 = 100$
Part H: $1 \times 100 = 100$
Part S: $1 \times 100 = 100$
Part P: $1 \times 100 = 100$
Part P: $1 \times 100 = 100$
Part P: $1 \times 100 = 100$
Part A: $1 \times 100 = 100$

Time elements, generally referred to as lead times, are determined for each item. Lead times represent either the time required to produce the part internally, or the time needed to order the part. Assume that lead times are:

E = one week
S = two weeks
H = two weeks
P = three weeks
A = one week

If we know when product E is required, we can construct a time schedule specifying which parts are needed and when they must be ordered and received, as in Figure 6-3. In this way the MRP is developed, based on the demand for product E, knowledge of how E is manufactured, and the time needed to obtain each part.

Obviously, it would be impossible to develop an MRP manually for hundreds or thousands of items, as a great deal of computation is required. In addition, large amounts of data must be available concerning inventory status and product structure. The MRP, therefore, requires a computer program based on the logic used in the above example.

Inventory Control Status

An inventory control status file contains data for each item in inventory. Some companies maintain extensive data files for individual items. The information commonly maintained in an inventory control status file is illustrated in Table 6-3. The item master data segment includes: item identity, item characteristics, planning factors, safety stock, and pointers to other files. This file is kept up-to-date by posting inventory transactions as they occur, including stock in and out, scrap losses, wrong parts, and canceled orders.

Shop Floor Control in MRP

The objective of shop floor control in MRP is to manage orders through the production process to make sure they are completed on time. Shop floor control assists materials management in adjusting to day-to-day problems such as breakdowns and materials shortages. When problems arise, materials management must make decisions based on job priorities obtained from shop floor control systems.

The shop floor control system requires feedback reports on all jobs as

Week

		1	2	3	4	5	6	7	8	9	10	11	12	13	
E	Gross Requirements													100	Lead Time 1 week
	Order Placement												100		
S	Gross Requirements											100			Lead Time 2 weeks
	Order Placement									100					
H	Gross Requirements							100				200			Lead Time 2 weeks
	Order Placement					100				200					
P	Gross Requirements				100	100			100						Lead Time 3 weeks
	Order Placement	100	100			100									
A	Gross Requirements									100					Lead Time 1 week
	Order Placement								100						

Figure 6-3. Materials requirements plan for completing 100 units of product E in period 13.

Table 6-3. Common information found in inventory control status file.

Item master data segment:
Item identity
Item characteristics
Planning factors
Safety stock
Pointers to other files

Inventory status segment:
Gross requirements—
  control balance or past-due field
  time-phased data fields
  total
Scheduled receipts—
  control balance or past-due field
  time-phased data fields
  total
On hand—
  current on hand
  allocated on hand
  projected on hand fields
  total (ending inventory or net
    requirements)
Planned order releases—
  control balance or past-due fields
  time-phased data field
  total

Subsidiary data segment:
Order details—
  external requirements
  open (shop and purchase) orders
  released portion of blanket orders
  blanket order detail and history
  other (user's choice)
Records of pending action—
  purchase requisitions outstanding
  purchase-order changes requested (quantity, due date)
  material requisitions outstanding
  shop order changes requested (rescheduled due dates)
  planned (shop) orders held up, material shortage
  shipment of item requested (requisition, etc.)
  other (user's choice)
Counters, accumulators—
  usage to date
  scrap (or vendor rejects) to date
  detail of demand history
  forecast error, by period
  other (user's choice)
Keeping-track records—
  firm planned orders
  unused scrap allowance by open shop order
  engineering change action taken
  orders held up, pending engineering change
  orders held up, pending raw material substitution
  other interventions by inventory planner

Source: Orlichy, *Materials Requirements Planning,* with permission pp. 181–183.

they are processed. Workers must notify the system as each process is completed. Then a priority list is prepared for each job in the work center, and each work center works on the highest-priority job. If materials or machines are unavailable, the next highest priority is run. The shop floor control system requires valid due dates on all orders. The system is highly dependent on proper priority and capacity planning.[11]

Job priorities make it possible to adjust production to meet schedules through the use of dispatching rules. The production lead time for a job can be drastically decreased or increased because of the large amount of time spent in work-in-process. If a job is behind schedule, its priority can be increased until it is back on schedule, or a job can be slowed down if it is ahead of schedule. Thus, lead times are not fixed, but can be increased or decreased on the basis of priority, and the shop floor system provides managers with important information for making lead-time decisions.

Capacity Planning

Capacity planning is used to check the validity of the master schedule. This is done either by rough-cut capacity planning (sometimes called resources planning) or by shop loading. To determine rough-cut capacity, the approximate machine and labor hour requirements are estimated directly from the master production schedule without using component explosion. Shop loading uses a full component explosion for capacity planning. Detailed routing loads shop orders against work centers to give future projections of the work force and machine hour requirements for all work centers, including materials handling requirements. If adequate capacity is unavailable, the master schedule or capacity is adjusted to obtain a feasible master schedule.[12]

MATERIALS MANAGEMENT INFORMATION FROM MRP

The MRP program derives its information from the inventory file, master production schedule, and bill-of-materials (see Figure 6-4). The program determines the number of products from the master production schedule that will be needed in each time period, and then generates a list from the bill-of-materials, containing descriptions of materials and parts needed to make each product in the master schedule. The inventory file program serves as a check on the quantities of all materials and parts currently on hand and on order, and the MRP program then computes the quantities of each item needed. The net requirements are offset to different time periods to allow for manufacturing and supplier lead times.

Although a master production schedule theoretically satisfies anticipated customer demands when it is initially prepared, it often happens that

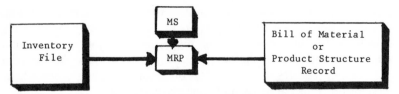

Figure 6-4. Sources of information for MRP.

finished inventories cannot meet actual demand, and that manufacturing capacity is insufficient to support the master production schedule; so the MRP schedule is checked against the capacity requirement plan (CRP). The CRP helps determine the personnel and equipment resources, such as materials handling, needed to meet the MRP. Computer simulations make exhaustive comparisons of networks to ensure the feasibility of the MRP's scheduled output. Together, the MRP and the CRP establish the specific materials and capacities needed, and show when they are needed.

Lead Time

Lead time is the interval between the determination that more materials are needed in stock, and the time when the materials are actually received. Lead time can be divided into operation time and interoperation time. Operation time involves setups, run time, and materials handling time, including transit and waiting time. Lead times must be defined for each part and operation in order to determine specific capacity requirements for specific time periods. Lead time is critical to successful production and materials management because it directly affects the amount of work-in-process and thus affects materials management requirements.

It is essential to establish accurate and reasonable lead times before implementing MRP. The actual lead time for a given operation may vary above and below the normal lead time. Lead times can be lengthened by shop loads, breakdowns, rework, and so on, or can be shortened by expediting. Thus, lead times can be managed, planned, and controlled.

Time-Phasing

Time-phasing is scheduling to produce or receive materials so they will be available in the time periods when they are required, not before or after. It is the opposite of placing replenishment orders at the time when inventory levels reach the order point, whether or not inventory is needed immediately. For independent demand items that are ordered in response to a forecast, this time-phasing is referred to as order point. The same time-phasing logic is fundamental to dependent demand items of MRP systems.

The order point is triggered when the projected on-hand quantity of an item drops below the safety stock level. A planned order is released at a time corresponding to the lead time for the item.

Table 6-4 illustrates the logic of a time-phased order point system. At the beginning of week 1 there are 20 units on hand. If we add 40 units received and subtract the requirements for week 1, the ending inventory is 40 units. During the eight-week period, stock may equal but not fall below the safety stock level of 20 units. Because lead time is one week, the order release is scheduled· to occur one week earlier than the exhaustion of stock. The 40-unit order is assumed to be received at the beginning of the week so that safety stock is not used unless something unusual happens.

The Use of Bill-of-Materials

MRP puts the bill-of-materials to special use, providing part of the product specifications and a basic framework for the entire planning system. Often the existing bill-of-materials defines the product from a design point of view, and is not usable for MRP; then it must be redefined for material planning. With MRP, the bill-of-materials becomes the prime input to the master production schedule, which is put together in terms of the bill-of-materials (e.g., assembly numbers, etc.). When an MRP system is being created, the master production schedule and the bill-of-materials must be developed together for proper coordination.

Lot Sizing

Determining proper lot sizes is always important to management, but under MRP different considerations may apply. Independently calculated lot sizes, based on cost factors alone, may not match actual manufacturing requirements or materials handling requirements and other operations. If

Table 6-4. Planned order release.

Assume: Order quantity lot = 40
Lead time = 1 Week
Safety stock = 20

					WEEKS				
	0	1	2	3	4	5	6	7	8
Requirements		20	20	20	20	20	20	20	20
Receipt		40		40		40		40	
On hand at end of week period 20		40	20	40	20	40	20	40	20
Planned order			40		40		40		

the requirement is for 75 pieces, it is more important to make that quantity than the economic lot size. For MRP, then, discrete lot sizes may be preferable to the regularly calculated economic lot size.

The MRP Computer Program

The MRP computer program operates as follows:[13]

1. From the master production schedule it determines the number of end items required in each time period.
2. Replacement parts that are not included in the master production schedule, but are deducted from the inventory status files, are included as end items.
3. Using the bill-of-materials file, the master production schedule and replacement parts are exploded into gross raw materials required during specific future time periods.
4. The gross material requirements are modified by the amount of on-hand materials and those on order for each period. The net requirement of each material is determined; if net requirements are greater than zero, an order must be placed.

Net requirements =
   Gross requirements − Inventory − Safety stock −
Inventory allocated to other uses (i.e., scheduled and planned receipts)

5. The net requirements are offset to different time periods, to allow for lead times at each step in the production process and supplier lead times.

The resultant transactions are used to update the inventory status file and primary reports. The primary outputs of an MRP system dynamically provide the scheduled requirements for the future. These outputs are:

- A planned order schedule: the planned quantity of each material to be ordered in each time period. Purchasing uses the schedule to place orders with suppliers, and the schedule serves as a guide to suppliers for future production schedules.
- Order releases: authorizations to produce the materials identified in a planned order.
- Changes to previously planned orders: changes in quantity, cancellations, delays, or advancements to a different time period.

MATERIALS MANAGEMENT WITH THE MRP SYSTEM

MRP is a technically sound system, but its use can challenge materials management. Many materials managers experience problems and even outright failures with MRP. The following discussion will help one to effectively use MRP.

Issues

An MRP system raises many concerns, affecting every segment of materials management. By its very nature an MRP system always produces massive changes within an organization, including the establishment of new communication lines and methods and new procedures for materials management. Major issues for MRP system users are suggested in Table 6-5; managers must pay careful attention to all of them.

Table 6-5. Key issues for materials management using an MRP system.

Completing the operating model
- policies
- measurements
- systems

Recognizing the magnitude of change expected
- timing
- individuals with MRP experience as critical resources
- key individuals carrying heavy loads

Transition problems
- old and new systems support
- trust in individuals; no "watchdog"
- reports not available initially

Attention of senior materials management
- need to see value of behavior changes
- proper rewards from management

Adequate funding to complete the program
- high enough priority required

Undertaking many other changes at this time
- divisionalization
- improved material management
- new quality emphasis
- reduced cost of manufacturing
- increased new product introductions
- improved return on operating assets

Materials Management Changes

Use of an MRP system requires that materials management provide:

- Sufficient education for all system users.
- Clear objectives.
- Development of software "tailored" to specific company needs.
- Acceptance of the system as a valid materials management tool.
- Proper communication of the system to all.
- A supportive environment to motivate participation in system use.
- Adequate time to implement the system.
- Adequate rewards for system use.

The changes the system brings will be accepted if they are presented properly and have the support of top materials management. For an MRP system to be useful to materials management, individuals must change not only their procedures but also their views. Sometimes job responsibilities will change.

Table 6-6 lists the concerns that materials management must address

Table 6-6. Areas of concern for materials management with an MRP system.

Changes
- Identifying available resources.
- Revising internal priorities.
- Assigning new responsibilities.
- Selecting leaders; staffing for new responsibility.
- Meeting need for education.
- Getting commitments.
- Achieving high file data integrity.

People
- Obtaining agreement on change.
- Assigning new responsibilities.
- Revising job descriptions and measurements.
- Retraining people to accept system discipline.
- Giving up traditional practices.

Operation
- Taking formal approach to planning and execution.
- Reallocating and shifting resources.
- Measuring and correcting activities.
- Maintaining bill-of-materials and inventory data integrity.
- Resisting pressures on the production plan.
- Resisting end-of-month push.
- Resisting cuts in vital areas.
- Putting the system's integrity above any short-term crisis.

with an MRP system. Use of an MRP represents major change in the materials management philosophy:

- MRP formalizes the materials management planning process, from top management to the unit level.
- It imposes greater discipline on materials management.
- It creates a service-oriented relationship between work centers.
- It requires a massive project-oriented education and training program.
- It demands that upper materials management take an active role in its use.

Unfortunately, the benefits of MRP may not be obvious to all levels of materials management. For example, one MRP benefit, reducing materials handling time, may take six to nine months to be realized. The handling time may actually increase initially and then decrease.

To ensure materials management acceptance of an MRP, the system must involve all levels of materials management. Thus MRP requires:

- Solid commitment (stable organization).
- Internal communication.
- Clearly identified responsibilities (accountability).
- Measurable objectives, including periodic monitoring of progress.

Applying MRP

Successful application of an MRP system requires changes in procedures and job skills at all levels of materials management. Table 6-7 lists some specific actions needed for success. MRP is a formal system that requires strict adherence to procedures; materials managers must acquire basic knowledge and skills for operating the system. MRP is a valuable tool, currently being used successfully by many companies. These companies thoroughly planned and laid proper groundwork before using MRP sys-

Table 6-7. MRP requirements for success.

- Involve material managers in all divisions/functions.
- Establish project managers and teams.
- Develop operating procedures.
- Develop and conduct internal/external training programs.
- Develop communication links and user groups.
- Establish decision-making and issue-resolution forums.
- Obtain materials management agreement to overall implementation plans and priorities.
- Define policies for an interdivisional/functional operating environment.
- Establish implementation proceedings.

tems. Table 6-8 is a checklist for companies involved in installing MRP systems. After installing an MRP, management must operate the system effectively. This requires materials management to be concerned about lead times, requirements, lot sizing, and other factors.

Table 6-8. MRP checklist.

	Yes	No
Data Integrity		
1. Inventory record accuracy 95% or better.	___	___
2. Bill of material accuracy 98% or better.	___	___
3. Routing accuracy 95% or better.	___	___
Education		
4. Initial education of at least 80% of all employees.	___	___
5. An ongoing education program.	___	___
Technical		
6. Time periods for Master Production Scheduling and Material Requirement Planning are 1 week or smaller.	___	___
7. Master Production Scheduling and Material Requirements Planning run weekly or more frequently.	___	___
8. System includes firm planned order and pegging capability.	___	___
9. The master production schedule is visibly managed, not automatic.	___	___
10. System includes capacity requirements planning.	___	___
11. System includes daily dispatch list.	___	___
12. System includes input/output control.	___	___
Use of the System		
13. The shortage list has been eliminated.	___	___
14. Vendor delivery performance is 95% or better.	___	___
15. Vendor scheduling is done beyond the quoted lead times.	___	___
16. Shop delivery performance is 95% or better.	___	___
17. Master Schedule performance is 95% or better.	___	___
18. There are regular (at least monthly) production planning meetings with the general manager and his staff, including: manufacturing, production and inventory control, engineering, marketing, and finance.	___	___
19. There is a written master scheduling policy which is adhered to.	___	___
20. The system is used for scheduling as well as ordering.	___	___
21. MRP is well understood by key people in manufacturing, marketing, engineering, finance, and top management.	___	___
22. Management uses MRP to manage.	___	___
23. Engineering changes are effectively implemented.	___	___
24. Simultaneous improvement has been achieved in at least two of the following three areas: inventory, productivity, and customer service.	___	___
25. Operating system is used for financial planning.	___	___

Scoring Information
Give yourself 4 points for each "Yes" response.

90–100 points = Class A	50–70 points = Class C
70– 90 points = Class B	0–50 points = Class D

Classes of MRP Applications

Although MRP is easy to understand conceptually, companies use it to varying degrees. The different degrees of application of MRP systems can be described as:[14]

Class D — Computer success
Class C — Used for order launching (mainly hot lists, not scheduling).
Class B — Used for scheduling (still uses hot list, particularly at end of billing period).
Class A — Credible system (no hot list; foreman believes dates and is meeting master schedule).

Wight defines Class A use as follows:

Area	*Performance*
• Master schedule	• Less than 5% rescheduled; 95%+ accomplishment
• Material planning	• Pass acid test
• Shop and purchasing	• 95% on time or earlier delivery
• Scheduling	• 95% accuracy of scheduling plans
• Stockroom	• 95% record accuracy
• Engineering	• 98% bill-of-materials accuracy
• Sales	• 95% cumulative group forecast accuracy

Sophisticated management at all levels is required to utilize MRP successfully.

DISTRIBUTION REQUIREMENTS PLANNING (DRP)

A distribution requirements plan (DRP)[15] is a scheduling tool that calculates orders many months into the future using the MRP format. DRP optimizes planning for both orders and product distribution by determining the aggregate time-phased net distribution requirements at the same point in the materials flow as in the MRP master production schedule. MRP is a scheduling technique for manufacturing; DRP applies MRP principles and techniques to distribution. Integrating distribution planning with manufacturing planning ensures that supplies will be available for distribution when needed, and that manufacturing resources are used most effectively. Under an order-point system, inventory at the central warehouse can become inadequate overnight if two or more branch warehouses reach their order point at the same time. DRP avoids this problem by projecting branch warehouse requirements by period and generating planned orders for the central warehouse. As branch warehouse orders are predicted, the central warehouse can place orders with the factory to meet these requirements.

DRP is especially beneficial to materials management when it is desirable to ship large quantities at relatively infrequent intervals. DRP is based on future time-phased requirements rather than past sales, and maintains most safety stocks at the central warehouse. It enables materials managers to allocate resources and capacity, limit resources, and meet total organizational requirements in a manner consistent with overall corporate goals.

Relationship of DRP Objectives to Materials Management

DRP serves specific objectives in regard to materials management functions. With DRP, materials management is able to plan how many people and how much equipment will be needed each month to receive, store, and ship inventory, which is calculated in pounds and cubes.

DRP controls distribution costs by reducing rush orders that require special handling and shipment to distribution centers, and avoiding back orders that enable complete orders to be shipped. DRP reduces inventories by maintaining accurate and current information. By knowing what is required and when, materials managers can reduce the need for distribution warehouse space. DRP provides better coordination between materials handling, manufacturing, and the marketing network.

DRP's purpose is to improve service by meeting customer delivery dates and reducing customer complaints. DRP indicates what is needed and then provides for execution of the plan. Because the objective is to meet customers' expectations, DRP provides advance notice when products will be unavailable; materials management then can be planned accordingly. A DRP also enables earlier preparation by materials management when new products are introduced and promoted. Through DRP, materials management has a better working relationship with other company functions because all functions are working with the same information. Causes of problems are usually more evident, and solutions easier. In short, DRP helps avoid confusion.

DRP complements MRP, as both have the same objectives. DRP provides accurate information for MRP master scheduling concerning current requirements of the distribution system. Utilizing the same system, materials management is able to work effectively with different units. Non-DRP distribution systems generally ignore materials management and are concerned with allocating available inventory to meet distribution center requirements. Inventories may be limited or unavailable at times; frequent shortages may create problems in controlling the distribution network. The objective of a DRP system is to integrate materials management plus other functions such as manufacturing into product distribution, to ensure that inventory is available.

DRP-scheduled orders assist materials managers in developing cash flow projections. Anticipating related labor, equipment, and other resources, DRP complements materials management by providing information needed for forecasting future activities.

Operating a DRP

The information required for DRP includes:

- A forecast of product demand by periods.
- A calculation showing how long the inventory balance on hand will last.

If safety stock is maintained, it is subtracted from the inventory balance before the latter calculation is made. In-transit shipments are added to the inventory balance. The inventory balance plus the in-transit shipment is used to calculate the next shipment and to determine when it is to be delivered. Shipping lead time includes processing of the order, packing, in-transit time, and time needed for receiving the product at the distribution center. The date when the distribution center places the order must reflect the time needed for order processing, mailing orders, and receiving orders.

Figure 6-5 shows a distribution and manufacturing operation with three warehouses and sales direct from the factory warehouse. The lead time, shipping quantity, forecast demand, projected orders, and projected on-hand balance by week for each warehouse are given in Table 6-9. In Table 6-9 the distribution center (regional warehouse) has 100 units of the product on hand, a safety stock of 40 units is required, and the forecast demand varies between 16 and 24 units per week. The lead time is one week, and the order quantity is 60 units, which makes a full pallet. In this example, the on-hand balance is reduced by the quantities forecast to be sold each week. In the first week, 100 units are on hand at the beginning of the week, and 20 are forecast to be sold during the week. Therefore, the projected on-hand balance is 80 at the beginning of the next week. Stock reduction continues to be projected until the projected on-hand balance goes below the safety stock of 40 in Week 3. The distribution manager needs to have more product delivered in Week 3 to keep from dropping below safety stock. The replenishment lead time for this item is one week, and 60 are shipped from the central supply to the distribution center. Table 6-9 shows

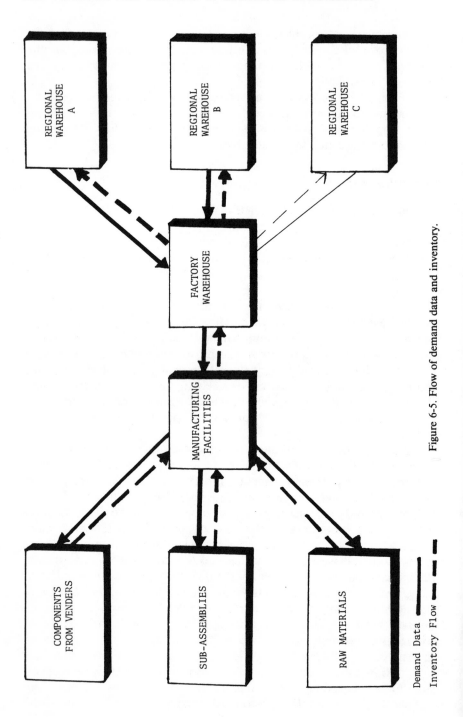

Figure 6-5. Flow of demand data and inventory.

Demand Data ▬▬▬▬
Inventory Flow ▬ ▬

Table 6-9. DRP for a distribution center.

On-hand balance 100
Safety stock 40
Lead time 1 week
Order quantity 60

	WEEK							
	1	2	3	4	5	6	7	8
Forecast	20	24	18	22	24	20	16	24
In transit								
Projected on hand 100	80	56	98	76	52	92	76	52
Planned shipments— receipt date			60			60		
Planned shipments— shipment date		60			60			

the planned shipment ship date and the planned shipment receipt date, or when items are to arrive at the distribution center.

DRP projects regional warehouse requirements by period and generates planned orders for the factory warehouse. DRP can predict when regional warehouse orders will jointly occur, and can plan an order from the factory warehouse to the manufacturing facility to meet distribution requirements. DRP is based on future time-phased requirements rather than on past sales, which makes future forecasts critical. By carefully calculating and predicting future shipping dates, DRP provides materials management information for planning at the central warehouse and distribution centers. These projections help to ensure that products are available at the distribution centers when needed for a planned period, such as a year.

Briefly, DRP can do the following:

1. Determine when inventory and shipment-in-transit will be depleted.
2. Use the projected order quantity required by the distribution center to determine planned shipments to the distribution center.
3. Use the planned shipment lead time to determine the date for planned shipments from the warehouse to the distribution center.
4. Determine projected on-hand balances, including planned shipments.
5. Repeat the process for the planning horizon or the forecasted demand (a year or more).

This process is carried out for each distribution center, to determine when and what the warehouse should ship to the distribution center to meet the forecasted demands. Information from DRP gives materials managers the necessary data for planning and allows them to react to changes. Actual sales often differ from forecasts, and materials management must be able to take these changes into account. A DRP makes such adjustments repeatedly for each product at the distribution center. In most DRP applications, such replanning occurs weekly. DRP constantly replaces, updates, and revises the plan based on the best available information, thereby keeping true needs up-to-date. Changes in lead times, safety stocks, order quantities, and forecasts, as well as changes in sales, can all affect planned shipments.

DRP and Master Production Scheduling

A master production schedule (MPS) is a summary statement of production rates; it is a plan for components and raw materials, and is used to determine capacity requirements of the work center. The MPS is a starting point for scheduling all manufacturing and serves as a focal point between a company's distribution and manufacturing systems (see Figure 6-6). The most common problems between manufacturing and distribution are those in which the MPS is unable to meet distribution demands; these problems can be solved by proper use of DRP, MPS, MRP, and CRP. DRP can help to solve problems in the distribution network; for example, if product demand exceeds inventory quantities, shipment can be achieved by eliminating a special promotion, using safety stocks, or shipping alternate quantities to customers. Manufacturing problems can be solved by overtime or extra shifts, or by using alternate machines and changing production runs. Another alternative is to change the MPS, but this is usually done only as a last resort because the normal objective is to meet the MPS.

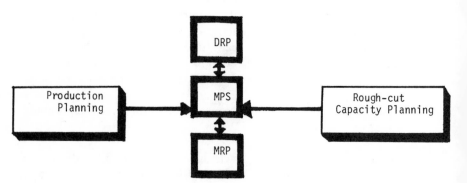

Figure 6-6. Relationship of MPS to other planning activities.

DRP and MRP tell manufacturing how distribution operates, and tell distribution how manufacturing operates. Both programs use the same principles, procedures, and logic, and they generate similar reports. This common arrangement enhances communication, understanding, and teamwork.

With DRP, MPS, and MRP, customer service objectives are shared by everyone. More important, these planning activities make it possible to identify common managerial problems while there is time to correct them.

MATERIALS MANAGEMENT AND DRP

A DRP uses the same information format as an MRP. It includes:

- Accurate forecasts (such as the demand used in the MPS).
- Scheduled receipts (in-transit shipments).
- Planned orders (orders scheduled for future shipment and/or items scheduled to be manufactured in the future).
- Planned shipments, added to the projected on-hand balance.

Information Included in DRP

Information in a DRP that is vital to materials management includes:

- *Balance of inventory on hand:* For maximum benefit, DRP inventory records must be at least 95% accurate. To achieve this degree of accuracy, personnel must be educated and be made accountable, and inventory must be counted periodically.
- *Safety stock:* Inventory is used to cover situations where sales exceed forecasts.
- *Lead time:* The time required from the release of an order until it is received in the warehouse, lead time includes releasing the order, packing, loading, shipping, and unloading. In many situations, this time interval can be compressed.
- *Order quantity:* The major factors that determine order quantities are frequency of shipment, FOB, materials handling and storage practices, total weight, and volume.
- *Order policies:* The methods used to calculate the planned order quantities are termed order policies. A fixed-order policy, specifying equal order quantities, is the most common type; but with DRP, order policies are based on *what* is required and *when*.

DRP Benefits to Materials Management

DRP helps to resolve numerous materials management problems, in such areas as:

- Transportation, scheduling, and loading.
- Planning for stock buildup in warehouses in advance of promotions or seasonal or special sales.
- Alerting the materials organization to warehouse-related problems, such as anticipated labor strikes or relocation or remodeling of facilities.

Any complete distribution planning system must recognize the importance of scheduling inventories from the point of supply until orders reach the customers. DRP helps companies schedule and replenish inventories more effectively, resulting in on-time deliveries and better customer service. Distribution must not only schedule and manage inventories in the network, but must be concerned with how inventories are handled. In many companies, materials management cost is the major element of total product cost, and recently materials management costs have risen faster than many other elements of product costs.

DRP provides many opportunities for cost savings in materials management. Substantial savings can be achieved in managing the company's transportation network, for example. To take advantage of rate structures and to eliminate unnecessary handling and shipping, managers must know what is to be shipped and when. DRP provides data on planned shipments, by date and quantity, for all products, including information on equipment being utilized, such as half-full loads.

Additional benefits of incorporating DRP into the system are:

- DRP is a simulation of what is going to happen—forecasts and planned orders show what materials are going to be handled so that managers can plan to meet requirements.
- Materials management, marketing, and manufacturing can work closely together and help each other solve problems.
- DRP information allows materials managers to develop budgets for specified areas, such as transportation and equipment purchases.
- DRP provides a schedule of arrivals in pounds, cubes, and dollars.
- DRP provides action messages if shipments are reduced or canceled.
- DRP combines shipments to distribution centers.
- DRP combines shipments from suppliers.

Materials management utilizes a very valuable resource—time; but efficient use of time requires that it be scheduled. By making planning opportunities visible, DRP can be used to develop a materials management planning report. Based on such a report, a schedule can be established for the plant and the entire distribution network. Materials managers must assure adherence to schedules in order to stablize inventory levels, meet production schedules, and achieve company marketing goals.

DRP uses computer support to control a large number of products, and can help individuals to avoid the pitfalls of a total materials management system. Although they cannot make decisions, computers can provide useful information when accurate inputs are used.

RELATIONSHIPS WITH OTHER MANAGEMENT FUNCTIONS

MRP and DRP are not just systems to schedule production and distribution; they are accurate, detailed simulations of an entire operation, and can be considered as a way to implement a materials management system. They also have important uses as planning and budgeting resources for materials management, and can be used to anticipate many other requirements, including certain physical operations whose results can be examined.

Inventory

Inventories are among the largest assets of many companies, but can also be their most manageable resource. DRP and MRP provide information needed to accurately predict future inventories. With a projected on-hand balance for every product, components can be restocked efficiently at all locations.

Financial Planning

MRP and DRP allow finance to utilize the same plan and information that manufacturing and marketing use, and to measure the use of financial resources against the same plan that operations is using. If inventories are larger than anticipated, production is greater than planned or sales have decreased. Finance can readily determine the reasons for the difference and make needed adjustments in financial resources. Without formal planning systems such as MRP and DRP, managers have no way to predict what information they will need to justify budgets and plan for variances. Independent forecasts, or those based on historical experience, are independent of the system that actually determines what will occur. Because the two systems are not connected, they do not give consistent information. The most obvious benefit of MRP and DRP is in budgeting costs; the information they supply provides a basis for recommending changes in operations and indicates areas for cost savings, thus helping to determine future cash needs for the planning period.

Forecasting and Planning

MRP and DRP are only as good as the information on which they are based. Inventory projections must be based on correct data if they are to be used for effective management. Sales forecasts and production plans are seldom perfect, but the objective of good planning is to take the best information available and refine it, through continual revision and evaluation based on changing conditions. Through this process, a company's forecasting and planning can reach a high degree of accuracy.

Valid predictions can be developed for manufacturing by using MRP. Projected on-hand inventories for components and subassemblies can be extended by cost to give projected inventory values. Such information is used in managing the financial aspects of a company, and can be used to determine the effects of various actions on a company's financial situation. In addition to its applications in budgeting and financial planning, DRP can help in forecasting warehousing space requirements for the coming year. Inaccurate predictions of warehousing space requirements (by location) can result in added costs for materials handling, product damage, obsolescence, lost products, increased accounting, and related problems.

DRP can be used to forecast the number of hours required for materials handling, labor, and equipment by location, including the hours required to load and unload materials based on planned orders. Extending planned orders by labor hours generates reliable capacity requirements projections for materials management. This is equivalent to capacity requirements planning (CRP) in a manufacturing operation. Routings in the manufacturing operation specify all procedures performed, the equipment used, and the number of hours required, including times for materials handling. For a materials manager, these forecasts of labor and equipment needs in the system, by location, are extremely important. Too much or too little capacity in a given area can be expensive and create many problems, especially in a company where peak seasons are important to financial plans and budgets.

Managerial Relationships

A DRP introduces a new approach to managing distribution of products. The DRP reflects new sets of values:

- *Accurate data:* Three sets of data are critical to the DRP system and must be accurate: inventory records, description of the distribution system, and master production schedule.

- *New management direction:* Managers need to be educated to understand DRP; their past experience and past training are inadequate.
- *Planning:* DRP requires that managers establish sales forecasts, master production schedules, and customer service objectives.
- *Delegation of responsibility:* Specific people must be accountable for accomplishing plans. For example, manufacturing is responsible for adhering to the master production schedule, and marketing is responsible for selling products. For proper utilization of DRP, these responsibilities must be set forth, and people must understand their accountability.
- *Common plans:* DRP requires that materials management, manufacturing, marketing, and finance use the same plans and the same data. All groups must work together as a team.
- *Decision information:* DRP provides managers with accurate information for making decisions, so that they no longer need to rely on guesses and intuition. Decisions must reflect an overall company point of view, and all operations must evaluate the impact of their decisions in terms of benefit to the whole company.
- *Improved communication:* DRP provides the vehicle for an effective communication system between work groups and all levels of management.
- *Increased productivity:* DRP improves productivity by establishing a formal system.

DRP relates to total materials management in significant ways:

- DRP provides information needed to plan materials management activities.
- DRP informs all managers of what is going to happen; planned and committed orders indicate what is going to be handled and when.
- Because information is accurate, it can be used to develop materials organization budgets and justify equipment proposals.

DRP ties planning for production and marketing together by determining the aggregate net requirements at the master production schedule (MPS). DRP is based on future time-phased requirements rather than on past sales and is especially beneficial when handling costs make it advisable to move large quantities at relatively infrequent intervals.

SUMMARY

The wide use of material requirements planning (MRP) has had an important impact on materials management. MRP is a technique for scheduling the material required to meet production goals for each time period.

Recently, in order to schedule distribution operations, distribution resource planning (DRP) has evolved. Both DRP and MRP facilitate materials management, giving a logical tie between materials management and production and sales.

MRP follows a specific sequence. A master production schedule develops from orders and indicates the number of products to be made for each period, showing the quantities of material required and the number of inventory units on hand. From these data, the MRP program prepares planned order schedules, order release requirements, and reschedules as required. The MRP program derives its information from the inventory file, master production schedule, and bill-of-materials. Materials management can use the information of the MRP in scheduling the operation.

Successful use of an MRP system requires an understanding of its special requirements and of materials management changes, procedures, and job skills needed, as well as the degree of its application in the company.

A distribution requirements plan (DRP) is a scheduling technique that calculates orders for many months into the future using the MRP format. The DRP optimizes planning for both orders and product distribution by determining the aggregate time-phased net distribution requirements at the same point in the materials flow as in the master production schedule of the MRP. DRP is especially beneficial to materials management when it is desirable to ship large quantities at relatively infrequent intervals. The benefit for materials management is that DRP is based on future time-phased requirements rather than on past sales, and maintains safety stocks at a central warehouse. DRP helps to make the best use of the total materials resources.

Materials management can use MRP and DRP for planning and budgeting its resources and anticipating the effects of other operations, such as production, inventories, and financial requirements. These systems do more than just schedule production and distribution; they give accurately detailed simulations of the entire operation.

NOTES

1. Monks, *Operations Management Theory and Problems,* p. 486.
2. Orlicky, *Material Requirements Planning,* The New Way of Life in Production and Inventory Management, p. 21.
3. Cook and Russell, *Contemporary Operations Management,* p. 382.
4. Schroeder, Anderson, Tupy, and White, "A Study of MRP Benefits and Costs," pp. 1–6.
5. *Material Requirement Planning,* A.P.I.C.S. Training and A.P.I.C.S. BUCS-MONT.
6. Cook and Russell, *Contemporary Operations Management,* p. 384.
7. Orlicky, *Material Requirements Planning,* The New Way of Life in Production and Inventory Management, p. 41.
8. Orlicky, *Material Requirements Planning,* The New Way of Life in Production and Inventory Management, pp. 180–185.

9. Ibid.
10. *Material Requirement Planning,* American Production and Inventory Control, p. 57.
11. Bevis, "A Management Viewpoint on the Implementation of a MRP System," pp. 105–108.
12. "A.P.I.C.S.: Capacity Planning and Control Study Guide," pp. 1–9.
13. Gaither, *Production and Operations Management,* pp. 537–538.
14. Oliver Wight, Oliver Wight Limited, 85 Allen Martin Drive, Essex Junction, VT 05452.
15. This section is based on the outstanding writing of Oliver Wight, and André J. Martin, Oliver Wight Limited Publications Incorporated, 85 Allen Martin Drive, Essex Junction, VT 05452; *Distribution Resource Planning—Distribution Management's Most Powerful Tool,* Prentice-Hall, Englewood Cliffs, NJ 07632, 1983.

BIBLIOGRAPHY

Anderson, John C., Schroeder, Roger G., Tupy, Sharon E., and White, Edna M. *Materials Requirements Planning: A Study of Implementation and Practice.* ISBN: 0-935406-03-4/ LC: 81-68514. A.P.I.C.S., 1981.

"APICS: Capacity Planning and Control Study Guide." *Production and Inventory Management,* Vol. 16, No. 1 (1975), pp. 1–9.

Berry, W. L., Vallmann, T. E., and Whybark, D. C. *Master Production Scheduling: Principles and Practices.* ISBN: 0-935406-21-2/LC: 82-236025. A.P.I.C.S., 1979.

Buffa, Elwood S. *Modern Production/Operations Management.* New York: John Wiley and Sons, 1980.

Cook, Thomas M., and Russell, Robert A. *Contemporary Operations Management.* Englewood Cliffs, New Jersey: Prentice-Hall, 1984.

Fogarty, Donald W., and Hoffmann, Thomas R. *Production and Inventory Management.* Cincinnati, Ohio: South-Western Publishing Co., 1983.

Gaither, Norman. *Production and Operations Management.* Hinsdale, Illinois: The Dryden Press, 1980.

Martin, André J. *Distribution Resource Planning—Distribution Management's Most Valuable Tool.* Englewood Cliffs, New Jersey: Prentice-Hall, 1983.

Material Requirement Planning. American Production and Inventory Control, 1973, p. 57.

Material Requirement Planning. American Production and Inventory Control Training, and A.P.I.C.S. BUCS-MONT Chapter, Washington, D.C.

Monks, Joseph G. *Operations Management Theory and Problems,* 2nd ed. New York: McGraw-Hill Book Co., 1982.

Orlicky, Joseph. *Material Requirements Planning—The New Way of Life in Production and Inventory Management.* New York: McGraw-Hill Book Co., 1975.

Plossl, George, and Wight, Oliver. *Material Requirements Planning by Computer.* A.P.I.C.S., 1971.

Schroeder, R. G., Anderson, J. C., Tupy, S. E., and White, E. M. "A Study of MRP Benefits and Costs." *Journal of Operations Management,* Oct. 1981, pp. 1–6.

Tersine, Richard J., and Campbell, John H. *Modern Materials Management.* New York: North-Holland Publishing Co., 1977.

Wemmerlou, Urban. *Capacity Management Techniques for Manufacturing Companies with MRP Systems.* ISBN: 0-935406-44-1/LC: 84-70268. A.P.I.C.S., 1984.

Wight, Oliver. *MRP II: Unlocking America's Productivity Potential.* Essex Junction, Vermont: Oliver Wight Limited Publications, 1981.

Part 3

PROCUREMENT, MATERIALS FLOW, AND DISTRIBUTION

7
Purchasing

Purchasing is essential to all organizations—manufacturing, nonmanufacturing, profit-making, nonprofit, and government. Its responsibility is to obtain purchased materials and services in the required quantity, at the right time (delivery), within desired quality specifications, and at a minimum total cost. Purchasing is a key subfunction within a materials management organization, uniquely involved in frequent contacts with different groups. It must cooperate closely with other materials management subfunctions to accomplish mutual objectives. Purchasing also has frequent contacts with other company functions such as engineering, marketing, quality assurance, finance, and manufacturing, as well as important contacts with suppliers of goods and services. Good communication with these various groups is essential; the relationships are illustrated schematically in Figure 7-1.

Purchased materials and services costs are among the largest capital expenditures in industry. The ratio obtained by dividing purchased materials and services costs by total cost of goods sold (dollars) indicates the significance of the purchasing function. This percentage will vary, depending upon the industry. Within an average manufacturing company, purchased materials and services account for 55 percent of total product dollars. This figure has increased as manufacturing processes have been mechanized and automated, becoming more material-intensive and less labor-intensive. In the more labor-intensive industries, such as health care and mining, the percentage may be 20 to 25 percent; but industries such as food processing and furniture manufacture have higher percentages for purchased materials and services, such as 75 to 80 percent.

Wise and skillful control of purchasing is critical to a company's success. Purchasing's efforts to obtain materials and services at realistic total costs have often made the difference between profit and loss, between success and bankruptcy.

PURCHASING OBJECTIVES

Almost every seminar, course, or lecture on purchasing summarizes purchasing objectives—namely, to obtain the right material or service at the

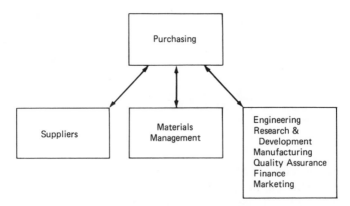

Figure 7-1. The purchasing communication relationships.

right time, in the right quantity, delivered to the right place, including the right service, and at the right price. Today, persons oriented to total materials management often delete "the right price" and replace it with "the right total cost." As purchasing attempts to accomplish its objectives, certain trade-offs must be recognized and analyzed. The materials manager must consider purchasing objectives and balance their trade-offs with those related to other materials subfunctions, to best serve the company.

Minimize Total Materials Costs

It can be counterproductive for purchasing to seek the lowest price; obtaining the lowest price may mean ignoring other costs that counteract any savings. To minimize total materials costs, purchasing must work with other materials management groups. Inventories are a good example of this. Purchasing can appear heroic when buying large quantities of material at appropriate quantity discounts, as this generally lowers costs, while also reducing the possibility of material shortages. However, these cost savings may be offset and eliminated by other costs such as the cost of carrying excess inventories. Buying in large quantities also can negatively affect a company's cash flow. Purchasing must work closely with inventory control to optimize costs while balancing inventories.

Purchasing can minimize total costs in areas other than material price, such as considering the FOB point when comparing quotations. (FOB is the abbreviation for "free on board," also referred to as "freight on board." "Free on board" is the preferred term, as the Uniform Commercial Code, adopted by all 50 U.S. states, defines it as such.) The FOB point in a quotation indicates to the buyer how transportation costs will be paid and determines the transfer of title for goods. The FOB point and transportation costs are important considerations in purchasing's efforts to minimize total costs.

Provide an Uninterrupted Flow of Materials and Services

One of the most common causes of complaint everywhere is material shortages or stockouts. Such shortages are extremely costly, producing tangible losses due to machine downtime, personnel downtime, decreased productivity, and lost customers. They also increase tension among company employees, impair communication between purchasing and suppliers and various company employees, and strain relationships with suppliers. Alternative transportation modes commonly are used to avert material shortages, for example, air freight shipment rather than truck transportation. Although air shipment often effectively eliminates material shortage problems, it also increases costs. Alternative, more costly, transportation modes should be used primarily when they will reduce total materials costs, and/or when they are needed to provide prompt deliveries to cus-

WHEN I SAID 'TIMELY PURCHASES' DUDLEY, I DIDN'T MEAN BUYING LOTS OF CLOCKS!

tomers. Purchasing should provide an uninterrupted flow of materials and services to the company without incurring additional costs. Good planning and good communication with all company groups and suppliers are a vital part of accomplishing this objective.

Provide Consistent, Good-Quality Purchased Materials and Services

Purchasing must consistently be aware of quality trade-offs in materials and services. Quality is related to both suitability and cost: purchasing should endeavor to obtain the best required-quality materials and services at the lowest cost. Purchasing personnel often say there are three important factors involved in every purchasing decision: quality, service, and price; and they generally agree that quality is the most important factor. Materials managers recognize that buying items at lower prices is not always less expensive—reduced quality may result in reworked parts or unhappy customers. Without good quality, good service and good prices are obtained in vain.

Purchasing should work closely with individuals responsible for quality specifications. For example, product specifications are required from design engineers and quality control engineers to ensure that suppliers have adequate information for quotes and for production of high-quality materials. Similarly, in purchasing services, such as cleaning services for offices, it is necessary to obtain definitive information from the appropriate designated source (office manager or maintenance supervisor) to ensure that quality standards are maintained.

Develop Favorable Supplier Relations

Good supplier relations are invaluable to the purchasing group and to the company as a whole. Reliable suppliers are important resources, contributing directly to a company's success; so purchasing should develop good rapport with suppliers.

Relationships with suppliers can be enhanced by treating them in a fair and equitable manner. The benefits of this type of association are mutual: suppliers will enjoy increased sales, and the company will get better service, more helpful research, greater cooperation in cost reduction programs, and faster resolution of problems. Like anyone else, suppliers respond best to individuals with whom they have good interpersonal relationships.

Develop Reliable Suppliers

One benefit of developing reliable suppliers is obtaining alternate sources of supply. Purchasing cannot wait until a supplier experiences some calamity (a labor strike or an equipment failure) before developing alternate sources. To find and develop competent suppliers purchasing must constantly search for new ones and carefully evaluate their qualifications. It may be necessary to visit the supplier and/or other companies for which they provide materials or services. A team of company personnel may be needed to help a buyer assess a supplier. This team could include quality control engineers, industrial engineers, accountants, and other suitable resource people. A periodic evaluation of suppliers is required to ensure that they are being responsive as well as responsible. Purchasing should continually monitor costs, delivery, and quality of purchased materials and services.

Optimize Purchasing Productivity and Costs

Productivity is as important for purchasing personnel as it is for all others in the company. Purchasing management must endeavor to train and help develop highly competent personnel. Capable personnel increase the department's productivity and serve as a reservoir of employees available for transfer to other material management groups and to other company functions. Development of better systems will also aid productivity. A good example of this is the current use of computers to increase purchasing efficiency. Interacting with other groups, computers can provide and receive vital data.

Purchasing costs should be kept at the lowest practical level. Travel, telephone, supplies, computer, and overhead are just a few examples of these costs. New procedures, methods, and equipment should be developed and instituted to minimize purchasing costs and increase productivity.

Maintain Good Informational Records

Reliable information is essential to the proper functioning of all departments, and especially important to purchasing. Decisions that directly affect the profitability of the company are based upon information purchasing receives from other materials subfunctions as well as other company groups. If the information is not reliable, resulting decisions may not be correct.

Many types of information affect purchasing decisions. All records must be reviewed and kept up-to-date. Consider, for example, the importance of timely information regarding supplier lead time. If the records show four weeks of lead time for an item that requires six weeks, then inventories will be exhausted before new supplies are received (assuming that safety stock is not large). In the reverse case, if the records showed four weeks of lead time and the actual time were two weeks, supplies would be received too early.

Up-to-date information is necessary on prices, discounts for quantity purchases, and transportation costs. Decisions on whether a company should make or buy, how much should be ordered, and which company offers the least total cost will be enhanced by accurate current information.

Cooperate with Other Departments

No department is an island in itself, and this is particularly true of purchasing. The success of purchasing, in accomplishing its objectives, is directly dependent upon its cooperation with other departments—both other materials management subfunctions and other major company functions (manufacturing, finance, and engineering). Relationships with these other groups are further discussed later in this chapter.

TYPICAL ACTIVITIES AFFECTING MATERIALS MANAGEMENT

The types of activities performed by the purchasing group vary from company to company. The assignment of activities depends upon the company's organization, size, and geographical dispersion. It is important to the success of the materials management group that all purchasing activities be assigned, and that all individuals be fully informed of their responsibilities.

Policies and Procedures

Development of policies and procedures is an important function of the purchasing department. Policies are broad, overall guidelines that assist a manager in decision making by delineating the span of consideration. They are guides to thinking as well as to action. Procedures are step-by-step guides to action or tasks that must be performed in order to accomplish an objective. Procedures are derived from policies. The use of policies and procedures ensures uniform approaches to decision making (policies) and accomplishing an objective (procedures). They eliminate the need to "reinvent the wheel" for each new decision or objective, and they facilitate communication and coordination of efforts by the various groups. Another advantage of written policies and procedures is that they establish clearly defined responsibilities.

Policies. Centralization of the purchasing function is essential for the attainment of company objectives (profit, operating efficiency, and reduced duplication of efforts). Centralization, in this context, is related to who has authority to perform the purchasing function, rather than the location of personnel. In some companies, various individuals in nonpurchasing positions (engineering, production, warehousing, and accounting) perform purchasing functions. In a total materials management organization, centralization is accomplished by assignment of a purchasing managerial position, reporting to the head of materials management, with clear responsibility for all purchasing functions. Establishing a company policy of centralized purchasing entails development of a series of internal and intradepartmental policies related to lines of authority, communication channels, and general departmental relationships.

Policies concerned with buyer–seller relationships are pertinent to primary purchasing functions. Many companies have established policies concerning scheduled times for salespeople to visit buyers. Provision is made to allow exceptions for individuals from out of town and for special appointments. Established policies on competitive bidding serve as a guide to buyers, both before and after the issuance of requests; these policies deal with such matters as confidentiality of supplier prices (government buyers having a mandatory seal bid and public opening policy do not have any options), bid revision, visits to supplier facilities, and exceptions for use of supplier contracts rather than normal purchase orders.

Procedures.   Procedures can be developed after policies are established; they are designed to improve the performance of personnel and minimize red tape. Although personnel may feel too constrained by them, procedures are meant to limit the ways that work is performed in order to optimize results. Employees should be encouraged to develop innovative methods, as true improvements can be used to revise procedures.

Typically, purchasing procedures cover all of the various departmental activities. For example, most companies use a standard, serially numbered purchase order form. The procedure for using this form would outline all pertinent information regarding completion of the form, including such information as description of material, quantity, date required, and authorized signature. Another typical procedure would cover the processing of rush orders. Some points included in this procedure would be limits to verbal requisitions and orders, use of purchase order numbers, and arrangements for premium transportation costs.

Many companies have policy and procedure manuals, which are an aid to good performance. However, if a manual is not kept up-to-date, its effectivity will be negated. A carefully maintained policy and procedure manual offers many benefits. It is an essential part of a company training program, for both new employees and those transferred into and within the purchasing department. Such a manual is useful for explaining work relationships and responsibilities to others within the materials organization as well as other groups.

Established policies and procedures allow for management by exception, and help guide normal operations. Then purchasing management decisions are required only when an exceptional problem arises.

Selection and Evaluation of Suppliers

Selection of capable suppliers is one of the most important responsibilities of purchasing professionals. Materials management systems depend upon a continuing supply of purchased goods and services; the process of seeking, evaluating, and selecting suppliers is continual. Company products and processes are always changing, necessitating the development of new suppliers. Also, additional suppliers for existing purchased items will be needed in order to obtain lower costs, better quality, on-time delivery, and improved technical services. Continuing supplier communication and evaluation are necessary after the selection process.

Developing Supplier Sources. The initial step in obtaining competent new sources of supply is to develop prospective suppliers. Some of these sources are:

1. *Salesmen contacts:* Buyers talk with salesmen regularly even when there is no immediate need for a product. Supplier information is then available when required at a future date.
2. *Purchasing contacts:* Contacts with individuals performing purchasing activities for other companies can be an invaluable source of prospective suppliers. Membership in professional societies, such as the National Association of Purchasing Management, Inc., helps to expand these contacts.
3. *Trade directories:* These publications list suppliers according to the products they make. They include *Thomas' Register of American Manufacturers* and *Conover-Mast Purchasing Directory.* The local telephone directory offers a quick source of information.
4. *Catalogs:* Carefully maintained files of supplier catalogs can be very useful. It is essential that the catalog file be kept current to maintain its effectiveness.
5. *Trade shows and conventions:* Periodically, different national and international groups conduct trade shows or conventions where many suppliers display their products. They offer good, concentrated exposure for buyers to new products, services, and suppliers.

More and more often buyers are being required by company policy, or by law, in the case of large government contracts, to increase purchases from socially and economically disadvantaged (minority) suppliers. These suppliers may be found in directories and other sources. Another aspect of purchasing from socially and economically disadvantaged suppliers is the development of acceptable long-term suppliers.[1] Methods used by some successful companies to solve external problems are illustrated in Figure 7-2.

Evaluating Suppliers. Evaluation of suppliers is critical to obtaining an uninterrupted flow of materials and developing reliable suppliers. The type

TECHNIQUE	BENEFITS TO MINORITY FIRMS
Breaking purchases into small quantities	Order size is within capacity and capability limits
Allowing longer leadtimes on materials	Provides protection against late deliveries
Providing longer quotation times	Quotations are received on time and proper information is provided
Providing special payment terms	Cash flow problems are minimized
Simplifying paperwork requirements	Time is spent on productive work versus paper-shuffling
Helping minority vendors secure raw materials	Provides assurance that material received is of good quality, competitively priced, delivered on time
Awarding long-term contracts to minority vendors	Assurance of steady business allows better planning for future financing
Providing prepayment on large dollar or long-leadtime items	Cash flow problems are reduced
Helping minority vendors develop effective purchasing practices	Helps firms to become cost competitive
Requiring suppliers to utilize minority vendor sources	Expands opportunities for business
Paying a price differential	Gives minority vendor time to become cost-competitive for a temporary period

Figure 7-2. Minority suppliers—solving external problems. (Source: Larry C. Giunipero, "Helping Minority Suppliers Become Better Sources," *Purchasing World,* Nov. 1, 1981, p. 63. Reprinted with permission, *Purchasing World,* copyright International Thomson Industrial Press, Inc.)

of evaluation required varies, depending upon the nature, complexity, and dollar amount of the item being purchased. For example, a buyer will devote very little time to evaluation of a low total cost purchase for which standard items are available in catalogs. Conversely, any purchase of large-dollar items or complex materials would require additional investigation. The following factors should be considered when evaluating suppliers:

1. *Financial condition:* The credibility of suppliers depends upon their ability to maintain financial stability. The best suppliers are financially strong. It is essential that a buyer obtain financial information to determine whether or not the supplier will be capable of performing satisfactorily. One source of financial information is credit reports. A service such as Dun and Bradstreet provides valuable information for supplier assessment. Additional information can be obtained from supplier financial statements, including the income statement and balance sheet.

2. *Quality:* Both total materials management and overall company management regard supplier quality as a primary requirement. All industries, including service, manufacturing, and distribution, need to receive purchased products and services that comply with individual company specifications. The buyer must assume responsibility for considering whether suppliers can consistently deliver good quality. If the supplier cannot provide the required quality, then cost and other factors are not a consideration.

3. *Personnel:* People are among the most important resources in any company. Much of the success or failure of suppliers depends upon the quality of their personnel. It is therefore necessary to assess suppliers' capability to perform based upon their having a sufficient number of qualified personnel. The buyer should meet with various company executives, particularly the materials manager, and evaluate the depth and capability of management. Another concern is labor relations. Strikes, slowdowns, poor quality, and late delivery can result from poor relationships with employees.

4. *Service:* The term service-related can be interpreted in various ways by suppliers. When evaluating service, a buyer would certainly want to consider a supplier's ability to comply with scheduled delivery dates. Other important service-related evaluations include the supplier's ability to provide qualified technical assistance, to extend equitable warranty provisions, to provide unit loads that allow for efficient materials handling, and to take prompt action regarding defective materials, as well as the supplier's willingness to stock materials to minimize the buyer's company inventory and to provide good communication about present or future problems.

5. *Plant visits:* The buyer may visit a supplier's facility to determine the supplier's capability. This visit can be conducted by an individual, or, if the purchase is very critical, in conjunction with a team of company experts (such as an industrial engineer or a quality control engineer). The visit could include a review of equipment, processes, quality control procedures, the material management organization and systems, and other critical factors. The evaluation team's visit can be made more effective by having the supplier provide some basic information before the team's visit. One purchasing department, for example, asks suppliers to complete an extensive form (illustrated in Figure 7-3). They use the form to decide whether a visit should be made, or how extensive an analysis the evaluation team should make.[2]

6. *Supplier rating:* Supplier ratings should be developed periodically as a monitor of performance. They provide a quantitative basis for comparing competing suppliers. The total materials management philosophy promotes the use of objective techniques for measuring and comparing existing suppliers. An example of a weighted-point plan for supplier evaluation is shown in Figure 7-4. With this plan, individual performance factors are weighted according to their importance to the company.[3] The major performance factors selected in this case were quality, total cost, and service (see Figure 7-4). Assume a supplier's monthly performance to be as follows: 3% rejected for poor quality; total cost of $50 per unit, compared with the lowest offer of $50 per unit; and two service failures (one late shipment, one split shipment). Figure 7-4b shows the computation of the supplier rating.

Make or Buy Decisions

Many companies are organized to distribute products or services produced by other companies. Their company policy is to buy rather than to make. Manufacturing companies periodically are faced with the decision of whether it is more beneficial to make or to buy a product. Making the product can entail complete vertical integration, producing the product from the initial extraction of basic materials to its completely finished form. For example, the Inland Steel Company mines iron ore, produces cold rolled steel through the various stages of manufacture, and then fabricates completed steel containers. Other manufacturing companies purchase components and materials, and complete the product within their facility. Make or buy decisions are also necessary in service businesses. For example, a hospital must decide whether it should maintain

VENDOR CAPABILITY SURVEY

SURVEY DATE ________

COMPANY NAME ________ ☐ CORPORATION ☐ PARTNERSHIP

ADDRESS ________ ☐ OTHER ________

PHONE NO ________ DATE ESTABLISHED ________ STATE OF INCORPORATION ________

SUBSIDIARY OF ________ DIVISION OF ________

CREDIT RATING ________ SECURITY CLEARANCE ________

OFFICIALS (OWNERS)	TITLE	KEY PERSONNEL	TITLE

☐ MASS PRODUCTION ☐ JOB SHOP ☐ MACHINING ☐ FINISHING ☐ ASSEMBLY

☐ TESTING ☐ ENGINEERING ☐ RES & DEV ☐ OTHER ________

NORMAL PRODUCTS OR SERVICES	DEFENSE	COMMERC

CUSTOMER REFERENCES	ITEMS PRODUCED FOR THEM

FACILITIES	SQUARE FEET	OWNED	LEASED	LEASE EXPIRES	PERSONNEL		UNION	NON UNION
					DIRECT	INDIRECT		
OFFICE AREA								
ENGINEERING AND LAB AREA								
MANUFACTURING AREA								
TOTAL								

UNION AFFILIATION	LOCAL NO	CONTRACT EXPIRATION DATE

EQUIPMENT
ATTACH LIST OF MACHINE TOOLS, SPECIAL TEST AND OTHER EQUIPMENT. GIVE GENERAL CONDITION AND INDICATE WHETHER OWNED, LEASED, OR GOVERNMENT FURNISHED

EQUIP LIST DATED

Figure 7-3. Form for soliciting preliminary evaluation data from suppliers. (Source: Stuart F. Henritz, Paul V. Farrell, and Clifton L. Smith, *Purchasing: Principles and Applications,* 7th ed., © 1986, p. 100. Reprinted by permission of Prentice-Hall, Inc., Englewood Cliffs, New Jersey.)

(a) Assume performance plan to be as follows:

Factor	Weight	Measurement formula
Quality	50	100% − Percentage of rejects
Total cost	25	$\dfrac{\text{Lowest cost offered}}{\text{Actual cost paid}}$
Service	25	100% − 10% for each failure

(b) Computation of a supplier rating would be as follows:

Factor	Weight	Actual performance	Evaluation	
Quality	50	3% rejects	$50 \times (1.00 - .03) =$	48.5
Total cost	25	$50	$25 \times \dfrac{\$50}{\$50} =$	25.0
Service	25	2 failures	$25 \times [1.00 - (2 \times .10)]$	= 20.0
			TOTAL RATING	93.5

Figure 7-4. Example of a weighted-point plan, and application.

people and facilities to provide services, or purchase them, including such diverse requirements as laundry, printing, and food services.

Another aspect of the make or buy decision involves both making and buying a product or service. In this case the company elects to do both. The question then is, "How much do we make, and how much do we buy?" A company may use this strategy when production control needs to increase capacity without changing its facilities and personnel.

Purchasing is responsible for providing the supplier-oriented information required to analyze the relative advantages and disadvantages of any make or buy decision. This involves coordination among materials management groups and any other groups that help to develop input for the decision, including industrial engineering, manufacturing, quality assurance, and finance.

Major Factors in Make/Buy Decisions. Some important considerations in deciding whether to make a product or provide an internal service, versus buying the product or service, including the following:

1. *Quality control:* In making a product, quality can be controlled best within the company. However, if special equipment or processing methods are required, they may be incapable of producing the desired

quality level internally—so the item must be bought. Sometimes suppliers produce at too high a quality level and are unwilling to provide the desired quality level at a lower price—so the item is made. Purchasing a product or service can be a means for obtaining high-quality items when the company has no experience in making them, or when the company lacks, or does not wish to invest in, equipment that can provide the desired quality levels.

2. *Volume required:* If the desired quantity is low, and/or the item or service is not unique, the company normally purchases it. This is commonly true of items such as building maintenance supplies and standard catalog parts. Occasionally, a company must make small quantities of an item if supplier costs are prohibitive, or if no one else will produce it. As the required quantity of a product or service increases, greater economies are possible, a consideration that can lead to a make decision.

3. *Facility capacity and capability:* A major factor in many make or buy decisions relates to existing facilities. The type and capacity of equipment and/or buildings currently available could swing the decision in either direction. New capital may not be available to expand facilities, a circumstance that would dictate a buy decision. On the other hand, in periods of reduced sales, a company may elect to make a previously purchased item because of excess facility capacity.

4. *Labor capacity and capability:* A firm may decide to buy rather than make if the labor skills required are not available within the company, if supplier labor rates are much lower, or if labor resources are being fully utilized and additional labor is not available. A make decision could be influenced by factors such as the desire to maintain a skilled labor force during a depressed business period.

5. *Company mission:* If companies see themselves as part of an industry that distributes products, they automatically are in a buy situation. Some companies do not wish to make certain products or provide services because they want to limit their efforts to other product/service areas. Upper management often clearly states the latitude of the company mission, and it affects make or buy decisions.

6. *Cost comparison:* The make or buy decision should be approached objectively. It requires a quantitative analysis of various costs related to both purchasing the item and providing it internally. Internal costs include materials, direct and indirect labor, and overhead (supervision, utilities, engineering, and buildings). Some companies apply overhead costs to a make or buy decision very cautiously, as supervisory costs do not necessarily increase if additional work is performed in a department. In such cases, overhead costs for supervision may not be applicable to the decision.

A midwestern manufacturer of electromechanical products experienced some unexpected benefits during a make or buy analysis. The company was at the limit of its manufacturing capacity but needed more electronic coils. An entire department was making the coils, requiring a significant amount of space, equipment, and personnel. The purchasing department was given the problem and asked to find suitable suppliers. When price quotations were received and total purchase costs developed, management was surprised to find that the total cost of purchasing the item was considerably less than the internal manufacturing costs. Purchase orders were issued, and the company used supplier coils to satisfy their additional needs. Then, after a suitable period of time, the company evaluated its supplier. Not only were the supplier's costs lower, but its product quality was superior to the company's and the supplier service was exemplary. Further investigation revealed that the company's equipment was not as modern or as automated as the supplier's equipment. A study was made to determine whether the company should be making coils, and as a result, the coil winding department was eliminated. Not only were manufacturing costs reduced, but some badly needed space was provided, and skilled employees could be transferred to other operations.

Supplier Relations

The purchasing department must recognize that supplier relations are vital to the company's success. A negative relationship can produce problems and costs for materials management, whereas a positive relationship will provide substantial current and future benefits. The progressive purchasing professional views suppliers as major company resources — as critical to operations as other company resources, including machines, money, and personnel.

Purchasing personnel have frequent supplier contacts, by all methods of communication, both oral (in person and by phone) and written. Often the first contact sets the tone of the relationship. Purchasing must convey the impression that suppliers are an important company asset. Initial contacts with a supplier include product indoctrination, product cost development, and supplier evaluation. Sometimes during discussions with a supplier the salesperson will offer inducements that would compromise the buyer's ethics. Such a conflict must be clarified immediately.

Many companies are expanding their communications with suppliers to maximize the benefits of their association. For example, companies may conduct open houses for suppliers. Suppliers are invited to visit the company on a particular day, when they are presented with a program informing them of future company plans. The program may include a welcoming speech by the chief executive officer, information related to materials management plans, discussion of new products, projections of future sales, discussion of the need for supplier input regarding cost reduction, and displays of both existing and prototype products and parts. Usually a luncheon is provided. Open houses can be conducted for both existing suppliers and potential new ones. Reportedly, these open houses not only have improved supplier relationships, but also have provided input for significant cost reductions.

Another way to improve communication is to use "supplier guides," which provide various materials management policy information to suppliers. These guides can include material on contacts with other departments, ethical standards, and visit hours. Figure 7-5 shows supplier guides used by Norton Company and GTE Products Corporation.

Product Quality

Purchasing professionals regard product quality as the number one consideration in any purchasing decision. This does not mean that purchasing should always obtain the best possible quality; it may be very detrimental to company profits to obtain quality that exceeds product specifications. Purchasing should obtain the best-quality product, considering the function that must be performed, at the least possible total cost.

The responsibility for specifying quality does not belong to the purchasing department. Purchasing may sometimes seem to be defining quality, when in fact it is just pursuing a clear-cut definition. Description and definition of product quality are the responsibility of various groups, depending on the product involved. Quality specifications for manufactured parts, subassemblies, and products are prepared by the engineering department. The quality of many items must be specified by the user department. For example, the maintenance department prescribes what type of grease will be used for lubricating machines; the materials manager establishes requirements for consulting services; and the office manager determines typing paper quality. An exception is found in the retail trade: a buyer of men's clothing for a department store is responsible for both defining the quality and buying the product.

Purchasing is responsible for checking the completeness of the product description and follow-up between the supplier and the department responsible for product definition. The description of a product that purchasing provides to the supplier can take a number of forms, including manufacturer's brand name, standard specifications, performance specifications, and samples.

Product quality can be defined simply by identifying a particular manufacturer's brand or trade name. This approach relies on the integrity and good name of the supplier. If the initial purchase is of the desired quality, it

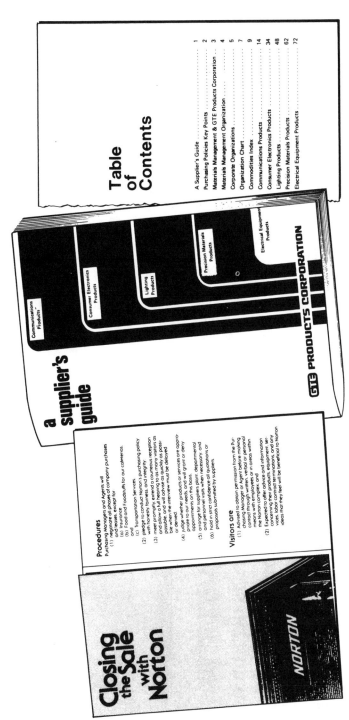

Table of Contents

Figure 7-5. Supplier guides, typical companies. Supplier guides used by companies range from the succinct pamphlet provided by the Norton Company to the comprehensive booklet of the GTE Products Corporation. (Source: "Tell Suppliers Who, What and Where," *Purchasing World*, Apr. 1982, p. 47. Printed with permission of the Norton Company and of GTE Products Corp., and with permission of *Purchasing World*, copyright International Thomson Industrial Press, Inc.)

241

is reasonable to expect that the manufacturer will maintain the quality level. The use of brand or trade names reduces the cost and time involved in developing written specifications. However, the use of brand names can limit the buyer's selection of sources. This can be overcome by adding the phrase "or equal" to a brand name.

Specifications are detailed descriptions of the general characteristics of an item. Different types of specifications are used to delineate quality requirements. Standard specifications are developed by both government and nongovernmental agencies. The National Bureau of Standards is an example of a government agency. Nongovernmental agencies developing specifications include the Underwriters Laboratories (U.L.) and the Society of Automotive Engineers (S.A.E.).

Performance specifications detail the performance or use of an item. They place the responsibility for providing a satisfactory product on the supplier. The proper use of performance specifications depends upon securing reliable suppliers. Engineering drawings are used to supply details beyond a descriptive text; they provide various views of the item, with dimensions and tolerances. Engineering drawings also are useful to incoming inspection personnel, for an accurate check of purchased items.

Quality definition can be minimized by using a sample of the item to be purchased. This alternative means of describing quality is relatively simple but could lead to difficulty. It may not be easy to assess whether delivered products match the sample if subjective judgment is required. For example, samples are used for judging visual quality, such as the color and grain of wood finishes.

Although the purchasing group is not responsible for quality specification, it is responsible for procuring proper quality. The key to achieving quality control in any company, according to Dr. W. Edwards Deming, is the purchasing function. His reasoning: without quality control on incoming parts, little can be done in-house.[4] It is the buyer's task to keep purchased material cost at the lowest possible point consistent with required quality. Purchasing must continually audit, question, and suggest changes that will benefit the company. This task can be maximized only by having qualified purchasing personnel whose suggestions are considered credible by engineering and other user departments.

Price Determination

Determination of the price to be paid for an item is one of the principal purchasing department functions. The purchase price is only one part of the total cost of an item, but it is an extremely significant part of total cost. A buyer must take a broad view and examine the prices of various suppliers, to obtain the right price. Any price analysis must consider the level

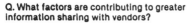

Q. What factors are contributing to greater information sharing with vendors?

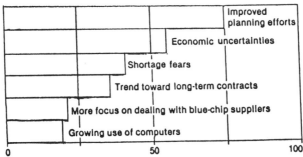

Improved planning efforts

Economic uncertainties

Shortage fears

Trend toward long-term contracts

More focus on dealing with blue-chip suppliers

Growing use of computers

0   50   100

Figure 7-6. Trend toward increased buyer–supplier communications. (Reprinted from *Purchasing Magazine*, March 26, 1981. Copyright by Cahners Publishing Company, 1981.)

of quality and service obtained. A professional buyer should be knowledgeable about supplier pricing, in order to minimize company costs. Suppliers use different means for pricing products; supplier price determination is not simple. Two approaches used are the cost approach and the market approach.

Cost Approach. The cost approach to price determination involves computation of all applicable costs of a product plus an appropriate profit. For an existing product, the costs can be fairly well defined. For new products, which have never been produced before, costs must be estimated. Most cost systems include direct material, direct labor, manufacturing overhead, and general and administrative costs.

Direct materials consists of all purchased material used in making a product; normally this includes materials such as raw materials, parts, packaging, and paint. Direct labor consists of all work performed in making a product; this includes labor costs such as fabrication, assembly, and finishing. Manufacturing overhead consists of all costs related to making a product that cannot reasonably be identified with individual products; it includes costs such as supervision, maintenance, materials handling, operating supplies (e.g., grease for a machine), and tooling. General and administrative costs consist of various expenses incurred for functions such as sales, promotion, legal services, and executive salaries.

Some buyers use an analytical tool called break-even analysis to determine the supplier's dividing point between profit and loss. Figure 7-7 shows a break-even chart. A buyer may use this technique to assist in determining the structure of a supplier's price. It can also be used to assist in predicting future price decreases, increases, and sometime quantity price

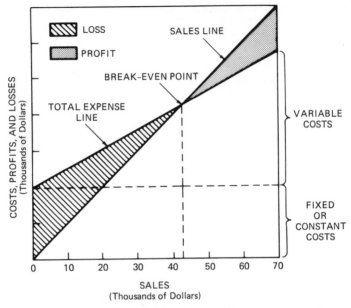

Figure 7-7. Break-even chart.

differentiation. Information such as this can be very useful to a buyer in developing a purchasing strategy. For example, when the supplier is operating well above break-even and sales are increasing, prices can be reduced.

Market Approach. This approach to pricing essentially consists of setting a price based upon the marketplace or willingness of purchasers to pay a price. Price may not be directly related to cost. Prices vary depending upon demand and supply. If demand is high, relative to supply, then prices will rise; if demand is low relative to supply, prices will decline. Figure 7-8 shows demand and supply curves. The reader can review any current economics book to understand the basic assumptions of these curves.

Suppliers establish market prices by various methods. A market research study employs questionnaires or tests of the market to determine possible demand and prices. Another method utilizes prices based upon an industry leader, whereby the supplier keeps prices pegged to a competitor's prices, depending upon factors such as quality and service. Another technique develops prices based upon other related products.

Knowledgeable buyers are aware of strategies for coping with market prices. For example, it is common for U.S. buyers to find another market by purchasing products from foreign suppliers. Another technique is to select suppliers who offer nonprice incentives such as higher quality, rapid

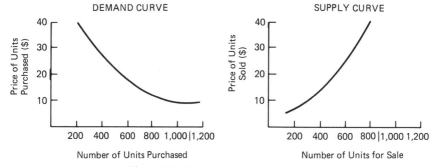

Figure 7-8. Demand and supply curves.

delivery, and cost concessions for transportation, payment discounts, and design engineering.

Negotiation

Negotiation is defined as "to confer, bargain, or discuss with a view to reaching agreement."[5] Purchasing personnel use this form of communication to reach acceptable agreement or compromise with the supplier. Unfortunately, the negotiation used in modern purchasing practices is often misunderstood; too often it is falsely regarded as haggling or chiseling. Negotiation should provide an opportunity for both buyer and supplier to benefit from the transaction. As with other business transactions, one side may benefit more than the other, according to its skill and knowledge. However, most successful long-term negotiations satisfy both sides and provide a framework for a mutually beneficial relationship.

Successful negotiation requires an appreciation and understanding of the emotional aspects of the process. Personal contacts take place between the buyer and the supplier. Negotiations can be performed by individuals or by teams of people representing both groups. The buyer must learn as much as possible about the supplier and plan strategies in advance for possible positions. One valuable source of information is the performance data available from supplier evaluation programs.[6] Other important sources include materials management and other group personnel and data.

A skillful buyer understands negotiation techniques and how to employ these techniques to achieve optimum results. Many tactics can be helpful to a buyer in negotiation. Some useful techniques include the following:

1. *Arrange for negotiation meetings to be conducted at your location.* There is a psychological advantage to having the supplier come to

your facility meetings. It is similar to sitting at the head of a table or sitting at a desk while someone else is standing. Try to isolate members of the supplier team by seating buying members between them.

2. *Allow the supplier to do most of the talking.* Salesmen cannot remain silent. Suppliers may talk themselves into making more concessions than they had planned to do. Also, their silence may make buyers seem to be in a stronger position than they really are. Concessions often result if the supplier fears a loss of business.

3. *Possess all necessary, reliable information.* The buyer should have all necessary data, which should be accurate. Lack of information or faulty information can place the buyer at a disadvantage.

4. *Know your goals.* Buyers should know what they want and keep their goals in mind. They should analyze in advance the concessions that the suppliers can reasonably be expected to provide.

5. *Negotiate with someone of high authority.* It is often a waste of time to negotiate with suppliers who do not possess the authority to make concessions. Most individual salesmen have a limited percentage leeway on price, and lack the authority to negotiate other important terms such as credit, quality, and transportation.

6. *Allow the supplier to retreat gracefully.* Follow the Oriental philosophy of allowing the other person to "save face." For example, if you detect errors in supplier information, do not accuse anyone of deliberate falsification to obtain sales leverage. Simply suggest that a revision is required.

7. *Plan ahead.* Prepare the agenda for the negotiation meeting to your advantage. Make sure that all members of the team are fully briefed; explain facts, individual roles, and planned strategies. The team leader should be in control of the action at all times.

8. *Avoid any premature climax.* Eventually negotiations will reach a climax. Buyers do not want to force suppliers into the position of saying, "Here are my terms; take them or leave them." This could eliminate the possibility of further discussions. The suppliers might then feel compelled to stand by their original offer.

9. *Divert attention if suppliers hit weak points.* During negotiations the suppliers may detect and mention a weakness in a buyer's presentation. Buyer team members must be ready to shift the focus to minor points that later may be conceded.

10. *Refrain from moving too fast.* The negotiation process is used mainly for major purchases, because of its time-consuming nature. It is inadvisable to rush the proceedings. Do not give the suppliers the impression that you are in a hurry; it is best to put them in a position to conclude negotiations by providing concessions.

Timing of Purchases

Cost, availability, and other factors often depend upon the timing of purchases. Under normal, stable market conditions, timing is predictable. However, in many circumstances markets must be watched very closely to optimize company objectives. The buyer may perform four types of buying.

Hand-to-Mouth Buying.   This type of purchasing considers buying materials or services in smaller than normal quantities. It is literally obtaining supplies on a hand-to-mouth basis. There are different reasons for doing this. Often purchasing will forecast a drop in prices, and purchase quantities are reduced in order not to accumulate too great an amount of higher-priced items. Manufacturing companies also utilize hand-to-mouth buying when engineering changes are contemplated, to minimize the obsolescence of materials. Another practical reason for companies to use hand-to-mouth purchasing is that their cash flow may necessitate inventory reduction. This precaution may increase long-term costs, but business people often say, "If we don't take care of our short-term cash flow, there may not be any long-term considerations because the company will be bankrupt."

Current Requirement Buying.   This type of purchasing is the most common. The company is generally obtaining required items most economically, balancing all individual costs such as quantity discounts, carrying costs, stockout costs, and ordering costs. Just-In-Time systems are an example of this, in which a company arranges to receive materials in lot sizes that optimize flow through all operations.[7] (Current requirement lot size determination is discussed in Chapter 4.)

Forward Buying.   This approach consists of purchasing in excess of current company requirements, but it does not include purchases made in order to realize speculative profits. Forward buying is an essential part of successful purchasing, and to be effective it must consider all trade-off costs related to buying excess inventory. Some of the reasons for forward buying are:

- To provide an "insurance policy" for possible strikes or similar developments.
- To reduce purchase costs by buying during an unstable market, when costs are lower.
- To attain economies through quantity discounts and favorable transportation rates.
- To protect the company against risks of forecasted shortages of materials.

Speculative Buying. Here the purchased quantities are considerably beyond current requirements or those of forward buying. This approach is utilized when the objective is to profit from forecasted price changes. Just where the line of distinction between speculation and gambling is drawn is a matter of individual judgment.[8] It is questionable whether speculative buying, which entails high risk, should be a purchasing department function. If a company decides to do speculative buying, it should be the result of an executive decision, with the appropriate policy established. Purchasing personnel may be part of a committee responsible for speculative buying decisions.

Purchasing Research

Materials managers have recognized the value of purchasing research in improving purchasing decisions. It requires the systematic collection, classification, and analysis of data. The tasks of this activity vary considerably, depending upon the company products and operations. Activities could include development of purchasing systems related to administration of the overall function, study of long-range material requirements, development of suppliers who provide new materials for both present and future products, and the forecasting of materials cost data and price trends for long-range financial planning. Another major research function is to work with other company groups to develop changes in product design to improve profit.

Purchasing research has yielded dividends in the prevention and reduction of material and service costs, as well as in material planning. Purchasing procedures and activities have been improved, enhancing the productivity of the entire group. In cases where both corporate and plant purchasing organizations exist, the development of data pertinent to mutual buying interests sometimes has resulted in tremendous cost savings.

LEGAL ASPECTS OF PURCHASING

Purchasing personnel are involved in legal aspects of business on a daily basis. Contracts, both verbal and written, generally commit a company to over 50% of its yearly expenditures. It is essential that the company be protected in these transactions by legal counsel. The purchasing department must develop a good relationship with the legal staff. Also, buyers must know basic principles of law that relate to their activities. Buyers are not required to be lawyers, but it is not true here that "A little bit of knowledge is a dangerous thing."

Purchasing Agent Legal Status

Purchasing personnel are agents of the company. The law of agency permits agents to be given authority to act on behalf of a company. As an agent, the buyer can legally bind the company to enforceable contracts, both verbal and written. The law requires an agent to operate within the bounds of authority; so it is essential for purchasing personnel to know the types of transactions in which they are authorized to represent the company.

The general rule of agency has been described as follows:[9]

Whenever one person has (1) held another person out as the first person's agent authorized to act for the first person in a given capacity or (2) has knowingly and without dissent permitted such second person to act as though he were the first person's agent, or (3) where the first person's habits and course of dealing have been such as to reasonably warrant that such second person was the first person's agent, it will be presumed that there is an agency so far as it may be necessary to protect the rights of anyone who has relied upon the actions of the first person.

Purchasing authority may be regarded as "actual" or "apparent." Actual authority includes acts that the buyer has been authorized to perform, which are usually part of the job assignment. It also includes by implication all authority necessary, usual, and proper to perform the job. The problem with actual authority is that any person dealing with a buyer has no knowledge of his or her actual authority. Apparent authority relates to the authority that a seller, acting in good faith, could reasonably expect that a buyer would have, similar to the authority of similar agents in similar companies. It is also referred to as "custom of the marketplace."

The use of apparent authority raises questions of the liability of both the company and the buyer. For example, if it is customary for buyers in a manufacturing company to have the authority to purchase metal stampings, then a seller has the right to believe that a buyer has this authority. If a buyer goes beyond the authority he or she has been granted in purchasing stampings, then the seller can generally hold the company liable for the buyer's action; however, the company could bring suit against the buyer for going beyond his or her actual authority. If the seller knew that the buyer was exceeding delegated authority, the seller would have no recourse against either the buyer or the company.

Laws Related to Purchasing

There are numerous laws related to purchasing activities besides the law of agency. A few of those are listed below.

Uniform Commercial Code. The Uniform Commercial Code (UCC) covers most of the transactions involved in the purchase and the sale of goods and services. The UCC has been enacted into law by all the U.S. states except for Louisiana. It has been effective in eliminating most of the important differences in commercial laws within individual states, and has provided new statutory provisions to augment prior laws. Examples of UCC provisions are as follows:

- Normally a written notice is required for all orders of $500.00 or more.
- A contract exists if both buyer and seller behave as though there were a contract. For example, assume a seller receives a purchase order and starts work, and then the buyer decides the item is not required and wishes to cancel the order. According to UCC, a contract exists because both parties behaved as if there were one.
- The code provides a definition of "reasonable" period of time for an offer to remain open.
- A seller may exclude or modify the implied warranty for a product. An example of this is including a statement such as, "This product is offered for sale as is."

Sherman Antitrust Act. This law prohibits business monopolies. Companies cannot lawfully make price agreements that restrain trade except in cases of exemption and cases that do not affect interstate commerce.

Clayton Act. This law prohibits price discrimination between different buyers where it would lessen competition or tend to create a monopoly. It also provides an important point for labor unions, in that they are not considered an article of commerce and not subject to antitrust laws.

Robinson-Patman Act. The Robinson-Patman Act made it mandatory for all buyers to receive the same quantity discounts. The law provides that a seller is allowed to sell a given product to different buyers at a different price only when the price variation is justified by some difference in the seller's production costs or distribution costs. It also prohibits the seller from knowingly inducing or receiving an illegal discriminatory price. Regarding this point, John E. Murray, Jr., noted authority on the legal aspects of purchasing, stated: "As a professional buyer, you are entitled to seek the best price you can get. However, if you knowingly induce a price which you know other buyers cannot get and you pressure the vendor into the deal because you have the vendor over a barrel, you may encounter the Robinson-Patman Act."[10]

VALUE ANALYSIS USES FOR PURCHASING AND MATERIALS MANAGEMENT

Value analysis is a management technique utilized to coordinate the talents of various organizational members to conduct in-depth investigations. This structured approach has been successfully applied to accomplish significant cost savings. The basic philosophy behind value analysis is to identify unnecessary cost in a material, a part, a component, or an entire unit that can be eliminated without negatively affecting the item's function. Lawrence D. Miles, from the purchasing group of the General Electric Company, is generally credited with developing this technique.

Organization and Administration

Value analysis can be organized and administered by using either full-time personnel or part-time employees of the materials management organization. Company size determines the type of staffing. Considering that potential cost savings sometimes equal eight to ten times the salaries of analysts, it can be a very good investment. Where value analysis is organized as a separate materials staff function, the full-time analyst is responsible for training various personnel, coordinating team efforts, and performing work on individual projects.

A committee approach to developing suitable projects and improvements can prove effective in all companies. This type of organization can stimulate worthwhile ideas, but the committee should not be too large, or it will be ineffective. Normally four to six members will suffice. Typically committee members are composed of representatives from all major functions of the company (materials management, engineering, finance, and manufacturing). No more than one member of a major function should be on a team.

Another approach to organizing value analysis is to have full-time staff specialists assigned to the materials group. These individuals concentrate on developing cost reductions, using input from materials management personnel and members of other major company functions. The staff specialist not only must be very capable technically, but should possess human relations skills. It is important to obtain the cooperation of various contacts, for both idea development and successful implementation.

Results of value analysis efforts normally are presented in periodic reports. These reports describe individual projects, typically including statements of project goals and information on interim developments in such areas as product design changes, cost comparisons, supplier inputs, and progress in achieving goals. Value analysis achievements should be publicized to provide recognition of individual and team efforts and to promote improvement consciousness among the entire organization. Bulletin boards, company papers, and meetings are common vehicles for publicizing results.

Analysis Techniques

The basic question, which is integral to value analysis, is, "What is this part, assembly, or product worth?" Answers are developed by evaluating an item in terms of the function that it performs and its value. Alternative methods are explored, and the "best way" is determined. The structured approach of value analysis provides various quantitative and qualitative analysis techniques. All participants are trained to use analysis procedures. Training sessions are most successful when limited to small groups. These meetings are basically workshops where participants get hands-on experience. The analysis techniques used by individual companies vary greatly. Some effective ones are described below.

Design Analysis. Using this technique, a complete product or component is disassembled on a table in the meeting room, or individual parts are mounted on a plywood board. Each part is placed to show its relationship to the total unit. The basic idea is to aid objective analysis of each part's function and the development of better and more economical designs.

Brainstorming. This technique is used to stimulate creative thinking in the value analysis group. This approach encourages group development of product improvement ideas, which are recorded as fast as they are suggested, without any detailed review. One person's suggestion will stimulate a new and different idea in another team member. When the group can no longer develop ideas, each suggestion is considered in detail.

Checklist. Use of a checklist helps to stimulate analytical thinking. Analysts review questions concerned with the basic purpose of items; the approach ensures a careful investigation. Some typical questions are:

- Is the item's cost proportionate to its function?
- Can tolerances be changed without impairing the function?
- Can a standard part be substituted or built into the design?
- Is there another method that could be used to lower costs?
- Can the item be eliminated or combined to reduce labor and materials handling costs?

The following example of a value analysis application was a contest winner.[11] The Amoco Oil Company analyzed vent installations, which

amount to a thousand each year at a Texas City refinery. A major installation cost was for labor, as the original vent consisted of three separate
components that had to be welded together (see Figure 7-9). Value analysis
developed an extended body gate valve. Now only one part has to be
stocked; but, more important, labor costs were considerably reduced because only one field weld now is required, instead of three. Total savings is
more than $30,000 annually.

INTERNATIONAL SOURCING

U.S. companies historically have relied on imported goods and services
much less than companies in other countries have, as all or most U.S.
needs could be obtained from domestic sources. This situation has been
changing dramatically. Since World War II buyers have steadily increased
their purchases of imported items, so that in 1986 offshore buys were 11
percent of overall demand — a percentage that had nearly doubled over 15
years.[12] Figure 7-10 illustrates the dramatic increase in imports between
1979 and 1986.

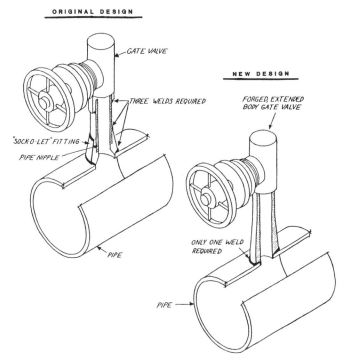

Figure 7-9. Example of value analysis application. (Reprinted from *Purchasing Magazine,*
June 26, 1986. Copyright by Cahners Publishing Company, 1986.)

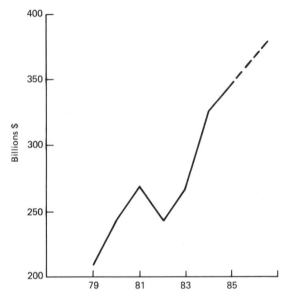

Source: United States Department of Commerce, FT 990,
"Highlights of U.S. Export and Import Trades.

Figure 7-10. United States imports. (Source: United States Department of Commerce, FT 990, "Highlights of U.S. Export and Import Trades.")

Reasons for International Sourcing

The reasons for buying from foreign companies vary from one domestic company to another. All of them relate to the total materials management objective of obtaining a better value for monies expended. A strong dollar may have some temporary significance. Buyers who have purchased imported goods and services generally give the following reasons for offshore buying.

Cost.   Total costs for some imported items are less than for U.S. products. Foreign companies can deliver at lower cost because of their low labor costs, high productivity, efficient equipment and/or processes, low material costs, low overhead costs, availability of monetary subsidies, and dumping practices.[13] Savings of 20 percent or more are often cited by purchasing executives. Foreign sellers consistently have been fiercely competitive in order not to lose their lucrative U.S. markets.

Quality.   Product quality improvement now is being emphasized more in U.S. companies. Offshore products are being purchased to obtain higher, and in some cases more consistent, quality. Some buyers complain that they cannot obtain required tolerances or specifications from domestic sources. High foreign quality levels can be attributable to improvements in equipment and processes, good quality control systems, employee-involvement programs (such as quality circles), and positive attitudes.

Technology.   Foreign companies are rapidly increasing their technical capability. In previous years, the United States was an exporter of technology, and it still is; but now it also is importing some technology at a rising rate. Research and development in foreign countries have contributed to new products, processes, and productivity. Many sources have formed teams in the interest of developing new technology, including government, private, and company sponsors.

Continuity of Supply.   Domestic buyers must broaden their geographical sourcing in order to meet company requirements. Overseas suppliers can provide both primary and backup needs, which in some cases are necessary because of inadequate or nonexistent domestic sources. For example, one buyer had to obtain material from a foreign steel mill because U.S. mills would not roll special sections in small quantities. The United States also depends largely on offshore sources for some raw materials, such as chrome and platinum from South Africa.

Competition.   The continued growth of industrialized countries and previously underdeveloped nations has resulted in new sources of goods and services, and has stimulated competition. Foreign suppliers in the American markets have caused domestic companies to improve facilities, increase operating efficiencies, and improve product quality. One buyer indicated that his company uses lower import prices to keep a lid on domestic quotes.[14]

Access to Foreign Markets.   More and more countries are requiring offset or countertrade before they will purchase goods from another country. This "we will buy from you only if you buy from us" policy has led many U.S. companies to make foreign purchases in order to enhance their ability to sell abroad.

Organization

Each company that decides to become active in international sourcing must determine how to organize the group responsible for foreign purchasing activities. There are many alternatives and trade-offs involved. It is important to decide whether purchases will be made through an intermediary or by direct contact with the supplier, or by some combination of the two methods. No organization is etched in stone; periodically, each group must review its organization of international sourcing activities to determine whether change is needed.

Intermediary Resources. Companies have successfully used groups that specialize in providing foreign buying services. This alternative does not require hiring additional people, and it is especially effective if internal personnel do not have overseas buying experience. Its cost-effectiveness depends upon the volume and frequency of international sourcing.

Trading Company. A trading company is basically a type of import broker. The U.S. buyer purchases from the trading company, which typically locates sources and arranges shipping, insurance, and other details necessary for obtaining goods for the buyer.

Import Broker. An import broker represents a company in obtaining foreign goods on a fee basis. Services provided vary, depending upon the contracting company's requirements. Normally the import broker will locate foreign suppliers and process required paperwork. Title for all purchases is given to the company buying the items.

Import Merchant. A contract is drawn up between the import merchant and the buying company, whereby the import merchant will locate foreign suppliers, purchase the goods in its own name, and arrange for delivery to the buying company. An invoice is sent to the buyer for the previously agreed-on price, which includes a fee for import merchant services.

Internal Resources. Many American firms use internal resources to perform international sourcing. The extent to which they allocate their resources to this depends upon how aggressive the management has decided to be. Figure 7-11 shows the spectrum of internal resource allocation alternatives, from highly aggressive to less aggressive approaches.

Corporate buying office(s). Some of the larger American companies, including IBM, GTE, AT&T, and Apple, have procurement groups located overseas. These firms report savings of 10 to 20 percent.[15] The corporate buying office is responsible for various activities, including identifying sources, taking orders from domestic operations, and placing orders. Staffing is a major consideration. Most companies are increasing their use of nationals from host countries because they are familiar with local language

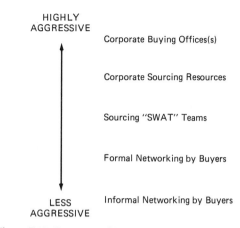

HIGHLY
AGGRESSIVE

Corporate Buying Offices(s)

Corporate Sourcing Resources

Sourcing "SWAT" Teams

Formal Networking by Buyers

LESS   Informal Networking by Buyers
AGGRESSIVE

Figure 7-11. Spectrum of international sourcing alternatives.

and customs, local governments prefer them, and it is less expensive to use local staff than to send Americans overseas.

Corporate sourcing. This approach is similar to using corporate buying offices, in that personnel are located in designated areas such as Europe, Latin America, or Asia. The two methods differ primarily in the assignment of responsibilities. The corporate sourcing function is responsible for identifying potential sources and obtaining initial quotes; purchase orders are issued by domestic purchasing managers. The corporate sourcing group may assist in follow-up and expediting. This alternative is costly because of fixed costs such as offices, salaries, and other operating expenses.

Sourcing "SWAT" teams. An alternative that reduces the degree of company commitment and still provides for concentrated offshore buying activity uses sourcing "SWAT" teams. Personnel with varying technical and commercial skills are recruited within the company. Assignment to a team is temporary, usually for a stipulated number of months. The team is responsible for identifying potential suppliers and obtaining initial quotes. This alternative does not require any additional personnel, and it exposes various individuals to the international marketplace. Disadvantages include lack of coverage for unmanned functions that volunteer team members have left, and loss of continuity with suppliers as personnel move on to new assignments.

Formal networking by buyers. This alternative provides formal communication within a company between individuals who are involved in overseas purchasing activities. A corporate clearinghouse function, which may include a purchasing council, is used to organize and stimulate networking. Newsletters and reports can be circulated within the company, containing a variety of information obtained from company sources, such as supplier names and addresses, costs, and so on. This alternative minimizes cost while stimulating international sourcing activities.

Informal networking by buyers. In an informal networking system, individuals within a company who are involved in overseas purchasing contact each other, and exchange relevant information, with no particular structure. This activity can be effectively augmented by contacts with purchasing professionals from other companies, through local association meetings of the National Association of Purchasing Management (N.A.P.M.) and the Purchasing Management Association of Canada (P.M.A.C.).

Cultural Differences

In international sourcing, it is vital to understand the culture and business customs of the people with whom one comes in contact. American business people often have exercised poor judgment in this regard. For example, a purchasing manager from a U.S. company visited a Japanese company executive in his private office. The two sat down at a cocktail table in the office area and proceeded to make small talk about the weather, national points of interest, and the like. However, the American was interested in negotiating a contract, and periodically tried to change the subject—a mistake due to his unfamiliarity with Japanese business customs. It would have been wiser for him to follow the host's lead; efforts to steer the conversation to business topics were considered poor manners, and diminished the host's respect for the visitor.

Although many individuals in other countries speak English, business people must make sure that there is mutual understanding of all topics discussed. A questionnaire on the subject of international communications was completed by American business people with extensive experience in overseas trade. Fully 80 percent reported difficulties in conducting business with foreigners because of the latters' misunderstanding of American English.[16] The use of slang words can cause miscommunication, and even "standard" English words may have different connotations in different countries. Some Americans have taken accelerated foreign language instruction to improve their communication skills. Results of such efforts vary, depending upon the individual's linguistic capability and the country. For example, if a visitor to France spoke poor French, the French host might be irritated; but in Japan such a situation could provide the opposite result, as the Japanese feel complimented if visitors attempt to use their language.

The N.A.P.M. international group produced a filmstrip/cassette intended to indoctrinate purchasing professionals in international business customs. Eight rules are suggested to improve relationships with Japanese contacts:

1. Arrange for high-level introductions.
2. Maintain surface harmony.
3. Avoid embarrassing others.
4. Appearance is very important.
5. Be patient—progress will be slow.
6. Use business cards in Japanese.
7. Speak Japanese, if only a little; at least know common greetings, good-bye, and thank you.
8. Give little mementos and gifts.

ETHICAL STANDARDS

Purchasing agents are legal agents of the company, and as such are required to be loyal to the employer and diligent in the performance of their duties. They are not allowed to gain any personal advantage. Among the various organizational functions, purchasing has more regular contacts with suppliers than any other member of the company. These contacts often involve large sums of money, requiring purchasing personnel to maintain high ethical standards.

The National Association of Purchasing Management (N.A.P.M.) has been diligent in promoting the professionalism of its members. A national committee of N.A.P.M. is dedicated to the development of a code of ethical conduct for the association. The principles and standards of purchasing practice of N.A.P.M. are general guides for the buyer (Figure 7-12).

Each company should develop an explicit policy for all employees in respect to what constitutes ethical conduct. This policy would include everyone, not just materials management personnel; it would encompass anyone with a potential conflict of interest, including members of the engineering, finance, and marketing functions.

Probably the most common ethical questions concern gifts and entertainment. Inducements provided by suppliers can include free meals, tickets, or liquor—items of relatively low cost; or they can be very valuable, including television sets, new cars, or even large gifts of cash. The acceptance of costly items is clearly a violation of ethics, as it would obligate the buyer (or any other company employee) to favor a supplier.

1. To consider, first, the interests of his company in all transactions and to carry out and believe in its established policies.

2. To be receptive to competent counsel from his colleagues and to be guided by such counsel without impairing the dignity and responsibility of his office.

3. To buy without prejudice, seeking to obtain the maximum ultimate value for each dollar of expenditure.

4. To strive consistently for knowledge of the materials and processes of manufacture, and to establish practical methods for the conduct of his office.

5. To subscribe to and work for honesty and truth in buying and selling, and to denounce all forms and manifestations of commercial bribery.

6. To accord a prompt and courteous reception, so far as conditions will permit, to all who call on a legitimate business mission.

7. To respect his obligations and to require that obligations to him and to his concern be respected, consistent with good business practice.

8. To avoid sharp practice.

9. To counsel and assist fellow purchasing agents in the performance of their duties, whenever occasion permits.

10. To co-operate with all organizations and individuals engaged in activities designed to enhance the development and standing of purchasing.

Figure 7-12. Principles and standards of purchasing practice, prepared by the National Association of Purchasing Management.

The Center for the Study of Ethics in the Professions at Illinois Institute of Technology conducted a nationwide survey of purchasing practices for N.A.P.M.'s Ethical Standards Committee.[17] In one part of the survey, respondents were given a list of "favors" and asked to indicate which had been offered them by vendors, those that would be acceptable (would not involve an ethical problem) to them if offered by the vendor, and those they actually had accepted. Figure 7-13 shows the survey results.

According to N.A.P.M., gifts and kickbacks should not be accepted, nor should buyers purchase from friends or family relations because, in such circumstances, a buyer's loyalty could be misdirected.[18] Some companies and most government agencies have policies that prohibit accepting gifts. Suppliers are sent letters thanking them for their support and indicating the company policy regarding favors. This is usually done before Christmas.

	Offered by Vendors	Rated Acceptable	Actually Accepted
Lunches	98%	90%	87%
Advertising Souvenirs	96%	92%	87%
Dinners	90%	70%	76%
Tickets (Sports, Theater)	86%	60%	19%
Christmas Gifts	85%	50%	49%
Trips to Vendor Plants	83%	51%	34%
Golf Outings	74%	47%	33%
Food and Liquor	65%	29%	9%
Discounts on Personal Purchases	46%	21%	9%
Small Appliances	33%	6%	5%
Vacation Trips	26%	2%	1%
Clothing	15%	3%	3%
Large Appliances	13%	1%	—
Loans	3%	1%	—
Automobiles	2%	1%	—

Figure 7-13. Offers, acceptance, and actual acceptance of "favors." (Source: Ernest D'Anjou, "IIT Completes Ethics Survey for N.A.P.M.," *National Purchasing Review*, Jan.–Feb. 1979, p. 4.)

Concerns Other Than Gifts

Requesting Quotations with No Intention to Buy. Buyers sometimes will obtain quotations only to satisfy company policy regarding the minimum number of quotations. They may know in advance that a requested quote will be higher than other requested quotes and will justify purchasing from a particular supplier. Also, a quote may be requested only to be used to obtain a lower price from another supplier. These practices are unethical because there is no intention to purchase anything from the supplier who is spending money to develop the quotation.

Providing Erroneous Information to a Supplier to Induce Lower Prices. A dishonest buyer may try to use false information to obtain lower prices. Such fictitious information could relate to other quotations, long-term company plans, or other pertinent information.

Allowing a Supplier Favored Treatment. Except for government agency quotations, all supplier information is considered confidential. No one supplier should be allowed to examine all quotations. Also, if one supplier is allowed to revise quotations, the same opportunity should be available to all.

Creating a Conflict of Interest. Purchasing personnel may be charged with a conflict of interest if they do business with any company in which they have a substantial equity position, or in which relatives or friends have a similar interest. Buying from these companies can cause divided loyalties on the part of the purchasing agent.

Double Standards. Any discussion of ethical standards would be incomplete without some mention of the use of "double standards" in companies. That is, different standards of behavior are practiced for various groups within the same company. One must be concerned with how a company can justify a policy stating that purchasing personnel should not accept gifts or entertainment from suppliers if their sales representatives are allowed, or encouraged, to give gifts to their customers.

RELATIONSHIPS WITH OTHER MATERIALS MANAGEMENT SUBFUNCTIONS

Purchasing is a vital part of the materials management team effort, and good communication and cooperation between purchasing and other materials management subfunctions are essential to the success of the entire group. Some of the important relationships are reviewed below.

Inventory Control

Purchasing and inventory control should work together to optimize inventory levels and minimize total cost, communicating with each other continually. Deliveries of purchased material will be delayed if inventory control is late in requisitioning needed materials. This delay can lead to premium transportation costs, as a result of efforts to speed up materials delivery. Air freight has often served as a means for collapsing the delivery time for materials that were requisitioned late, but it is a costly alternative. Also, vendor relationships can be strained if purchasing is constantly trying to expedite deliveries.

Production Control

Production control depends upon purchasing for the proper flow of supplier materials. Late deliveries can deprive production of vital resources. Any disruption in production operations due to lack of material affects production control's credibility and the morale of both production and production control personnel.

Physical Distribution

Physical distribution is responsible for making on-time deliveries to the customer, but these deliveries also depend upon purchasing performance.

Late supplier deliveries can delay customer shipments. Physical distribution can contribute to good purchasing by minimizing incoming transportation costs, which depends upon meaningful communication between purchasing and the transportation group. Historically, there has been a lack of communication between the two groups.[19] Total materials management provides a meaningful bridge between them. Transportation must be achieved with minimum freight costs, on-time delivery, and minimum damage, which all require proper relationships with the traffic and transportation group. With the help of traffic and transportation, purchasing can provide specific delivery instructions for purchase orders. This information will eliminate the use of ambiguous terms such as "best way," and lead to use of low-cost, reliable carriers.

Receiving and Stores

A common complaint of receiving and stores personnel pertains to receipt of supplier materials without appropriate paperwork by purchasing, authorizing receipt of the material. Confusion and time-consuming discussions result. Purchasing often justifies the lack of paperwork, blaming it on requisitions that required rush phone calls to obtain needed materials. However, buyers normally have little excuse not to use an alternative means of communication to inform receiving and stores of rush orders.

Getting accurate counts and detecting damage can be difficult. Receiving and stores must provide accurate information on the quantity and condition of all materials; otherwise purchasing will use erroneous information.

Materials Handling

Materials handling must optimize the use of space, equipment, and people. Its objectives can be enhanced if materials handling design personnel designate the unit load condition for all major purchased items. They should specify the size of loads, containment or packaging, stacking patterns, and quantity per load; then purchasing can obtain materials by considering optimum loads. Unit load drawings and instructions should be provided to purchasing, for use in obtaining quotations. Buyers can contribute to improve materials handling systems by assisting materials handling design personnel in the procurement process. In some organizations operating and materials handling design personnel do not have faith in purchasing's capability to provide adequate assistance in such areas as supplier development, price determination, and product comparison; but groups that have established good relationships with purchasing have been able to save time and obtain better values.

RELATIONSHIPS WITH OTHER COMPANY FUNCTIONS

The purchasing function has frequent contacts with many groups, as indicated in Figure 7-1. In these constant interactions, mutual credibility and cooperation are essential to success. Use of the total materials management philosophy helps to minimize friction among the groups.

Marketing

Marketing depends upon purchasing for many inputs. Purchasing can best aid the marketing group by buying at the lowest total cost to aid in competitive selling. Purchasing also must prepare accurate material cost estimates for sales quotations. Purchasing can help to determine the degree of quality that can be "built into" a product, related to cost. Buyers are constantly interviewing supplier salesmen, and are aware of the effectiveness of different sales techniques and methods. Discussion of these sales approaches can aid the company's marketing program.

Like other materials management subfunctions, purchasing requires good sales forecast information from marketing. Purchase quantities and quantity discounts are related to the sales forecast. Purchasing also is involved in reciprocity—purchases by the company from its customers. Purchasing and marketing should work closely together to ensure that reciprocal purchases (1) are not illegal, and (2) contribute to the overall profits of the company.

Finance

Finance is responsible for various aspects of financial planning such as budgets, cash flow, and working capital. The purchasing function provides accurate procurement plans to finance. Purchasing should not incur contractual obligations involving large, unplanned sums of money without contacting the finance group. Even if a purchase appeared extremely beneficial with respect to overall costs, the company's financial condition might not warrant the expenditure.

Copies of purchase orders usually are routed to the accounting section of finance. These forms should be correlated with accounting forms and procedures to avoid duplication. Purchasing depends upon the finance group for prompt payment of approved invoices. Delays in payment of invoices, taking unauthorized cash discounts, and other sharp practices can jeopardize valuable relationships with suppliers. Companies in financial straits frequently have difficulty with suppliers who demand COD payment or advance payment. In some cases such a supplier will not do business with the company. All of these problems affect purchasing personnel.

Manufacturing

The purchasing function is vital to efficient manufacturing operations, which require a smooth, uninterrupted flow of purchased materials, equipment, and services. Purchasing should communicate well with manufacturing regarding the disposition of critical purchases. Purchasing may communicate with manufacturing directly or through other materials management subfunctions such as production control. Purchasing also aids manufacturing efficiency through value analysis or other cost and operational improvement programs.

Manufacturing can aid or hinder the buyer's effectiveness, depending upon its attitudes and actions. If manufacturing personnel do not make products according to the bill-of-material, inventory control can be affected, and premature stockouts may result, causing unnecessary expediting by purchasing personnel.

Engineering

Most of the contacts and communication between purchasing and engineering relate to product design and specifications. Purchasing provides an important communication link between suppliers (existing and new) and engineering, and can support engineering by providing information and services such as alternative design costs, new product/process availability, and prototype samples. Supplier information regarding tolerance problems and product improvement suggestions is channeled to engineering for its consideration.

Engineers tend to be independent thinkers and to operate independently, but engineering must keep purchasing "in the picture" at all times to derive maximum benefits from their relationship. Engineers should discuss their needs and arrange contacts with suppliers through purchasing; then buyers will be better informed of future and present product requirements, and will be able to properly support engineering. Also, specifications then can be written that will drastically reduce the number of possible suppliers and control costs. Engineering should help purchasing to develop realistic specifications that allow economical procurement of materials from more than one efficient, optimum-cost supplier.

Quality Assurance

Purchasing must relate quality assurance's complaints and recommendations to the supplier if materials are rejected on incoming inspection.

Prompt buyer follow-up will reduce problems of material availability and supplier relations. Sometimes, because of an immediate need for rejected materials and a lack of inspection personnel, quality assurance will request purchasing to arrange for the supplier to perform 100 percent inspection of rejects on the premises. Purchasing will then communicate with the supplier and quality assurance in developing work schedules, providing facility arrangements, and other coordination of functions.

Quality assurance personnel assist purchasing by visiting supplier facilities and evaluating their performance capabilities. They may advise the supplier on quality control methods and techniques that will minimize inspection costs. Quality assurance provides incoming inspection acceptance criteria to purchasing, which then communicates with the supplier. Occasionally, suppliers will challenge quality specifications after materials are rejected; or they may maintain that certain specifications were not communicated to them, or that parts were damaged in transit. The buyer is responsible for satisfying these complaints, providing fair treatment to the supplier. Purchasing also must have prompt action from quality assurance in inspecting incoming materials. Delays generally impact the warranty period, and could cause difficulties with warranted adjustments.

SUMMARY

The purchasing subfunction of materials management is responsible for a majority of monetary expenditures in most businesses. With this high level of capital outflow, companies require wise, skillful administration and performance by the purchasing group. The success of most enterprises depends on close cooperation between purchasing and other materials management subfunctions, as well as all other major functions in the organization.

A major objective of buyers is to minimize total costs of purchased products and services. Providing an uninterrupted flow of procured items reduces possible losses due to downtime, decreased productivity, and poor customer service. The group is responsible for obtaining good-quality materials and services. Other buying objectives include developing reliable suppliers, promoting favorable relationships with suppliers, optimizing the purchasing group's productivity and procurement costs, maintaining good records, and cooperating with personnel of other departments.

The assignment of purchasing activities varies from company to company, but departmental responsibilities should be known by all members of the organization. Supplier contacts are basic to any procurement function. Other purchasing activities include supplier development, evaluation, and negotiation, analyzing make or buy decisions, obtaining required product quality, timing purchases to optimize company costs, and performing worthwhile research.

Purchasing personnel must be knowledgeable about legal aspects of the business. They have authority as agents to bind the company to both oral and written contracts. Buyers should be familiar with various laws, including the Uniform Commercial Code, Sherman Antitrust Act, Clayton Act, and Robinson-Patman Act.

Lawrence D. Miles, a member of the General Electric Company's purchasing group, developed value analysis, a cost reduction program. Value analysis has been implemented in various companies to stimulate worthwhile ideas. Analysts are trained to review parts, subassemblies, or products and use quantitative and qualitative procedures for "attacking" product costs. Some of the techniques employed include design analysis, brainstorming, and checklists.

As agents of the company, buyers are responsible for performing their job ethically. The National Association of Purchasing Management (N.A.P.M.) recognizes that its members are involved in decisions about large sums of money. N.A.P.M. has developed principles and standards of purchasing practice to aid purchasing professionals maintain ethical standards.

NOTES

1. Giunipero, "Helping Minority Suppliers Become Better Sources," p. 63.
2. Heinritz, Farrell, and Smith, *Purchasing Principles and Applications,* p. 99.
3. Dobler, Lee, and Burt, *Purchasing and Materials Management,* pp. 125–126.
4. Gottlieb, "Purchasing's Part in the Push for Quality," p. 75.
5. David B. Guralnik, ed., *Webster's New World Dictionary* (New York: World Dictionaries/Simon and Schuster, 1984), p. 952.
6. Bonneville, "Vendor Analysis Packs a Punch in Negotiations," p. 33.
7. Hahn, Pinto, and Bragg, "'Just-In-Time' Production and Purchasing," pp. 2–10.
8. Leenders, Fearon, and England, *Purchasing and Materials Management,* p. 328.
9. Farrel and Aljian, *Aljian's Purchasing Handbook,* pp. 4–6.
10. Murray, "Purchasing and the Law," p. 22.
11. "VA Contest Winners," p. 103.
12. "More to Imports than Bargains," p. 102.
13. Dumping refers to the sale of a product at a lower price abroad than in the originating company's country. This practice is illegal in the United States, but difficult to control.
14. "More to Imports than Bargains," p. 102.
15. Russell, "How To Buy In Asia: Rule I," p. 88A16.
16. Axtell, *Do's and Taboo's around the World,* p. 139.
17. D'Anjov, "IIT Complete Ethics Survey for N.A.P.M.," p. 2.
18. Felch, "Proprieties and Ethics in Purchasing Management," section 4.7, p. 3.
19. Dillon, "Wanted: More Cooperation between Purchasing and Traffic," p. 66.

BIBLIOGRAPHY

Axtell, Roger E. *Do's and Taboo's around the World.* Elmsford, New York: Benjamin Co., 1985.

Bonneville, David. "Vendor Analysis Packs a Punch in Negotiations." *Purchasing World,* Mar. 1983.

Carter, J. R., and Cagne, J. "The Do's and Don'ts of International Countertrade." *Sloan Management Review,* Spring 1988.

Cayer, S. "Building a World-Class Supplier Base is the Number One Priority." *Purchasing,* Apr. 1988.

D'Anjov, Ernest. "IIT Completes Ethics Survey for N.A.P.M." *National Purchasing Review,* Jan.–Feb. 1979.

Dillon, Thomas F. "Wanted: More Cooperation between Purchasing and Traffic." *Purchasing World,* July 1985.

Dobler, Donald W., Lee, Lamar, Jr., and Burt, David N. *Purchasing and Materials Management.* New York: McGraw-Hill Book Co., 1984.

Farrel, P. V., and Aljian, G. W., eds. *Aljian's Purchasing Handbook.* New York: McGraw-Hill Book Co., 1982.

Felch, Robert I. "Proprieties and Ethics in Purchasing Management." *Guide to Purchasing.* National Association of Purchasing Management, 1986.

Guinipero, Larry C. "Helping Minority Suppliers Become Better Sources." *Purchasing World,* Nov. 1981.

Gottlieb, Daniel W. "Purchasing's Part in the Push for Quality." *Purchasing,* Sept. 10, 1981.

Hahn, Chan K., Pinto, Peter A., and Bragg, Daniel J. "'Just-In-Time' Production and Purchasing," *Journal of Purchasing and Materials Management,* Second Quarter 1983.

Kraker, J. "Materials Managers Change Their Stripes." *ENR,* Mar. 1988.

Leenders, M., Fearon, H., and England, W. *Purchasing and Materials Management.* Homewood, Illinois: Richard D. Irwin, 1985.

"More to Imports than Bargains." *Purchasing World,* Mar. 1986.

Murray, John E., Jr. "Purchasing and the Law." *Purchasing World,* Aug. 1981.

Russell, John F. "How to Buy in Asia: Rule I." *Purchasing,* Apr. 11, 1985.

"Suppliers and the Just-In-Time Concept." *Journal of Purchasing and Materials Management,* Winter 1984.

"VA Contest Winners," *Purchasing,* June 26, 1986.

8
Receiving and Stores

It once was thought that the receiving and stores functions were relatively unimportant, that anyone could work in these capacities. This kind of thinking led to poor supplier relationships, inaccurate inventory records, lost materials, unhappy customers, and other problems. Receiving and stores are vital to a well-run materials management program. The personnel within these groups must be educated, responsible, and capable individuals.

Receiving and stores activities are common to all businesses in all industries. Probably the only companies where they would be of minor importance are service-oriented; and even those businesses must receive and store items such as supplies, spare parts, and paper forms. The organization of receiving and stores varies, depending upon the company size and the nature of the business. These functions are grouped under one general supervisor in many companies, to achieve a good material flow, maximize labor and equipment capacity, and ensure the ready availability of materials. Some companies separate receiving and stores to improve their checks and balances, or because of the size and location of various groups.

RECEIVING AND STORES OBJECTIVES RELATED TO MATERIALS MANAGEMENT

Receiving and stores groups perform basic service functions in physically moving and controlling materials. They service the operating departments by organizing the timely delivery of required materials. Another significant function is performing custodial and controlling activities for the numerous materials being processed and stored, including raw materials, supplies, work-in-process, and finished goods. Control of finished goods inventory is normally part of the physical distribution function. Rational, attainable objectives are necessary for these activities to achieve adequate control of business resources.

Optimize Materials Flow

A smooth flow of materials, from receiving to incoming inspection (if applicable), to stores, and then to operations, is necessary to ensure uninterrupted company functions. A good physical layout and materials handling design will help to achieve this goal. It is also necessary to develop and implement effective control systems, with their accompanying paperwork.

Poor materials flow in both receiving and stores often is due to bottlenecks. For example, both the size and the location of staging areas may be inadequate. These areas, which are temporary storage locations for materials, are not always fully utilized and at times may even by empty; but they must be available when needed. Some companies, for instance, do not provide enough space for staging materials received by truck or rail; and if no staging space is available when a truck is unloaded, employees will move materials into other areas such as aisles. The resulting bottlenecks contribute to poor flow, damaged materials, OSHA violations, and loss of both employee and equipment capacity.

Another type of bottleneck, not necessarily obvious to the observer, involves poor labor utilization. A typical example often occurs when freight cars are unloaded. Two laborers may be assigned to palletize cartons for a forklift truck driver who removes loaded pallets. If the laborers' speed exceeds that of a driver, they are obligated to wait until the driver returns to remove a load.[1] The laborers then work at the slower pace of the driver to remain occupied at all times, and their productivity is lowered.

Just-In-Time (JIT) systems are a good example of modern techniques that require efficient receiving. The receiving department is the first, and probably easiest, place for JIT operations to be stalled. If materials are delayed, misdirected, or totally blocked, tight JIT schedules will collapse like a row of dominoes. Dana Corporation's Lancaster, Pennsylvania, assembly plant found that using bar codes on incoming shipments reduced previous delays of up to a day to four hours.[2]

Improve Accuracy of Information

The receiving and stores functions are a basic source of much of the information used to drive the materials program. It is essential that there be accurate documentation of incoming materials. A basic rule is that no material is accepted, issued, or moved without accompanying authorization, which normally consists of a copy of the purchase order. Inaccurate recording of information on incoming material, such as quantity, item, and condition of the material, can cause difficulties in purchasing, inventory control, and production control.

The stores function must maintain accurate records for various reasons; it is essential, for example, to be able to find existing inventory items. Stories abound describing losses of items in company stockrooms and the time-consuming efforts required to find them. The resulting confusion and chaos represent just part of the costs. Operating departments often lose both personnel and equipment capacity, and customer orders are delayed. These losses can be avoided by instituting and maintaining reliable systems, such as a location numbering system, and by proper personnel training.

Another stores problem concerns inaccurate physical counts of items in storage. Stockroom personnel must be able to provide accurate item counts; otherwise unnecessary purchases, production line stoppages, and incorrect financial reports can result. Physical control techniques that are effective in curtailing this problem are discussed later in this chapter.

One company defined inventory accuracy as having the exact quantity of an item, identified by a part number, in the exact location to match the record. Company management instituted a program that included education of employees, stockroom security, a locator system, a transaction control system, and a cycle count system. Inventory accuracy increased from 64 percent to 95 percent. Elimination of physical inventories provided six additional workdays and resulted in $10,000 worth of cost savings. On-time delivery to customers for stock items increased from 40 percent to 99 percent. That company clearly found that information accuracy yields significant benefits.[3]

Minimize Costs

Many receiving and stores activities influence costs, either directly or indirectly. One area of potential cost-effectiveness is space utilization. Efforts must be made to fully utilize all space, both on the floor and in the air. A common complaint of management is that "there is no space." In reality this means floor space, which may indeed be fully occupied. At the same time, however, the space above ground level may be unused—the type of space often referred to as "cube space" or "air rights." Facility costs can be reduced by proper utilization of cube space in both receiving and stores.

Receiving and stores have many opportunities to reduce labor costs. A good example is found in companies that are improving their paperwork flow and completion time by using computer terminals. Figure 8-1 shows a printer that provides receiving personnel with computer-generated receiving documents. Another way to reduce cost is to locate the receiving and shipping docks next to each other, to maximize both labor and equipment utilization. Having effective storage layout and order picking systems in the stores area helps to lower labor costs by eliminating unnecessary movement of employees.

Inventory obsolescence, and its costs, can be greatly reduced by developing a report that pinpoints inactive materials. Management also can take

Figure 8-1. Automatic printer generating computerized receiving documents. (Courtesy Ace Hardware Corporation.)

appropriate action to eliminate surplus inventories. Surplus materials are current items used for production and/or sales whose inventory quantities are excessive for normal future operations and sales. The first step in identifying surplus materials is to develop a report that relates material quantities available to normal demand. This information is obtained by dividing the currently available quantity by forecasted monthly usage. Such identification and disposal of obsolete and surplus materials will provide additional funds and space.

The receiving and stores activities can help reduce operations costs. Operations personnel often are inactive, awaiting materials that are in receiving or stores. Prompt service from receiving and stores will eliminate unnecessary downtime for both personnel and equipment.

Minimize Damage

Wherever there is volume handling of materials, the possibility of damage to the materials increases. Receiving and stores activities can help to minimize the damage by utilizing effective handling procedures, using appropriate materials handling and storage equipment, and implementing programs to train employees and improve morale.

Requirements for protecting the stored materials may vary considerably. Some materials must be protected from dampness and extreme changes in temperature. Other supplies should be stored away from light and odors. Food processors must be careful of vermin infestation. Many fragile materials such as glass, bagged sugar, and electronic components require special handling. Planning for the maximum protection of materials against all causes of deterioration or destruction is an essential part of the receiving and stores operations.

Damaged materials within a stockroom are a constant source of embarrassment. Some supervisors try to ignore such material and hide it from others. Instead, damaged materials should be visible to everyone as a reminder of the need to improve stockroom procedures. Employee training and continual communication with individuals involved in damaging materials will help reduce the damage.[4]

Improve Paperwork Systems

The paperwork systems used for receiving and stores vary considerably from crude minimal forms to sophisticated, on-line computer systems. Some companies try to save money by limiting paperwork, only to experience a lack of control, inventory inaccuracies, lost materials, and poor communication. On the other hand, some companies implement extensive computer systems, complete with terminals in all areas, that are effective in controlling receiving and stores activities.

No single paperwork system is good for all companies. Many factors must be taken into account—the size of the company, volume of receipts and stores, variety of items handled, sophistication of management, and various other considerations. Any paperwork system used for receiving and stores should relate to the overall system used for control of materials management operations. Nor is a computer system the only solution to documentation problems—a good manual system is sufficient for some companies. In fact, in most situations a good existing manual system is a prerequisite for instituting a successful computer system.

All companies need to improve their paperwork systems in order to simplify control of receiving and stores activities. These paperwork systems should require minimum employee preparation time, but it is also critical that pertinent information and records of transactions not be lost in the interest of minimizing work efforts. The use of "bare bones" systems should not be allowed to compromise data integrity.

Provide Good Working Conditions

The work environment for employees in receiving and stores normally should be similar to that of any other plant or warehouse employee. Most other materials management personnel are located in office areas, for example. Working conditions that provide a healthy, pleasant work environment will ensure high employee morale and good performance.

Good housekeeping is essential. Prescribed rules should be rigidly enforced to ensure orderliness and cleanliness in receiving and stores areas. Potentially troublesome materials, such as small pieces of wood, spilled liquids, and steel strapping scraps, should be removed from floor areas and aisles. Good housekeeping contributes to employee morale and positive work attitudes and is important in providing a safe work environment.

Because the majority of tasks in these areas require materials handling, every effort should be made to reduce physical fatigue through the use of mechanization and automation. Mental fatigue also can be reduced, if supervisors provide a healthy and pleasant work environment.

TYPICAL RECEIVING AND STORES ACTIVITIES

The receiving and stores functions often have reported to inventory control, purchasing, or manufacturing management; but in recent years this practice has been declining as receiving and stores matured into a major subfunction of total materials management. Although receiving and stores activities are numerous and diversified, the two major aspects of these functions relate to clerical and materials handling activities. All other materials management subfunctions, as well as other company functions, depend upon these groups performing their activities carefully and expediently, to avoid errors and provide essential materials flow.

Receiving

The receiving department is the first group within the company that is physically involved with any incoming materials. Therefore, it is the first "line of defense" in assuring that the materials received are what the company ordered. This activity normally does not include product quality assurance; in most companies, product quality determination is the responsibility of the inspection or quality assurance department.

Any discrepancy that is not found by receiving, and is allowed to filter through the system, will result in increased costs, wasted time in various departments, and possible future difficulties with both customers and suppliers. Poor receiving procedures can mean acceptance of unordered material, inaccurate counts, and misidentification of products. Unfortunately, these errors stay in the system until they are discovered in the taking of physical inventories, or until more severe problems arise when the products are ordered for use.

Receiving operations, documents, and reports influence many groups within the company. For example, the purchasing department uses delivery information to evaluate timely delivery by suppliers; and normally the accounts payable section of the accounting department uses receiving documentation as a check against incoming department invoices. In one hospital, doctors ordered items individually instead of working with the purchasing department to obtain purchase orders—with resultant confusion and many lost personnel hours. The materials manager at the hospital decided to use the receiving department as a means of screening these unauthorized purchases, and sent a memo to all concerned stating that the receiving department was not to receive any item for which there was no purchase order.[5] The wayward doctors soon "got the message" and began to place orders through the purchasing department.

Receiving Activities—Functions and Flow. The basic responsibility of receiving personnel is to perform their various activities in such a manner that all incoming materials are processed accurately and expeditiously. Figure 8-2 illustrates the typical flow of receiving activities, which are discussed in the following paragraphs. In actual practice, many of these activities are combined to obtain efficient operations.

Unload. Initially receiving department personnel unload the carrier vehicle (truck, freight car, etc.). Some companies maximize dock capacity and minimize manning requirements by working with carriers, scheduling incoming vehicles. This helps to provide a balanced schedule, which is beneficial to both the carrier and the receiving company. The unloading of carrier vehicles and the unitizing of loads are in many cases still performed by manual handling. In some situations, workers unload material directly onto a conveyor that moves it to another location. Often companies receive unitized loads,[6] which permit the rapid mechanized unloading of vehicles.

Verify Items and Quantity—Freight Bill and Purchase Order. A freight bill is prepared by the carrier. It includes information such as the number of containers, gross weights, and a general description of articles shipped. It is essentially a contract between shipper and carrier to ensure safe handling of shipments. All unloaded materials must be initially verified, using the consignee's copy of the freight bill. At this point in the processing of incoming materials, receiving basically ensures that the number of cartons, bags, drums, or other units agrees with the quantity shown on the freight bill. This first step in the receiving process establishes carrier and supplier liability, and identifies discrepancies.

A very important check is made at this time, using the receiving copy of the company's purchase order, to determine whether the items were actually ordered by the company. Periodically, suppliers make errors in ship-

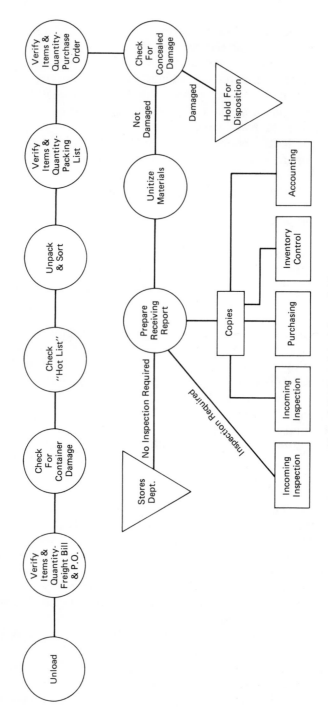

Figure 8-2. Flow of receiving activities.

ments. One mistake is to ship the wrong materials to a customer. Receiving must be alert and return materials that were not included in the company purchase order. If incorrect materials are allowed to enter the system, unnecessary cost and confusion will follow. Another type of check is being instituted by cost-conscious materials management groups at this point: receiving checks the scheduled receiving date shown on the purchase order to determine if the shipment is being received too early, according to company procedures. The shipment is returned to the supplier if it has not arrived within the time period allowed for early shipment. The practice of stopping shipments that are received well in advance of their need benefits companies by reducing financial costs and storage congestion.

Check for Container Damage. All containers are checked for external damage. Any damage to containers can indicate damage to the internal contents. If receiving personnel find evidence of container damage, it should be reviewed with a carrier representative and noted on the freight bill or a receiving document. It is important that personnel perform this check prior to signing for receipt of the material, in order to establish carrier liability for damages.

Check Hot List. In many companies, certain incoming materials are urgently needed to satisfy internal or customer requirements. Often, company personnel have devoted considerable time to expediting the shipment of materials and have paid premium costs for transportation, such as air freight. To alert all pertinent personnel to the significance of these materials, a "hot list" is completed and constantly updated. If any items in an incoming shipment are found to be on the hot list, receiving personnel give them preferential treatment in processing.

Unpack and Sort. All containers that have mixed contents are carefully unpacked and the materials sorted for ease of examination. The items are also separated to allow faster processing at a later point in the receiving function. For example, a container may have materials destined for delivery to several different departments. Separation, considering the destination, will reduce materials handling.

Verify Items and Quantity—Packing List. The supplier's packing list itemizes all products included in a shipment, giving sufficient detail to allow receiving personnel to identify each product. The packing list is used to verify all items and quantities. Often materials are received in standard containers in uniform quantities. There is no need to open and count every one—spot checks are usually sufficient. Any discrepancy is noted on the supplier's packing slip.

Verify Items and Quantity—Purchase Order. A copy of all purchase orders is maintained in a receiving department file. Receiving checks each item included on the packing list to determine if the items conform with the purchase order. The next verification is to verify that the quantity received matches the quantity ordered. If too little material is received, there may have been a supplier error or a partial shipment.

Check for Concealed Damage. The term concealed damage pertains to any material damage that is discovered after the carrier has left. This damage should be reported to the carrier as soon as possible. A carrier representative will be asked to review the material, and the carrier will require a completed damage form. It is important that all damaged material be stored in a specified, restricted area so that it will not mistakenly enter the system as good material. Also, the disposition of this material should be determined quickly to avoid excessive storage.

Unitize Materials. All incoming materials that are not received in a unit load condition should be unitized, whenever feasible, to reduce materials handling and storage costs. The unitizing activity may be physically performed at different times in the receiving procedures. One common location is at the docks, when a large quantity is received. For example, a truckload shipment of nonunitized cartons can be stacked by receiving personnel on pallets. Unitizing for small quantities may be performed after verification activities. It is desirable to place these materials in a container that is compatible with both materials handling systems of stores and quantity requirements of operations. Unitizing may commonly be accomplished using pallets, wire containers, stretch wrap material, plastic containers, and a variety of other equipment.

Prepare Receiving Report. Many companies use a standard form to record all materials received, which must be completed by receiving personnel. It may be a multiple-copy form, prepared as part of the original purchase order for ease of completion and distribution. Some companies use a copy of the purchase order to record this information. They duplicate copies of the purchase order containing receiving information and distribute them to all pertinent groups. Copies are normally provided to the following:

1. Accounting—to provide a document to use in checking invoices.
2. Inventory control—to give information regarding the disposition of incoming materials.
3. Purchasing—to indicate the receipt of purchased materials and provide information for supplier evaluation.

4. Incoming inspection — to provide information for use in scheduling work loads.

Stores

The area for stores activities is referred to by various names, including stockroom, storeroom, and warehouse. The basic stores function is to store material temporarily. Ideally, a company would have no stores function — material would flow smoothly from receipt through all operations and then to a customer. In many companies, the practice of total materials management has effectively reduced the stores function by minimizing inventories. However, very few companies have eliminated the stores function. Having raw materials supplies, work-in-process, and finished goods inventories enhances company operations and permits economies such as those obtained through quantity purchase discounts, as well as optimum utilization of labor and equipment. Normally, finished goods inventory is part of the physical distribution organization.

Symptoms of Poor Control. The proper control of materials in stores areas is essential for efficient total materials management. Conversely, poor control of stockrooms will create many problems for materials management as well as other company functions such as manufacturing, marketing, and finance. It is important to recognize the symptoms of poorly controlled stores areas in order to provide needed corrective action.

Inaccurate inventory records. Poor data integrity in inventory records is a common symptom of an improperly controlled stockroom. Many inventory control problems result from inaccurate stockroom counts, stores personnel dispersing the wrong material (so that the recorded quantity of one material is too high and the other too low), and illegible paperwork. Corrective action includes the use of cycle counting (discussed in detail later in this chapter), improved employee training, and the use of scales instead of manual counting. One company initiated a program to gain control of inventory costs, recognizing the need for accurate parts count in the program. The stock consisted of 24,000 different SKU's (stock keeping units), ranging from nuts to heavy forgings. An important means of achieving the goal of 95 percent accuracy was to use electronic scales instead of manual counting. This method improved counting accuracy and eliminated tedious work that had contributed to employee fatigue and errors.[7]

Lost material. When we lose personal possessions — whether temporarily or permanently — we experience both anger and frustration. But when material is lost in a stockroom, the losses produce more than unpleasant emotions; these losses can mean ordering additional materials, schedule changes, lost time for people and equipment, and unhappy customers. The possibility of losing materials can be reduced by instituting an improved location numbering system, developing an efficient paperwork system, and providing good storage systems. Probably the chief way to reduce such losses, along with many other stockroom problems, is to maintain good employee morale through a healthy work environment.

Damaged material. Excessive material damage is a problem in many stockrooms for many reasons. Frequently it is due to the negligence of mobile equipment operators. It also can result from dampness, improper temperature, vermin infestation, or water leaking from a roof. Improper facilities, such as narrow aisles and poor storage systems, are another cause. Very often, damage is not discovered until the material is withdrawn from storage for use, when it causes confusion and many of the other problems that occur with lost material. Corrective action includes proper employee training and controlling temperature and moisture in the physical facility. Stock rotation can be important for materials that have a short shelf life.

Obsolete and surplus material. The presence of obsolete and surplus material is an expensive problem for any company. Obsolete inventories exist for various reasons. One common cause is engineering changes, where schedule dates do not allow for the use of remaining inventories. Another is the decision to eliminate a product. Surplus material results from overprocurement, uncontrolled production operations, and general inefficiency. One company had an inventory of rod stock that, considering projected average consumption, represented over six years' supply — an amount far in excess of inventory control limits.

Whatever the cause, this material is costly because of the stockroom space it occupies as well as its potential sale value. Corrective actions required to reduce such waste include better communication between materials management and design engineering, closer control of purchase quantities, and use of color coding for all incoming materials.

Materials stored in aisles. Material left in an aisle is a symptom of poor design and management of stores facilities. Such storage practices, even if temporary, contribute to ineffective material flow, safety problems, damaged materials, and poor housekeeping. A glaring example of this situation occurred in a company that manufactures electromechanical devices. Because of a poor layout, there was insufficient storage space, and loaded pallets were placed in the pallet rack aisle. There they blocked the visibility and accessibility of items stored in the racks, creating a safety hazard. Also, stockroom personnel stepped on these materials to obtain items behind them, damaging the products.

The need for aisle storage results from many types of faulty facilities design, including insufficient storage space and improper staging areas. Stockroom supervisors are responsible for some aisle crowding. Lack of employee training, poor worker attitudes, and improper allocation of supervisory time to the stockroom are just a few aspects of this employee-oriented problem. Corrective action to reduce or eliminate aisle storage would include improved facility design (to provide proper staging areas and storage systems) and good supervision (by a supervisor conscious of employee morale needs who would provide the proper degree of supervision).

Physical Control. An essential part of stores activities is maintaining physical control of materials. Physical control involves (a) assuring that materials are secure and that the proper procedural methods are being employed to provide the best storage methods; and (b) instituting techniques that will yield the desired data integrity for all stores-related information. Every business must be conscious of the need to improve physical control of stores operations in order to support a successful total materials management program.

Stockroom Security. Investment in materials represents a substantial portion of the total current assets of most companies; so a company should employ effective means for controlling the materials stored in stockrooms. In general, the more valuable materials and those that can be used for personal or home use require greater security. Any large, heavy, and expensive items that have little utility, such as castings or forgings, require little security. Unauthorized removal of materials from the stockroom can be due to either pilferage or company use.

A consultant described one case of the uncontrolled removal of stock for company use. While reviewing the stockroom with the company's president, the consultant saw a well-dressed man, in a three-piece suit, carrying a clipboard and selecting items from stock. "You certainly must pay your order pickers well in this company, judging by the way that man is dressed," said the consultant. The president replied, "Oh, no! That's not an order picker. He's one of our salesmen. Probably selecting some stock to be used as samples." "Does he give anyone a list of what he takes?" asked the consultant. "Not normally. It is only one or two pieces of a few items that he takes," said the president. The president did not recognize that the uncontrolled removal of stock by anyone, including sales personnel, affects stockroom security. Other common examples of unauthorized stock removal include people obtaining materials without a requisition on a night shift, with no stockroom personnel on duty, and employees obtaining material from the stockroom to replace units damaged during operations. The cost of pilferage and burglary amounts to millions of dollars a year. Consequently, security is a top-priority management issue. Companies have been intensifying their efforts to improve security systems. Tight procedural controls are one element of a successful program. Good housekeeping reflects management commitment to security, as out-of-place stock will be noticeable in a clean, orderly stockroom or warehouse. Establishing a uniform pallet caseload number will make short pallet loads easily visible. Softsel Computer Products, Inc., of Inglewood, California, uses motion detectors, keeping their high-value merchandise section under constant camera surveillance.[8]

Storage Methods. Companies institute various methods to control stockroom materials and maximize resource utilization. One of these methods is *addressing systems,* also commonly called *location numbering systems.* A good addressing system is essential for control of materials in a stockroom. The number of different addressing systems varies only with the imagination of individuals developing them. One good system locates materials in storage by identifying, in sequence: (1) aisle, (2) slot or floor storage section, and (3) elevation or shelf level. For example, assume an item is to be found in shelving, location 08-04-C. Referring to the schematic layout in Figure 8-3a, our first consideration is finding aisle 08, and next, the slot or section of shelving, 04. (Note that this addressing system is the same as used by a postman, where homes or buildings have odd numbers on one side of the street and even numbers on the other side. This "postman system" is easy for people to understand and remember.) Once we reach 04, our final consideration in locating the item is the shelf level. Refer to Figure 8-3b, which illustrates a front view of the shelving unit.

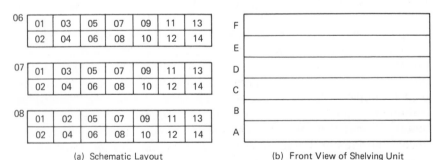

(a) Schematic Layout   (b) Front View of Shelving Unit

Figure 8-3. Addressing system. (a) Schematic layout; (b) front view of shelving unit.

Starting with the bottom shelf and going upward, we find shelf C as the third one. In some companies, numbers are used instead of letters to indicate the shelf level.

Another consideration in physically controlling materials is whether there is a stockroom or not. The storage containment system can be either closed or open. In either case, there are trade-offs. In a *closed containment system*, materials are physically controlled in a stockroom. The stockroom should be strictly controlled. The closed system provides the strongest security and greatest degree of data integrity, but it does require fixed stockrooms and additional materials handling. With an *open containment system*, sometimes referred to as *four-wall inventory*, there is no stockroom. The big advantage to the open system is that material is stored close to the point of use. There is no restriction, in terms of fencing or doors, to obtaining material. Also, there is a minimum amount of materials handling, in moving material to the work area and in worker access. The major disadvantage of an open system is that there is virtually no control of material.

The material storage location system is important from the viewpoints of space utilization, ease of training, and error potential. There are three basic material storage location systems: fixed, random, and combination.

A *fixed*[9] *storage location system* uniquely identifies each individual storage location at the home of a specific item. If there is no material in stock at the moment, no other material can be placed in that location. Referring to the pallet rack shown in Figure 8-4, only A12 material can be stored as shown, with fixed storage. This system makes it easy for store personnel both to store and to find specific materials, with a relatively simple type of addressing system. It also reduces paperwork and sources of error. Fixed storage's main disadvantages are an inability to maximize space utilization (empty spots remain empty) and a lack of flexibility when expansion of space is required for an item.

A *random storage location system* allows all material to be stored in all storage locations. As soon as a material is depleted, such as A12 in Figure 8-4, another incoming material can be stored in that location. Advantages of random storage are that it provides for FIFO (first in, first out) material rotation, and that there is no limit to its flexibility in expanding or contracting space for an item. The biggest advantage to random storage is maximum space utilization, which is especially important with expensive equipment, such as automated storage retrieval systems. The disadvantages of random storage are: the paperwork system and employee input must be accurate, or there will be more errors; more information must be recorded on every transaction; and there can be a lag in information for order pickers when new material comes in and is located. Simulation studies have shown that fixed storage can require from 20 percent to 60 percent

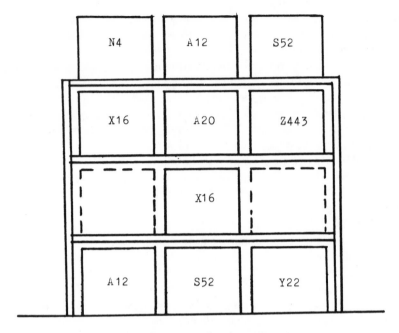

Figure 8-4. Storage location system.

more slots (storage locations) than are required for random storage.[10]

The third possibility is a *combination storage location system*. This system provides some of the advantages of both fixed and random systems. Referring to Figure 8-4, combination storage would provide for levels A and B to be fixed storage and levels C and D to random storage. Levels A and B would provide easy access and fewer errors in order picking. Overflow material for items stored in a picking location on levels A and B, such as A12, can be stored in any nearby location on levels C and D.

Cycle Count. Total materials management, to succeed in any business, must establish a high level of data integrity. The annual physical inventory, commonly relied upon by accounting and inventory control for accurate updating of inventory quantities, is a costly exercise in frustration in most companies, even if management does not recognize it as such. The annual physical inventory is often inaccurate, a cause of general confusion; it can result in lost material, and lead to an untimely lapse in operations. The inaccuracy of daily stores activities often detracts from material management's credibility. Inventories may vanish—although not without explanation. They may be stolen, evaporate through chemical processes, or be damaged beyond repair. One important factor in employee theft is that individuals are given the opportunity to steal through lax security.[11] Accurate counting techniques are essential to control these problems.

It is necessary to maintain the integrity of stores operations on a continuing basis, the technique of cycle counting is used to provide for accurate inventories. Cycle counting is a system that involves continuous counting of stores material throughout the year. Specific materials are selected to be counted each day. The frequency of counting an individual item depends on the degree of control desired, using the ABC system, which is discussed in Chapter 4. Figure 8-5 illustrates a cycle counting plan for various materials. The frequency of counts and the acceptable tolerance counts for A, B, and C items would vary according to individual company needs.

The first phase of cycle counting is to check the physical quantity for each item on a daily list. This quantity is compared with the amount shown on the inventory records. If there is a discrepancy that exceeds the acceptable tolerance level, which is usually established to minimize labor costs for the desired level of data accuracy, the next phase is invoked. Reconciliation—or, more dramatically, the "Sherlock Holmes" phase—is then performed.

Reconciliation is an important phase of cycle counting. Its function is to determine the source(s) of errors and correct them. Very often the same error reoccurs. When the error source is discovered and individuals are told how to correct it, the problem seldom reoccurs. For example, a materials manager told the story of a cycle counter who was trying to find an error. During the investigation, a conversation with a stockroom employee revealed that one person always wrote a number one that looked like a seven. This meant that 111 would read as 777, an error of 666. When asked why this was not previously reported, the employee replied, "The boss is not interested in what we have to say." Obviously, this problem went beyond record accuracy.

Development of a cycle counting program is recommended in two distinct phases. Before full-scale cycle counting is initiated, a small sample

Cycle Counting Plan

Type	Frequency of Counts	Counts per Year	Acceptable Tolerances
A	12 week cycle	4	0%
B	24 week cycle	2	±2%
C	50 week cycle	1	±5%

Source: Ernest D'Anjou, "IIT Center Completes Ethics Survey for N.A.P.M.", *National Purchasing Review*, January-February, 1979, p. 4.

Figure 8-5. Cycle counting plan.

of items is selected that can be cycle-counted repetitively to detect and correct major causes of error at the beginning of the program. When the test sample can be maintained error-free at a predetermined percent, the second phase, the full-scale cycle counting program, is started. Another more recent improvement to cycle counting programs is specifying tolerances for acceptable counts as both a percentage quantity deviation and an absolute dollar value deviation. Expressing the tolerance as a percentage quantity deviation alone has not proved effective as a common denominator for measuring the record accuracy of high-usage-value "A" items and low-usage-value "C" items.[12]

Both high and low tolerances are independent of safety stock, as properly applied safety stock is a valid requirement based on uncertainty of demand or supply, but not uncertainty of inventory balance. Safety stock is not a substitute for inventory accuracy.[13]

Storage Systems. Many good, basic storage systems are available for stores operations, and few properly designed stockrooms or warehouses can effectively use only one system. Primary considerations in developing an efficient stockroom involve which storage system should be used, and how much of each type of system is required. Faced with the wide selection of storage systems currently available, individuals responsible for stockroom design should recognize the advantages and disadvantages of each. A knowledgeable stockroom or warehouse designer balances trade-off considerations to select the best application for both present and future operations. Some of the basic storage systems, and major points regarding their usage, are discussed below.

- *Shelving* (see Figure 8-6):
  - Maximizes space for small-size items and small-quantity items.
  - Requires trays to contain material on shelf.
- *Mezzanine shelving* (see Figure 8-7):
  - Increases equipment costs.
  - Provides ability to manually pick on two levels.
  - Requires means to move material up to and down from mezzanine.
- *High-rise shelving—no mezzanine* (see Figure 8-8):
  - Eliminates possibility of manually picking second level.
  - Reduces employee fatigue.
  - Requires order picker trucks.
- *Floor storage* (see Figure 8-9):
  - Provides best ratio of aisle to storage cube.
  - Requires uniform material in a single row, which means it is best for high-quantity storage.

Figure 8-6. Shelving. (Photo courtesy of Equipto, Aurora, Illinois.)

- Requires well-designed loads to avoid tipping and damage to bottom load.
- Allows use of stacking frames for fragile material.
- *Conventional pallet rack* (see Figure 8-10):
  - Provides ability to use cube space.
  - Protects individual loads.
  - Provides access to individual loads.
  - Allows hand-stacking of large items.
  - Reduces aisles with side-load fork trucks (example: reducing aisle from 12 feet to 5½ feet).
- *Two-deep pallet rack* (see Figure 8-11):
  - Provides better ratio of aisle to storage cube than conventional pallet rack.
  - Requires same material in both locations for maximum labor and equipment utilization.
  - Requires fork truck with extended reach capability.

Figure 8-7. Mezzanine shelving. (Photo courtesy of Equipto, Aurora, Illinois.)

Figure 8-8. High-rise shelving—no mezzanine, using order pick truck. (Photo courtesy of Equipto, Aurora, Illinois.)

Figure 8-9. Floor storage. (Courtesy Signode Corporation.)

- *Cantilever rack* (see Figure 8-12):
  - Maximizes storage space for long, irregular-shaped items, and for materials that vary in length.
  - Increases rack cost.
- *Flow rack* (see Figure 8-13):
  - Provides FIFO material movement.
  - Increases equipment cost.
  - Allows increased order pick productivity, as it provides more pick positions per foot.
  - Requires uniform material in a single row and aisles for both stocking and picking.
- *Drive-in rack* (see Figure 8-14):
  - Increases equipment cost.
  - Requires same material in entire row.
  - Maximizes space use for large-quantity loads of fragile products or materials.
  - Requires constant monitoring to prevent mixed material in the same slot.
- *Automated storage retrieval system* (*AS/RS*) (see Figure 8-15):
  - Increases total equipment costs.
  - Eliminates labor costs for storage and retrieval of material.
  - Reduces lighting, heat, and insurance costs.

Figure 8-10. Conventional pallet rack. (Courtesy Ace Hardware Corporation.)

- Allows use of rack-supported buildings which reduces the number of years that the building can be depreciated.

Stockroom Layout and Materials Handling. Efficiency in the stockroom layout and in materials handling is essential to the achievement of overall stores function objectives. Many of the problems of both new and existing stockrooms can be attributed to faulty layout and poor materials handling. Development of an efficient storage facility depends directly on the prior study of all operations. This requires an in-depth analysis of all stores activities, for both present and future time periods. The analysis of future

Figure 8-11. Two-deep pallet rack. (Photo courtesy of Equipto, Aurora, Illinois.)

Figure 8-12. Cantilever rack. (Courtesy Ridg-U-Rak.)

Figure 8-13. Flow rack. (Courtesy Rapistan, a Lear Siegler company.)

requirements should cover a minimum of five years. The study can be extended beyond five years, depending upon the company's projected growth, new product plans, and other vital factors. Some important considerations in planning an efficient storage facility are discussed below.

Maximize space utilization. The maximum utilization of stores space is directly related to the optimum use of cube space, whereas a key to cube space use is to design and implement efficient storage systems. The first consideration is to use all available space, stacking as close to the ceiling as allowed. This can be accomplished with an effective storage system; for example, when floor storage is well designed, materials can be stacked as high as possible. Some packaging is not strong enough to sustain the weight of multiple stacked units; but in these cases the package can be improved, or alternative storage systems, such as a drive-in rack, can be used. A critical factor in storing materials near ceilings is the limitation that fire insurance companies impose to ensure proper operation of the automatic sprinkler system. The distance between sprinkler heads and material is specified, depending upon the type of materials stored and the sprinkler system capacity.

Space also is maximized by eliminating lost space due to any excess distance between the top of materials and the shelves or pallet rack beams. Modern shelving and pallet racks are adjustable, to ensure efficient space utilization. Some companies install equipment with one large standard

Figure 8-14. Drive-in rack. (Courtesy Ridg-U-Rak.)

opening. The advantage is that all items fit into the standard space; but because stored materials vary in height, this added flexibility may prompt trade-off costs of unused space. Materials and storage openings should be reviewed to determine standard opening sizes that will provide flexibility and maximize space usage.

Figure 8-15. Automated Storage Retrieval System (AS/RS) with an Automated Guided Vehicle System (AGVS) used for delivery and removal of storage units. (Courtesy of Eaton-Kenway, Inc.)

Optimize equipment and labor resources. The optimum use of equipment and labor is as important to stores operations as it is to all other phases of a business. Reducing the distance traveled by mobile trucks and operators is one way to optimize equipment and labor resources. There are many ways to reduce travel distance, one being to minimize the amount of truck travel without a load. To obtain a high percentage of loaded truck travel, the stores layout and communications systems must be efficient. Mobile trucks may be equipped with two-way radios, so that drivers have constant contact with the dispatcher. Also, if the dispatcher uses a CRT (monitor screen) computer terminal, needed information is readily available to the truck driver, eliminating unnecessary travel to gather instructions and check data (see Figure 8-16).

Labor use can be facilitated by increasing the use of materials handling equipment and reducing manual handling. Both labor and equipment use can be optimized by locating materials in a stockroom in ways that mini-

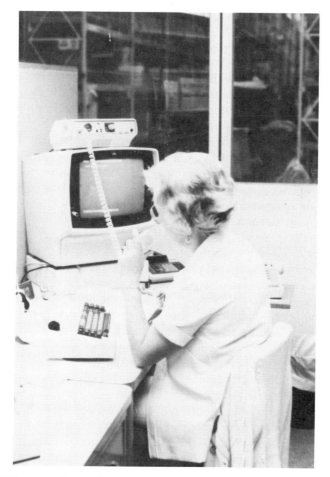

Figure 8-16. Stores employee using a computer terminal (CRT) and two-way radio. (Courtesy Ace Hardware Corporation.)

mize movement. Fast movers (materials frequently picked) should be stored in locations where they can be stocked and picked with minimum travel distance. Slow movers (infrequently picked materials) should be stored in less accessible locations. Very large, heavy items should be stored, when practical, near doors and aisles close to the point of disbursal.

Provide proper staging areas. Staging areas, or temporary storage spaces, are vital to all business operations. As materials flow from one area to another, there normally is an immediate need for space to store material temporarily until the next function is ready to use it. For example, assume that all the work on incoming material has been completed by the receiving group, and the material is ready to be stored. Receiving personnel must be able to store the material in order to remove it from their operating area; at the same time, stores employees should not have to depend on others' schedules to move materials into their area. The use of a staging area allows stores to move material at times that are convenient for their activities. Also, temporary storage is necessary because of the time required for determination of proper storage locations and document preparation.

A staging area is required between stores and all departments serviced by them. Typically there are two staging areas, incoming and outgoing. A lack of appropriate staging space will contribute to inefficient operations in the various departments. Some common problems due to inadequate staging areas include congested work areas, blocked aisles, inefficient labor and equipment utilization, and damaged materials.

Minimize aisle size. There are many trade-offs in planning proper aisles. Wide aisles help to provide good material flow. Aisles that are too narrow can cause congested operations and loss of labor and equipment productivity. It is like trying to park a car where parking lot aisles are too narrow; additional time is needed to maneuver the auto into the parking space. In such cases, the parking lot planner probably thinks that the additional parking time and effort are less important than maximum space utilization. However, most current industrialists emphasize maximum labor and equipment utilization.

Fortunately, the use of cube space for material storage can be increased in direct proportion to aisle size reduction. As new types of equipment have been developed, stockroom planners have been able to have their cake and eat it too! Narrower aisles have been incorporated into layouts, but do not reduce employee and equipment productivity. In fact, in many instances, layouts using new narrow-aisle equipment have provided increased space, labor, and equipment utilization.

Aisles should be designed according to a number of commonsense suggestions: designing them as straight as possible, minimizing intersections, using column boundary lines (keep columns out of aisles), identifying aisles with three- or four-inch-wide floor line markings, and providing for two-way traffic.

Maximize flexibility in layout and systems. Storage areas undergo periodic changes because of the introduction of new materials, elimination of other materials, contraction and expansion of material quantities, and changes in equipment and systems. It is essential that the stockroom layout, systems, and procedures provide enough flexibility to adjust to changing operating conditions.

Stockroom layout and storage systems should provide for future expansion requirements. If this logic is not incorporated at the earliest development stages of stockroom design, there may be serious problems later. Potential difficulties include costly relocation of equipment, storage systems that do not relate to new materials/products, and the inability to provide building expansion in the desired direction because of the poor location of fixed, costly-to-move equipment.

Proper flexibility in layout and systems requires close examination of the key trade-offs involved. One example concerns the design of a shelving storage layout. A normal aisle for manual order picking would be 3'0" wide, using 7'0"-high shelving units. However, a company may initially decide to trade off additional costs incurred by using a wider aisle to gain the flexibility that would allow future expansion, using operator-driven trucks in conjunction with increased shelving height. The trucks could pick materials at a 14'0" level, thereby enhancing operator productivity.

RELATIONSHIPS WITH OTHER MATERIALS MANAGEMENT SUBFUNCTIONS

Receiving and stores personnel have regular contact with individuals working in other materials management subfunctions. The effectiveness of total materials management depends upon supportive activities and good communication between these subfunctions.

Purchasing

Purchasing can support receiving and stores activities by obtaining materials in unit loads conducive to internal operations. This will eliminate the time required to rehandle materials and improve space utilization. Receiving and stores can benefit from improved scheduling of purchased-materials deliveries; employee and equipment work-load problems are reduced by the more uniform receipt of materials. Purchasing personnel assist receiving and stores by buying all needed equipment and supplies. They also perform an important activity in arranging the prompt disposition of rejected and obsolete materials, which provides usable space.

Receiving and stores can aid purchasing activities by providing prompt and accurate information about incoming materials. This is essential for purchasing's supplier evaluation and for expediting deliveries of hot items. Receiving department personnel can assist purchasing by maintaining courteous relationships with supplier personnel.

Inventory Control

Inventory control assists receiving and stores operations by ordering materials in quantities related to standard unit load capacities (e.g., not making the mistake of ordering 5300 gizmos when standard containers hold 5000). This is essential for effective materials control, reduced materials handling, and maximum space utilization for both purchased and manufactured materials. Inventory control can help to reduce stores problems by maintaining constant control of inventory levels. Excessive inventories generally compound stores operating difficulties. If inventory control succeeds in achieving data integrity, there will be fewer phone calls to the stockroom asking, "Count how many gizmos we have."

Receiving and stores are a vital link in inventory control's network to ensure inventory accuracy. They should contribute errorless information on incoming and work-in-process materials, cycle counts, stock locations, and potential obsolete materials. Reducing the damage to materials during in-house handling will decrease inventory control problems. Receiving personnel can also assist inventory control by promptly rejecting shipments of unordered and nonacceptable materials.

Production Control

Production control can reduce stores materials handling by providing accurate information on disbursals to operating departments. Communications between the two groups regarding unit-load quantity requirements can also reduce materials handling, as well as material damage and loss. If production control effectively communicates disbursal priorities to stores, better utilization of personnel and equipment will result, as well as a decrease in the often irritating stores problem of rushing to pick and disburse materials that were not ordered properly.

Receiving and stores can aid production control by maintaining a high level of data integrity. Material ordering discrepancies are reduced, as are material shortages and subsequent rescheduling. Production control schedules are enhanced by minimizing damage to materials and ensuring correct disbursals. Receiving and stores should have physical control of materials at all times in order to provide operations with needed materials. Loss of materials disrupts schedules and creates confusion throughout operations.

Physical Distribution

Physical distribution personnel perform various activities that affect receiving and stores operations. The traffic and transportation group can cooperate in scheduling incoming material receipts by both common carrier and company trucks, so that receiving operations can operate efficiently. This same group can help in expediting damage claims. Elimination of shipping errors can reduce returns of goods.

Accurate receiving and stores information helps to improve finished goods order-picking operations. Stores department storage of materials in unit loads and prepackaged items aids order-picking and shipping operations. Receiving personnel must carefully identify customer-returned materials to reduce problems of customer communication regarding physical distribution activities.

Materials Handling

The materials handling group develops optimum materials handling systems for receiving and stores. Effective systems increase employee productivity, reduce space requirements, and improve material flow. Well-controlled materials handling systems reduce receiving and stores problems such as lost or damaged materials, as well as potential employee safety hazards. The development of materials handling specifications for purchased materials can enhance receiving and stores operations. Receiving and stores personnel can aid individuals responsible for the physical movement of materials throughout the facility by maintaining accurate information, stacking materials in a safe, stable manner, and adhering to schedules.

RELATIONSHIPS WITH OTHER COMPANY FUNCTIONS

Because receiving and stores handle incoming materials first, their performance affects all other company functions. Similarly, the effectiveness of other company functions impacts upon receiving and stores operations. Some common interdepartmental relationships are reviewed below.

Marketing

Receiving and stores can aid marketing through efficient performance of operations. The prevention of material damage by receiving and stores will facilitate on-time deliveries to customers. Accurate records help provide customers with desired quantities of materials and proper credits for returned goods. Receiving and stores play essential roles in the total materials management effort to minimize product costs. Success here helps marketing to maintain a competitive position through lower and/or consistent product pricing.

Marketing operations can directly affect receiving and stores activities by selling obsolete materials and providing accurate sales forecasts. The sale of obsolete materials makes additional space available. Accurate sales forecasts minimize required inventory levels and reduce the possibility of generating more obsolete materials. Marketing can also aid stores by adhering to established schedules; schedule changes generally increase the stores work load and the number of work errors.

Finance

Receiving and stores activities are directly related to the finance function through control of company assets. Accurate record keeping by receiving and stores personnel provides finance with the factual information (such as assets included in balance sheets) required for management of company financial activities. By minimizing material damage, reducing duplicate purchase orders, and decreasing material loss, receiving and stores lower material costs, allowing finance to channel company monies to other areas. Accurate records on incoming materials will ensure correct payment to suppliers, thereby avoiding supplier overpayment and payment for materials received without an order.

Finance can help receiving and stores operations by allocating monies for necessary equipment, personnel, building space, and supplies. If finance does not function at an optimum level, a reduction in cash flow and other monetary problems may result. Then there will be less money available for the entire company, including receiving and stores. Receiving and stores depend upon finance for monies to improve employee working conditions (e.g., minimize employee fatigue through the use of mechanical handling equipment), increase departmental productivity, and increase employee safety.

Manufacturing

Manufacturing depends upon receiving and stores for the uninterrupted flow of materials in order to maximize operational requirements. They need to receive the right material, in the right quantity, at the right time, at the right place. Any shortcoming here will result in manufacturing losses, involving employee productivity, machine capacity, and schedule maintenance. Receiving and stores should provide the manufacturing group with continuous communications about expedited hot list materials and any potential problems.

Receiving and stores operations are affected by manufacturing. Manufacturing can reduce receiving and stores problems by proper control and identification of materials sent to the stockroom (such as placing returned parts in the proper container). Correct information from manufacturing about schedule requirements can help to reduce duplicated work, improve employee scheduling, maximize materials handling equipment utilization, and improve data. Problems of data integrity arise in stores when manufacturing withdraws materials from the stockroom without the necessary forms. This may occur when a company is operating with work shifts that have limited operations, sometimes called skeleton shifts.

Engineering

Engineering relies upon receiving to properly identify materials, perform punctually, and route incoming sample products and other materials to its attention—especially materials that are being expedited. Engineering affects receiving and stores operations primarily through product design activities; the use of existing standard parts in any new product design will decrease the number of parts in inventory. Thus engineering aids receiving and stores activities by reducing materials handling, minimizing paperwork requirements, and improving space utilization.

Quality Assurance

Quality assurance relies on receiving to check incoming shipments for materials that were not ordered and for obvious transportation damage. These checks will reduce the inspection work load. Careful handling by both receiving and stores will reduce damage to materials and the number of rejects by inspectors. Receiving should cooperate with incoming inspection in planning the sequence of processing materials, allowing both groups to maximize employee productivity.

Quality assurance is responsible for assuring that all materials in the stockroom are of approved quality. If this is not accomplished, there will be additional work for receiving and stores personnel. The receiving and stores groups rely upon quality assurance, cooperating with purchasing and other company functions, to obtain prompt action regarding the disposition of rejected materials. Delays could cause problems of congested storage areas and of rejected materials being confused with good-quality materials. The quality assurance function must be accurate and definitive in preparing paperwork, especially in differentiating between acceptable and rejected materials. If defective material enters operations, it can be a source of confusion for receiving and stores employees.

SUMMARY

The receiving and stores subfunctions, which are common among all businesses, perform the initial activities of total materials management in the physical movement and control of materials. These subfunctions contribute the first link in the data integrity chain that provides materials management subfunctions and other company functions with information vital to their performance. Therefore, it is critical for all companies to consider the receiving and stores groups as major activity areas.

Receiving and stores objectives relate primarily to achieving a smooth flow of materials to provide uninterrupted company functions. The efficiency and effectiveness of company activities also are enhanced by competent receiving and stores personnel, who can help to maximize company profits in many ways, such as minimizing space and labor costs, reducing material damage, and improving paperwork systems. It is vital for receiving and stores to achieve good employee working conditions, to enhance morale and productivity.

Receiving activities, which involve the initial flow of materials into the facility, include checking and verifying the correctness of these materials. These activities begin with the physical unloading of materials from incoming vehicles, and continue with verifying items and quantities, checking for hot list or urgently needed items, and unpacking and sorting materials from containers with mixed contents. At this point all items can be verified by using the supplier's packing list and the company's purchase order. Materials are checked for damage, loose materials are unitized, receiving reports are prepared, and materials are delivered to either incoming inspection (if required) or the stores department.

The basic stores function is the temporary storage of materials. Control of these stored materials is an essential element of this activity. Poor stores control can be detected and corrected by responding to its symptoms. Inaccurate records are a common symptom of poor control; other indications include lost material, obsolete and surplus materials, and material stored in aisles. Companies are focusing on improving the physical control of material. Stockroom security is a critical part of this control. Addressing or location numbering systems, physical stockroom design, and storage location systems also contribute to control of materials. Cycle counting is one method used to increase materials management data integrity. This system is employed both to correct inaccurate inventory record quantities and to eliminate the causes of inaccuracies.

Most stores operations employ a variety of storage systems to stock materials efficiently. The process of selecting appropriate storage systems from the wide selection of equipment available requires a review of all trade-offs, including space utilization, material protection, equipment utilization, and employee productivity. Some good, basic storage systems are shelving, pallet racks, cantilever racks, flow racks, drive-in racks, and automated storage retrieval systems.

Stockroom layout and materials handling efficiency is essential in achieving overall stores objectives. Planning an optimum facility requires in-depth analysis, and the consideration of present and future requirements. Maximum employee productivity and space utilization are two prime factors in stockroom design. Other critical considerations include the optimum use of equipment, proper staging areas, the minimum aisle size that can provide the desired materials flow, and maximum flexibility in layout and systems.

NOTES

1. Ackerman and LaLonde, "Making Warehousing More Efficient," p. 95.
2. Maraschiello, "JIT and the Receiving Room," pp. 36–37.
3. Thompson, "How to Achieve and Maintain Inventory Accuracy," p. 44.
4. Ackerman, *Practical Handbook of Warehousing*, p. 438.
5. The only exceptions, during the initial period after this change, were emergency items needed to ensure a patient's health.
6. Unitizing is the process of taking various items or bulk material and arranging and/or constraining them so that they can be moved and stored as a single unit. This can be accomplished by using pallets, containers, and other equipment.
7. "Scales Give MRP the Accuracy It Needs," p. 59.
8. Harrington, "Is Your Warehouse Secure?" pp. 72–73.
9. Sometimes referred to as "dedicated."
10. Salvendy, White, and Kinney, *Handbook of Industrial Engineering*, p. 10.4.5.
11. Frey, *Warehouse Operations*, p. 148.
12. Jordan, "Cycle Counting for Record Accuracy," p. 385.
13. Burch, "Cycle Counting and Inventory Accuracy," pp. 66–70.

BIBLIOGRAPHY

Ackerman, Kenneth B. *Warehousing, a Guide for Both Users and Operators.* Washington, D.C.: The Traffic Service Corporation, 1977.

Ackerman, Kenneth B. *Practical Handbook of Warehousing.* Washington, D.C.: The Traffic Service Corporation, 1983.

Ackerman, Kenneth B., and LaLonde, Bernard J. "Making Warehousing More Efficient." *Harvard Business Review,* Mar.–Apr. 1980.

"An Inside Look at Warehouse Management." *Traffic Management,* July 1985.

Apple, James M. *Materials Handling Systems Design.* New York: The Ronald Press Co., 1972.

Birkner, E. C. "Undercovering Extra Storage Space." *Professional Builder,* Apr. 1988.

Burch, J. D. "Cycle Counting and Inventory Accuracy." *Production and Inventory Management Review,* Sept. 1981.

Frey, Stephen L. *Warehouse Operations: A Handbook.* Beaverton, Oregon: M/A Press, 1983.

Green, James H., ed. *Production and Inventory Control Handbook.* New York: McGraw-Hill Book Co., 1970.

Harrington, Lisa H. "Is Your Warehouse Secure?" *Traffic Management,* Aug. 1986.

"Hydraulic Leveler Improves Dock Safety." *Traffic Management,* July 1987.

Jenkins, Creed H. *Modern Warehouse Management.* New York: McGraw-Hill Book Co., 1968.

Jordan, Henry H. "Cycle Counting for Record Accuracy," American Production and Inventory Control Society, *1980 Conference Proceedings.*

Maraschiello, Bill. "JIT and the Receiving Room." *Handling and Shipping Management,* Aug. 1986.

Nelson, Raymond A. *Computerizing Warehouse Operations.* Englewood Cliffs, New Jersey: Prentice-Hall, 1985.

"Random Slotting Techniques and Their Applications." *Material Handling Engineering,* Apr. 1985.

Salvendy, Gavriel, ed., White, John A., and Kinney, Hugh D. *Handbook of Industrial Engineering.* New York: John Wiley and Sons, 1982.

"Scales Give MRP the Accuracy It Needs." *Modern Material Handling,* Aug. 1982.

Thompson, Richard L. "How to Achieve and Maintain Inventory Accuracy." *Production and Inventory Management,* First Quarter 1985.

Twede, Diana, and Goff, James. "Are You in Packaging or Warehousing?" *Warehouse Review,* Summer 1984.

Warehouse Accounting and Control. Ernst & Whinney with Cleveland Consulting Associates, National Council of Physical Distribution Management, 1985.

9
Materials Handling

Materials handling is not a new endeavor. The first humans who inhabited the earth were faced with the problem of transporting both themselves and the materials needed for their existence. The movement of materials is basic to all business and personal activities. Through the years people have learned to apply mechanical principles such as the wheel, lever, and inclined plane to provide for easier, faster, and safer movement. Basically, materials handling is the art and science of implementing movement in an economical and safe manner. Industrial focus upon materials handling did not develop until the early 1900s. It is now recognized as a major activity that warrants review, systematic analysis, and refinement.[1]

Why is materials handling important to total materials management? That question can be answered by asking another question. Why are the veins and arteries essential to the human body? The answer to this question is fairly simple. All the vital elements of the human system depend upon the proper flow of blood through the body. Similarly, a total materials management system depends upon well-organized and integrated materials handling to provide the proper flow of materials to all essential parts of the business.

History has recorded continual progress in materials handling. Probably one of the greatest feats in the ancient world was construction of the pyramids in Egypt. Another ancient engineering marvel was construction of the pre-Inca temple near Cuzco, Peru. Stones weighing up to 20 tons were quarried from the bottom of the valley and moved over 2000 feet up to the temple site. Eli Whitney, in 1800, developed one of the early examples of mass production by standardizing musket design and arranging work tables for progressive assembly. In 1913, the Ford Motor Company instituted the first mechanized progressive assembly line. World War II stimulated the implementation of materials handling mechanization. Companies that had government cost-plus contracts were encouraged to make capital expenditures for materials handling equipment. Progress in current modern facilities is evident in the use of both mechanized and automated materials handling equipment, to provide desired efficiencies.

Materials handling systems are the key component in modern automated operations. Peter F. Drucker states that in the United States and

Europe automation still is seen as something for the "big boys." However, in Japan automation has been found advantageous for both large and small companies. Drucker believes that the payoff from automation is both fast and high. Automation builds quality standards and quality control into every step in the process. Quality savings outweigh the savings in payroll and manpower and are likely to repay the costs of automation within two or three years. Other economic benefits are derived from a reduction in downtime of people and facilities, when production is changing from one model or part to another. Reduction of downtime means less cost for "not doing" and provides additional capacity to generate revenues.[2]

MATERIALS HANDLING OBJECTIVES RELATED TO MATERIALS MANAGEMENT

Materials handling does not manufacture a product, using operations such as shaping, cutting, or assembly. It does not improve the quality of raw materials, work-in-process, or finished goods inventories. However, over the years, as companies performed various work-related tasks, it became necessary to develop or find suitable equipment to handle materials. Initially, this equipment provided solutions to various individual problems, such as movement of heavy loads, storage of large quantities of materials, and use of available building space. As company operations became more complicated and business volume increased, the need developed for materials handling systems. These systems had to satisfy objectives related to the total materials management program: providing integrated systems, minimizing total costs, improving working conditions, and improving productivity.

Provide Integrated Materials Handling Systems

Materials handling is common to all types of businesses, both in the office and in operations. Manufacturing, distribution, service, government, and transportation are just a few of the areas that require materials handling activities to channel an enormous volume of materials. Materials handling activities can be found at all levels of a business. Figure 9-1 illustrates the wide range of activities. Handling starts with an individual work area, involving one person. A work center requires movement between various employees. Materials then flow within individual work centers, and then between work centers. Movement continues through various departments. Companies with multiple facilities transport materials between various locations. The overall flow network involves materials movement among the segments of a cycle that starts with suppliers and ends with the ultimate consumer.

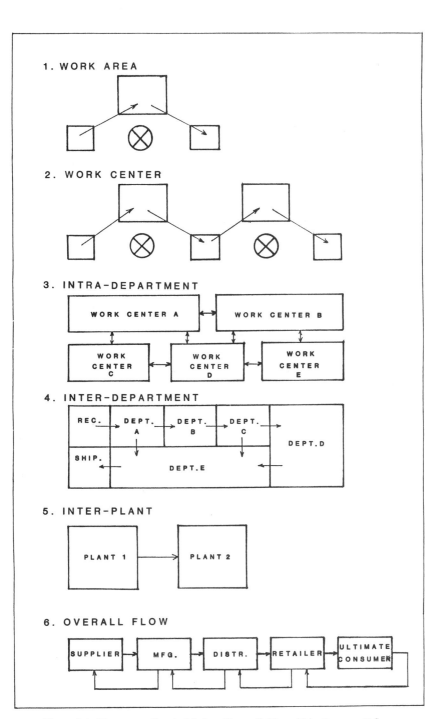

1. WORK AREA

2. WORK CENTER

3. INTRA-DEPARTMENT

WORK CENTER A

WORK CENTER B

WORK CENTER C

WORK CENTER D

WORK CENTER E

4. INTER-DEPARTMENT

REC.

DEPT. A

DEPT. B

DEPT. C

DEPT.D

SHIP.

DEPT.E

5. INTER-PLANT

PLANT 1

PLANT 2

6. OVERALL FLOW

SUPPLIER

MFG.

DISTR.

RETAILER

ULTIMATE CONSUMER

Figure 9-1. The range of materials handling activities within the overall flow.

Considering the numerous and diverse business activities that require materials handling, it is logical to have an objective that considers integrating all these facets. Significant gains in cost savings, productivity, customer service, and reduction of bottlenecks can result from an integrated materials flow system. It is critical that all individuals involved in materials handling and plant layout have an integration orientation. They must recognize that changes in one part significantly affect other elements of the overall flow network.

The cause-and-effect relationships created by changes in the flow network span all levels of the business. For example, one electronics manufacturer discovered that their customers were receiving damaged products. Assemblies were being packaged on the assembly line, and the final solution was to use a different configuration for inner protective packaging, which required enlarging the package size. However, this change on the assembly line affected storage in the physical distribution area; the larger packages did not fit into the flow rack that previously was used to store and pick these units.

Another example of the need to think in terms of multiple network elements concerns a food distributor. Pails were originally stacked individually in a truck for shipment to customers. A unit load program was instituted to provide for wrapping and strapping individual pails into one large unit load. This change permitted higher storage of materials and faster loading of trucks. However, the "improvement" brought immediate customer complaints. Some customers did not have equipment capable of handling the new unit loads. Their receiving personnel were spending more time unpacking the unit loads, and they faced the new problem of disposal of scrap unitizing materials.

Minimize Total Costs

Materials handling represents a major portion of total costs for every type of business. Depending upon the nature of the industry, materials handling may account for 20 to 35 percent of product costs.[3] This activity is an obvious target for any materials management cost containment or reduction program. Reducing its total materials handling costs allows a profit-oriented business to maintain a competitive edge over its competition. Nonprofit businesses can channel these savings to other segments of the organization that have justifiable, perhaps urgent, needs for additional funds.

Total materials handling costs can be minimized by various approaches. The most common method is to directly reduce an existing expense item. For example, a midwestern company that used electric lift trucks to move materials through its facility was able to reduce its total trucking costs by replacing older units, which were slow and required frequent maintenance, with newer, highly productive units. Another approach is to invest in equipment that will reduce materials handling activities by individual employees. For instance, an electronics company purchased a new assembly conveyor that reduced handling time for each employee, and achieved a labor savings of $12,000 per year, so that the new materials handling equipment was paid for in less than two years.

To control materials handling costs, analysts first must identify general sources of potential savings. All company operations should be reviewed to target possible cost-reduction projects. The major sources of materials handling costs are space, labor, inventory, equipment, and waste.

Space. Improvements in space utilization can reduce costs. Often, the first solution to apparent overcrowding is to construct an addition or build another facility. A more positive approach is to look for alternative solutions that would involve more efficient use of the existing building. One of the most effective options is to make use of air rights or cube space. By increasing the storage height from 12 feet to 16 feet, one company increased its space utilization by 33 percent.

Space costs also can be controlled by changing the size of storage aisles. Changing from a counterbalanced truck to a side-loader truck could permit a reduction in aisle width from 10 feet to 5½ to 6 feet (a 40 percent savings). Frequently, the empty space above operational areas can be given new uses, such as conveying waste materials or production parts and assemblies.

Labor. There are many opportunities to reduce handling costs in labor-intensive operations. This is true for both manual labor employees and more highly paid, skilled employees. The use of mechanized systems can be an effective means of cost reduction. For example, a Chicago electronics company originally required incoming inspection personnel to transport loads of materials to and from their workbenches. A conveyor system was installed to perform this materials handling activity, which resulted in a 15 percent labor cost reduction.

Automated systems can considerably reduce labor costs. Many applications exist in manufacturing, government, distribution, and transportation. For example, the United States Postal Service installed automatic mail handling and processing equipment to reduce labor costs and improve flow. The Yamazaki Machinery Works in Nogoya, Japan, operates 18 machining centers on a night shift, with only a night watchman present.[4]

Inventory. Most businesses strive to minimize inventories, as inventory reduction offers tremendous cost-reduction opportunities. Materials management programs that have been instituted to accomplish this objective include Kanban, Just-In-Time, and material requirements planning (MRP). These programs all depend on having an optimum flow of materials for successful results. Dependable materials handling systems can provide the required materials flow.

Dramatic reductions in inventory have been achieved by installing new materials handling systems. The Schweizer Turbochargers Company implemented an MRP system that called for installation of two automated storage retrieval systems (AS/RS). The equipment was justified by a 30 percent inventory reduction. The General Electric Company uses a minicomputer in one facility to direct a truck operator. The truck is equipped with a terminal that provides instant communication. The total system has resulted in a 50 percent reduction in work-in-process inventory as well as other benefits.[5]

Equipment. Improvements in materials handling equipment can reduce costs. Numerous illustrations can be found in the transportation industry. For example, in cargo ship loading and unloading, every day that a ship is in port means increased costs for the operating company; so it is critical that loading and unloading be performed expeditiously. Vessels called container ships, designed to transport containers that hold large amounts of materials, are being used because they can be loaded and unloaded in record time.

An AS/RS unit installed by Bethlehem Steel Corporation exemplifies the many cost-effective features of materials handling equipment. It is 105 feet high, and allows storage of 6200 coils in less than 90,000 square feet. Manual effort has been virtually eliminated in this unit. The use of a computer in conjunction with the AS/RS has reduced order picking time and eliminated product damage. Power and free conveyors are used to carry coils from production. Coils can go directly to storage, bypass the AS/RS, and continue to a processing area, or they can move directly to shipping.[6]

Product Quality. Successful materials management systems require good-quality materials. To avoid the negative effects of product damage, quality control systems of the future increasingly will depend upon properly selected and designed materials handling methods.[7] One of the most common ways to reduce costs is to decrease damage to materials. Concentrated efforts to eliminate the waste of damaged materials through better handling techniques and practices will yield substantial results. Damage control should start with the initial layout design of the materials handling system. Another deterrent to materials damage is an effective personnel training program.

Some materials are more susceptible to spoilage than others; so materials handling systems have been designed to consider the shelf life of stored items. For example, flow racks provide FIFO (first in, first out) rotation of stock, ensuring early dispersal of the older stock. Another method of reducing waste costs relates to scrap materials. Selective handling of scrap, where values and volume warrant it, will result in higher scrap revenues. Separation of scrap can be beneficial with different types of materials, including metals and corrugated box materials.

Improve Working Conditions

Improving employee working conditions is a basic objective of total materials management. There is excellent justification for directing attention to this area, involving humane considerations as well as the profit motive. Good employee working conditions contribute to the general success of an organization. Companies that have instituted productivity improvement programs have found that focusing on areas related to materials handling, such as providing safe work areas, reducing employee fatigue, and enhancing the quality of the work life, is an extremely effective means of improving productivity.

Safety. Mechanization of materials handling reduces the possibility of accidents. Manual handling is a common cause of feet and back injuries, as well as hernia, and takes a toll in medical expenses, lost productivity, and reduced customer services. For example, back injuries associated with industrial jobs account for about 25 percent of all lost job time and result in an annual expenditure of more than one billion dollars for compensation payments, according to one insurance company study.[8]

The primary way to reduce materials handling accidents is to develop and implement a safety program, which can be part of a general safety program. Some safety requirements are stipulated in Occupational Safety and Health Administration (OSHA) standards. Rules and procedures for safe handling should be developed and monitored. These regulations will cover areas such as housekeeping, use and maintenance of mechanical handling equipment, unitization, and storage. Training programs should be conducted to instruct employees. Posters (see Figure 9-2), booklets, safety committees, meetings, and articles in company newsletters are among the many ways of stimulating employee safety consciousness.

Quality of Work Life. There are numerous ways to improve the work environment. One goal of this effort is to increase the level of employee satisfaction. Most workers devote a high percentage of their total productive hours to their firm's activities; so it is important that the hours spent at work be as pleasing as possible.

Figure 9-2. Posters used to promote materials handling safety. (Courtesy the National Safety Council.)

The materials handling function can do much to improve the quality of the individual's work life. Volvo, the Swedish automobile manufacturer, has become well known for its success in this area. The key to its most publicized achievement, at the Kalmar assembly plant, was a mechanized materials handling system. A "Kalmar wagon" was developed to carry the auto body from one assembly area to another. This assembly wagon made it possible to replace the conventional fixed-speed assembly line's rigid control with a much looser manufacturing process, in which the auto stops at various assembly stations during long periods, creating new possibilities for reorganizing assembly work. Kalmar proved to the world that the possibilities for humanization of the workplace are endless, and that monotonous jobs can be improved to provide employees with a better work environment. The materials handling system enhanced the quality of the work life in many ways; it reduced fatigue, improved job satisfaction, provided flexibility in work organization within assembly groups, and created a small workshop atmosphere in a large manufacturing facility.[9]

Improve Productivity

Business publications refer continually to "productivity." Productivity can be defined as:

1. The ratio of effective or useful output to the total output in any system.
2. The relationship between the amount of work accomplished and the amount of labor necessary to accomplish it.
3. The efficiency of people/machines.

Productivity is important to all countries as they compete in world markets. Increases in productivity can significantly affect the average citizen's standard of living. At the individual company level, productivity is a means for minimizing costs and providing positive benefits in competition with other firms. The output per man-hour for U.S. manufacturing has been climbing steadily, rising between 1981 and 1987 to equal West Germany, but it lags behind that of Japan (see Figure 9-3).

A major objective of materials handling is increased productivity, which can be accomplished in many ways. The use of flow racks can reduce walking by employees in picking warehouse orders. Replacement of defective and/or older-model equipment will reduce downtime for employees and equipment, as well as improve operational efficiency. Increasing materials flow by installing new materials handling systems will eliminate bottlenecks and yield a greater output. Reducing damage to materials, by better handling methods and procedures, will decrease material shortages and improve customer service. There are countless other ways to improve productivity through materials handling innovations.

MATERIALS HANDLING PRINCIPLES

The College-Industry Council on Material Handling Education (CIC-MHE) is an independent organization that prepares and provides information, materials, and activities to support materials handling education and research. CIC-MHE, supported by the Material Handling Institute, Inc., developed 20 principles of materials handling. *Webster's New World Dic-*

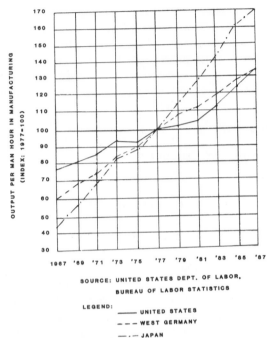

SOURCE: UNITED STATES DEPT. OF LABOR,
BUREAU OF LABOR STATISTICS

LEGEND:
_____ UNITED STATES
_ _ _ WEST GERMANY
—.— JAPAN

Figure 9-3. U.S. productivity is increasing but lags behind that of other industrial nations.

tionary defines a principle as "a fundamental truth, law, doctrine, or motivating force, upon which others are based." These 20 principles represent experience accumulated by practitioners over a long period of time. In many respects they are simply applications of common sense.

The CIC-MHE principles can be applied as building blocks for the analysis and design of any new facility or the redesign of an existing facility. These fundamentals are an invaluable resource for materials management personnel seeking materials handling design improvements. It has been said that anyone indoctrinated with the 20 principles can walk through almost any existing building and develop beneficial short-term and long-term improvements.

1. Orientation principle: *Study the system relationships thoroughly prior to preliminary planning in order to identify existing methods and problems, and physical and economic constraints, and to establish future requirements and goals.* Typical applications of the orientation principle are:
   A. Review the entire facility from the point of incoming materials through various operations and outgoing shipments to be familiar with all existing materials handling equipment and practices.

B. Use basic analytical techniques, such as from–to charts, flow process charts, and product quantity charts to determine potential improvement areas.

C. Determine management's long-term plans regarding new products, changes to existing products, forecasted customer demand, and financial constraints.

2. Planning principle: *Establish a plan to include basic requirements, desirable options, and the consideration of contingencies for all materials handling and storage activities.* Typical applications of the planning principle are:

A. Provide appropriate staging areas for temporary storage of materials at strategic locations.

B. Design materials handling systems that provide for accumulation, where operational volumes can vary.

C. Consider providing manual overrides for automated operations in case of equipment failure.

3. Systems principle: *Integrate those handling and storage activities that are economically viable into a coordinated system of operation including receiving, inspection, storage, production, assembly, packaging, warehousing, shipping, and transportation.* Typical applications of the systems principle are:

A. Avoid rehandling by using the materials handling system to transport materials through as many operations as possible.

B. Coordinate handling activities with suppliers, customers, and transportation carriers.

C. Provide alternative handling methods for emergency situations.

4. Unit load principle: *Handle product in as large a unit as practical.* Typical applications of the unit load Principle are:

A. Consider development of optimum-size unit loads to increase productivity of equipment, storage space, and personnel.

B. Design unit loads for safe storage and handling.

C. Provide suppliers with specifications for unit loads that are desirable for internal receiving, storage, and dispersal.

5. Space utilization principle: *Make effective utilization of all cubic space.* Typical applications of the space utilization principle are:

A. Use pallet racks, stacking frames, and other materials handling equipment to provide higher storage.

B. Design corrugated cartons to allow use of floor storage space at maximum heights, without damage to materials.

C. Reinforce floors to allow heavier floor loading and provide for higher stacking of materials.

6. Standardization principle: *Standardize handling methods and equipment wherever possible.* Typical applications of the standardization principle are:

A. Establish and adhere to standard container sizes.

B. Determine and specify standard equipment specifications in order to reduce spare parts inventories and decrease training time for maintenance personnel and operators.

C. Develop written procedures that provide standard methods for all handling activities.

7. Ergonomic principle: *Recognize human capabilities and limitations by designing materials handling equipment and procedures for effective interaction with the people using the system.* Typical applications of the ergonomic principle are:

A. Reduce load sizes or use mechanized equipment whenever loads are too heavy for manual handling.

B. Select materials handling equipment that provides readily accessible controls and gauges that can be easily seen.

C. Design materials handling systems that reduce employee body movements to reduce fatigue and injury.

8. Energy principle: *Include energy consumption of the materials handling systems and materials handling procedures when making comparisons or preparing economic justifications.* Typical applications of the energy principle are:

A. Reduce the amount of energy required for heating building areas by employing automated storage retrieval systems (AS/RS).

B. Establish a preventive maintenance program to assure equipment operating at peak efficiency and to reduce energy costs.

C. Eliminate heat loss by sealing gaps around overhead dock doors and insulating the doors.

9. Ecology principle: *Minimize adverse effects on the environment when selecting materials handling equipment and procedures.* Typical applications of the ecology principle are:

A. Select materials handling equipment for enclosed operations that does not generate dangerous fumes.

B. Design materials handling systems that conform to OSHA (Occupational Safety and Health Act) sound level regulations.

C. Establish housekeeping procedures and regulations to provide a good employee environment.

10. Mechanization principle: *Mechanize the handling process where feasible to increase efficiency and economy in the handling of materials.* Typical applications of the mechanization principle are:

A. Use wire guidance systems for narrow-aisle trucks to reduce operator driving activities.

B. Reduce employee fatigue and increase productivity by using mechanized materials handling equipment instead of manual handling.

C. Avoid excessive mechanization or automation.

11. Flexibility principle: *Use methods and equipment that can perform a variety of tasks under a variety of operating conditions.* Typical applications of the flexibility principle are:
   A. Employ random-path flow conveyors where a variety of products can be assembled on the same line, at the same time.
   B. Use wire containers, which can contain a variety of materials, can be stacked to high levels, and can be stored in racks.
   C. Recognize the flexibility afforded by lift trucks that use a variety of attachments.

12. Simplification principle: *Simplify handling by eliminating, reducing, or combining unnecessary movements and/or equipment.* Typical applications of the simplification principle are:
   A. Utilize basic industrial engineering methods for motion economy.
   B. Develop materials handling procedures and flows that eliminate rehandling.
   C. Minimize employee walking by strategic location of materials, equipment controls, etc.

13. Gravity principle: *Utilize gravity to move material wherever possible, while respecting limitations concerning safety, product damage, and loss.* Typical applications of the gravity principle are:
   A. Employ gravity flow conveyors to provide nonpowered movement and FIFO materials rotation.
   B. Use roller conveyors, wheel conveyors, chutes, etc., between operations.
   C. Use spiral chutes to move materials between floors.

14. Safety principle: *Provide safe materials handling equipment and methods that follow existing safety codes and regulations in addition to accrued experience.* Typical applications of the safety principle are:
   A. Develop, promulgate, and enforce safety rules, regulations, and work methods.
   B. Inspect equipment regularly to ensure that safety devices are operating as desired.
   C. Maintain aisles that are unobstructed, without debris and wet or oily conditions.

15. Computerization principle: *Consider computerization in materials handling and storage systems, when circumstances warrant, for improved material and information control.* Typical applications of the computerization principle are:
   A. Use computer-controlled automated guided vehicle systems (AGVS) for automatic routing and positioning and to provide efficient materials flow.
   B. Employ computers to generate directive information to mecha-

nized order picker operations, using video display and keyboard consoles on board the truck.

C. Integrate various islands of automation by means of conveyor transfer and storage using programmable controllers.

16. Systems flow principle: *Integrate data flow with the physical material flow in handling and storage.* Typical applications of the systems flow principle are:

A. Use move tickets to provide manual control systems, where applicable, to maintain information regarding materials movement and storage.

B. Employ AS/RS systems for both automated materials movement and inventory control.

C. Design automated routing of parts from one work station to another and maintain accurate production and inventory records through the use of automatic identification systems.

17. Layout principle: *Prepare an operation sequence and equipment layout for all viable system solutions; then select the alternative system that best integrates efficiency and storage.* Typical applications of the layout principle are:

A. Identify major objectives and factors for the materials handling system to provide standards for comparison of alternative solutions.

B. Utilize the input of others in generating viable alternative layout designs.

C. Apply quantitative techniques such as queuing theory and simulation to evaluate, compare, and test the feasibility of alternative solutions.

18. Cost principle: *Compare the economic justification of alternative solutions in equipment and methods on the basis of economic effectiveness as measured by expense per unit handled.* Typical applications of the cost principle are:

A. Select a common, convenient, standard unit to ensure equitable comparisons.

B. Use the economic justification for the selected alternative solution as a basis for future audit.

C. Recognize that maximum economy in expense per unit handled is not always the overriding goal, as in the case of need for higher production and safer working conditions.

19. Maintenance principle: *Prepare a plan for preventive maintenance and scheduled repairs on all materials handling equipment.* Typical applications of the maintenance principle are:

A. Require daily inspection of equipment by operators using easily completed check sheets.

B. Provide adequate maintenance facilities and qualified personnel.

C. Maintain maintenance records for individual pieces of materials handling equipment.

20. Obsolescence principle: *Prepare a long-range and economically sound policy for replacement of obsolete equipment and methods with special consideration to after-tax life-cycle costs.* Typical applications of the obsolescence principle are:

A. Establish a company policy regarding replacement of materials handling equipment.

B. Develop a yearly budget for replacement of materials handling equipment.

C. Do not allow supervisors to fall into the habit of "string saving," continuing to keep older, less productive equipment.

MATERIALS HANDLING PROBLEM ANALYSIS

Many aspects of a total materials management system depend upon and are affected by materials handling. Closely observed, materials handling problems are actually a class of engineering systems design problems. Handling systems are not isolated entities, but in most cases form the structure that ties together all the interrelated segments of an operating system.[10]

Plant layout and materials handling are intimately related. Plant layout is responsible for the physical arrangement of all aspects of a facility; so any analysis of materials handling problems must include plant layout considerations. In many respects the total industrial or commercial facility can be compared to a living organism (see Figure 9-4). The different parts of the anatomy are different components of the facility.[11]

Problem Definition

Materials handling problems must be clearly identified so they can be solved. A review of existing operations is made, beginning with receiving activities and continuing through all operations, until final shipment. The observer constantly asks the standard industrial engineering "why" questions: what, where, when, who, and how? A check sheet can be used to stimulate ideas and for notations. Figure 9-5 is a checklist of materials handling constraints used when reviewing existing operations. Ray Bartlett, a materials handling authority, refers to constraints as "no-no's" and "yes-yes's," to differentiate between aspects of buildings and materials that are allowable and those that are not, in the design of materials handling systems. Constraints must be considered in every systems design for the end result to be effective. Ignoring any of the no-no's can lead to a

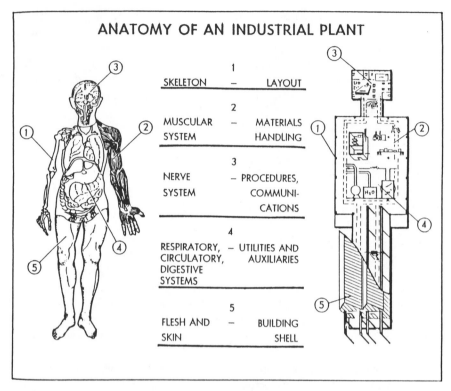

Figure 9-4. Comparison of an industrial facility with a human body. (Source: Richard Muther and Lee Hales, *Systematic Planning of Industrial Facilities,* Vol. I, Management & Industrial Research Publications, Kansas City, Missouri, 1979, pp. 2-3.)

nonoperative system in a worst-case situation, or at least result in inefficient operations.

The individual reviewing operations, using checklists as aids, should realize that a "yes" does not necessarily mean that a problem exists; it may well be that the symptom of a problem is discovered. Only further study and good judgment will determine if the problem is real, and if it is worthwhile to pursue a solution. A clear definition of each problem should be developed and reviewed. The scope and the objectives of each study must be defined in order to control resolution efforts.

Analytical Techniques

Reliable information is the foundation of sound decision making; so the data collection and analysis phase of problem solving is very important.

MATERIALS HANDLING CONSTRAINTS CHECK LIST			
FACILITY _____ DEPT./AREA _____			
OBSERVER _____ DATE _____			
POTENTIAL CONSTRAINTS	**CHECK**		**COMMENTS**
	YES	**NO**	
1. FLOOR LOAD CAPACITY			
2. ELEVATOR SIZE & CAPACITY			
3. FRAGILE MATERIAL			
4. FIRE CODE STORAGE HEIGHTS			
5. HAZARDOUS MATERIALS			
6. SECURITY REQUIREMENTS FOR ITEMS SUBJECT TO PILFERAGE			
7. TEMPERATURE CONTROL			
8. SIZE OF DOOR OPENINGS			
9. FLOOR CONDITION			
10. OBSTRUCTIONS			

Figure 9-5. Materials handling constraints checklist.

Development of relevant data is often viewed as a tiresome, unpopular task; but the determination of a worthwhile solution depends upon conscientious efforts at this point. Data collection is a costly process, in terms of both labor costs and time. It may not be reasonable to devote $10,000 for expenses and ten months of time to an analysis that will save $15,000. Decisions must be made concerning which existing data are available and pertinent, and what new information should be obtained.

Worthwhile data can be derived by using both graphs and operations research analytical techniques. Information sources are extensive, and include the following:

1. Industrial engineering standards
2. Operational data
3. Management personnel
4. Accounting department
5. Marketing department
6. Engineering department
7. Equipment supplier
8. Handbooks

From–To Chart. The from–to chart (see Figure 9-6) is a matrix used to collect and summarize information regarding material movement between related activities. It can be used for many purposes, including establishing material flow patterns, comparing alternative flow patterns, pinpointing bottlenecks, and determining candidates for mechanization and automation.

Flow Process Chart. The flow process chart is a step-by-step record of activities performed to accomplish a task (see Figure 9-7). Symbols are used to indicate which of four categories (operation, transport, inspect, or storage) the individual activities pertain to. The flow process chart is useful for analysis and for determining improvements such as combining operations, eliminating unnecessary handling, simplifying the method, or changing the sequence or routing.

Flow Diagram. The flow diagram is a graphical record of the steps in a process, similar to a flow process chart, except that the symbols are superimposed upon a layout of the area being studied (see Figure 9-8). It is useful for obtaining a macro perspective on the entire activity. The flow diagram can help detect potential improvements, explain changes, and act as a supplement to the flow process chart.

Product Quantity (PQ) Chart. The product quantity chart is a graphical record of various products, parts, or materials produced or used for a

FROM \ TO	A	B	C	D	E	F	TOTALS
A		15		20	5	4	44
B	2		5	8	10	4	29
C				9		12	21
D	10		6			9	24
E		12	18				30
F	8		15				24
TOTALS	20	27	44	37	15	29	172 / 172

FROM-TO CHART

Facility _____   Dept./Area _____

Observer _____   Date _____

Figure 9-6. From-to chart.

particular time period. Quantities should be related to standard unit loads. The PQ chart can be developed into a curve (see Figure 9-9). Typically this curve indicates items that are fast-movers (A), medium-movers (B), and slow-movers (C). The A's may be candidates for automated or highly mechanized material handling, the B's for mechanized handling, and the C's for manual handling. Some C's may have the potential for further grouping, which would make them candidates for mechanized handling.

Simulation. Because many materials handling problems and their various solutions are extensive and complicated, special analytical techniques have been developed to simplify their treatment. Simulation, one of the most popular, allows the analyst to perform experiments with a computer model that represents the proposed design. Monte Carlo simulation is most applicable to handling problems because it uses random number generators to develop sample data. The computer generates a series of occurrences that have the same statistical characteristics as the system being studied. This paper analysis is much simpler, faster, and less costly than installing a materials handling system and then trying to correct deficiencies.

Part Name	Automotive Transmission	Part No.	101	Date	
Process	Audible Test	Dept.	Ind. Eng.	Analyst	REM

◯ = Operation   ⇨ = Transportation   D = Storage   ☐ = Inspection

_____Present_____ Method

Symbol	Description	Distance Moved	P.U. & L.D.	How Moved
⮕1	Load overhead conveyor		1	Man
⮕2	On overhead conveyor	189		Power
⮕3	To roller conveyor	3'	1	Man
◯1	Fill with grease			
⮕4	On roller conveyor	4'		Gravity
D1	On roller conveyor			
⮕5	To test stand	4'	1	Man
□1	For noises			
⮕6	To roller conveyor	5'	1	Man
⮕7	Down roller conveyor	4'		Gravity
D2	On roller conveyor			
⮕8	To drain rack	5'	1	Man
◯2	Remain drain plug; place protector tube; drain; replace plug			
⮕9	To bench	7'	1	Man
◯3	Tighten plug			
⮕10	Shove along bench	5'		Man
D3	On bench			
⮕11	Shove along bench	6'		Man
D4	On bench			
◯4	Place gearshift dust seal grease front and rear face			
⮕12	Load on overhead conveyor	4'		Man
⮕13	To paint booth	20'		Power

Figure 9-7. Flow process chart. (From: *Productivity Management* by Gorden K. C. Chen and Robert E. McGarrah. Copyright © 1982 by CBS College Publishing. Reprinted by permission of CBS College Publishing.)

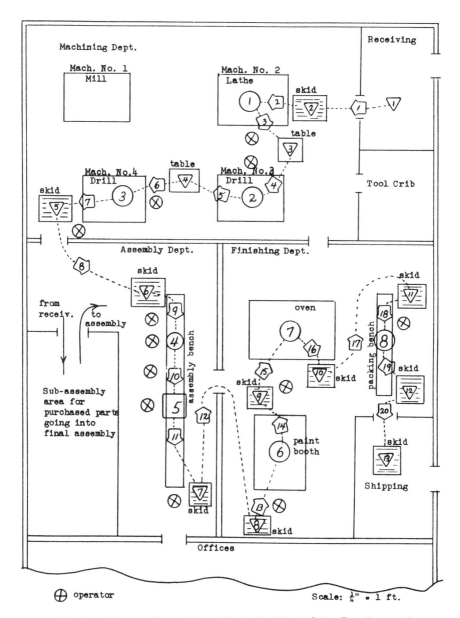

Figure 9-8. Flow diagram. (Source: James M. Apple, *Material Handling Systems Design.* Copyright © 1972 John Wiley & Sons, Inc. Reprinted by permission of John Wiley & Sons, Inc.)

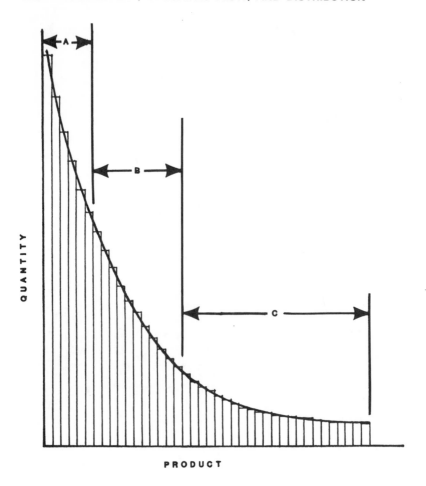

Figure 9-9. Product quantity (PQ) chart.

Simulation has a wide range of applications in solving materials handling problems. One company, for example, used it for monorail systems design. The performance of complex monorail systems is affected by many variables—changes in schedules, production queues, and processing times; carrier routings and travel times; and delays at converging paths. After computer simulation was used to determine bottlenecks where carriers would stack up, modifications were made that improved system performance.[12] Simulation is also being used to design AS/RS facilities; a computer study can develop critical design factors such as optimum height, number of aisles, and conveyor design. The system then can be tested for existing business levels as well as forecasts of future demand.

Waiting Line Analysis. Waiting line analysis, or *queuing theory,* has broad application in materials handling problems. It develops information regarding queues at various locations in the system and the amount of time that will be wasted under varying conditions. Whenever something must wait because of the randomness of another entity, waiting line analysis may be utilized to determine the following:[13]

1. The average length of the line.
2. The average number of units in a line.
3. The average length of time spent in line.
4. The average length of time spent in the system.

Waiting line analysis has been applied to the design of complex food distribution center conveyor systems to eliminate bottlenecks in the system. Other applications include the study of common carriers being loaded and unloaded at truck docks, to determine the number of docks required. Incoming materials waiting for inspection can be reviewed to determine the need for longer buffer conveyors, additional inspection stations, and different quality control techniques.

Selection and Justification of Solutions

Whenever there is more than one feasible solution to a problem, a quantitative comparison of the approaches is needed. Because of the large expenditures associated with these projects, a thorough understanding of materials handling factors is essential. Economic analysis is critical in determining the best solution to a problem. It is also important in preparing a justification of capital expenditures for consideration and approval by upper management. Basic methods of cost comparison are discussed below.

Payback Period. The most commonly used method for economic analysis, payback period is the easiest method to compute and understand. It computes the time period required for estimated project savings to equal the investment. A serious shortcoming is the assumption that one alternative is better than another because it pays for itself more rapidly. For example, system A's payoff period is two years, but the life expectancy of the system is only four years. System B may be a better investment, in spite of a three-year payback, because it will continue to operate and produce earnings for ten years. The payback period method is a good screening device to select high-profit alternatives and reject alternatives of limited potential benefit.

Return on Investment (ROI). The ROI method of analyzing alternative costs is also called the *accounting method* because its concepts are used in conventional accounting practice. Unlike the payback period method, it takes into consideration the equipment's useful life. Normally it relates net profit after taxes and depreciation to the total investment, thus indicating what each alternative will earn with respect to the investment.

Discounted Cash Flow (DCF). Another common method of evaluating alternatives, discounted cash flow computes the total present worth of cash flow over the project's life, using an interest rate equal to the company's minimum required rate of return on investment. The term discounted refers to present worth calculations. This method considers the present value of money after interest payments have been added to it over a period of time. Basically, it finds the interest rate that discounts future earnings of the project alternative down to a present value equal to the project cost.

MAPI. MAPI refers to the Machinery and Allied Products Institute, which sponsored the development of this method. The MAPI technique measures how a company will profit with or without the proposed equipment or system. It uses an adjusted after-tax rate-of-return criterion. A systematic calculation of various factors is made. Charts and forms are available from the Machinery and Allied Products Institute to help simplify the mechanics of calculation.

Comparing Methods—Payback, Return on Investment, and Discounted Cash Flow

The following comparison is from Raymond A. Kulwiec's *Basics of Material Handling,* Published by the Material Handling Institute, Inc. This example is for the purpose of illustrating basic methods of cost comparison. The information provided does not necessarily reflect current tax laws including but not limited to the tax rate, depreciation rates, and availability of investment credits.

Consider the following situation: A proposed system for updating an existing operation requires the purchase of equipment at a total cost of $100,000. The equipment is estimated to have a useful life of ten years, with no salvage value. An annual cost savings of $25,000 is anticipated from the new system. A 10% investment tax credit can be used. In other words, up to 10% of the cost of the new equipment can be deducted from applicable income taxes. A tax rate of 48% is assumed. Three different economic measures of feasibility will be used to evaluate the proposed project.

Payback. Data for the payback calculations are illustrated in Figure 9-10. Years are shown from the year of purchase, 0, to the last year of operation, 10, across the top. All figures in parentheses are negative values. For example, the $100,000 purchase in year 0 represents a negative cash flow or outflow. The 10% investment credit reduces the outflow to a net of $90,000. The first operating year's savings of $25,000 is a cash inflow. Federal tax on the savings is 48% of $25,000, or $12,000.

Another tax factor that must be considered is depreciation. For the payback analysis, an 8-year double declining balance method is used. (In this method, a declining periodic charge for depreciation is made throughout the life of the project, with greater amounts being taken during the early years.) In year one, the depreciation is 25% of $100,000, or $25,000. Taxes are reduced by 48% of this figure, or $12,000. This tax reduction is considered a cash inflow. Thus, the net result for the first year is a cash inflow of $25,000. The cumulative cash inflow is shown as ($90,000) + $25,000, or ($65,000).

The same elements are operative in year two, except that the depreciation inflow has decreased. At the end of year five, the cumulative cash flow is a positive inflow of $12,000. At this point the net savings have exceeded the equipment investment by $12,000. The payback period is therefore somewhere between years four and five, and is interpolated at about 4⅓ years.

Return on Investment. Data for this method are illustrated in Figure 9-11. Depreciation for the ROI calculation is straight line, meaning that equal depreciation charges are taken during each year of the project life. Also, the investment tax credit does not appear in the calculations. (When ROI is used, investment tax credit generally appears in a tax expense account.) The year's depreciation charge of $10,000 is deducted from the savings of $25,000 to yield an operating income of $15,000. The 48% of tax of $7,200 is subtracted from this figure, leaving a net of $7,800.

Average capital investment for the year is shown in the final column. It is the average of the net investment in equipment at the beginning and

Year	0	1	2	3	4	5	6	7	8	9	10
Purchase	(100)										
Investment credit	10										
Cost savings		25	25	25	25	25	25	25	25	25	25
Tax effect—											
Cost savings		(12)	(12)	(12)	(12)	(12)	(12)	(12)	(12)	(12)	(12)
Depreciation		12	9	7	5	4	4	4	3		
Net cash flow	(90)	25	22	20	18	17	17	17	16	13	13
Cumulative	(90)	(65)	(43)	(23)	(5)	12	29	46	62	75	88
Payback	Approximately 4⅓ years										

Figure 9-10. Payback period. (Source: Raymond A. Kulwiec, *Basics of Material Handling,* published by The Material Handling Institute, Inc., 1981, p. 42.)

Year	Income	Straight-line depreciation	Income tax at 48%	Net return	Average Investment
1	25	10	7.2	7.8	95
2	25	10	7.2	7.8	85
3	25	10	7.2	7.8	75
4	25	10	7.2	7.8	65
5	25	10	7.2	7.8	55
6	25	10	7.2	7.8	45
7	25	10	7.2	7.8	35
8	25	10	7.2	7.8	25
9	25	10	7.2	7.8	15
10	25	10	7.2	7.8	5
Total	250	100	72	78	500

Return on investment is 78 ÷ 500 = 15.6%

Figure 9-11. Return on investment (ROI). (Source: Raymond A. Kulwiec, *Basics of Material Handling*, published by The Material Handling Institute, Inc., 1981, p. 42.)

end of the year. For example, the net investment is $100,000 at the beginning of the first year, and $90,000 at the end after the $10,000 depreciation charge is deducted, so the average investment is $95,000. Total return for the ten-year period is $78,000, and the total average investment is $500,000. The return on investment is $78,000, and the total average investment is $500,000. The return on investment is $78,000 divided by $500,000 or 15.6%. In order for the project to be acceptable, this figure must meet the firm's minimum ROI criterion.

Discounted Cash Flow. Data for this method are illustrated in Figure 9-12. This approach uses the same basic data as payback. The double-declining-balance method of depreciation also is used, as is the 10% investment tax credit. Cash outflow in year 0 is $90,000. In year one, there is a net cash inflow of $25,000. In year two it is $22,000, and in the tenth year it is $13,000. With the depreciation method used, the total tax depreciation charges have been deducted in the first eight years, so no tax savings are realized from that source in the final two years.

Year	0	1	2	3	4	5	6	7	8	9	10
Purchase	(100)										
Investment credit	10										
Cost savings		25	25	25	25	25	25	25	25	25	25
Tax effect —											
Cost savings		(12)	(12)	(12)	(12)	(12)	(12)	(12)	(12)	(12)	(12)
Depreciation		12	9	7	5	4	4	4	3		
Net cash flow	(90)	25	22	20	18	17	17	17	16	13	13
Discount factor	1.00	.85	.73	.62	.53	.46	.39	.33	.28	.24	.21
Present value — cash flow	(90)	21	16	12	10	8	7	6	4	3	3
Cumulative	(90)	(69)	(53)	(41)	(31)	(23)	(16)	(10)	(6)	(3)	-0-

The discount factor above is 17% annually.

Figure 9-12. Discounted cash flow. (Source: Raymond A. Kulwiec, *Basics of Material Handling*, published by The Material Handling Institute, Inc., 1981, p. 42.)

The total net cash inflow for the ten operating years is $178,000. A discount factor (percentage equivalent to an interest rate) must now be found that will produce present values for the cash inflows that will approximately equal the initial outflow of $90,000. Determined basically by trial-and-error procedures, this figure will represent the rate of return on the cash flows over the life of the equipment.

An annual discount factor of 17% produces the numbers shown in the line labeled *Present value — cash flow*. Note that the total of the present value numbers for the ten operating years equals $90,000. The cumulative total, as shown on the bottom line, is 0.

When different projects are being compared with the DCF method, the one having the highest discount factor will be most favorable. For instance, if the cost savings were $31,000 annually instead of $25,000, the net cash flow would be about $3,000 higher each year. A higher discount factor would then be needed to reduce the cash flows to a cumulative present value of $90,000.

TYPICAL EQUIPMENT AND APPLICATIONS

Materials handling problem analysis normally involves some type of equipment. Materials management personnel responsible for developing solutions must become acquainted with the large and constantly increasing types of available materials handling equipment and their application. Frequently, an individual piece of equipment cannot accomplish the desired results. A beneficial solution often requires various pieces of equipment that together comprise an integrated system. Therefore, the designer must have knowledge of individual pieces of equipment, optimum use of the equipment, and how to integrate one piece of equipment with other. Flexibility is an essential feature of handling equipment. Equipment may be required to move materials over many different paths, accommodate significant changes in sales volume, and handle a variety of products. Flexibility has its trade-offs. For example, special-purpose equipment can lower unit costs, but it may not be able to handle a variety of products or apply to different applications. Current trends in equipment provide low-cost handling as well as flexibility. For instance, automatic guided vehicle systems have increasing application in conventional plants and warehouse operations and also serve as an integral part of flexible manufacturing systems.[14]

Conveyors

One of the most widely used types of materials handling equipment is the conveyor, partly because of the large selection available. Conveyors provide for continuous or intermittent materials flow from point to point over fixed paths. There are many basic types of conveyors. The stationary conveyor consists of rollers, wheels, or balls over which material moves. These conveyors can be either power-driven or gravity types. Conveyors with moving surfaces use power to move materials along using surface flow. Typical moving surfaces include belts, chains, slats, and buckets. Underfloor tows move wheeled vehicles by mechanically powered tracks. Pneumatic tubes move materials by pressure or vacuum.[15] Examples of conveyors are shown in Figure 9-13.

Conveyors are adaptable to many applications. They can transport almost any size, shape, or weight of material, either as individual items or grouped in a container. Material can be moved at floor level, overhead, vertically, on an incline, or spirally. Some transport systems load in sequence, whereas others allow one load to bypass another to change routings, or to shunt materials out of the main movement path without otherwise impeding the flow. Figure 9-14 presents an example of the many conveyor applications within an automated factory.

Figure 9-13. Illustration of power belt, gravity skate wheel, and gravity roller conveyors. (Courtesy Rapistan, a Lear Siegler company.)

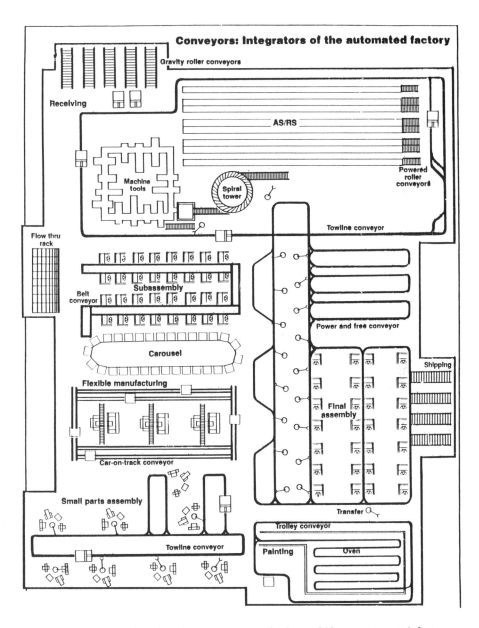

Figure 9-14. Illustration of typical conveyor applications within an automated factory. (Source: "Conveyor Systems," *Modern Material Handling,* Aug. 5, 1983, p. 51, copyright 1983 by Cahners Publishing Company, Divison of Reed Publishing USA.)

Industrial Trucks

Trucks, another kind of commonly used materials handling equipment, are powered or manually operated vehicles used to move materials intermittently, in a variable path. The most popular type, a fork lift, offers great versatility through the use of attachments, which enable it to handle tasks beyond basic fork handling. Some common attachments are roll clamps, slipsheet handling, cranes, rotating forks, and rams. A manually operated truck is not economical for long-distance movement; it is primarily effective for loading and unloading carriers, storage, and movement between operations.

The wide variety of available trucks can be used for all types of facility layouts. Industrial trucks include manual pallet trucks, walkies (low lift and high lift), counterbalanced, narrow-aisle with outriggers, turret-type side loaders, tow tractors, order pickers, and personnel carriers. Trucks are powered by electric motors, gasoline, LPG, or diesel-fueled engines. Examples of industrial trucks are shown in Figure 9-15.

Cranes, Monorails, and Hoists

Cranes, monorails, and hoists are used for vertical, intermittent movement of materials between points within an area defined by supporting rails. Hoists are the lifting mechanism. Monorails have a single overhead track that provides a runway for the hoist. Monorail systems allow vertical

(a)

Figure 9-15. Industrial trucks. Standup rider, counterbalance truck (a); standup rider with outriggers (b); and highlift walkie (c). (Courtesy The Raymond Corporation, Greene, N.Y. 13778.)

(b)

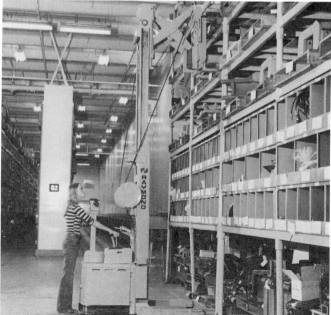

(c)

Figure 9-15. (continued)

movement of varying size and weight materials over a fixed area, and a monorail network can provide movement to various locations. Bridge cranes utilize two supporting rails that allow movement of materials in an area bounded by the rails. They are effective for handling materials over a broad area such as a bay, series of bays, or department. The jib crane has a horizontal beam, pivoted on one end, that is supported by a cantilever mast; it can move materials vertically in an area bounded by the horizontal beam's arc. Jib cranes can cover up to 360 degrees of a circle. Figure 9-16 gives examples of cranes and hoists.

Robots

The Robot Institute of America defines a robot as "a reprogrammable, multi-functional manipulator designed to move material, parts, tools, or specialized devices through variable programmed motions for the performance of a variety of tasks." Robots have the ability to duplicate the move-

(a)

Figure 9-16. Jib crane (a) and bridge crane (b). (Courtesy Abell-Howe Company.)

(b)

Figure 9-16. (continued)

ments of the human arm, while lifting loads weighing hundreds of pounds and following computer instructions. They are able to handle materials of various sizes, shapes, weights, and degrees of fragility, and some have visualization capability. Robots can be electrically or hydraulically powered, and controlled by simple or sophisticated programmable controllers, high-speed microprocessors, or minicomputers. They require little maintenance and are rated 98 percent or higher uptime.[16] Materials handling applications for robots have been increasing rapidly. Some of the uses for robots include palletizing, depalletizing, transfer between conveyors, movement between machines and conveyors, and transfer to and from carousels. Figure 9-17 shows a robot application.

Automated Guided Vehicle Systems (AGVS)

AGVS vehicles are battery-powered guided units that are equipped to follow a predefined, flexible guide path while towing or carrying a load. Their control system allows for a virtually unlimited number of computer-controlled operations to load, unload, accelerate, stop, start, and select

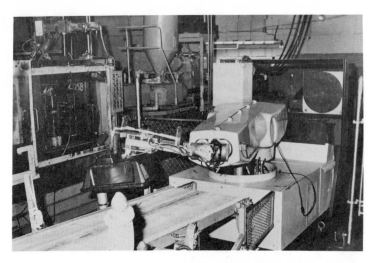

Figure 9-17. Industrial robot. (Courtesy of UNIMATION Incorporated, a Westinghouse Company.)

travel paths, without human intervention. The ease with which these vehicles can be altered and expanded places them among the most flexible materials handling equipment for the automated factory or warehouse.[17] In addition to providing flexible handling capabilities, the system offers management real-time-based information for decision making. Figure 9-18 shows an AGVS application.

Automated Storage Retrieval Systems (AS/RS)

The concept of a completely automated warehouse has been a reality for many years. In the United States, high-rise storage units are normally 100-foot structures; in Europe they reach 120 feet. Typically, the AS/RS consists of vertical storage racks constructed of structural steel. Narrow aisles allow a storage and retrieval machine to travel back and forth. The machine has the capability to move loads in and out of racks. It is remotely controlled by computer, and can also be manually controlled. There are many advantages provided by AS/RS units. Buildings may have the rack support walls and roof which allows management to expense the cost, rather than incur a long period for depreciation, which reduces short-term tax costs. In comparison with the conventional fork trucks used for warehouse operations, the AS/RS is designed to increase material handling productivity, maximize storage density per square foot of floor space,

Figure 9-18. Automated guided vehicle system. (Courtesy Mannesman Demag Corporation.)

reduce labor costs, provide accurate information, and reduce damage and pilferage. The major disadvantage is the high cost of an AS/RS installation. However, many companies have found that AS/RS units will provide a worthwhile return on their investment.

Automatic Identification Systems (AIS)

In these systems intelligent sensors provide the basis for accounting, tracking, and movement control for automated operations in modern facilities. These systems relate information and materials flow to obtain the benefits of total integration. Basically, a code is used to identify material, and, in many cases, materials received from suppliers already have been coded. The coded materials can be automatically tracked and moved by reading devices through all required operations until shipment, while information is maintained on location, quantity, quality, processing, and so on. Other benefits of AIS include reduced waiting time, more accurate inventory control records, and reduced inventory levels. Applications of these systems are increasing, following the adoption, in 1981, of the Uniform Container Symbol for distribution, and implementation, on July 1, 1982, of the LOGMARS program by the U.S. Department of Defense. (LOG-MARS requires each outer container shipped to any U.S. Armed Services to contain a bar code and an optical character code.) The basic types of automatic identification systems are bar codes, optical character recogni-

Figure 9-19. Examples of automated identification systems. (Upper photo courtesy Cognex Corporation; lower photo courtesy Accu-Sort Systems, Inc.)

tion (OCR) magnetic stripes, vision systems, transponders, and voice recognition. Figure 9-19 shows some AIS systems.

Unitizing Equipment

A large variety of equipment is available for unitized materials handling. Bulk material or individual pieces may be packaged, contained, or placed on a surface (i.e., pallet) to provide for ease of movement and storage.

Figure 9-20. Pallet loads, containers, and stacking frames in storage rack. (Courtesy Ace Hardware Corporation.)

Advantages of unitized loads include reduced cost, maximum space utilization, and better materials flow. Pallets are one of the basic types of unitizing equipment; materials used in pallets include wood, plastic, and metal. Pallets allow stacking of individual materials to form a load. Containers, which are made of wire, plastic, metal, corrugated cartons, wood, or sheet metal, are used to retain materials. Some designs can be nested when empty or stacked for higher storage. Stacking frames, attached to pallets, are useful for load retention and for stacking one irregular or fragile unit load upon another. Strapping or wire provides a means to bind a load. Plastic, steel, and fiber commonly are used for this purpose. Another means of unitizing is film wrapping. In shrink-wrapping, plastic film is used to enclose a load; then heat is applied to form a tight load casing. Stretch wrapping uses plastic film to encase a load without the application of heat. Unitizing equipment is shown in Figure 9-20.

RELATIONSHIPS WITH OTHER MATERIALS MANAGEMENT SUBFUNCTIONS

Materials handling provides the essential flow of materials that enables individual materials management subfunctions to effectively accomplish their objectives. Whether the materials handling design function is a part of materials management or some other function (e.g., industrial engineering), communication between design personnel and other materials management subfunctions is very important. Some of the relationships are reviewed below.

Inventory Control

Inventory control is closely associated with materials handling, and should communicate contemplated changes in inventory levels that can affect storage system requirements. This is especially critical when large increases in inventory are anticipated, and materials handling design personnel must provide for the increased capacity. Inventory control should consider input from materials handling on optimum unit loads when determining requisition quantities. Incorporation of unit load quantities in inventory control planning will ensure minimum handling costs and maximum storage space utilization. Materials handling systems relate closely to inventory control's effort to minimize material levels. They can provide the throughput necessary for Just-In-Time and other reduced-inventory programs.

Production Control

Production control should cooperate with materials handling in determining unit load sizes and quantities, in order to facilitate disbursement to production operations and maximize the use of critical manufacturing space. Scheduling difficulties are often encountered because of bottlenecks. Materials handling designers can provide improvements that will solve some of these problems. The success of production control and inventory control systems such as MRP depends upon whether the handling and storage system is designed to complement the manufacturing plan. A well-known appliance manufacturer installed a highly sophisticated MRP system that failed to satisfy original expectations simply because management did not consider the importance of materials handling. They overlooked answers to critical questions such as: how are materials and supplies to be transported and moved from storage to point of use, how are they to be stored, and does the existing system have the capability to meet new requirements?[18]

Purchasing

Purchasing policies can affect inventory levels, which in turn have an effect upon materials handling methods and costs. Buyers can positively influence supplier delivery methods and schedules, as well as load configurations, which can improve handling. Purchasing should provide information to materials handling regarding new packaging materials and processes. Cooperatively, the two groups can develop packaging and unit loads that will improve protection for both receipts and shipments. Materials handling and purchasing should cooperate in the purchase of new handling equipment and disposal of obsolete or deficient equipment. Their joint activity is especially critical for large and complex materials handling systems that are not purchased as turn-key (with one supplier responsible for providing the total system); non-turn-key systems require the purchase and delivery of many individual items. Purchase of materials handling equipment as individual components can considerably reduce the total costs involved, although other trade-offs can nullify these benefits. These trade-offs underscore the importance of the two groups working closely together in analyzing alternative plans.

Receiving and Stores

Receiving and stores can indicate areas where new materials handling design projects are needed. They also should provide input into the development of any new handling system to ensure that it is user-oriented. Receiving and stores play a critical role in the initial stages of installing and implementing any new handling system. Their cooperation, in complying with procedures and assisting with debugging (corrective action), can contribute to the success of a new installation. Materials handling is an integral core activity of receiving and stores operations; it is essential to have the optimum materials handling design for activities such as unloading, sorting, storing, retrieving, and transporting. There are numerous applications for both mechanized and automated systems in receiving and stores operations.

Physical Distribution

Physical distribution includes a broad range of operations involving the storage, order picking, packing, and shipment of finished goods; and materials handling is an integral part of each of these activities. Like receiving and stores, physical distribution operations primarily involve materials handling activities. The design and handling of unit loads for shipment to customers requires cooperative action by the two groups. Customers also have substantial input regarding unit loads. Mechanized and automated handling designs are used effectively for storage, order picking, packing, and loading operations. Some of the current systems for automated picking of finished goods can select and assemble individual items (e.g., jars, cans, and containers) as well as full cases. Automated sortation systems can feed materials to conveyors that transport them directly into carriers.

RELATIONSHIPS WITH OTHER COMPANY FUNCTIONS

Materials handling represents a major portion of business costs, so there must be effective communication between the materials handling group and other company functions. A review of some of the common interdepartmental relationships follows.

Manufacturing

Manufacturing demands on materials handling capabilities are numerous. Production schedules, work standards, and goals cannot be met without suitable materials handling support. Materials handling is an essential force in minimizing costly downtime of both machines and labor. As manufacturing operations increasingly utilize high technology and automated equipment, they become more dependent upon sophisticated materials handling systems to provide reliable and timely material movement. In continuous production systems, materials handling is an integral element of the production process. High-technology manufacturing capability can be achieved only if the materials handling group has the ability to support it through state-of-the-art design.

Materials handling design personnel must have cooperation and communication from manufacturing in order to accomplish their supporting role. Manufacturing's short- and long-term plans must be transmitted to the materials handling group. Changes in product size, shape, weight, and so on, should be known in order for materials handling to provide suitable handling equipment. Also, any significant variations in volume requirements must be communicated to allow for appropriate changes in handling systems. Manufacturing should cooperate with materials handling in the design and implementation of new systems. The input of manufacturing is essential to the development of materials handling systems that satisfy production requirements.

Quality Assurance

Currently there is a strong emphasis on improving product quality. The quality assurance group requires teamwork from materials handling to accomplish this objective. Handling systems must be designed to minimize product damage in all stages of operations, starting with receiving and continuing through company processes, including shipment. Materials handling systems designed for inspection operations can be instrumental in reducing the time and cost of inspection. They provide for orderly work performance, and maintain the all-important flow of materials through inspection stations and areas. Inspection procedures can be enhanced by using efficient methods to move and identify materials.

Materials handling depends upon information from quality assurance in order to properly design a totally integrated handling system. The two groups can jointly determine locations and handling requirements for inspection, salvage, and repair stations. In some modern automated operations, inspection activities are included in the handling system. For example, a midwestern clothes distribution center uses laser scanning and automatic weighing to check incoming containers; these devices can detect merchandise errors and automatically convey containers to an inspection station.

Finance

Among its various objectives, finance must maintain accurate records and financial statements. Finance personnel rely on materials handling design employees for systems whose procedures and equipment will provide accurate inventory counts, give the correct location of materials, and minimize damage so that company assets shown in the balance sheet will be accurate. Materials handling improvements in package design and scanning devices can ensure the accuracy of inventory information, which in turn ensures the correctness of financial statements. Materials handling becomes a critical contributor to company profits, as reflected in the income statement, by developing and implementing cost-effective handling systems.

Materials handling needs the cooperation of finance to perform its function. Accounting information is essential for material handling programs. Cost studies and records must be accumulated to provide the data needed for intelligent assessment of alternative solutions and for justification of new systems as well as changes to existing systems. Materials handling requires the assistance of finance for such information as the preferred method(s) for cost comparison, current carrying cost percentage, and various tax consequences.

Marketing

Marketing is closely related to materials handling because marketing must obtain sufficient operating capacity, and be capable of achieving optimum throughput, to ensure timely customer shipments. Materials handling systems are critical to this objective. Marketing also needs package designs that are low-cost, protect the product, and perform as a merchandising tool. Customers often request that products be shipped in unit load configurations that complement their handling and storage operations. Materials handling can be termed an internal marketing "tool" in that it provides marketing with essential means to satisfy customers.

Materials handling, like all other groups within the company, depends on marketing for accurate sales forecasts, which are used as a basis for establishing quantity requirements. Many aspects of handling equipment decisions relate to volume; concerns include the degree of mechanization and automation, flexibility or fixed use of equipment, and permanency of operations. As sales volume increases, it is necessary to plan materials handling systems for new facilities and expansions to existing facilities. Materials handling must have close communication with marketing to provide fast, decisive responses to customer requirements.

Engineering

Various engineering groups have contact with materials handling. The design engineer needs input from materials handling about product design changes that may improve materials handling systems. For example, an electronics company was fabricating electrical contacts using a punch press, but the handling of individual pieces coming out of the press was time-consuming and caused considerable damage. Consultation with the design engineer produced a change in the contact design that allowed automatic collection, and this single change considerably improved materials handling operations. Industrial engineering also requires the cooperation of materials handling, with regard to material flow in developing a facility layout. Handling is a critical aspect of process and methods engineering in developing the workplace layout, work flow, and work standards.

Materials handling depends on information from engineering to properly develop its functional systems. Plans for new products should be communicated as early as possible so that materials handling can focus attention on required changes to existing equipment and/or new equipment needs. Industrial engineering supplies information on operational time and labor costs as a basis for comparing different handling systems. Plant engineering can make important contributions to the development of materials handling systems in the areas of equipment structure, installation, and maintenance. The more sophisticated handling systems, in particular, require plant engineering input during the design stage. For example, plant engineering should be included in all phases of an AS/RS program to ensure long-run success.

SUMMARY

Materials handling is basic to every business, and is an important activity throughout the organization. The subfunction is a vital part of total materials management. Just as the human body depends upon veins and arteries for its blood supply, an industrial or commercial facility requires a well-organized, integrated materials handling system to provide materials flow to all of its operations. History has recorded continual progress in materials handling, starting with such feats as the building of the Egyptian pyramids. Through the years new equipment and techniques have been developed. Current state-of-the-art handling technology is included in automated factories and warehouses.

As a company's operations become more complicated and business volume increases, materials handling must satisfy a myriad of demands. There are many significant objectives for materials handling in satisfying business requirements, a primary one being to minimize total handling costs. Because materials handling represents a large portion of total costs for most businesses, it is a prime area for cost reduction. Other materials handling objectives include providing integrated materials handling systems, improving working conditions, and improving productivity.

The College-Industry Council on Material Handling Education (CIC-MHE) developed 20 principles of materials handling. These building blocks can be very helpful in analyzing and designing improvements for new and existing facilities. The principles are an invaluable resource for both veteran engineers and individuals who have had little experience working with materials handling design. Some of the principles relate to planning, systems, unit load, space utilization, energy, mechanization, simplification, safety, and computerization.

Materials handling problem analysis is initiated by defining the problem. A review of existing operations will show where improvements are needed. Checklists can stimulate ideas during the review. The data collection and analysis phase is an essential part of problem solving. Various analytical techniques are useful in this activity, including from–to charts, flow process charts, simulation, and waiting line analysis. The selection and justification of a problem solution is the final task in problem resolution. An economic analysis normally is required to evaluate alternatives and justify company expenditures. Common methods for performing economic analysis include payback, return on investment, discounted cash flow, and MAPI.

Problem solutions will normally involve some type(s) of materials handling equipment. The experienced handling systems designer has knowledge of the various types of equipment that are available and how they are used in various applications. Among the equipment used for materials handling are conveyors, industrial trucks, cranes, monorails, hoists, robots, automated guided vehicle systems, automated storage retreival systems, automatic identification systems, and unitizing equipment. Each of these can be used individually or as part of a larger integrated handling system.

NOTES

1. Apple, *Materials Handling Systems Design*, p. 3.
2. Drucker, "Automation Payoffs Are Real," p. 14.
3. Allegri, *Materials Handling*, p. 1.
4. White, "Factory of Future Will Need Bridges between Its Islands of Automation," p. 62.
5. "Tight Controls and AS/RS Slash Inventory by 30%" and "Terminal on Truck Reduces In-Process Inventory by 50%," *Modern Materials Handling*, Jan. 20, 1982, pp. 58–61.
6. "Why We Specified a 105-Ft. AS/RS," *Modern Materials Handling*, Sept. 7, 1981, pp. 70–72.
7. Gilbreath, "Increasing Product Quality through Better Design of Materials Handling Procedures," p. 58.
8. Kroemer, "Back Injuries Can Be Avoided," p. 37.
9. Lindholm and Norstedt, *The Volvo Report*, pp. 63–66.
10. Thomas P. Cullinane and James A. Tompkins, 1981 American Institute of Industrial Engineers/Material Handling Institute, Inc., *Seminar Proceedings*.
11. Muther and Hales, *Systematic Planning of Industrial Facilities*, Vol. I, pp. 2–3.
12. "Monorails," *Modern Materials Handling*, Nov. 5, 1982, p. 59.
13. Thomas P. Cullinane and James A. Tompkins, 1981 American Institute of Industrial Engineers/Material Handling Institute, *Seminar Proceedings*.
14. Roywan, "Flexibility—How The Trade-Offs Are Changing," p. 35.
15. Kulwiec, *Materials Handling Handbook*, p. 1132.
16. Schwind, "Robots: A Flexible Solution for Tough, Unitizing Jobs," pp. 36–40.
17. Tompkins and Smith, "Keys to Developing Material Handling System for Automated Factory Are Listed," p. 52.
18. Shaver, "A Firm Hold on Material Handling," p. 45.

BIBLIOGRAPHY

"AGVS Provides Wang New User Benefits," *Transportation and Distribution*, Sept. 1987.
Allegri, Theodore H. Sr. *Materials Handling*. New York: Van Nostrand Reinhold Co., 1984.
Apple, James M. *Materials Handling Systems Design*. New York: The Ronald Press Co., 1972.
Ballakur, A. "Streamlining Material Flows for Just-In-Time Applications." *1986 Fall Industrial Engineering Conference Proceedings*, Institute of Industrial Engineers, Dec. 1986.
Drucker, Peter F. "Automation Payoffs Are Real." *Wall Street Journal*, Sept. 20, 1985.

Gilbreath, Sidney, III. "Increasing Product Quality through Better Design of Materials Handling Procedures." *Industrial Engineering,* July 1986.

Hill, J. M. "The Changing Profile of Material Handling and Controls," Parts 1 and 2. *Industrial Engineering,* Nov. and Dec. 1986.

Kroemer, K. H. E. "Back Injuries Can Be Avoided." *National Safety News,* Feb. 1980.

Kulwiec, Raymond. *Basics of Materials Handling.* Pittsburgh, Pennsylvania: The Material Handling Institute, 1981.

Kulwiec, Raymond A., ed. *Materials Handling Handbook.* New York: John Wiley and Sons, 1985.

Lindholm, Rolf, and Norstedt, Jan-Peder. *The Volvo Report.* Stockholm, Sweden: Swedish Employer's Confederation, 1975.

Muther, Richard, and Hales, Lee. *Systematic Planning of Industrial Facilities.* Vol. I. Kansas City, Missouri: Management & Industrial Research Publications, 1979.

Roywan, Mike. Editorial: "Flexibility—How the Trade-offs Are Changing." *Modern Materials Handling,* Sept. 20, 1983.

Schwind, Gene. "Robots: A Flexible Solution for Tough Unitizing Jobs." *Material Handling Engineering,* Sept. 1983.

Shaver, North C. "A Firm Hold on Material Handling." *Production and Inventory Review,* Nov. 1982.

Soltis, David J. "Using Automatic Identification Systems: Weakness and Future Trends." *Industrial Engineering,* Apr. 1985.

Tompkins, J. A. "The New IE Challenge: Integration of CIM Through Material Handling." *1986 Fall Industrial Engineering Conference Proceedings,* Institute of Industrial Engineers, Dec. 1986.

Tompkins, James A., and Smith, Jerry D., *The Warehouse Management Handbook,* New York: McGraw-Hill Book Co., 1988.

Tompkins, James A., and Smith, Jerry D. "Keys to Developing Material Handling System for Automated Factory Are Listed." *Industrial Engineering,* Sept. 1983.

White, John A. "Factory of Future Will Need Bridges between Its Islands of Automation." *Industrial Engineering,* Apr. 1982.

10
Physical Distribution

Physical distribution, often referred to as distribution, is the materials management subfunction most closely related to finished goods. In the context of total materials management, physical distribution is defined as all activities related to finished goods, starting with their receipt from the company's manufacturing facility and/or from a supplier, and concluding with the delivery to a customer. Coyle, Bardi, and Cavinato[1] define physical distribution as "the movement and storage associated with finished goods from manufacturing plants to warehouses and to customers." This vital subfunction may include the following activities: receiving, storage, materials handling, order assembly/picking, packaging, shipping, and transportation.

Physical distribution has responsibility for inbound as well as outbound transportation. It is equally important to optimize service and costs for materials received by a company and for finished goods shipped to customers. Distribution can use all its technical knowledge and expertise in traffic and transportation to coordinate the external movement of materials.

Physical distribution activities involve providing the customer with the right product at the right place at the right time in the right condition for the right cost. The cost of physical distribution components represents a significant portion of product cost and has a decided impact on overall price levels. A single component, transportation, on the average accounts for 20 cents of every customer dollar.[2] Accumulated movement and storage costs in the United States account for roughly 20 percent of the gross national product.[3] It is not surprising that physical distribution was usually part of the marketing organization before the advent of total materials groups. It is still included with marketing in some companies.

PHYSICAL DISTRIBUTION OBJECTIVES RELATED TO MATERIALS MANAGEMENT

Current and past publications on distribution/logistics indicate that the goal of physical distribution is to increase profits by reducing distribution costs. The objective of maximizing profits is the same in physical distribution as in all other materials management subfunctions and every other function in a company. Distribution can also play a significant role in minimizing costs for nonprofit organizations, thereby providing funds for needed projects.

Stating that the goal of distribution is to increase company profits may be an oversimplification. In the following discussion we review the major distribution objectives that contribute to a successful business.

Provide Good Customer Service

Distribution can help maximize the sales volume by providing the best possible overall customer service. Other company functions also contribute to reliable customer service, but distribution is the final group in the business process that impacts directly on the customer. Distribution is often justly blamed when a customer does not receive good service.

Traffic Management magazine sponsored a study by the management consulting firm of Shycon Associates, Inc. to review the opinions of purchasing and distribution personnel regarding customer service. Figure 10-1 illustrates common customer service complaints made by respondents. Late delivery of products was the number one complaint, accounting for 44 percent of all problems. Product or quality errors, which can be distribution-related, accounted for 31 percent. Another 12 percent of respondents complained about products delivered in damaged condition. Purchasing managers sometimes impose penalties for service infractions. Among the responding companies, 76 percent reported taking action against suppliers for repeated failures. Figure 10-2 illustrates some of the penalties imposed for customer service failures. The most common action taken was to reduce the overall volume of business (29 percent). The ultimate loss of all business with a customer was a significant 18 percent. These two pie charts illustrate the important role that physical distribution plays in the customer service function.[4]

Optimize Total Distribution Costs

Physical distribution and total materials management share the common objective of optimizing total costs. It is impossible to study these costs without considering the dynamics of a business enterprise and its many trade-offs. Comparison of various alternatives will provide the single best solution to optimize total distribution costs. For example, if a company can reduce order processing time by using a more efficient system, it can increase transportation time and still provide adequate customer service.

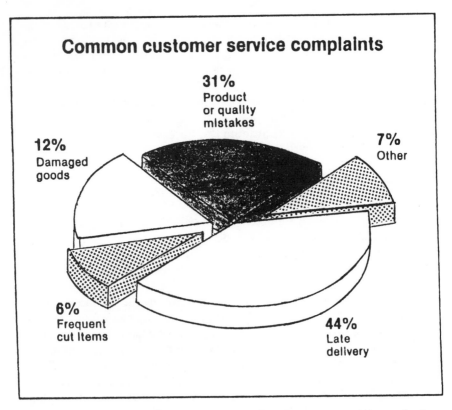

Figure 10-1. Common customer service complaints. (Source: "Does Your Customer Service Program Stack Up?" *Traffic Management*, Sept. 1982, p. 56. Reprinted by permission of *Traffic Management*, a Cahners Publication.)

This can be cost-effective if order processing improvements cost $80,000 and transportation costs are reduced by $120,000. However, another trade-off must then be considered, namely, the effect on inventory carrying costs.

There are other trade-off considerations: (1) the consolidation of distribution centers will decrease inventory and facility costs while increasing order fill rates, but it will delay shipments to customers; (2) the use of premium-priced transportation may result in increased sales and higher income; (3) a reduction in packaging costs may result in increased product damage and increased customer complaints; (4) increasing the customer service level will result in higher operating costs; and (5) investment in improved warehouse lighting may decrease order picking errors and reduce accidents. In each instance, all of the dynamic factors must be taken into consideration and evaluated to determine the best distribution solution.

Penalties for customer service failures

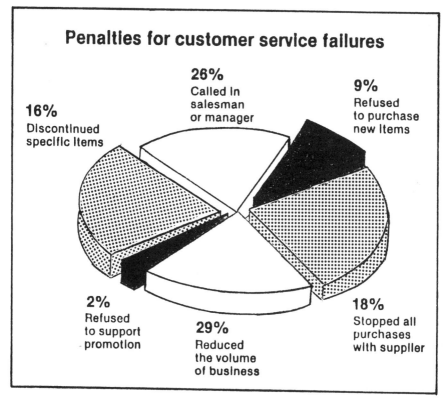

26%
Called in
salesman
or manager

9%
Refused
to purchase
new items

16%
Discontinued
specific items

2%
Refused
to support
promotion

29%
Reduced
the volume
of business

18%
Stopped all
purchases
with supplier

Figure 10-2. Penalties for customer service failures. (Source: "Does Your Customer Service Program Stack Up?" *Traffic Management,* Sept. 1982, p. 57. Reprinted by permission of *Traffic Management,* a Cahners Publication.)

Minimize Finished Goods Inventory

The most expensive inventory per cubic foot is finished goods inventory. It is estimated that finished goods represents 40 percent of total inventory for the Fortune 500 list of top manufacturing companies.[5] Thus, it is not surprising that a vital objective for distribution is to minimize finished goods inventory. Once again, trade-offs must be evaluated. A trend in many industries is for companies to reduce their materials inventories and ask the supplier to perform an inventory-holding function. This may be a condition of continuing to sell a product. The supplier company must then consider the trade-off costs of maintaining a pipeline inventory for the customer, which involves having additional finished goods or sufficient capability to produce the items quickly.

Another critical factor in determining how much finished goods inventory should be stocked is the relationship between safety stock levels and customer service. Company presidents who declare that 100 percent customer satisfaction is their goal generally are not aware of its consequences on inventory. An optimum service level should be established, based upon a trade-off of profits generated by increased sales and the costs of maintaining increased inventory. Figure 10-3 illustrates the relationship between customer service and inventory investment.

Provide Dependable, Timely Delivery to Customers

Establishing credibility with customers is a key factor in every company's marketing program. Figure 10-1 indicates the importance of providing dependable, timely deliveries; customer dissatisfaction because of delayed shipments represented the greatest number of complaints. The second largest source of complaints was product or quality errors. Here, operations and quality assurance should improve their monitoring of products, while distribution must concentrate on eliminating shipping errors. The third most common customer complaint was damaged goods. Distribution can

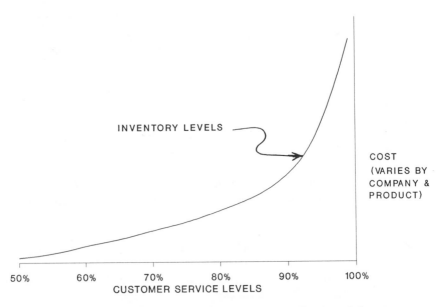

Figure 10-3. Relationship between customer service level and inventory investment.

improve dependability of shipments by reducing internal and product damage.

Decentralization of distribution centers may be a viable solu..ɹ to shipment problems. The management of Intercraft Industries Corporation, the world's largest manufacturer of picture frames and framed art, wanted to provide rapid, reliable deliveries to customers. They changed from having just one central distribution center, in Chicago, to multiple units in various locations throughout the United States, thereby improving customer service by providing rapid, reliable deliveries. Intercraft also gained in flexibility; they could adapt more quickly to regional customer preference trends by adapting inventories rapidly to reflect local buying preferences.[6]

Determine and Provide the Best Transportation Services

Optimizing transportation services for individual applications is critical to total materials management. The purchaser has a variety of choices and considers various trade-offs in selecting the best buy. Some of the variables are delivery time, cost, travel distance, product fragility or perishability, potential pilferage, amount of materials handling, frequency of shipment, and size of shipment. The primary transportation modes are truck, rail, water, pipeline, and air. The various means of transportation provide different service capabilities.

Dr. Bernard J. LaLonde, in discussing transportation in the twenty-first century, predicts that there will be a substantial reconfiguration of the system. The buyer will be able to purchase a range of services from one seller and receive a single invoice for the entire purchase. Elimination of regulatory constraints will allow the emergence of a transportation conglomerate. Elimination of paperwork, single-source accountability, longterm contractual relationships, and automated communication interfaces are among the expected benefits for transportation purchasers.[7]

Minimize the Order Cycle

An important criterion for measuring customer service is the length of an order cycle. The order cycle begins when the customer orders materials and ends with customer receipt of the materials. As an order cycle is decreased, the inventory that is required decreases. Thus process and safety inventories, and implicit inventory costs, are reduced.

Physical distribution influences the length of an order cycle in several ways. Order processing activities may include receipt and recording of data, inventory checks, determination of supply location, selection of transportation mode, and other activities, depending upon the firm's organizational structure. The order cycle can be reduced by improving the communication system for these activities. Also, selective use of different transportation modes can shorten the cycle. In some instances, use of premium-cost transportation may be warranted to reduce inventory cost and improve customer service.

Implement Computer Applications to Improve Physical Distribution Operations

The computer is playing an increasingly important role in improving physical distribution operations. Transportation activities that can be improved by using computers include bill of lading preparation, shipment routing, freight rating, carrier payment, and truck fleet routing. Other computer applications are being implemented for order entry/processing, inventory control, warehousing, order picking, materials handling, and shipping activities. The benefits derived from computer applications include improved customer service, reduced operating and record costs, faster communications, maximum space utilization, and tighter control of assets.

Distribution resource planning (DRP) uses computers to integrate manufacturing and distribution operations. (See Chapter 6.) DRP represents a new way of thinking about a company's entire distribution function, and it can be useful in many areas, including inventory control, transportation planning and scheduling, maximizing cube/weight utilization of transportation modes, planning and scheduling distribution center personnel and equipment, budgeting, and space allocation.[8]

Utilize Analytical Techniques to Improve Physical Distribution

For physical distribution to be an integral part of the materials organization, it must make effective use of appropriate analytical techniques to improve operations. Various quantitative techniques are available; some that have been successfully applied are linear programming (mathematical models for solving linear optimization problems), simulation (utilizing representative data to reproduce in a model various conditions that are likely to occur in the actual system), the delphi method (a forecasting technique where the opinions of experts are combined in a series of questionnaires), and queuing theory (the collection of models dealing with waiting-line problems). With increasing education, especially beyond the undergraduate level, personnel will be more inclined to use such techniques.

TYPICAL PHYSICAL DISTRIBUTION ACTIVITIES

Activities assigned to physical distribution vary among different organizations, sometimes because of the location of physical distribution within the company structure. A firm committed to a total materials management function will include distribution within that function, whereas a marketing-oriented company may include distribution within the marketing organization, where it may be responsible for marketing-related activities such as order entry/processing. Also some activities vary according to whether physical distribution is centralized or decentralized. With centralization, distribution centers may have broad responsibilities, including inspection, inventory control, and order processing.

Order Processing

The flow of information from customers into a company is critical to customer service. If the order processing system is not efficiently organized, customers may be unhappy. This situation can lead to further problems such as excessive expediting, premium transportation costs, and lost sales. Order processing is normally a marketing responsibility because of its close relationship to the customer, but may be included in the physical distribution group as part of a total materials management organization. A simplified example of the order processing sequence is shown in Figure 10-4.

In the past, customer orders were transmitted by means of sales order forms, delivered by mail, teletype, telephone, or personally by a salesperson. A manual system provides flexibility, which can be useful for low-volume operations, or where special considerations are involved. Automated information flow, now widely used, has many benefits. It provides greater lead time for completing orders because it reduces total processing time. Expediting time and resultant costs are reduced. Automated order processing improves the integrity of information and reduces clerical costs by increasing productivity. Computerized order processing systems also provide important information to other groups within the company. For example, finance can obtain data required for cash flow analysis, and credit checks can be automated by applying predetermined logic for acceptance and rejection.

An example of automated order entry is the system used by an east coast company, which sells to retail drugstores. The company is committed to daily delivery service to customers. With automation, their sales more than doubled within a six-year period; at the same time, the after-tax net tripled. Approximately 95 percent of orders are received through the automated order-entry system. The key element in this system is a portable data

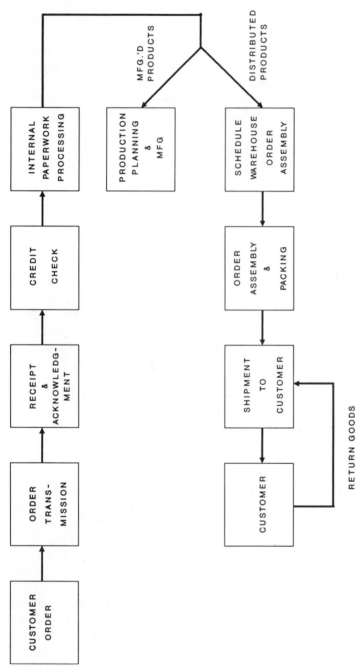

Figure 10-4. Order processing sequence.

terminal that is hand-held by store personnel as they walk through the aisles. The unit is capable of reading bar-coded shelf labels; quantity is the only manual entry. Order data are held in the unit's memory and later transmitted to the main office by placing the memory pack into the system's communication module. Information is sent through telephone lines. At the distribution center, orders are received, items are sorted on each order to picking sequence, and hard copies are made on peripheral printers. The copies are immediately assigned to pickers, who gather items for shipment.

A major order processing decision relates to inventory allocation in the situation where demand exceeds supply. In that case, the system must be able to allocate products among customers. It must be flexible enough to provide inventory allocation at any time on the order cycle. For example, some customers require specific quantities and cycle times and would like the inventory allocated in an early part of the cycle. Other customers may be willing to trade-off inventory guarantees for price discounts.[9]

Dow Corning Corporation, a worldwide manufacturer and marketer of silicone products, has effectively used computers for order processing. Customer service is part of the company's marketing organization, whereas transportation and physical distribution are part of the materials management group. Since the start of centralized order entry, customer service and traffic departments have worked closely to develop mutually beneficial policies and practices. Consequently, Dow Corning now makes fewer but larger shipments with substantial freight savings for customers, while reducing internal handling and paperwork costs.[10]

Finished Goods Inventory Control

Chapter 4 covered the subject of inventory control in detail. Finished goods inventory control is discussed further here because it is an integral part of the physical distribution network. Finished goods constitute the most costly inventory category. Because of the high costs associated with maintaining these inventories, it becomes critical to any company's profit structure to minimize them.

In many respects the effort to minimize finished goods inventories leads to a struggle between the supplier and the customer in which each tries to get the other to maintain higher inventories. The seller can carry less if the customer maintains higher inventories and vice versa. Customers expect suppliers to maintain large inventories to accommodate their needs. This is especially true of companies that are instituting Just-In-Time or similar types of systems. In order to provide more frequent, smaller orders, the supplier must either have a very responsive supply source (internal or external) or maintain larger inventories.

The activities of total materials management in controlling finished goods inventory are vital to a business from the viewpoints of customer service, profits, and continuity of operations. Many variables and trade-offs must be evaluated. Some of the important considerations are carrying costs, stockout costs, the order cycle, and the number of decentralized distribution centers.

Carrying Costs. Carrying costs are the costs associated with holding finished goods. They normally include such elements as interest on capital or opportunity costs, storage and handling costs (e.g., warehouse space, heat, and fork trucks), insurance, taxes, depreciation, and obsolescence costs. Total carrying cost percentages will vary depending upon the component elements, 25 to 35 percent being common. If carrying costs are 30 percent, a company incurs an annual cost of $300,000 for every $1,000,000 of finished goods inventory. The high costs associated with maintaining finished goods stock have caused firms to establish or revise policies to control this stock.

Stockout Costs. One might assume that because of the high cost of maintaining finished goods inventories, with their high carrying cost expenses, inventory levels should be kept at a bare minimum. However, the physical distribution group has a responsibility to satisfy customer demand. Failure to have sufficient finished goods can be just as bad as maintaining an excess. A stockout occurs when customers want to buy goods that are not available. Stockout costs are difficult to compute or even to estimate, but they are real and critical factors in establishing finished goods inventory levels.

To determine the cost or penalty for a stockout, one must analyze possible customer reactions to the seller's shortage of merchandise. Johnson and Wood categorize customer responses as follows:[11]

1. The customer says, "I'll be back," and this proves to be so.
2. The customer says, "Call me when it's in."
3. The customer buys a substitute product that yields a higher profit for the seller.
4. The customer buys a less expensive substitute that yields a lower profit.
5. The customer asks to place an order for the item that is out of stock (back-order) and asks to have the item delivered when it arrives.
6. The customer goes to a competitor.

These customer responses can be placed in three major categories: (1) the sale is delayed; (2) the sale is lost; (3) the customer shifts his or her

Determination of The Average Cost of a Stock-out

ALTERNATIVE	LOSS*	PROBABILITY*	AVERAGE COST*
#1 Brand Loyal			
Customer	$ 0.00	.10	$ 0.00
#2 Switches and			
Comes Back	$ 37.00	.65	$ 24.05
#3 Lost Customer	$1200.00	.25	$300.00
Average Cost of a Stock-out		1.00	$324.05

*These are hypothetical figures.
Source: James C. Johnson and Donald F. Wood, *Contemporary Physical Distribution & Logistics*, PennWell Publishing Company, Tulsa, Oklahoma, 1982, p. 266.

Figure 10-5. Determination of the average cost of a stockout. (Source: James C. Johnson and Donald F. Wood, *Contemporary Physical Distribution and Logistics*, Macmillan Publishing Company, New York, 1986, p. 254.)

business to a competitor. Assuming that alternative number one occurs 10 percent, alternative number two 65 percent, and alternative number three 25 percent of the time, these percentages can be used to determine the average cost of a stockout. Figure 10-5 illustrates this calculation. A delayed sale results in no loss although repeated occurrences can have long-term consequences. If a customer switches to a competitor and comes back, the result is a lost sale. The most damaging result is a lost customer. These individual costs are totaled to provide the average cost of a stockout.

Order Cycle. Minimizing the order cycle is another distribution objective. Order cycle time is an important consideration in determining company inventory policy because a decrease in order cycle time affects the amount of finished goods inventory required. A shortened order cycle reduces the requirements for process and safety stock; the company can respond more quickly to increases in demand with a shorter cycle, before the demand accumulates to a high level. A shorter order cycle period also reduces order lead time. As a result, safety stock can be reduced without diminishing the efficiency of customer service. Figure 10-6 illustrates the relationship between required inventory and order cycle length.[12]

Decentralized Distribution Centers. Finished goods inventory strategies become more critical as the number of distribution centers increases with geographical dispersion. The amount of stock in different locations will affect service levels, total inventory carrying costs, and transportation costs. Centralized control of inventory gives an overall perspective that makes it possible to optimize trade-off costs, customer service levels, transportation costs, and so on.

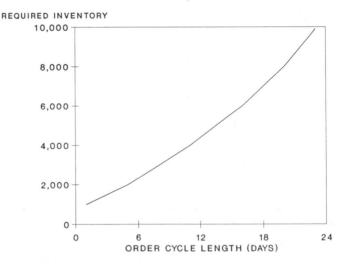

REQUIRED INVENTORY

Figure 10-6. Relationship between required inventory and order cycle length. (Source: Roy Dale Voorhees and Merrill Kim Sharp, *Transportation Journal*, Fall 1978, a publication of the American Society of Transportation & Logistics, Inc.)

Centralized inventory planning should be done by product group rather than by warehouse location. For example, in one company two planners were responsible for controlling all products in three distribution centers. A problem developed when the two planners began to compete for the plant's inventory; each planner tried to obtain more materials and earlier delivery in order to achieve higher service levels than the other provided. This competition had a detrimental effect on the overall service picture. The problem was resolved by assigning each planner sole responsibility for a line of products handled by all distribution centers. This solution eliminated the internal conflict and improved service by making the best use of total resources.[13]

Materials Handling and Packaging

Materials handling and packaging design are essential activities of physical distribution operations. Chapters 8 and 9 provided considerable information on the handling and packaging of products for distribution. This section concentrates on some of the current handling and packaging topics that are pertinent to distribution activities.

Containerization. Containers are shipping units that are usually 8 feet wide, 8 feet high, and 10, 20, 35, 40, or 48 feet long. They are constructed of waterproof components and are capable of moving a variety of material in one large unit load. These containers are adaptable to various modes of transportation, and so are referred to as "intermodal." Figure 10-7 illus-

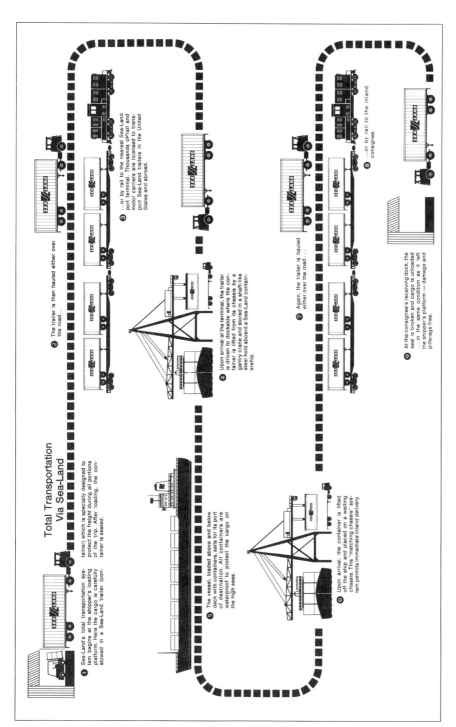

Total Transportation Via Sea-Land

1. Sea-Land's total transportation system begins at the shipper's loading platform. Here the cargo is carefully stowed in a Sea-Land trailer (container) which is specially designed to protect the freight during all portions of the trip. After loading, the container is sealed.

2. The trailer is then hauled either over the road...

3. ... or by rail to the nearest Sea-Land port terminal. Thousands of rail and motor carriers are licensed to transport Sea-Land trailers in the United States and abroad.

4. Upon arrival at the terminal, the trailer is driven to dockside where the container is lifted from its chassis by a gantry crane and stored in a shaft-like steel hold aboard a Sea-Land containership.

5. The vessel, loaded above and below deck with containers, sails for its port of destination. All containers are waterproof to protect the cargo on the high seas.

6. Upon arrival, the container is lifted off the ship and placed on a waiting chassis. This "matching chassis" system permits immediate inland delivery.

7. Again, the trailer is hauled either over the road ...

8. ...or by rail to the inland consignee.

9. At the consignee's receiving dock, the seal is broken and cargo is unloaded ...in the same condition as it left the shipper's platform — damage and pilferage free.

Figure 10-7. Intermodal container movement. (Courtesy Sea Land Service, Inc.)

trates intermodal container movement. An estimated two million containers and about 500,000 chassis are currently in use worldwide, with U.S. companies having about 600,000 containers and an estimated 42,000 chassis. Between 35 and 50 percent of all containers are owned by leasing companies.[14]

Loading Materials. Loading methods for trucks, freight cars, and containers should ensure protection for all materials within the carrier. A specific loading plan can be designed to provide adequate bracing or cushioning to protect against the various forces exerted from each mode of transportation. Inflatable dunnage bags made of rubber or craft paper typically are used to maintain load stability. Loading methods for intermodal trailer shipments, as suggested by the Association of American Railroads, are illustrated in Figure 10-8.

Potential Transportation Hazards. Materials handling techniques for cargo protection must consider the mode(s) of transportation, as individual modes have different potential transportation hazards. For example, freight being transported in ships is exposed to a wide variety of motion. There are six classes of shipboard movement—rolling, pitching, yawing, heaving, swaying, and surging—which can differ greatly in severity. Highway freight is subject to shocks in braking and in impact with docks, swaying on curves, and general vibration. Railroad transportation hazards include acceleration and deceleration, humping impacts, swaying on curves, and vibration.

Handling and Packaging of Hazardous Materials. The handling, packaging, and shipment of hazardous materials require special consideration. Hazardous materials are those materials that may cause harm to persons or property in the event of an unintential release from their containers. Designated categories include explosives, compressed gases, flammable liquids, oxidizers, poisons, radioactive materials, and corrosive materials. Tariffs cover specific rules and regulations concerning the packaging, marking, placarding, and handling of hazardous materials.

Packaging. There are basically two types of packaging: industrial packaging, which protects products for shipment, and consumer packaging, which is designed for sales appeal. Physical distribution is concerned with consumer packaging to the extent that an inadequate design might result in damage claims; but this is normally a marketing responsibility. Distribution's primary emphasis and responsibility involve industrial packaging, the exterior protection of products.

SEGREGATE IRREGULAR LOADING

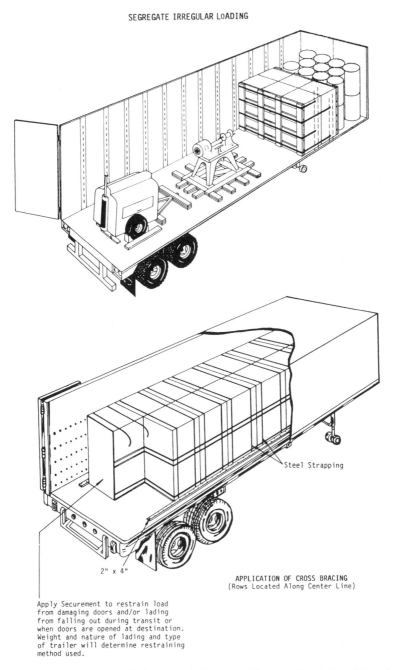

Steel Strapping

2" x 4"

APPLICATION OF CROSS BRACING
(Rows Located Along Center Line)

Apply Securement to restrain load
from damaging doors and/or lading
from falling out during transit or
when doors are opened at destination.
Weight and nature of lading and type
of trailer will determine restraining
method used.

Figure 10-8. Loading methods for intermodal shipments. (Courtesy Association of American Railroads.)

The cost of product loss and damage in the distribution environment exceeds 5 billion dollars annually. Each physical distribution activity (packaging, materials handling, and transportation) adds to the complexity of the problem.[15] In materials handling processes such as the unloading and loading of trucks, packages are subject to shock, the severity of which depends upon many factors such as product weight and size and the method of movement — manual, mechanized, and automated. The various modes of transportation similarly have their own hazards, as mentioned above. A primary goal of packaging is to reduce damage through improved design.

Packaging involves many trade-offs. For example, a change to lightweight materials might increase packaging costs, but it could also result in lower freight charges or permit an increase in marketing area by the use of air shipments, and/or allow a reduction in the number of distribution centers. Packing materials, used to protect or orient products within a package, can be improved by the use of costlier materials that produce a net savings by reducing damage. Only after careful study of actual field conditions should packaging performance criteria be finalized; this will permit the long-range attainment of an economic balance between the cost of packaging and other physical distribution costs such as in-transit damage.[16]

An interesting trade-off involves product fragility. Figure 10-9 illustrates a case where increasing the cost of a product by improving weak design components can lower packaging costs and reduce total costs while providing the customer with a better product. Line $0-N$ indicates the previous product costs. Lines $N-P$ and $P-S$ show previous interior and exterior packaging costs. The total previous cost (line $0-S$) achieved damage control objectives. Line $0-L$ indicates an increase in product cost to improve the design of weak components. Lines $L-F$ and $F-G$ show the resulting new interior and exterior packaging costs, which have been considerably reduced by having a better product. The same percent of safe arrival is achieved with the improved product, while the total cost curve $(0-G)$ equals 70 percent of the original cost.

Warehousing

General concepts of warehousing were discussed in Chapter 8. Finished goods warehousing includes many activities also found in the raw material or work-in-process material stores operation. When a company is involved in manufacturing, the activities related to finished goods are often relatively uncomplicated. The materials are easier to count, less numerous, and more orderly than raw or process materials. Whether the company is manufacturing or purchasing the products it distributes, warehousing

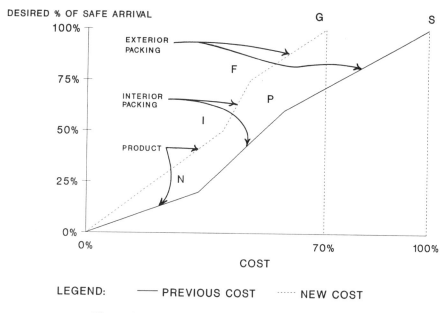

DESIRED % OF SAFE ARRIVAL

LEGEND: ⎯⎯ PREVIOUS COST ⋯⋯ NEW COST

Figure 10-9. Trade-off of product costs versus packing costs.

operations are a key activity in achieving customer service, inventory control, and cost containment objectives.

Basic Role of Distribution Warehousing. The primary function of a warehouse is to store materials temporarily so that they are available to meet customer demand. This can be a relatively simple task until customer demand increases, in both quantity and geographical dispersion. The effort then becomes more complicated, in terms of both providing good customer service and minimizing total costs. Periodic analysis of warehousing requirements is critical to achieving marketing objectives. The following list of pertinent considerations was adapted from Charles A. Taff's recommended elements for physical distribution analysis:[17]

- Markets to be served
- Desired customer service levels
- Number of warehouses
- Location and size
- Products and their quantities in inventory
- Products and their quantities to be made at specific plants[18]
- Decisions on additional plants to be built[18]

The finished goods warehouse/distribution center is one stage in the movement of materials from the manufacturing plant and/or supplier to the customer. Figure 10-10 illustrates this relationship. Each company must determine how many warehouses/distribution centers will best suit its particular requirements. This decision does not remain static over long periods of time; it must be reviewed periodically to determine whether it is appropriate to increase or decrease the number of warehouses.

In its "middle-of-distribution" role, the warehouse has many functions. Decisions on the number and location of warehouses, products and their quantities in inventory, and so on, influence the effectiveness of these functions. One key function of the distribution warehouse is to allow consolidated shipments to customers. Rather than shipping individual items from different manufacturing plants and/or warehouses, the company can send a combined shipment from one warehouse. Maintaining customer service is another important warehouse function. The service level will depend upon such variables as how close a warehouse is to the customer and product availability. Warehouses can also be an insurance factor to protect against the possibility of plant or supplier labor strikes, fires, or transportation delays.

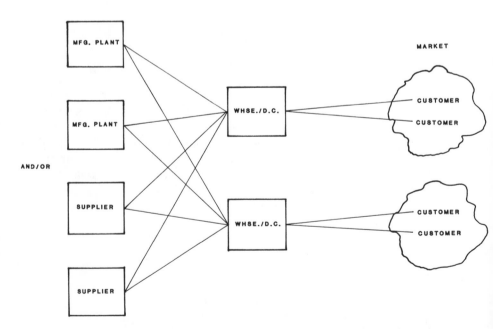

Figure 10-10. Warehouse/distribution center relationship to the distribution system.

Private versus Public Warehousing. Companies must decide whether to own a warehouse, to lease space from a public warehouse as needed, or to use some combination of the two alternatives. The private warehouse entails certain fixed costs such as capital investment, taxes, labor, and equipment. The cost of public warehouse use varies, depending on how much space is used, and is generally based on a charge per square or cubic foot. Figure 10-11 gives a cost comparison of private and public warehousing.

Many considerations other than cost affect the decision of private versus public warehousing. Private warehouses afford a company complete control, with greater security, better monitoring of perishable goods, and better control of customer service. Public warehousing, too, offers advantages, most notably the retention of capital. Space in public warehouses can be leased when needed, allowing a company the flexibility to expand, contract, or completely eliminate a warehouse location without any continuing costs. The cost of public warehousing is less than that of private warehousing for lower volumes, as indicated in Figure 10-11.

The public warehousing market is highly specialized to meet the needs of a variety of customers. Types of public warehouses include the following:[19]

1. *Refrigerated*—For storing materials requiring temperature control, such as perishable food items, chemicals, and biologicals.
2. *Commodity*—To hold a specific type of material.

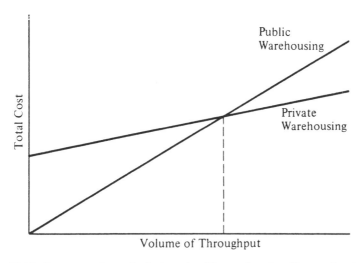

Figure 10-11. Cost comparison of private and public warehousing. (Source: Reprinted by permission from *The Management of Business Logistics,* Third Edition, by Coyle and Bardi; copyright © 1976, 1980, 1984 by West Publishing Company. All rights reserved.)

3. *Household goods*—For personal household belongings.
4. *General merchandise*—To store common materials not requiring special services or controls.
5. *Bonded*—Authorized to store materials upon which taxes or duty have not been paid.

Order Assembly

The mission of order assembly (often referred to as order picking) is to select all items required for a customer's order within a prescribed time frame. Although much has been written about the automatic warehouse, few fully automated applications actually exist. Therefore, our discussion will focus primarily on manual and combined manual and automated operations.

Information planning and management of order assembly activities are critical to a successful operation. Each company must decide on the best system for its particular needs, determining the degree of automation and the system's overall cost-effectiveness by weighing such variables as number of orders per day, order quantities, number of stock keeping units (SKU's), warehouse size and layout, and order processing time objectives. As their relative costs decrease, computers are playing a growing role in warehouse order assembly activities. An order picker may pick individual items manually, as illustrated in Figure 10-12, using a computer-generated order selection sheet. Computers increase order assembly productivity by determining the most efficient order picking sequence and route.

Besides generating order selection lists, computer systems can be applied to many other activities related to order assembly such as planning optimum personnel requirements and schedules. Some systems provide displays at the ends of flow racks to instruct order pickers as to what and how much to pick. The computer can automatically weigh completed order containers to verify the accuracy of counts, and can automatically accumulate quantities for batch picking. It can direct order pickers to the oldest stock when material is stored in multiple locations. The list of possible computer applications for order assembly activities is limited only by the user's imagination.

Order Pick Work Stations. Productivity can be increased by providing an order picker with information and materials at a fixed work station. Using such work stations, Motorola's Semiconductor Products Sector (SPS) doubled employee productivity and increased the warehouse's capability to process orders, as line item shipments increased from 87,000 to 140,000 per quarter. The majority of materials at Motorola are stored in an automated storage retrieval system (AS/RS). Individual bin-loads travel by

Figure 10-12. Manual order picking. (Courtesy Ace Hardware Corporation.)

conveyor from the AS/RS to ten individual work stations, directed by the computer. Each work station has a conveyor spur capable of holding three bin-loads. An order picker receives instructions from a computer terminal screen (CRT), as shown in Figure 10-13. As items are selected, the order picker keys information into the terminal providing the host computer with the capability to inform sales offices throughout the world of current inventory status. Conveyors move completed orders to inspection and then to the shipping department.[20]

Use of Take-away Conveyors or Trucks.   Because order assembly is very labor-intensive, industrial engineers have sought to reduce the amount of manual effort and increase worker productivity by increasing the degree of mechanization. Figure 10-14 illustrates some alternative systems for applying mechanization to assist order pickers. Where take-away (transfer) con-

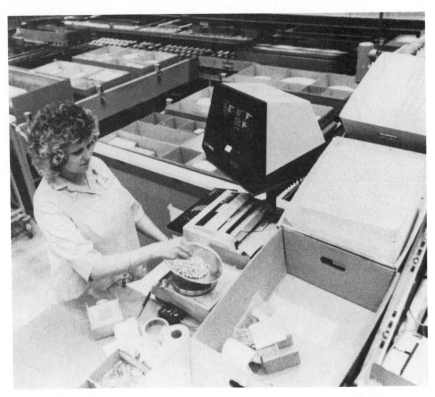

Figure 10-13. CRT used to provide instructions for an order picker. (Source: *Material Handling Engineering,* copyright by Penton/IPC, Inc.)

veyors are used, labels are applied to containers or packages bearing automatic identification system (AIS) coding. This system permits automated movement, sorting, and assembly. Examples A and D illustrate two configurations for storing pallet loads next to a conveyor that allow order selection for batch picking fast enough to empty a pallet load in less than one week. Example B shows a storage system for slow-moving materials, typically using pallet racks or shelving. Employees may use a cart (as in Figure 10-12) to accumulate items and then unload them onto a take-away conveyor. Example C, effective for materials that are not easily transported by conveyor, uses a nonpowered truck, powered truck, or tractor train for accumulation and transportation. Example E illustrates the use of flow racks in conjunction with a conveyor. This same design could also be used for a carousel and mini-load AS/RS.[21]

Use of Order Pick Trucks. Figure 10-15 illustrates the use of equipment that an employee rides in performing order picking activities, to increase

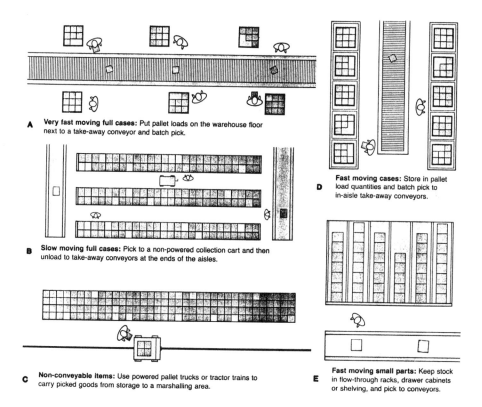

A Very fast moving full cases: Put pallet loads on the warehouse floor next to a take-away conveyor and batch pick.

B Slow moving full cases: Pick to a non-powered collection cart and then unload to take-away conveyors at the ends of the aisles.

C Non-conveyable items: Use powered pallet trucks or tractor trains to carry picked goods from storage to a marshalling area.

D Fast moving cases: Store in pallet load quantities and batch pick to in-aisle take-away conveyors.

E Fast moving small parts: Keep stock in flow-through racks, drawer cabinets or shelving, and pick to conveyors.

Figure 10-14. Take-away conveyor and truck applications. (Source: *Modern Materials Handling,* copyright 1983 by Cahners Publishing Company, Division of Reed Publishing USA.)

productivity and reduce employee fatigue. Example A illustrates hard-to-handle materials being placed on tractor trains. Example B is a high-speed picking system in which the order picker rides on a truck above a conveyor in the aisle. As items are picked, they move to the take-away conveyor. Example C shows an order pick truck operating in a narrow aisle guided by a wire embedded in the floor or by mechanical means. Example D illustrates an order pick truck, which is entirely operator controlled, traveling freely throughout the warehouse. Example E shows narrow-aisle trucks capable of loading and unloading full pallets. Other equipment allows the order picker to pick individual items and store them on a pallet.

Shipping

Receiving and shipping have some similar activities in that both work with docks and carriers. Frequently, the same type of materials handling equip-

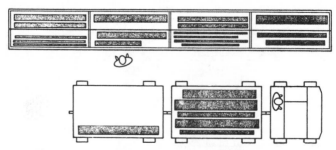

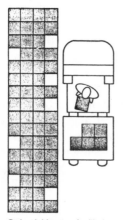

A **Tractor trains** permit a worker to pick and accumulate quantities of large, non-conveyable items.

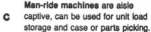

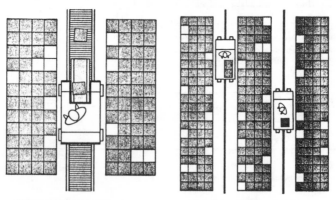

B **Pick car systems** include an in-aisle conveyor which carries individual cases to sorting.

C **Man-ride machines** are aisle captive, can be used for unit load storage and case or parts picking.

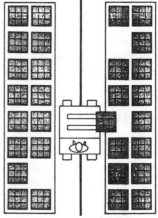

D **Orderpicking trucks** lift the operator to 30-ft heights, can travel freely from one aisle to another.

E **Hybrid trucks** are flexible-path vehicles that can lift the operator to heights of 50 ft.

Figure 10-15. Order pick truck applications. (Source: *Modern Materials Handling,* copyright 1983 by Cahners Publishing Company, Division of Reed Publishing USA.)

ment is used to unload trucks or freight cars as to load them. Many companies maximize the utilization of docks, equipment, and personnel by merging the two groups into a single department with one supervisor coordinating all tasks. Receiving processes incoming materials from many sources and performs checking and paperwork activities. Shipping also must carry out various checking and paperwork activities.

Shipping is the last company group involved with a customer's order before the customer receives it. Because this is the last chance to ensure proper shipment, shipping is responsible for making sure that the customer will receive all ordered materials in an undamaged condition. Thus, the shipping group is important in maintaining good customer relations. Consider the effect upon the company's sales when a customer receives an incorrect shipment (wrong items, wrong quantities), or when all the correct items are received but some are damaged.

Packing.   Packing activities often are included in shipping responsibilities. Packing personnel place individual items in a container, provide adequate cushioning materials for protection during shipment, and seal the container. Material in containers is subject to static and dynamic stresses, and packing materials serves to minimize damage due to these stresses by cushioning and dunnage (filling void spaces within the container). Among the inner packings in use are expanded polystyrene (popcorn), plastic-encapsulated air (air bubbles), various types of paper products, foam-in-place, molded polystyrene, and corrugated partitions (egg crating).

The choice of shipping modes is based upon the container quantity, size and weight, unit load configuration, destination, and so on. For containers being shipped by United Parcel Service (U.P.S.) or parcel post, appropriate shipping costs must be determined and metered labels applied. Many companies now use machines that automatically weigh a package, determine the transportation cost, apply a metered label, and maintain a record of charges. This system speeds the processing of small packages and reduces transportation costs by eliminating errors made in manual operations. Shipping can contribute further to cost savings by such measures as banding together two packages going to the same customer to reduce shipping costs. The shipping container must be properly labeled to ensure correct delivery.

Loading.   The loading of vehicles is an essential activity of the shipping department. Materials are loaded either manually or by the use of mechanization or automation. Cartons may be manually loaded to maximize carrier space utilization. Fork trucks are used to move and position unit loads in the vehicle. Overhead conveyors may be used to load products such as hanging garments, which are loaded onto monorail extensions in a truck. Conveyors on the floor of the vehicle also allow automatic loading and unloading operations. All materials must be secured within the vehicle. Improper loading increases transportation costs and product damage.

Documentation and Reports. The shipping group prepares and handles various types of documentation and reports. Most packages have a packing slip attached or enclosed, which the customer uses to verify receipts. Bills-of-lading, used in conjunction with truck shipments, contain information such as date, destination, number of cartons, type of material, and whether the shipment is being sent prepaid or collect. Air and rail freight require similar documentation.

The shipping department normally prepares reports for internal control and communication. The daily shipping report, which records basic information on all shipments for the day, can later be used to check total billings for a period, and provides a useful audit trail for tracking discrepancies. The product availability or on-hand report contains information regarding the status of items within the shipping department such as materials received, shipped, or on hand, and partially filled orders.

Transportation

The terms transportation and traffic are often used interchangeably. Transportation is an essential part of physical distribution and its most costly component. Its importance was shown by the effects of a four-day strike in 1982 by one of the railroad labor unions. The strike resulted in losses of $50 to $80 million a day, and its potential impact was so devastating that Congress ordered the labor organization back to work. Transportation accounts for a significant percentage of the GNP.

Transportation Modes. The many modes of transportation in the United States are competitive, both between and within modes. Of the 2,502,340,000 revenue ton-miles traveled in the transportation of freight in 1986, 25.1 percent went to highway carriers, 35.8 percent to railroads, 15.7 percent to water carriers, 23.1 percent to oil pipelines, and 0.3 percent to airlines.[22]

Railroads. Historically, railroads have transported the largest number of ton-miles of cargo within the United States, and projections indicate this situation will continue. This dominance is due to the railroads' ability to convey large shipments economically over long distances. The growth of highway systems has made it difficult for the rail industry to compete for short-haul traffic. Mined materials such as coal, stone, and gravel represent the highest percentage of carload shipments by rail.

Trucks. Highway transportation has expanded rapidly since World War II. The primary advantage of trucks is their flexibility in permitting door-to-door shipment, not only within the United States but also overseas. They can provide trailer-on-flatcar (TOFC) movement with good results. Motor carriers are presently facing problems that will affect the growth of the industry. The high labor intensity of trucking operations, coupled with an increased cost for labor, has caused financial difficulty, but improvements such as the use of double bottoms (one tractor pulling two trailers) have helped to control costs. Possibly the greatest threat to the motor carrier industry is an increase in the use of private carriers. As companies attempt to reduce their costs by operating their own trucks, the business volume decreases for the motor carriers.

Pipelines. The first domestic pipelines were operating in 1865. A major increase in pipeline use occurred between 1947 and 1958, when the share of total intercity freight ton-miles increased from 9.5 to 16.5 percent; and usage increased further to 21.0 percent by 1975. Pipelines are the fastest-growing mode of transportation, and the petroleum industry is their largest user, with almost 90 percent of all petroleum products being transported by this mode. Pipeline use can be maximized because pipelines can operate 24 hours per day, seven days per week. Their obvious major disadvantage is that there are limitations on the kinds of products that they can transport.[23]

Water. Water transportation in the United States involves both domestic traffic (movement on inland waterways and between mainland ports) and ocean traffic (between the U.S. mainland and Hawaii, Alaska, and Puerto Rico). It is the oldest method of transportation. The Great Lakes, rivers, and canals provide an inland waterway system over which ships and barges transport commodities such as coal, grain, and ore. Rivers had low water levels in 1988, due to weather conditions, which resulted in slow movement and sometimes stoppages of river barges. Barge traffic is one of the lowest-cost means of transportation. Water transport is also able to move large quantities of materials, although waterways spokesmen contend that U.S. ocean port technology is at least 30 years out of date.[24] Other major disadvantages are its limited areas of serviceability and slow speeds. Ocean transportation has advantages related to costs. Disadvantages include the time required and potential damages.

Air. Among the greatest advances in transportation are new developments in air freight technology. Jets have doubled the speed of earlier propeller-driven aircraft, while jumbo jets have more than tripled freight capacities. Most air freight is transported by companies such as United

Airlines and American Airlines, which are primarily in the business of passenger transportation; Flying Tiger and Airlift International primarily move freight. Air freight services are capable of transporting a variety of products, most of which are expensive, perishable, or emergency items. Air movement is very costly, with fuel costs having increased sharply in recent years.

Criteria for Selection of Transportation Modes. The selection of a specific mode of transportation is based on weighing the trade-offs for various alternatives. Some primary considerations are speed, dependability, and fuel efficiency.[25]

Speed. The fastest means of transportation is air freight, whereas motor carriers provide rapid service from one point to another. Rail transportation can be effective for longer runs. Water and pipelines are the slowest modes.

Dependability. Pipelines are the most dependable mode of transportation because they are not affected by weather conditions, and motor carriers are the next best. Air cargo has improved in dependability with the use of jet aircraft, but weather is still a problem. The railroads have been historically undependable, often because they must wait to accumulate cars. Water is the least dependable mode, because of weather as well as other delays.

Capability. Capability refers to the size, weight, and variety of products that the mode can physically accommodate. Water carriers have the greatest capability. Railroads are next, but they are limited in height by tunnels and bridges. Air carriers have been steadily increasing their capacity, but still are limited to airplanes such as the Boeing 747. Pipelines are the least capable mode because of their inability to transport a wide variety of products.

Fuel Efficiency. As its cost increased after the energy crisis of the 1970s, fuel became a significant factor in selection of transportation mode. Representatives of the various modes of transportation generally do not agree on calculations used to determine relative fuel efficiency. Carrier fuel efficiency ranks as follows, from most to least efficient: (1) pipelines, (2) water, (3) railroads, (4) trucks, and (5) air.

TRANSPORTATION MANAGEMENT

Transportation management is a key component of physical distribution within the total materials management function, in terms of both cost and service. According to a 1982 study, total distribution costs within manufacturing companies average 8.62 percent of sales. Transportation of finished goods constituted the largest component of distribution costs, 3.32 percent of sales, as shown in Figure 10-16.[26] Although the cost of transportation adds no value to a product, poor transportation management can mean increased costs and lost sales. Thus an efficient transportation department contributes to the company's profits and reputation, and must constantly keep informed of new developments in the discipline.

Principles of Transportation

A clear set of principles can aid in establishing an efficient transportation group. Marvin L. Fair and Ernest W. Williams, Jr. developed the following principles of transportation:[27]

1. *Continuous Flow.* The function of transportation is to convey goods and persons from origin to desired destination. The objectives of minimum cost and time require avoiding reverse or out-of-line movement and minimizing handling, interchange of equipment, and transfer of goods and persons.
2. *Optimum Unit of Cargo.* Within the capabilities of standard vehicles and cargo-handling accommodations and equipment, the cost of handling cargo tends to vary inversely with the size of the unit of shipment. The optimum size unit of cargo is the largest size which all accommodations and equipment can handle properly.
3. *Maximum Vehicle Unit.* The individual vehicle tends to get ever larger for two principal reasons. First, the operating costs of the

Physical Distribution Costs

COMPONENT	DISTRIBUTION COST PERCENT OF SALES
Finished Goods Transportation	3.32%
Warehousing	1.92
Order Processing/Customer Service	0.72
Distribution Administration	0.42
Inventory Carrying Cost @ 18%	2.18
Other	0.57
Total Distribution Cost	8.62%

Source: J.R. Davis, "Physical Distribution Costs: The 1982 Distribution/Service Data Base", 1982 Annual Proceedings, National Council of Physical Distribution Management, p. 55.

Figure 10-16. Physical distribution costs. (Source: J. R. Davis, "Physical Distribution Costs: The 1982 Distribution/Service Data Base," *1982 Annual Proceedings,* National Council of Physical Distribution Management, p. 55.)

vehicle do not increase in proportion to its size, and second, the costs of handling, dispatching, and documentation tend to remain the same regardless of size. Examples of this principle include the increase in trailer size and the use of large-size multiple units for barge and rail transportation.

4. *Adaptation of Vehicle Unit to Volume and Nature of Traffic.* The flow of traffic of any carrier tends to vary not only over an extended period of time but also during days of the week and hours of the day. The amount of equipment must be adapted to the traffic for maximum efficiency. For example, multiple units of freight cars and barges permit carriers to adapt the size of the vehicle unit to the volume of traffic. Also, new types of equipment such as rack cars for automobiles have reduced transportation costs.

5. *Standardization.* General-purpose, standardized equipment such as freight cars, trailers, and cargo ships can be used to transport a variety of materials economically in both directions of a trip. Although shippers often seek specialized equipment to meet their particular needs, the backhaul of such equipment tends to be empty. Standardization in transportation management applies not only to equipment but also to terminals, shops, and methods of operation.

6. *Compatability of Unit Load Equipment.* Unit load equipment placed in vehicles or containers should be of dimensions that readily fit and maximize cube space utilization as well as reducing load shift and damage to cargo.

7. *Minimization of Deadweight to Total Weight.* The cost of fuel in transport operations is directly related to the total weight of the unit of movement, whereas revenue relates only to the payload in the vehicle. The larger the transportation vehicle, the more favorable this ratio tends to be. Lightweight materials and proper design can help minimize the deadweight or empty weight of containers and transportation vehicles.

8. *Maximum Utilization of Capital, Equipment, and Personnel.* The intensive utilization of capital, plant, equipment, and personnel can be hindered by seasonal variations in business activity. Also, the imbalance of traffic between destinations causes empty vehicle movement. To reduce this imbalance, carriers may offer lower backhaul rates, may use vigorous promotion, or may merge. Utilization also refers to the percentage of time that a vehicle is moving with a load versus remaining idle.

Deregulation

Transportation management has experienced significant changes with government deregulation of carriers. Air freight carriers, railroads, and motor carriers were deregulated by the Air Cargo Deregulation Act of 1977, the Staggers Rail Act of 1980, and the Motor Carrier Act of 1980. Finding that the former regulatory structure had tended to inhibit market entry and carrier growth, and to cause operating inefficiencies and anticompetitive pricing, Congress passed these laws to promote competition within the various carrier industries. Deregulation was also intended to encourage minority participation, service to smaller communities, intermodal shipments, and a variety of quality and price options to meet changing market demands and the diverse needs of the shipping public.

Air Carriers. The 1977 Air Cargo Deregulation Act covers all-cargo aircraft only; it does not include passenger planes that also carry cargo. This law gave carriers with all-cargo operations the opportunity to broaden their coverage to all 50 states, Puerto Rico, and the Virgin Islands. It lifted restrictions on the size of aircraft that could be used for all-cargo service; as a result, Federal Express, Emery Air Freight, and other carriers purchased additional aircraft and started new schedules and services. The law also allowed airlines the freedom to establish freight rates as long as they were not unjustly discriminatory. Air carriers were not required to file tariffs or freight charges with the Civil Aeronautics Board (CAB).

Railroads. The Staggers Rail Act of 1980 granted new freedoms to U.S. railroads with regard to pricing, operations, and service. The act authorized railroads to enter into contract rates with shippers, thereby eliminating former contract uncertainties that had contributed to higher rail costs. As a result, volume shippers have reduced costs as much as 20 percent. The ICC deregulated both domestic and international piggyback rail movements in March 1981, allowing lower rates on TOFC (trailer-on-flatcar) and COFC (container-on-flatcar) traffic. Also, the role and importance of rate bureaus were reduced. The bureau cannot set rates charged by only one railroad, and only railroads that participate in carrying traffic may vote to change the rates.

Motor Carriers. Transportation managers gained an increased range of available services as the 1980 Motor Carrier Act made it easier for new companies to enter the trucking industry and for existing companies to expand their operations. Additional benefits are available to companies that support carrier applications for authority and in negotiating rates. Companies that are operating private fleets can obtain carrier authority for backhauls. They can be very competitive, with their rates sometimes covering only out-of-pocket costs.

The 1980 Act significantly affected pricing systems used by motor carriers—for example, permitting discounts for less-than-truckload (LTL) freight moving in single-line service (one carrier moving a load from origin

...1 for multiple-tender pickups (one carrier pickup at ... ...in the same area). Discounts began with class rates ...modities within one rate classification), and are now offered ...tion ratings (carrier taking exception to the normal classification ...establishing a higher/lower rate generally based on volume or a special condition such as fragile material). Other discounts also have been offered for deliveries to a carrier's dock and for FAK (freight-all kinds, or a flat rate for all types of materials loaded in a container or freight car).

Deregulation has also resulted in reduced costs for small shipments in the form of price discounts and/or improved service. Some carriers offer a refund if delivery is late, with a possible savings of 5 to 15 percent. Following the passage of deregulation laws, one metal building products manufacturer reported a 20 percent reduction in transportation costs. Their primary savings came from: (1) carriers contacting them and offering sizable reductions in rates, (2) discounts for LTL shipments, and (3) contract rates that included refund provisions.

Operational Improvement Techniques

Traffic managers apply numerous techniques to reduce transportation costs besides those resulting from deregulation. Some of these techniques are reviewed below.

Consolidated Shipments. This technique involves grouping smaller shipments together to form a full carrier load (e.g., truckload quantity). The benefit is reduced cost, but shipments may be delayed. For example, assume that four loads are going to the same company. The schedule and cost for shipping individual loads are shown in the tabulation.

ORDER	SHIPPING DATE	WEIGHT	RATE	COST
A	Monday	5,000 lbs.	$4.00 CWT*	$ 200.00
B	Tuesday	6,000 lbs.	$4.00 CWT	240.00
C	Wednesday	10,000 lbs.	$3.00 CWT	300.00
D	Thursday	9,000 lbs.	$3.00 CWT	270.00
TOTAL		30,000 lbs.		$1,010.00

*CWT refers to per hundred weight.

If, instead of individual shipments, all four orders were shipped on Friday in one truck, on one bill of lading, the cost would be 30,000 lbs. × $2.00 CWT or $600.00. Total savings would be $1,010.00 − $600.00 = $410.00, or 40 percent.

Another variation, *stop-off-in-transit,* involves grouping shipments going in the same general direction. In Figure 10-17, four company orders are

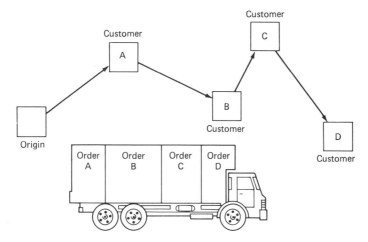

Figure 10-17. Stop-off-in-transit.

being shipped to different points in one truck. Using the same information as in the example above, the total cost of shipping a consolidated truckload would be $600.00. A charge of $25.00 per stop is added, for a total cost of $675.00. Deducting $675.00 from the previous cost of shipping individual orders ($1,010.00), the resultant savings is $335.00, or 33 percent.

Storage-in-Transit.   Storage-in-transit is a method of shipment whereby a freight car is held at some point before reaching its final destination. For example, suppose a freight car load of lumber is bought at a price well below market value, with no known customer at the time of purchase. The lumber is moved from the sawmill in Portland, Oregon, to a strategic point, Salt Lake City, Utah, where it can be subsequently shipped to a number of potential purchasers, as illustrated in Figure 10-18. The cost of shipping 100,000 lbs. of lumber from point A to B, and then to C, D, or E, would be $9.00 CWT or $9,000.00. Using storage-in-transit, the charges would be $5.00 CWT plus $500.00 storage cost, or a total cost of $5,500.00. The savings would be $9,000.00 − $5,500.00 = $3,500.00, or 39 percent.

Freight Bill Audit.   Many companies determine the correct transportation charges either prior to or after payment to the carrier, and then audit the freight bills to detect errors in weight and rate, or duplicate payments. Audits can be an effective cost-reduction technique, with an error factor of perhaps 2½ to 5 percent. Assuming a total of $10,000,000 in annual freight bills, identification of 3 percent error would yield a savings of $300,000.

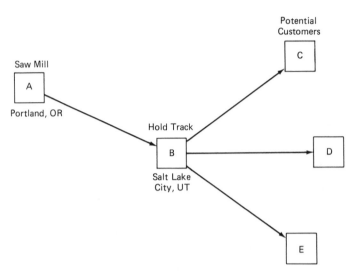

Figure 10-18. Storage-in-transit.

Private Trucking. The primary reason for using private trucking is to improve customer service and/or to reduce transportation costs. It gives the company greater control and flexibility in shipping products to customers. Other advantages include shorter transit times, reduced damage, and the use of drivers as salespeople or to promote good will. Disadvantages may include problems related to empty backhauls, capital investment requirements, vehicle maintenance, and labor unions.

Continuous Movement Program. Companies such as Xerox and U.S. Gypsum are realizing transportation savings of millions of dollars per year by utilizing the continuous movement program. This technique essentially allows a company to have private trucking operations without making any investment in equipment and without having drivers on their payroll. In a simplified version of how it works, the company contacts a common carrier or contract carrier and negotiates a guaranteed payment for the use of a truck for a specific period of time, typically seven to ten days. The carrier is paid for all miles driven, whether the truck is empty or full. The company's coordinator schedules the truck and informs the carrier's dispatcher. A continuous movement program reduces both the company's transportation cost per mile and total transportation costs.

For example, U.S. Gypsum contracts with a carrier for a continuous movement program for the use of a flat-bed truck. Their company coordinator schedules each leg or trip movement of the truck as follows: The truck starts at a plant in Ft. Dodge, Iowa, and picks up a load of gypsum wallboard. It delivers the load at a company facility in East Chicago, Indiana. Wallboard joint compound is loaded on the truck, which travels to a warehouse in Cleveland, Ohio. The truck dead-heads (travels empty) to Genoa, Ohio, where it picks up a load of bagged lime. The lime is then delivered to the plant in Ft. Dodge, Iowa, to end the contract. For companies that utilize a continuous movement program, it is critical to maximize loaded legs, and to minimize or eliminate empty backhauls.

INTERNATIONAL PHYSICAL DISTRIBUTION

International physical distribution is concerned with the control, storage, and movement of products shipped from the United States to other countries, and from other countries to the United States. International distribution is very different from, and more complicated than, domestic activities. With competition in world markets increasing rapidly, physical distribution becomes a key factor, affecting such areas as transportation, warehousing costs, materials handling, packaging, timely delivery, and documentation preparation.

Growth of International Operations

The United States conducts both import and export operations, trading with almost every country in the world, with a few exceptions that are usually based on political considerations. Trade with Canada and Mexico, two of the larger U.S. markets, is relatively simple because they are close to the United States, and all modes of transportation can be used. Trading with other countries involves longer transportation distances and fewer alternative shipping modes.

After World War II, many U.S. companies realized that trade with foreign countries was vital to their growth. Foreign markets offer vast opportunities to expand sales, whereas importation from other countries provides additional sources of raw materials, components, and finished goods. Foreign companies have recognized the advantages of opening new markets and developing new sources of supply. The expansion of world trade has increased competition between companies and fostered the growth of multinational firms.

United States companies have aggressively pursued markets in other countries as a means of increasing both sales and profits. Export statistics indicate the importance of this growing foreign market. In 1987, U.S. exports of merchandise amounted to $252.9 billion; this figure represents commercial activity only, and does not include military shipments. At the same time, imports from other countries had also increased, with imported materials for 1987 totaling $405.9 billion.[28]

Documentation

Processing documentation for export and import is much more complicated than for domestic transportation. For example, a domestic shipment may require only two documents, whereas an international shipment might require ten, including a bill of lading, letter of credit, customs entry, special customs invoice, consular documents, export declaration, packing list, insurance certificate, dock receipt, and shipping instructions.

Research conducted in 1988 showed the United States spending 7% of total product cost annually on transportation-related data in international trade. High documentation costs have prompted companies to develop sophisticated computer systems to minimize expenses. New Jersey–based Johnson & Johnson International devoted eight years to developing an integrated, on-line computer system capable of handling all export order processing and documentation. The new system takes an order from initial entry through purchasing, warehousing, and traffic activities, produces all the necessary traffic department documents, and provides distribution management with detailed reports of every transaction. It has improved data accuracy, eliminated the use of freight forwarders, and ended paperwork bottlenecks. The new system paid for itself in three months.[29]

Some companies lack the in-house expertise necessary to prepare required documentation for export and import shipments; these companies and some larger companies will require the assistance of outside specialists. International freight forwarders and import brokers can help such companies by managing their import/export operations. Their services include preparing documentation, arranging for insurance and carrier accommodations, and providing general consultation.

Packaging

International shipments are subject to greater potential damage than domestic movements. Frequent handling imposes additional stress and strain, requiring more stringent packaging to minimize in-transit damage. The amount of packaging varies, depending on the transportation mode(s). Air carriers have the advantage of not subjecting cargo to rough handling. In many cases, the packaging for materials shipped on international flights is the same as for domestic flights. However, the high rates charged for air cargo limit the use of this mode.

Ocean transportation frequently is used for international distribution because it is relatively inexpensive. However, ocean freight is subject to rough handling at the dock, tumultuous movements of the ship, climatic exposure at sea, and additional movements during the loading and unloading of delivery vehicles; so more stringent packaging is required for ocean transportation. Containers are often used to reduce potential damage.

Other factors that justify additional packaging costs for international shipments are increased travel distances and greater stockout risks. Lead time for international transportation is relatively long, and materials purchasers cannot readily replace delayed, lost, or damaged merchandise. Considering the travel distance, the increased chances of damage, and the potential stockout cost, both buyer and seller would want adequate packaging to be provided.

Package marking is critical to all international shipments. Damage can be limited by the use of international markings, as illustrated in Figure 10-19. These precautionary symbols provide instructions to handlers and

Figure 10-19. International pictorial markings. (Source: *Ports of the World,* 13th Edition, Insurance Company of North America and CIGNA Company, Philadelphia, Pa., p. 84.)

eliminate language barriers. Codes are used to conceal the identity of the shipper, the consignee, and the materials, in order to reduce pilferage.

ANALYSIS OF OPERATIONS

Developing a good physical distribution system requires comprehensive analysis and design. Analysis often begins with an audit of current operations and a forecast of future requirements. Its scope can vary widely; micro analysis might be limited to a specific activity such as order picking in a distribution center, whereas macroanalysis might include total national or international distribution operations. A determination of which data are required and how they can be obtained will affect both the study costs and quality of the analysis. Various analytical techniques are available, both manual and computerized, to provide guidance in decision making.

Analytical Techniques

Various analytical techniques can be used to plan an optimum distribution system to meet changing company conditions. Some common applications for quantitative tools are discussed below.

Number and Location of Distribution Centers. A classical distribution problem is to determine the best distribution network for a particular company—specifically, how many distribution centers are required, and where they should be located. For many manufacturing companies, such a study can be extended to determine how many manufacturing sites are desirable and what should be produced at each site. We will focus our discussion upon the most general application for both manufacturing and nonmanufacturing business—determining the optimum number and location of distribution centers.

Number of warehouses. The number of warehouses within a company's distribution network affects many aspects of its business. Generally, the customer service level increases with the number of distribution centers, while costs related to safety stock, buildings, and labor also increase. Thus, a key objective of physical distribution management is to minimize the number of warehouses while providing good customer service.

Some analytical techniques use computer programs to determine the number of distribution centers. One such method employs simulation to develop a mathematical system, or model, that evaluates possible operational characteristics by changing input information. Thus, simulation allows the evaluation of different alternatives without committing the company's actual resources.

Another tool used to determine the optional number of warehouse locations is the heuristic model. Heuristics attempts to formulate a good or near-optimum solution. By employing programming short-cuts, heuristics is simpler, is less expensive, and requires less computer time than simulation to develop a solution.

Reducing the number of distribution centers often yields significant benefits. For example, the U.S. Department of Defense changed its supply tactics in 1960. Most overseas Air Force bases had previously maintained their own supply and maintenance warehouses, but in 1960 individual supply locations were eliminated, and five major U.S. bases were chosen to provide materials to all locations, with electronic communications and air transportation servicing the overseas sites. This reduction in warehouses drastically reduced the requirements for expensive items, such as engines and electronics equipment.[30]

Site location.   There are many possible techniques for selecting the site for a distribution center, two common ones being the grid method and the center-of-gravity method. The grid method superimposes vertical and horizontal lines on a map, and locates customer sites within this grid system. A computer program, using simple mathematics, can then compute the various distances to determine the best warehouse location.

A simple example of the center-of-gravity method is illustrated in Figure 10-20. Here, too, a grid system is placed on a map containing customer locations. In the example, assume that the grid is in one-mile increments, each customer receives an equal number of products, and a straight line is

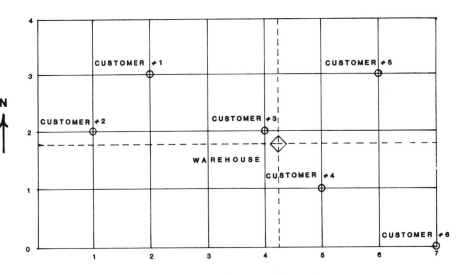

Figure 10-20. "Center-of-gravity" site location.

used for all distances. The warehouse location is computed by averaging the distances of each customer from the 0–0 point. The customers are located north of 0–0 at grid points 2, 3, 2, 1, 3, and 0. Dividing the total of 11 by six customer locations, yields an average north location of 1.8. The customers are located east of 0–0 at points 1, 2, 4, 5, 6, and 7. Dividing the total of 25 by six customer locations yields an average east location of 4.2. Therefore, the "best" location for a warehouse is at coordinates 1.8 north and 4.2 east.

Vehicle Routing.   Another common distribution problem is vehicle routing. Manual systems have been used to determine vehicle routing based on mileage between points derived from such sources as the *Household Goods Carriers' Bureau Mileage Guide.* Considering the high cost of fuel, labor, and vehicles, it is desirable to use computers to develop more efficient vehicle routings. Software programs for such purposes originally were developed primarily for large computers, but now software packages for smaller-capacity computers are available for purchase or for use on a time-sharing basis.

Computerized vehicle routing can provide sizable savings; according to one study, mileage reductions typically range from 5 to 30 percent of total miles driven. Any fleet that consists of ten or more vehicles, makes at least five stops per vehicle, and has specialized delivery requirements is a good candidate for computerized routing. Figure 10-21 shows how a wholesale liquor company improved its routing system by using a computer. Annual savings were approximately 15 percent of miles driven, or 7 percent of the company's annual transportation budget.[31]

RELATIONSHIPS WITH OTHER MATERIALS MANAGEMENT SUBFUNCTIONS

Physical distribution is an important component of any total materials management program. The members of the distribution group can be most effective as team members, and their relationships with other materials subfunctions should be close and supportive. Some of the key relationships are reviewed below.

Purchasing

A close relationship between physical distribution and purchasing improves inbound supplier shipments. Distribution can provide purchasing with a routing guide indicating preferred carriers for suppliers to use. The company can reduce inbound freight costs by utilizing carriers with whom the physical distribution group has established discount programs; these carriers can also provide more reliable on-time delivery. If the company

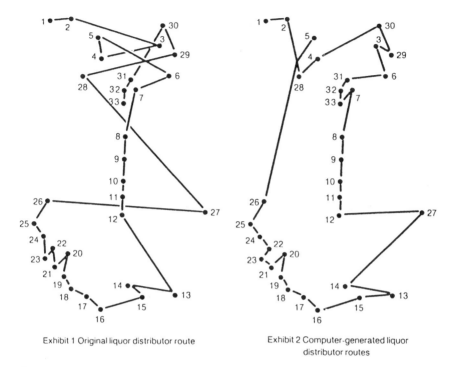

Exhibit 1 Original liquor distributor route

Exhibit 2 Computer-generated liquor distributor routes

Figure 10-21. Example of vehicle routing improvement using a computer. (Source: Reprinted with permission from *Handling & Shipping Management,* Aug. 1982 issue. Copyright © 1982, Penton Publishing, Inc., Cleveland, Ohio.)

maintains a private fleet of trucks, purchasing can ask suppliers with large shipments to contact the traffic department to see if company trucks are available, thus providing full backhauls for company vehicles. Physical distribution depends upon purchasing to provide a continuous flow of high-quality packing materials and other supplies, and to buy the equipment required for physical distribution operations.

Inventory Control

The relationship between physical distribution and inventory control varies, depending upon the organizational structure and delegation of responsibilities. If the company has a centralized system (in which inventory control responsibilities include all inventories), then inventory control is responsible for finished goods. Inventory control depends upon physical distribution to maintain highly accurate data for optimum control of expensive finished goods, and physical distribution requires that inventory control send timely authorizations to production control and/or purchasing for replenishment of inventory. Poor timing here can mean product deficiencies, which waste the time of order pickers and other distribution employees; but, on the other hand, products received too early at the distribution center can cause congestion. Inventory control should consider optimum unit load sizes in ordering, so that distribution can make efficient use of space, labor, and equipment. Companies that have decentralized the responsibility for finished goods inventory should encourage the transfer of technical knowledge between the inventory control and distribution groups.

Production Control

Production control activities have a pronounced effect upon physical distribution operations. Good scheduling and a good flow of finished goods provide physical distribution with required products, and enhance the efficiency of distribution activities in many ways, such as improved order picking, reduction of partial shipments to customers, and timely customer shipments. Control of finished goods flow to physical distribution points will help those facilities to utilize space efficiently and to relieve congested conditions. The physical distribution group must maximize the efforts of production control. If production control expends additional resources (e.g., expediting, production equipment, and labor) to obtain finished products for a customer, its efforts should be reinforced by an efficient physical distribution center.

Materials Handling

Materials handling design contributes to physical distribution operations. Most physical distribution activities are related to some aspect of materials handling; and the ultimate success of physical distribution operations, including optimum use of space, labor, and equipment, largely depends on the degree and efficiency of materials handling mechanization and/or automation. Physical distribution should provide user-related information and suggestions during the developmental stages of any new materials handling system, as well as positive inputs during the debugging period. Materials handling and distribution also interact in packaging design, to ensure that products are delivered undamaged to customers.

RELATIONSHIPS WITH OTHER COMPANY FUNCTIONS

Physical distribution's broad spectrum of responsibilities naturally puts it in contact with all major company functions, as the following review of some of its common relationships shows.

Marketing

Distribution's strongest ties are with marketing. The relationship is so close that in some companies distribution is included within the marketing organization. Physical distribution is the materials management subfunction that has contact with the customer, in its responsibility for storage and physical movement of finished goods; and marketing depends upon distribution to provide the customer with the right product, in the right quantities, at the right place, and in an undamaged condition. Thus, physical distribution is a critical element in marketing's effort to achieve customer satisfaction. Distribution's support of marketing is receiving greater emphasis, as many companies are reducing raw material inventories and insisting that suppliers hold inventory, or be capable of producing and distributing materials rapidly in response to demand.

Marketing, in turn, can influence the success of physical distribution operations. For example, as physical distribution copes with the problems of inventories in various distribution centers, poor sales forecasts from marketing can result in manufacturing or purchasing the wrong items or storage of finished goods in the wrong locations; so good forecasts are essential. Marketing also must provide good feedback regarding the distribution system's effectiveness. Accurate, objective assessments of customer problems help physical distribution to adjust elements of its system, to satisfy customers while maximizing company resources.

Finance

As part of its planning and reporting, the finance and accounting group depends upon physical distribution to provide accurate, reliable information about finished goods inventory, which, with its high dollar volume, is a critical company asset. In allocating company funds for various activities, finance also requires that physical distribution plan for long-term capital investments in facilities and equipment. "Surprises," such as the urgent need to expand a distribution center, can be harmful to a company's financial plan.

Physical distribution depends upon the accounting department for cost information regarding distribution-related activities. Often accounting systems are designed for developing financial statements and analyses for stockholders/owners or for tax purposes; so the distribution group should ask accounting to develop specific cost information, such as warehouse costs, that will provide the data they need to control operations. Also, because finished goods inventory can be very expensive—if there is too much or too little (resulting in lost sales)—distribution must coordinate inventory accumulation with finance. If the control of monies for finished goods inventory is too tight, it can cripple a distribution program.

Manufacturing

Manufacturing and physical distribution can differ over production run quantities. Long runs are desirable from a production viewpoint, to reduce setup cost per unit and increase labor efficiency; but extended runs are a problem for distribution because they result in excess inventory accumulation. In some industries, the manufacturing group tries to avoid seasonal fluctuations, which result in overtime and second shifts, and depends upon distribution for warehouse capacity to store excess production quantities during lower demand periods. This storage capacity allows production to proceed at a consistent level.

Similarly, physical distribution requires the cooperation of manufacturing to achieve maximum effectiveness. If production supervisors fail to conform to schedules and produce excess finished goods, distribution can have problems with congestion and poor space utilization.

Another area of cooperation is production information. Physical distribution is responsible for traffic and transportation for inbound, interplant, and outbound shipments, and needs timely and accurate information from manufacturing concerning the actual number of units produced, scrapped, and so forth, in order to properly schedule transportation activities. Last-minute searching for carriers for inbound or interplant shipments can result from manufacturing difficulties and poor communication.

Engineering

Engineering decisions on the introduction of new products affect the distribution group. The physical dimensions of new products impact such distribution concerns as storage systems and truck capabilities. Engineering should request input from physical distribution about how alterations in a product, such as changes in dimensions or weight, will affect the use of current equipment. In some companies, the design and testing of product packaging are part of engineering's responsibilities. In such cases, engineering must coordinate any prospective changes in packaging design with the physical distribution group because packaging will affect damage rates and storage system usage.

Quality Assurance

Physical distribution depends upon quality assurance to provide defect-free finished goods. Distribution must be able to assume that the products it ships to customers are of good quality. The sudden appearance of large numbers of defects could produce customer complaints and requests that company trucks pick up merchandise. Sometimes it is difficult to distinguish between items damaged in shipment, and items that were originally defective; thus defects can involve distribution in excessive damage claims and paperwork.

SUMMARY

The physical distribution group is generally responsible for the movement, storage, order assembly, packing, shipping, and transportation of finished goods going to the customer. Normally, distribution is also responsible for inbound transportation, working in conjunction with purchasing. Interplant movements are handled by distribution if multiple facilities exist. Physical distribution activities provide the customer with the right product, at the right place, at the right time, in the right condition, and at the right price.

A primary objective for the distribution group is to reduce costs and increase profits; providing good customer service, in conjunction with the company's marketing efforts, is also critical. Other objectives include optimizing total distribution costs, minimizing finished goods inventory, providing dependable, timely delivery to customers, determining and providing the best transportation services, and minimizing the order cycle.

The organization of physical distribution varies from one firm to another. Companies committed to the total materials management concept will include distribution within that function. Some companies may include it with marketing, because of the close association of distribution with customer service. The activities assigned to physical distribution also vary according to the individual company organization. Normally, its activities include order processing, materials handling and packaging, warehousing, order assembly, shipping, and transportation.

Transportation management is a key component of physical distribution. Transportation costs add nothing to product value, but poor transportation management can increase costs and reduce profits. A set of principles of transportation, developed by Marvin L. Fair and Ernest W. Williams, Jr., can help to improve traffic and transportation operations.

Laws passed by the U.S. Congress, beginning in 1977, have reduced government regulation of various carriers, creating many new opportunities for companies to reduce transportation costs and improve customer service. Other techniques for improving transportation services include consolidated shipments, storage-in-transit, freight bill audit, private trucking, and the continuous movement program.

International physical distribution activities have dramatically increased with the growth of importing and exporting since World War II, with documentation that is much more complicated than for domestic shipments. Freight forwarders and import brokers can assist companies in managing their international shipments. These shipments are subject to greater potential damage and require more stringent packaging than domestic shipments. Another factor that may justify added packaging cost with these materials is the length of time required to replace damaged materials, and the resultant stockout costs.

Good physical distribution systems require comprehensive analysis and design. Various analytical techniques, both manual and computerized, provide guidance for decision making. Some of these techniques are simulation, heuristics, center-of-gravity and grid site location, and computerized routing.

NOTES

1. Coyle, Bardi, and Cavinato, *Transportation,* p. 511.
2. Lieb, *Transportation: The Domestic System,* p. 4.
3. Gecowets, "Physical Distribution Management: What It Is — How It Got That Way," p. 90.
4. "Does Your Customer Service Program Stack Up?" pp. 54–58.
5. Whiting, "Public Warehousing and the 'Just-In-Time' Production System," p. 8.
6. "The Distribution Manager Takes on a Bigger Role," pp. 37–40.
7. Bernard J. LaLonde, "Transportation in the 21st Century," Washington, D.C., speech printed by The Warehousing Education and Research Council, Inc.
8. Perry, "The Principles of Distribution Resource Planning (DRP)," pp. 20–33.
9. Donald J. Bowersox, David J. Closs, and Omar K. Helferich, *Logistical Management,* Macmillan Publishing Company, New York, 1986, p. 132.
10. Farrel, "Dow Corning Puts Matrix Management to Work," p. 57.
11. Johnson and Wood, *Contemporary Physical Distribution and Logistics,* p. 253.
12. Voorhees and Sharp, "The Principles of Logistics Revisited," p. 69–84.
13. Michael P. Novitsky and C. Richard Polzello, "Improving Customer Service through Better Finished Goods Management," *1983 International Conference Proceedings,* American Production and Inventory Control Society, pp. 66–68.
14. Taff, *Management of Physical Distribution and Transportation,* pp. 285–286.
15. Sid Mott, "Packaging, Handling and Transportation — A Marriage for Profit," privately circulated paper, p. 1.
16. George Roshkind, "Management of Aspects of Packaging Adequacy Control (Testing)," *Proceedings* of Pack Info '83, 1983 International Packaging Week Conference, The Packaging Institute, U.S.A., Oct. 4–6, 1983.
17. Taff, *Management of Physical Distribution and Transportation,* p. 176.
18. For manufacturing companies only.
19. Tersine and Campbell, *Modern Materials Management,* p. 141.
20. Andel, "Linked Computers Break Records for Shipping Time," pp. 87–91.
21. "Manual Orderpicking Top Productivity is Within Your Reach!" pp. 54–55.
22. *Transportation Facts,* p. 32.
23. Bowersox, Closs, and Helferich, *Logistical Management,* p. 163.
24. VanWicklen, "Opportunity Rides the Rivers," p. 51.
25. Johnson and Wood, *Contemporary Physical Distribution and Logistics,* pp. 135–138.
26. J. R. Davis, "Physical Distribution Costs: 1982 Distribution/Service Data Base," *1982 Annual Proceedings,* National Council of Physical Distribution Management, p. 55.
27. Fair and Williams, *Transportation and Logistics,* pp. 90–100.

28. *Highlights of U.S. Export and Import Trade,* Ft 990, U.S. Department of Commerce, Dec., 1987, p. A-3.
29. Harrington, "World Trade Documents Enter the Age of Automation," pp. 33–35.
30. U.S. Congress, House Committee on Armed Services, *Review of Department of Defense Worldwide Communications, Phase I,* U.S. Government Printing Office, Washington, D.C., 1971, p. 20.
31. Hooban and Camozzo, "New Opportunities in Vehicle Routing," pp. 49–50.

BIBLIOGRAPHY

Ardel, Tom. "Linked Computers Break Records for Shipping Time." *Material Handling Engineering,* Mar. 1984.

Ballou, Ronald H. *Business Logistics Management, Planning and Control.* Englewood Cliffs, New Jersey: Prentice-Hall, 1985.

Bowersox, Donald J., Closs, David J., and Helferich, Omar K. *Logistical Management.* New York: Macmillan Publishing Co., 1986.

Christopher, Martin. *The Strategy of Distribution Management.* Gower Publishing (England), 1985.

Coyle, John J., and Bardi, Edward J. *The Management of Business Logistics.* St. Paul, Minnesota: West Publishing Co., 1984.

Coyle, John J., Bardi, Edward J., and Cavinato, Joseph L. *Transportation.* St. Paul, Minnesota: West Publishing Co., 1986.

Davies, G. J., and Gray R. *Purchasing International Freight Transportation Services.* Gower Publishing (England), 1985.

de Roulet, D.G., "Evaluating Third-Party Distribution Services," *Transportation and Distribution,* Apr. 1988.

"Does Your Customer Service Program Stack Up?" *Traffic Management,* Sept. 1982.

Fair, Marvin L., and Williams, Ernest W., Jr., *Transportation and Logistics.* Plano, Texas: Business Publications, 1981.

Farrel, Jack W. "Dow Corning Puts Matrix Management to Work." *Traffic Management,* Oct. 1982.

Gecowets, George A. "Physical Distribution Management: What It Is—How It Got That Way." *That's Transportation,* Oct. 1983.

Harrington, Lisa H. "World Trade Documents Enter the Age of Automation." *Traffic Management,* Oct. 1982.

Highlights of U.S. Export and Import Trade, Ft 990, U.S. Department of Commerce, Dec. 1987, p. A-3.

Hooban, J. Michael, and Camozzo, Bob. "New Opportunities in Vehicle Routing." *Handling and Shipping Management,* Aug. 1982.

Johnson, James C., and Wood, Donald F. *Contemporary Physical Distribution and Logistics.* New York: Macmillan Publishing Co., 1986.

Lieb, Robert C. *Transportation: The Domestic System.* Reston, Virginia: Reston Publishing Co., 1981.

Magee, John F., Copacino, William C., and Rosenfield, Donald B. *Modern Logistics Management.* New York: John Wiley and Sons, 1985.

"Manual Orderpicking Top Productivity Is Within Your Reach!" *Modern Materials Handling,* Jan. 20, 1983.

Perry, William. "The Principles of Distribution Resource Planning (DRP)." *Production and Inventory Management Review,* Dec. 1982.

Schneider, Lewis M. "New Era in Transportation Strategy." *Harvard Business Review,* Mar.–Apr. 1985.

"Software Masterpieces For Distribution." *Distribution,* 1985.

Taff, Charles A. *Management of Physical Distribution and Transportation.* Homewood, Illinois: Richard D. Irwin, 1984.

Talley, Wayne Kenneth. *Introduction to Transportation.* Cincinnati, Ohio: South-Western Publishing Co., 1983.

"The Distribution Manager Takes on a Bigger Role." *Traffic Management,* Dec. 1982.

Railroad Facts, Association of American Railroads, Washington, D.C., Sept. 1987.

Tersine, Richard J., and Campbell, John H. *Modern Materials Management.* New York: Elsevier North-Holland, 1977.

Tompkins, James A., and Smith Jerry D., *The Warehouse Management Handbook,* New York: McGraw-Hill Book Co., 1988.

VanWicklen, Paul F. "Opportunity Rides the Rivers." *Handling and Shipping Management,* May 1982.

Voorhees, Roy Dale, and Sharp, Merrill Kim. "The Principles of Logistics Revisited." *Transportation Journal,* Fall 1978.

Whiting, R. Scott. "Public Warehousing and the 'Just-In-Time' Production System." *Warehousing Review,* Winter Issue 1982.

Part Four

IMPLEMENTATION AND CONTROL OF MATERIALS MANAGEMENT

11
System Design and Computer Application For Materials Management

Systems and computers have provided materials management with dynamic control of the entire materials cycle, from procurement through shipment, with full lot/location traceability. The use of a functional design allows for "dock to stock" tracking, including the often overlooked functions of receiving, inspection, materials disposition, and vendor evaluation. This methodology has changed the way materials management operates in the organization.

SYSTEMS IN MATERIALS MANAGEMENT

A materials management system is an organized approach used to deal with problems involving a combination of skills from complementary disciplines, both managerial and technical, that require these special skills to be expended in a unified effort.[1] Thus, a system is made up of the interrelated elements of a work process. These elements, called subsystems, do not stand alone; each subsystem serves one or more higher-order subsystems, which fit together, supporting one another to achieve an objective. System elements may include personnel, machines, and nonphysical entities working in an interrelated fashion. The directed activity of a system is viewed as the processing of inputs and their transformation into outputs.

Briefly, the systems approach is a group of concepts, methods, and techniques used for problem solving, decision making, analyzing organizations and processes, and evaluating performance. In more formal terms, the systems approach involves:

- Defining materials management problems as decision-making situations consisting of constraints, resources, alternatives, and criteria for measurement.
- Analyzing how variables influence the decision result, and developing

models that describe the relationship of inputs and processes to outputs.

- Evaluating alternative solutions on the basis of different values, and, using these results, identifying preferred courses of action under various circumstances.

The Systems Approach

A materials management system, or any other system that contributes to the effectiveness and productivity of an operation, involves a rational process of planning and developing a group of related elements. This process is characterized by models, decision rules, information systems, and the role of materials management. A system is based on a creative process that questions the assumption on which old techniques have been built. It provides a new outlook and approach in order to produce innovations capable of bringing feasible solutions to problems such as those of materials management.[2]

Users of a system must consider the purpose for the system's existence as well as how it interfaces with other systems. A system proceeds from the particular to the general, with the design of the best system inferred by a process of induction and synthesis.

The systems approach entails a way of thinking that emphasizes the whole system, rather than individual parts striving to optimize a given problem (see Table 11-1.). A system's methodology has the following characteristics:

- It defines a problem in relation to the system to which it belongs.
- It views the system's objectives in relation to larger systems.
- It evaluates the extent to which a design diverges from the optimum design.

Table 11-1. System Analysis Versus Scientific Method Thinking.

SYSTEM ANALYSIS	SCIENTIFIC METHOD
1. Problem exists.	1. Problem exists.
2. Problem is embedded in the situation.	2. Problem has a single cause.
3. Problem requires alternative solutions.	3. Problem requires a single solution.
4. The solution has other effects that must be anticipated, in addition to its intended impact on the problem.	4. The solution has a direct impact on the problem.
5. Problem will not stay solved because the situation will change.	5. Problem will stay solved.

Adapted from David R. Hampton, *Contemporary Management* (New York: McGraw-Hill, 1977), pp. 21–25.

- It requires that planning, evaluation, innovation, and creative alternatives be initiated in the system.
- It involves inductive reasoning.
- It encourages the choice of alternatives that alleviate the unwanted effects of previous systems.

A system reflects management's policy, its attitudes, and its knowledge of the organization. These and many other factors must be considered in systems development.

Systems Analysis

Systems analysis is a comparison of alternatives with the objective of selecting the most desirable one. To permit a comparison, an analysis must identify the specific properties of the alternatives that will be compared. All elements of the alternatives must be taken into account, and data estimates are made for each element. Knowledge of the role of each element, and how it leads to a given alternative, is the central issue in systems analysis. The major elements of the system involved in the process are the first to be analyzed.

A system involves a set of objects, properties, and relationships, the objects of the system being its input, output, process, feedback, and restrictions. *Input* causes the operation of a given process, whereas the end result of the process is the *output*. The *relationships* between systems cause continuation of processes, and outputs in which humans are involved, or cause processes to be executed by human individuals. A system's *process* transforms inputs into outputs. *Feedback* compares actual outputs with objectives, and identifies any discrepancies between them. The discovery of significant differences provides a means of interacting with the basic process to achieve the system's objectives.

The system's *restrictions* establish the framework of the system, along with its other limitations. These limitations, called constraints of the system, must be consistent with its objectives. The various subsystems describe the system's scope. The system's boundary describes the inputs, processes, and outputs it requires to operate; it also includes all the resources required to operate the system—time, money, manpower, and materials.

Problems may exist in the actual conditions of the proposed system that will prevent increase, decrease, or change the output. These problems may be recognized through continuous monitoring and evaluation of the system's output. Their detection is made possible by prior knowledge of the desired behavior.

Solutions to problems are directed toward the system's operations. A solution may be found by using quantitative relationships, or, if they are at least partially known, qualitative relationships and elements of the problem. A solution results from analysis and evaluation based on cost, time, effectiveness, risk, and other factors.

The objective of systems analysis is to examine a situation and determine how the controllable variables relate to the results obtained. Systems analysis is not a one-time exercise. Once an operating system has been implemented, it must be reviewed continually to determine if the expected results are being achieved.

DESIGNING A MATERIALS MANAGEMENT SYSTEM

In the context of a systems approach, the term materials management includes all of the activities of the people involved in planning, evaluation, implementation, and control.[3] Each of these areas directly affects the others and the way the system will operate. Materials managers in effect become the system's designers, setting boundaries, establishing goals, and allocating resources. Each activity involves a sequence that constitutes the system process. Designers may not follow the same sequence in every case; a general systems approach is ever-changing and cannot be exactly defined.

A system's usefulness lies in its providing an objective frame of reference. Materials management requires a clear description of its operations, regardless of their complexity. The system is built on the premise that similarities exist between the way machine-like and man-dominated systems function. By using the analogy of a logically designed, machine-like system, the system suggests the way an efficient man-dominated system should operate.

Statement of Problem

The statement of the problem requires collecting information to define the problem as completely as possible.[4] The process begins by asking: what is the present system? The question does not presuppose that there is no existing method for coping with the problem. The existing method may not be working, or it may be poorly conceived. Its limitations must be defined carefully in order to document the problem. The nature of the existing system is determined through intensive data collection and interviewing that take advantage of every type of existing information. It is easier to discard useless information later, rather than to have insufficient information and have to collect additional data.

The statement of the problem concentrates upon the existing system, and may be descriptive or analytical. Descriptive statements set forth "symptoms" and a general understanding of the problem; such statements should be detailed and specific. Analytical material might include tables of data supporting a particular statement, or flow charts documenting an existing condition. The definition statement must include the following:

- Units whose needs are to be met.
- The kinds of needs to be met.
- Who will be involved in the system.
- Views or philosophy of groups involved.
- Methods that will be used to solve the problem.
- The system's boundaries or constraints.
- Comparison of resources available and needed.
- Recognition that the system design will not answer all questions.

A typical statement of the problem for a materials management system might express the need to "increase the efficiency of the physical flow of goods and services in the organization." This problem would involve a broad range of activities including production/operations, inventory control, management, financial purchasing, and marketing. Assume that the analysis of available information shows that the present materials management system is most susceptible, and indicates that a large number of immediate, critical, and costly problems are occurring. The ineffective management of materials handling is unquestionably a principal cause of inefficient operations, affecting all operations throughout the company. Despite its importance, the present materials management system has less top management involvement and consequently less formal development than other company operations. This area appears to offer greater opportunity for development, cost savings, and management improvement than other operations. The solution to this problem involves developing a total systems approach for materials management and design-related, integrated sybsystems throughout the company operations.

Materials Management Objectives

The objectives define the goals on which the proposed materials management system is to be postulated. The system's objectives are similar to a hypothesis, a tentative theory, or a suggestion set forth for the purpose of making the problems evident. An objective for the system is a result to be achieved. In stating the objective, we must consider the system's constraints, the specific limitations that add dimension to the objective and make the results meaningful. For any given objective, the constraints are imposed by the various activities of the organization. For example, materials management constraints might include policies of purchasing, sales, accounting, or manufacturing. Because materials management is a "service" function, it must maintain proper relationships with the departments that it serves so that the objectives are accomplished. Every important interaction must be considered in the system.

It is not an easy matter to define the real objectives of a materials management system. A common error is to emphasize the obvious, or to state objectives in vague terms. Objectives must be stated in sufficiently specific terms that a means can be designed to measure the performance of the system. System objectives ultimately must be stated in terms materials managers can use, or in terms of the functions the system is to perform. The objectives should be expressed so that they meet materials managers' information requirements. Descriptive statements, flow-charts, or any other means may be used to convey the objectives the system must meet. If possible, the objectives should be stated quantitatively rather than qualitatively, so that alternative systems designs and system performance can be measured for their effectiveness. In addition, the objectives should describe exactly what the system is supposed to accomplish and the means by which it will be evaluated.

Objectives stated in vague terms, such as "reduce materials handling time" or "avoid delays," must be restated in terms of the subsystems they affect. Murdick, Ross, and Cloggett provide the following suggestions:[5]

Subsystem	Objectives
Routing	Develop routing information and lines that can be used by materials management to determine materials handling requirements, status of production at each work station, effect of changes by rerouting.
Status	Establish a system that can be used by materials management and others to determine handling loads, effect of accepting additional work, handling overload in work centers, status of work-in-process handling.
Control	Establish an overall system that can be used by materials management to quickly determine materials handling times, costs, and overruns by work center.
Equipment	Develop equipment information that can be used by materials management to determine equipment status, maintain equipment capacity and utilization.

Upon examination, these materials management objectives cannot be divorced from the overall organizational objectives, both short- and long-term. Short-term system objectives are framed in terms of materials management planning, which must take into account the environment in which the business will be operating five to ten years hence. Thus the system design must anticipate the future environment.

Determining Requirements

Information requirements are fundamental to a good system design. All too often managers spend large sums on equipment for a materials management operation without first determining its real needs, because of the time and difficulty of determining specific requirements. A system's specific needs will, at various times and for various purposes, depend largely upon the production environment and the individual materials manager. One way to determine needs is to ask the individuals responsible for each area to write statements that detail:[6]

* Major activities/operations.
* Specific information about volume moved, timing, costs, etc.

If this can be done, the system is well on the way to being designed.

In addition, the production environment is largely responsible for the materials handling operation, which is a function of the company's size and the complexity of its production operations. Larger, more complex production operations require more formal materials management systems, and their requirements are more critical to the overall operation than those of simpler processes. The system must provide materials management information to top-level, control, and operational management. Each needs different types of information presented in different forms: top-level management needs a one-time report with summary; control-level management needs the exception report and a variety of regular reports for periodic evaluation; and at the operational management level, a formal report with fixed procedures is required, as are day-to-day reports to maintain operational control. In addition, individual materials managers' knowledge, technical background, leadership style, and decision-making ability will all affect the kind and amount of information they require.

Information generally can be obtained from the firm's files and accounting records. During this phase, planners begin to develop the new system by determining information sources for particular parts of the system as well as considering how they serve the overall, integrated information requirements. Various techniques of analysis and synthesis, such as input/output analysis, can be used to summarize and integrate the available sources of information, in order to avoid duplication.

Existing Materials Management System

A descriptive layout of the present situation is helpful in the initial phase of a study. Even the simplest problems inevitably offer choices, not only of objectives, but also of emphasis. One approach is to prepare descriptions of the organizational units affected by the problem under consideration.

Existing standard instructions may provide a starting point. If there are no written procedures, organizational charts, flow charts, and other such documents are a good place to begin. An analysis of the functional responsibilities in the light of specific problems provides a good approach to analyzing the existing system.

The first requirement generally is a well-developed flow diagram. This diagram broadly defines the system's elements from beginning to end. It also serves as a generalized model of the system, providing management the opportunity to look at the total problem early in the investigation.

Soon after analysis of the present situation has begun, a conceptualization of the system design begins to take shape. This conceptual design is the analyst's idea of how to attack the problem and of how the system should be redesigned. Inadvertently, materials managers may become involved in solving a problem even at the investigation stage; however, during this period, the primary goal should be to analyze the existing system.

Constraints

An important part of system design is to establish the system constraints. Planners define the conditions under which objectives may be attained by considering limitations that restrict the design. Because a constant review of objectives is necessary in considering the system constraints, the setting of objectives and establishing of constraints may be considered together as one process. Establishing constraints helps ensure that the system is realistic.

It is important to recognize the constraints that will have an impact on the system's design. Once they have been defined, appropriate allowances are made for them in the design. Illustrating the nature of constraints are these examples, which correspond to the system's objectives:

- Routings: Regardless of work station requirements, only full lots will be considered.
- Status: Workloads must be performed within a minimum of two hours.
- Equipment: Materials handling schedule will be identified by work stations only; any deviations from established schedules must have prior approval and not be decided by individual workers.

Constraints may be classified as internal or external to the organization (see Figure 11-1). Internal constraints include personnel needs and availability, resources, policies, and self-imposed restrictions. External constraints include customer orders, billing, services, and so on; government regulations; suppliers; and labor unions.

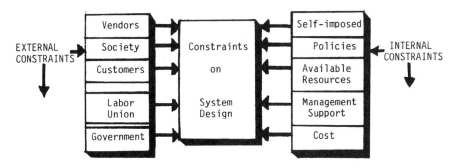

Figure 11-1. Constraints of a materials management system.

System Parameters

A workable materials management system has the same functional elements as any other system. In a general sense, it consists of input, process, and output — the three system parameters (Figure 11-2). Each parameter is a constant with variable properties and values that give specific character to the input, process, and output.

Input may be defined as the start-up component activities with which the system operates. The input for a materials management system consists of production data and materials. Data may include important information about component parts such as volume, types, and locations.

Output is the result of an operation or operations. The output of a materials management system is to optimize the efficiency of the company's materials management activities. This objective is accomplished according to the criteria of the company, which are defined in terms of the most efficient service materials management can provide to other company operations. A criterion is a standard measurement for analyzing the performance of a given alternative; it provides consistency in evaluating one condition against another. The company's requirements or criteria make it possible for materials management to stipulate the limiting factors that characterize the materials management system.[7]

The process is the activity of the system that transforms input into output. Machines, humans, functions, and operations all may be integrated into process performance. The system provides a grasp of the char-

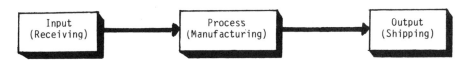

Figure 11-2. Relationship of input, process, and output for materials handling.

acteristics of the materials management operation, defining the logical sequence of operations and relationships and giving specifications as accurately as possible.

System Boundaries

In developing a materials management system, it is difficult to determine where materials management starts and stops — what is to be included and excluded. To some degree, this may be determined by the organization's definition of materials management, or it may be a subjective reflection of top management's opinion of what materials management should be doing. General statements about materials management may be of little value in specific materials management problems. In actual practice, an objective description of a specific problem is the first requirement for developing a materials management system.

One may view materials management in many ways. Top management would tend to view materials management in relation to the organization as a whole. Materials management would tend to view itself as an operating unit filling a variety of specific, hour-by-hour needs, whereas the managers of other departments that use materials management's services would tend to think of it in nonorganizational terms, perhaps looking at one or two special functions performed for them. These views are not contradictory but complementary, indicating alternative ways of defining the system.

A system needs to have its boundaries stated. The statement of boundaries determines the content of the system and creates a framework for its subsystems. Boundaries enable the materials manager to look at a problem as a whole and to concentrate on areas where evidence can be applied to the solution of the problem. The system's boundary restricts the scope of the problem to a size commensurate with the cost and time available and the amount of detail necessary to understand the process. The boundaries of a subsystem also should describe a problem of manageable size. Systems that include many subsystems will be proportionately more complex and will tend to be less easily managed and controlled than the simpler systems.

The condition of redundancy occurs when a system contains more elements than necessary to fulfill a requirement. The need for redundancy must be balanced against the cost and possible uncertainty generated by an excess of unnecessary data or processes. Unnecessary data are those for which there are no uses in the subsystem, or that are not essential to the solution. Repetitive data pertain to transactions that duplicate other transactions. Redundant data or processes may contribute to errors or to failure of the system or subsystem to operate.

Developing Conceptual Designs

The development of a system is a creative process that involves synthesizing knowledge into a particular pattern, or concept. The concept of a materials management system is a sketch of the structure of materials management that guides and restricts the form of the detailed designs. It includes the major handling operations, patterns of flow, channels of information, and the role of materials managers. The concept also must define the relationship of materials management to other operating systems. Various concepts may be developed.

Each alternative concept of the materials management system will offer advantages and disadvantages. Although one concept may dominate all others, there generally are several good designs that require careful evaluation. The procedures for evaluation are as follows:

- Compare present performance of the conceptual design with previously developed objectives.
- Examine flow charts and identify strong and weak points of each design.
- Develop a preliminary analysis of the system's output.
- Expand the design in greater detail.

At this point, sufficient development will have occurred for a more detailed description of the system to begin. This description includes a flow chart or other documentation of the materials management operations, showing the inputs and outputs, along with a narrative description of the operation. This phase involves the participation of materials managers in the system design to provide specific information from which the system's details can be further defined.

A general flow chart, indicating the overall structure of the materials management system, is illustrated in Figure 11-3. It describes the materials management process in broad terms, indicating only the main components of the system. The flow chart becomes the foundation upon which detailed specifications are developed, concerning particular steps, data, equipment, and people.

The input data specifications include sources of data — where they come from and who is responsible for producing them. Certain forms (e.g., sales order, production schedules, receiving forms often are used in collecting inputs for the operation systems, and they serve as important sources of input data.

Output data specifications include the content and form of the output documents. Such specifications are a direct function of information needs,

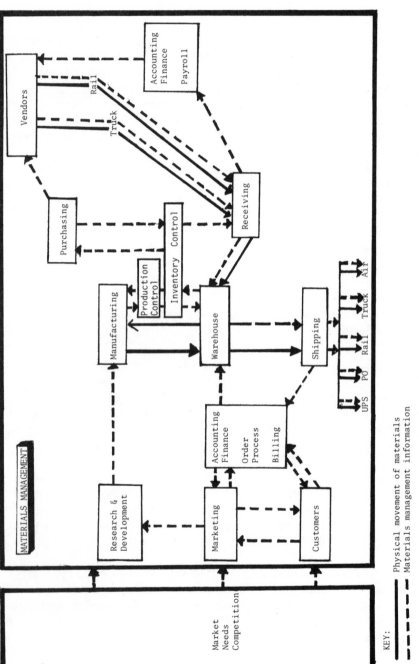

Figure 11-3. Conceptual design for materials management system.

and the documents should be constructed to fill these needs in a timely fashion. Output information should be presented in summary form. Other frequently used output forms are activity sheets and narrative descriptions, providing materials handling information on volumes, time relationships, and specific activity requirements.

Feedback/Control

Feedback is a means for the modification of a system to improve its performance. The purpose of feedback is control. Feedback/control is the comparison of output with the system's criteria. For example, in a materials management system the speed, handling, and timeliness of materials movement constitute the actual output. Because the system is designed to have materials at specific points in a plant at given times, specific priorities and times serve as the criteria. Control of the system is achieved by correcting the discrepancies between actual output and the established criteria (see Figure 11-4).

Feedback is output that is re-introduced as input into the process from which the output was derived. The feedback of the materials management system makes it possible to control the operation. Control is exercised over input, process, and output: controls over input check and verify materials in prescribed locations; controls over process verify the sequence of operations to see that they are proceeding in a prescribed manner and to detect processing errors; controls over output ensure conformance to the system.

Feedback/control is designed into a materials management system in a number of ways:

- Comparing shop job cards (direct materials tickets) with time schedules.
- Comparing purchase invoices with materials handling requests.
- Comparing shipping order data with materials handling.
- Comparing stock tickets that modify work-in-process with materials handling orders.

Interestingly, these feedbacks are generated as a result of the output of another subsystem.

Figure 11-4. Feedback/control in a multiprocess system.

The system design must provide for feedback actions to be sustained and become an important part of the system. Besides the feedbacks derived from the internal operation, there are other feedbacks that originate outside the system, such as sales, profits, materials costs, and so on. From the feedback, the control process determines what future action is to be taken, and which controls, rules, or procedures to use.

Controls can be applied with high reliability at various stages of the operation. Although the controls can entail a large number of very detailed rules, the objective of system design is to accomplish feedback/control with a minimum of system operations and complications. To do this, the underlying structure of the system must be designed to include problem solution, which is accomplished through the sound, established logic under which the system was designed. The system must be precise, yet complete enough to define all of the elements' requirements. Thus, any system must:

- Define elements in a consistent format.
- Include all elements in system input.
- Include complete input data.
- Include appropriate operations sequentially arranged.
- Maintain a consistency of input and process.

Any system must be rigorous, in the sense that it has been explored to the limit, and all required data have been considered and brought within the system.

IMPLEMENTING AND OPERATING THE MATERIALS MANAGEMENT SYSTEM

The development of a materials management system can be a time-consuming and expensive project. The cost of getting such a system on line and satisfactorily operating, and maintaining the system, is often comparable to the cost of bringing a new product to the market. Occasionally, development and implementation are carried out simultaneously. The operational testing of the system is a continuous process, but design changes should be considered only during major system changes. The main phases in implementation of a system are initial installation, testing, evaluation, and maintenance. Some of these activities can be undertaken simultaneously to reduce implementation time.

Planning Implementation

The planning and the action needed to implement a system are bound closely together. The first step in the implementation process is to develop a plan to implement the system. The major tasks consist of:

- Introducing the system to all levels of materials management.
- Organizing personnel for implementation.
- Establishing training programs for operating personnel.
- Redesigning and changing the layout of facilities as required.
- Acquiring required equipment.
- Testing the entire system.
- Completing changeover to the new system.
- Evaluating the management system.
- Providing system maintenance.

Most projects require the use of a network diagram such as PERT to accomplish the planned schedule. This requires an estimate of times required to complete events in the program, the starting date, and the sequence of events. Through PERT, the program's progress can be determined weekly or biweekly. When a large number of people and activities are involved in both regular operations and the introduction of a new arrangement of equipment, such detailed scheduling helps to minimize confusion.

Implementing a materials management system may involve a revision of facilities. This requires the preparation of layouts and detailed descriptions of changes in equipment and operations, probably involving production and other departments. This planning should begin immediately because a long lead time is needed to make these changes, especially when ongoing production must be maintained. The planning must consider space requirements for people and equipment, and the movement of people and equipment in the work process, as well as materials handling changes in routing, storage, and location of materials, and safety and environmental requirements for equipment. The detailed work flow depends upon the physical arrangement of facilities in relation to major production operations.

Organizing for the System

Once the implementation tasks have been defined, a project manager must be assigned to guide the actual implementation—in most cases, someone from materials management. Because the major concern of the new system is materials management, individuals from all levels must take an active part in its implementation; they are the ones who will operate the system and utilize its results. Thus, materials management must make sure that "all" personnel are involved in system implementation and consider it to be their system. The assignment of specific responsibilities to them allows materials management personnel to shape and construct the system they will operate and use. Without employee acceptance, a system will fail, because of employee inertia, apathy, resistance to change, and feelings of insecurity.

Installation Procedures

Detailed procedures for system installation are prepared. For example, new specifications may call for changes in production layout that require raw materials to be moved directly to production. In this case, a procedure must be developed for creating instructions, coordinating and integrating this portion of the materials management system with other parts of the manufacturing system, and working out problems with the people involved. A procedure for purchasing equipment must be established. Procedures must be developed for phasing in parts of the system and for operating them together. Clearly, procedures of this kind must be delineated in advance.

Training

A training program should be developed for materials management and related personnel, explaining the nature, goals, and benefits of using the system. The extent of training depends on the employees' level of participation in the development of the system. Specific attention should be paid to first-line supervisors and other employees who require a thorough understanding of the new system and what it is supposed to do. Because they will be directly involved in the operation of the system, they must learn how it will operate. These individuals will experience many changes in their work, and both they and their subordinates must accept these changes.

Certain professional support personnel — marketing, production, accounting, and other people who provide input to materials management or who are concerned with materials handling operations — also should attend training sessions. Even though these people will be working only indirectly with the materials management system, their training should involve an understanding of the complete system, furnishing direction for their own activities and giving them perspective on the system. People who perform the daily operational tasks of materials management will require a longer and more formal training program.

Acquisitions of Facilities

To a great extent, the detailed design of the materials management system will spell out the criteria for equipment and other requirements. If equipment criteria are not specified, an analysis must be performed to determine them. The acquisition of equipment is a complex subject, which will not be covered in this book, but can be found in many engineering economy books. Acquisition decisions involve many factors besides whether to buy or lease; decisions must consider usage rates, the company's anticipated replacement schedule, and vendors' options.

Developing Data

A vast amount of detailed information, both external and internal to materials management, must be collected for input into the system. Forms for providing correct information simplify the processing required (see Figure 11-5). The forms are needed not just for input and output but also

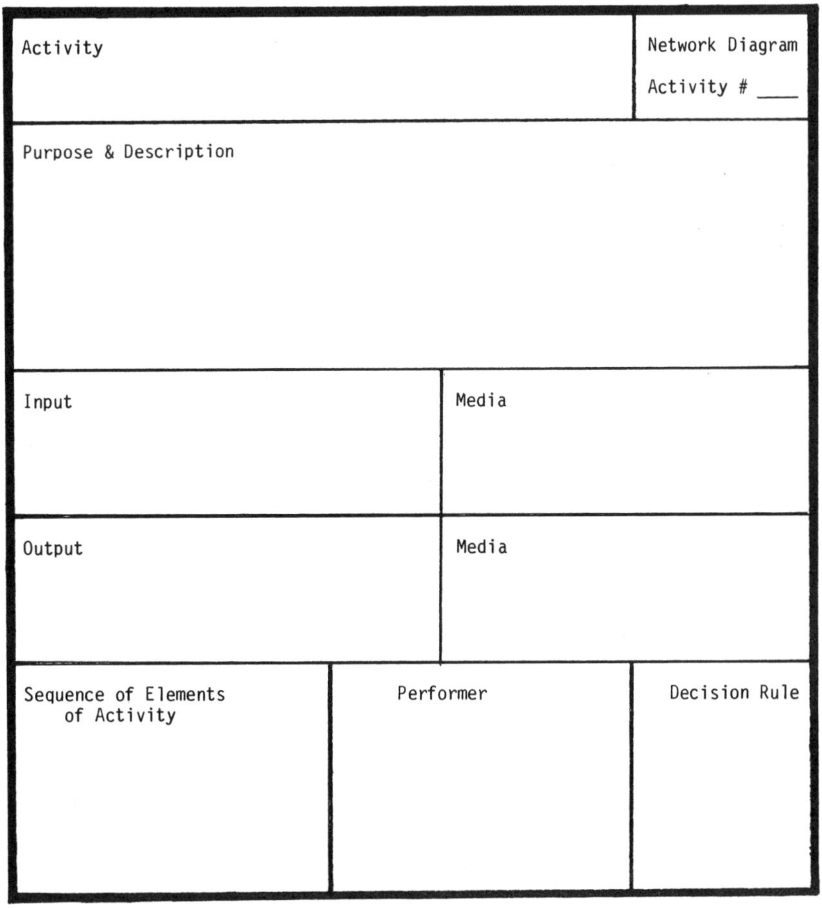

Activity		Network Diagram
		Activity # ____
Purpose & Description		
Input	Media	
Output	Media	
Sequence of Elements of Activity	Performer	Decision Rule

Figure 11-5. Activity design form.

for transmitting data at intermediate stages. Also, additional data can be included that were developed in the detailed design stage.

The actual data now are obtained and recorded for the initial testing and operation of the system. Whether data are obtained externally or internally, procedures must be developed for obtaining them, and responsibility for data maintenance should be assigned.

Testing the System

As each part of the system is installed, tests must be performed in accordance with previously established procedures. The testing during installation requires that line personnel perform actual operations or specially designed test problems. This is equivalent to the physical laboratory testing of parts of an engineered product before the construction of parts. Testing procedures must be developed on the basis of the design and test specifications. A test procedures should prescribe:

- Detailed segments to be tested.
- Test problems to be performed.
- When, by whom, and how the tests will be conducted.
- Evaluation of results and approval of modifications.

Tests made during the installation stage consist of component tests, subsystem tests, and total system acceptance tests. Components may be tested relatively independent of the whole system.

Tests for accuracy, range of inputs, frequency of inputs, usual operating conditions, human factor characteristics, and reliability are all of major concern. During testing, employees are further familiarized with the system before complete changeover is accomplished. Difficulties arising during the tests may lead to design changes that will later yield large benefits in the total system's tests and operations.

There is a considerable difference between the testing of a component and the testing of the system. System tests require verification of multiple inputs, complex logics, human interaction, widely varied equipment, and timing of humans with equipment, all interfacing with the system's many parts. Minor difficulties generally occur, requiring the redesign of procedures, work flow, and so on.

Changeover

Changeover is the point at which the new materials management system replaces the old system. It usually involves many last-minute changes, rearrangements, and new responsibilities. One difficulty is the need to maintain daily operations while the new system is being installed, and one possible solution is to plan for the new system to operate simultaneously with the old one. However, sometimes it is possible to have present operations and new operations integrated at regular work stations at the same time.

Despite thorough testing, there probably still will be problems. With adequate training of operating personnel, mass confusion can be avoided during this time. The provision of supervisory personnel may help to prevent changeover problems, and should last for several months. Programs may need improvement and changes to ensure a more efficient operation. The operational period exposes the new system to a variety of problems and conditions that could not be practically achieved during testing.

Materials Management System Manual

Written descriptions of the scope, purpose, information flow, and operating procedures of the system are necessary for troubleshooting, replacing subsystems, interfacing with other systems, training new operating personnel or materials management personnel, and evaluating and upgrading the system. The system manual allows new operators to be brought in and trained to operate the system, and provides a common reference for managers and designers.

Control and Maintenance of the System

System control and maintenance are the responsibility of the materials manager. Control involves operating the system as it was designed to perform. Often well-intentioned operators make unauthorized and undocumented changes to improve the system or develop their own procedures, thereby eliminating procedures that were designed to provide checks. Therefore, it is up to management at each level to provide periodic evaluations of the system for control purposes.

Directly related to the systems control process, maintenance is the ongoing activity that keeps the system efficient and effective. It is directed toward reducing errors due to design or environmental changes and improving the system's scope and services, and can take the form of emergency maintenance, routine maintenance, or improvements. It may necessitate changes in operating procedures, equipment, plant layout, raw materials, company policies, or decision-making requirements.

One important element of maintenance and control is monitoring the changes that constantly take place inside and outside a materials management environment. Numerous changes occur in response to regulations, agencies, services, customer requirements, new equipment, and inventory policies. Thus, there is a continual flow of new rules and changes that require constant updating of the materials management system. Also, changes in economic conditions may dictate changes in corporate policy; the direct internalization of these changes to materials management is an important part of a good system design. However, such changes are only partly predictable; so the materials management system must be evaluated periodically to ensure that all changes have been included in the system.

Timely reaction to such internal and external changes is very important in maintaining an efficient operation. The changes may be anything from routine to major adjustments in the materials management system. Changes in technology alone require continual system maintenance. In most systems, a full third of the work effort and cost goes to maintenance and control to ensure system effectiveness.

MATERIALS MANAGEMENT INFORMATION SYSTEM (MIS)

A materials management MIS provides relevant information to appropriate materials managers at the right time. This information helps them (a) plan both short- and long-term activities, (b) organize the tasks necessary for the plan, (c) monitor these tasks and activities to compare and control actual results with the plan, and (d) take necessary corrective measures. The MIS helps to manage and coordinate the activities of materials management.

Every materials management requires some form of MIS. Its degree of sophistication depends on: (a) the manufacturing environment in which materials management operates; (b) the size of the operation; (c) the organizational structure the materials management is part of; and (e) the value of data to be generated, and the extent to which they will be utilized by materials management and other managerial groups.

An MIS for Materials Management

A management information system (MIS) monitors and retrieves data from the environment, captures data from transactions and operations within materials management, and filters, organizes, and selects data and presents them as information to materials managers.[8] The MIS is then a process that goes beyond managing by piecemeal information, intuitive guesswork, and isolated problem solving to a level of systems insight, information, high-level data processing, and problem solving. It is especially important to the materials manager who always had many *sources* of information that the MIS provides a *system* of information. The MIS is an aid for materials management that involves materials managers, operating

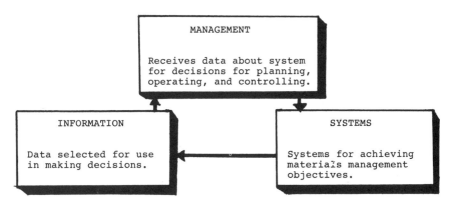

Figure 11-6. The three major parts of an MIS.

systems, and information (see Figure 11-6). The MIS captures both internal and external data and converts them to information for materials management decision making. The MIS assists materials managers in making decisions by making a common set of data and information available to all materials managers, thereby integrating the materials management system into the company. Thus, the company operates as a whole system, with all elements working toward common objectives.

The total system is composed of subsystems designed to carry out the activities supporting the company's objectives. In a manufacturing company, materials management is a subsystem that is itself composed of subsystems such as materials handling, warehousing, distribution, and receiving. These subsystems have two parts: the physical handling of materials and the processing of information. This processing of information is done by the operating information system, which ties the people and facilities together. Without it, there could be no operating system.

If the production structure is complex, materials management activities are correspondingly complex. An automobile, for example, will have over 10,000 parts, resulting in complex materials management activities and information needs. In addition, the environment makes the production dynamic. In a stable environment, there is relatively little complexity, and the materials management information can be correspondingly unsophisticated. In the automobile industry, however, demand fluctuates rapidly, especially where many different products are involved; in these companies materials management information needs are massive, and the information needs are complex. Because of this complexity, it has not been possible to provide materials management with the information needed for planning and control; materials management activities in the auto industry have been fragmented, and materials management information systems have been partial and inaccurate, failing to supply the timely information needed.

Materials Management MIS

The objective of a materials management MIS is to provide relevant, timely information for:

- Planning and decision making, to secure materials necessary for production and minimize material costs and safety stocks.
- Exercising control over materials management activities.

The relevant information needed for an MIS in materials management is obtained by:

1. Developing an understanding of aspects of the materials management function such as:
   - The variety of raw materials and the relative cost of raw materials compared to the final product.
   - The geographic remoteness of the sources of materials, suppliers, and the transportation network used for obtaining efficient, timely, and reliable supplies from suppliers.
   - The important economic and political constraints affecting supplies.
2. Becoming familiar with the company's management framework as it impacts the effectiveness of the materials management MIS; pertinent factors are:
   - The establishment of long- and short-term goals and objectives for materials management that complement the company's goals and objectives and are clearly conveyed.
   - Materials management operations, as reflected in the organizational structure by clearly documented position descriptions.
   - Performance estimates that have been revised to reflect actual operations.
   - Materials managers' major responsibilities and authorities, which are well defined and clearly documented.
   - Defined materials management interaction with production, finance, maintenance, inventory, and other groups.
   - Established policies for the following:
     Vendor relations.
     Commitment authority.
     Pricing, credit, and delivery.
     Security of supply.

Storage location.
Service levels.
Economic order quantities.
Reorder points.
Material requirements planning, material resources planning.
Materials management policies, to reflect an awareness of production and customer demand for handling of materials, requirements, and distributions.

The basic information required by materials management for an MIS includes:

1. The long-term materials management plan, including:
   • Technological changes affecting materials requirements.
   • Nature, location, and anticipated development of procurement sources, company-owned and operated, agents or brokers.
   • Future changes in availability (e.g., foreign suppliers).
2. The short-term materials management plan, such as:
   • Production schedules and production plan including suppliers' schedules, size of shipment, dependability, quality, and so forth.
   • Specific performance variables used for control and evaluation.
3. Operating materials management information:
   • Shipment and receipts: dates, partial shipments, back orders, in-transit location, carriers, purchasing variances.
   • Warehousing of large stock levels, stock mix, turnover space locations.
   • Form perpetual records: item description, stock number, location, quantity, supplies, purchasing, maintenance part, raw materials, work-in-process, finished goods.
   • Inventory receipts, issues and adjustment, and amounts committed to production.

In general, a materials management MIS is designed to (a) collect data, (b) record and store data, (c) provide for data retrieval, (d) process the data, and (e) transmit and present relevant information.

A simple version of an MIS for materials management is illustrated in Figure 11-7. The purpose of the materials management system is to accept requests from departments and to arrange to handle them promptly, accurately, and completely. Information is received, and information is produced as an output, as shown in Figure 11-7.

The MIS carries our individual operations and transactions required for day-to-day activity. It connects materials management to every operating information system. In Figure 11-7, the materials management operating

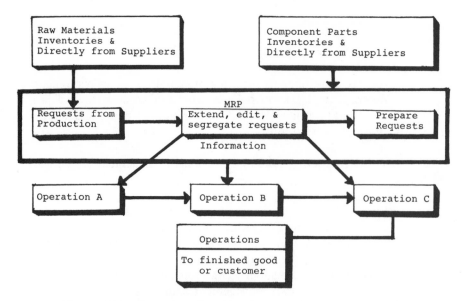

Figure 11-7. An illustration of an abbreviated materials management MIS.

system is interacting with data supplied from internal sources. Because materials managers make many requests and require many actions during an ordinary day, the materials management MIS captures and stores the required data, later converting this information into a form useful to the materials managers.

COMPUTER APPLICATIONS IN MATERIALS MANAGEMENT

Today's manufacturing environment, using, for example, Just-In-Time systems, increasingly needs for materials management to respond immediately, thus necessitating the use of computers. These changes in materials management are accelerating, requiring more and more information; so computers must be used to retrieve and to evaluate information, consequently, materials management personnel must have a working knowledge of computers and their use in information processing.

There are several prerequisites for an effective computer-based management system. First, there must be an organization for planning, control, and other functions that good management requires. Second, data must exist on resources, policies, operations, and performance. These data are the key to an understanding of the company's managerial operations process. To process data, the company's computer facilities must have sufficient capability to access and retrieve the data, enter information, and display it, as well as an organization for designing, maintaining, and managing the required systems and procedures.

Computer Characteristics

Computer functions consist of data input, processing, storage, and output. A computer accepts data in the form of computer language, and processes the data electronically. The function of entering data into the computer is usually performed by magnetic media (tape, disk, diskette), or by direct input from a terminal keyboard. The input devices read or sense the coded data and make them available in a form acceptable to the computer.

The central processor is the most significant component of the computer. Basically, it consists of a control section, which coordinates the system's components, and an arithmetic/logic unit, which performs tasks with remarkable speed and accuracy. The control section of the central processor directs and coordinates all operations called for by the instructions of the program. It controls the input/output units and the arithmetic/logic unit, transferring data to and from storage. Routine information is stored in the arithmetic/logic unit; it is through the control section that automatic, integrated operation is achieved.

The computer is like a huge electronic filing cabinet, completely indexed and instantly accessible. All data are placed in storage before being processed by the computer. Internal storage, or the computer's memory, permits the computer to store, in electronic form, data from input devices and instructions called programs that tell the machine what to do. The storage of the computer memory is divided into locations, each with an assigned address. Each location holds a specific unit of data, which may be a character, a digit, an entire record, or a word. When a data item is desired, it is obtained from its known location. External storage consists of disks, diskettes, magnetic drums, and magnetic tapes.

The computer processes data by using programs, which direct the processing unit to take data (input) and process them according to certain programmed instructions. Output devices produce the final results of computer processing. The information from the computer may be output on a variety of media: magnetic media, print on paper, signals for transmission over teleprocessing networks, graphic displays, microfilm images, and other special forms.

Computer Assembly Languages

As with natural languages, there are families of programming languages whose members are similar to and often explicitly derived from each other (Table 11-2). The basic purpose of an assembly language is to help create programs in machine code. This necessitates the use of all the capabilities

Table 11-2. Computer Assembly Languages Used in Materials Management.

ACRONYM	LANGUAGE	DESCRIPTION
ALGOL	Algorithmic Language	Developed jointly by users in the U.S. and Europe, this language is suitable for expressing solutions to problems requiring numeric computations for some logical processes.
APL	A Programming Language	A general language with complex notation and unusual but powerful operations. Notation is exceptionally compact.
BASIC	Beginner's All-Purpose Symbolic Instruction Code	A very simple language for use in solving numeric and business problems developed in on-line systems. Frequently used by nontechnical users.
COBOL	Common Business- Oriented Language	This is an English-like language that is the most widespread in use for business data processing problems.
FORTRAN	Formula Translator	Developed about 1957, this was the first language to be widely used for solving numeric problems. It is perhaps the most widely used language prior to 1970 and has been implemented on almost all computers. It is oriented to specific kinds of problems. For example, the solution to the problem: area of a circle $= r^2$ was written PI*R**2. Subsequent "generations" of FORTRAN have been FORTRAN II, IV, etc.
GPSS	General-Purpose Systems Simulator	A language for discrete simulation problems based on a block diagram approach.
PL/1		In wide use, generally limited to IBM equipment. For scientific, business, on-line, real-time.
RPG-II	Report Program Generator	A language to generate programs to prepare reports (usually only once) from existing data in the system.
SIMSCRIPT		Another language for doing discrete simulation problems. Based on FORTRAN.

Table 11-2. Computer Assembly Languages Used in Materials Management. (continued)

ACRONYM	LANGUAGE	DESCRIPTION
SIMULA	Simulation Language	ALGOL-based language widely used by international manufacturers of DP equipment.
PASCAL		A generalized programming language, easy to use, very powerful, and similar to ALGOL.

Source: Robert G. Murdick, *MIS: Concepts and Design,* © 1980, pp. 91–92. Reprinted by permission of Prentice Hall, Inc., Englewood Cliffs, New Jersey.

of the computer as effectively as possible while not requiring fixed parameters of the program that do not affect its efficiency or correctness, such as location in memory of the program and data.

Interface with Materials Management Facilities

Today, computers are being built into materials management facilities. Whole materials handling systems are controlled by computer systems that direct all the movements and activities of equipment such as AS/RS, AGVS, mini trains, and so on. These computers are utilized in materials management facilities because of their machine strength, speed, precision, untiring availability, predictability, reliability, and relative imperviousness to hostile environments. All of these materials handling systems interface with computers in highly structured industrial environments where practically all of the variability and decision making can be engineered out of the workplace. The present uses all involve repetitive, preprogrammable tasks, from the transportation in AS/RS to the picking of input-output stations in support of manufacturing operations that interface with automatic/robotic systems and flexible manufacturing systems (FMS). The next generation will have sensory functions enabling them to perform a broader range of tasks under less structured conditions. Their expected uses, with vision and improved feedback control, will include more of the materials management functions.[9] All of these capabilities interface with computers.

Eventually, most materials handling tasks performed by workers on the factory floor will be done by computer-controlled systems. Programmable materials handling automation is beginning to replace the current generation of manually controlled handling equipment. Potentially, it can significantly improve materials management productivity and company efficiency as a whole.

The increased use of computers for machine control depends on technology development. Computers already are having a tremendous influence on materials handling machine design, which is developing at an unprecedented rate with extremely significant advances expected in the next decade. Applications of programmable automation are becoming technologically feasible and economically efficient at an ever increasing rate. This development is directly related to the use of materials handling automated systems. Materials management must be trained to operate these machines and to make the results of programmed operations available in useful form (see Table 11-3, glossary of computer terms).

With these complex systems come many technological problems. Signals must be transmitted without excessive outside interference. To compensate for interference, a certain redundancy is introduced to recover the signal. The materials handling machines involved must be of stand-alone design. It is important to select the right computer to interface with the machines and to choose proper software for communicating with machines and computers.

COMPUTER AIDED MANUFACTURING AND
MATERIALS MANAGEMENT

Recent major developments in manufacturing automation have occurred in the areas of computer aided manufacturing (CAM), computerized machine centers, and industrial robots. Computer aided manufacturing is a sophisticated extension of direct numerical control of machine tools. In CAM systems, the computer not only directs machine movements, but also assists in data handling (see Figure 11-8). In the ultimate applications of CAM, all of the machines in a factory are run automatically by the computer, which also generates status reports on run time, quality levels, inventory levels, and so on.[10] Materials management has a key role in making each of these systems work.

Numerically Controlled Machines

The first numerically controlled, or NC, machines were controlled by punched paper tapes that instructed the machine to perform a sequence of operations. NC machines utilize punched instructions that are created by the software in a computer aided design (CAD) system, which is unique for each type and brand of machine. The paper tapes convey to the machine the instructions for making specific parts.

A computer numerical control (CNC) machine uses a dedicated computer and does not require paper tapes because machine instructions are stored electronically in the computer's memory. Programs can be created, edited, or changed, if necessary, on the machine. Thus the CNC machine

Table 11-3. Glossary of Computer Terms.

Access time: The time required to locate an item of data in storage and transfer it to the processor.

Accumulator: A register in the processor that holds sums, products, and so on; also used for comparing data.

Adder: The component of a machine that does arithmetic; it may or may not add by "counting."

Address: The designation of a storage location.

Address part of an instruction: The portion of an instruction that tells the machine where to find the data that are to be used in an operation, or where to store a result.

Address system: A term that designates the number of addresses contained in a single instruction.

Binary number system: A number system with only two digits, 0 and 1, in contrast to the decimal system which has 10 digits. All current machines are either decimal or binary. Arithmetic is done in a different manner with the binary system than with the decimal.

Bit: A bit is the least amount of information that can be represented as a zero or a one, as represented by a hole in a card or no hole; or as represented by a plus or minus electrical charge. Bits are grouped in patterns to represent coded characters. Bit is the abbreviated form of the words binary digit.

Branching: Automatic selection of appropriate alternate instructions.

Buffer: A register that can operate at (usually two) different speeds, thus permitting processing of data at high speed while simultaneously reading input and/or writing output; also, a temporary storage unit.

Control: The section of a data-processing machine that controls its operation. Most current machines may be manually controlled through a keyboard or a wired control panel, or they may be controlled by a stored program within the computer's memory.

Feedback: The technique of returning selected portions of the results produced by a processor to its own control section for the purpose of control, self-supervision, or modification of further processing.

Fixed word length: Storage designed to contain a specific number of characters for each addressable location.

Input: Information delivered to a machine; also, the section of the machine that "reads" this information.

Instruction: A word that is sent to a register in the control section of a machine, where it causes the machine to perform a particular operation. An instruction will consist of an operation code and one or more addresses. If all instructions for a particular machine have just one address part, then the instructions and machine are referred to as single-address. Similarly, a three-address machine will have three addresses and one operation code to each instruction. See also Address system.

Logical components: The sections of a processor capable of making comparisons, testing for algebraic signs, identifying zero or nonzero results, and so on.

Memory: The section of a machine used to store data and instructions.

Microsecond: One-millionth of a second.

Millisecond: One-thousandth of a second.

Modification: Altering the normal sequence of instructions by branching or changing the command or address portion of instructions.

Nanosecond: One-billionth of a second.

Operation code: The portion of an instruction that tells the machine what operation to perform.

Output: Information delivered by the machine; also, the section of the machine that "writes" this information.

Table 11-3. Glossary of Computer Terms. (*continued*)

Processor: The section of a machine that performs arithmetic, makes logical decisions governing control, and processes the data in storage.

Program: A list of instructions to the processor.

Read: A command instructing the machine to accept data from a specific input unit and place it in memory.

Record: A group of related data elements, sometimes called words.

Register: Any storage unit used for a specialized purpose; usually designed to contain a fixed number of characters.

Storage: The section of a machine that stores data or instructions; the memory section.

Storage location: The address of any specific area of memory. In a fixed-word-length machine, it refers to the address of a specific word. In a variable-word-length machine, it refers to the address of a specific character.

Stored program machine: One that is controlled by having an appropriate list of instructions stored in the machine just as data are stored. The machine refers to these instructions in a specified sequence, executing each before examining the next.

Variable word length: Storage designed to store words of any size in consecutive locations to make more efficient use of memory.

Word: A unit of information; a piece of data equivalent to a field in punched card terminology.

Word length: The number of characters in a word. See also Fixed word length; variable word length.

Write: A command to a machine to take information from memory and record it on some output media.

Source: Stanford I. Optner, *System Analysis For Business Management,* 3rd ed., © 1975, pp. 155–157. Reprinted by permission of Prentice-Hall, Englewood Cliffs, New Jersey.

performs the same functions as NC machines, but the methods of receiving operating instructions are different for the two types of machines.

With direct numerical control (DNC), a real-time computer controls more than one NC machine at a time. Several NC programs are stored in the memory of the central computer, which controls many NC machines

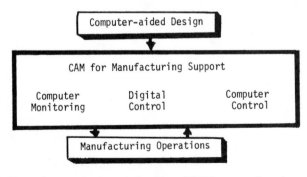

Figure 11-8. Block diagram showing relationships of CAM to manufacturing operations and CAD.

simultaneously, gathering feedback from each machine as to production rates and machine status. With a combination of DNC and CNC capability at each NC machine, programs can be downloaded from the central DNC computer to the individual CNC machines for operating. Thus less memory is required for each machine, for the program has to be created and loaded into only one machine. Such computer-controlled machine centers can perform many jobs that greatly reduce parts setup and handling, simplify the NC programming job, provide better part quality, allow less setup and rework, and require less operator attention and less operator skill.

The major advantage of using NC machines is the ability to accurately repeat each operation on every machine cycle. Human errors in machine control are inevitable over a long sequence of complex operations, but these errors can be reduced by eliminating human control in machining operations.[11]

Robotics

Robots are computer-controlled devices that automatically perform a programmed sequence of operations. The primary uses of robots mainly include various materials handling operations. Robots may operate by air pressure, hydraulic pressure, or electric motors, and are ideal replacements for manual materials handling operations involving repetitive, dangerous, or boring tasks. They can be programmed by software coding, or use the "teach mode" to perform tasks. In the teach mode, the operator moves the robot through a sequence of operations manually and instructs the robot to remember those movements. Robot software language may be either BASIC or FORTRAN, which makes programming of robots easy and efficient.

As they become more widely accepted and less costly, robots being used to perform many materials handling tasks that had required manual operators. Technological advances in developing their sense of touch and sight will bring about the widespread adoption of robots in materials handling operations. Typical applications of industrial robots include the following:

- Parts and handling: Robots perform a large variety of pick-and-place operations, moving work parts from one location and repositioning them at another.
- Machine loading and unloading: Robots are used with production equipment involved in stamping processes, forge presses, die-casting machines, injection molding machines, and metal-cutting machines. In most operations, the robot is set up to control and synchronize the equipment.
- Spray painting: A spray paint nozzle is attached to the robot, which is

programmed to move through a sequence of continuous motions to complete the painting operation.

• Welding: Robots perform both spot and continuous welding, mainly in fabrication.
• Assembly: Tasks robots perform are essentially an extension of pick-and-place motions.

Common ways of classifying robots are by physical configuration—whether point-to-point or continuous-path—and by the degrees of freedom of motion the robot possesses. The two principal robot configurations are polar and cylindrical. When used with NC machines, robots are either point-to-point or continuous-path.

The six basic motions or degrees of freedom in robot design are intended to emulate the versatility of human motion. These six basic motions include three arm and body motions and three wrist movements. Mechanical hand movement is not considered one of the basic degrees of freedom.[12,13] The arm and body motions are:

• Vertical traverse: up and down motions of the arm.
• Radial traverse: extension and retraction of the arms.
• Rotational: rotation about the vertical axis.

The wrist motions are:

• Wrist swivel: wrist rotation.
• Wrist bend: up or down movement of the wrist.
• Wrist yaw: right or left swivel.

Programmable Controllers and Microprocessors

Programmable controllers are microprocessor-based devices that can control many machine processes. These relatively inexpensive solid-state devices can be reprogrammed quickly to perform new tasks, and the different task sequences (programs) can be stored in the memory. Common processes for programmable controllers include: opening a conveyor door, turning on a conveyor to move parts, closing a conveyor door. The central computer can control any number of programmable controllers.

COMPUTERS FOR MATERIALS MANAGEMENT IN FLEXIBLE MANUFACTURING SYSTEMS

Flexible manufacturing systems (FMS) integrate many automation concepts and technologies into a single production operation. A typical operation might include the following features:

- Automatic materials handling between machines, — including part picking and part transportation.
- Numerically controlled machine tools, interconnected by an automated work part handling system.
- Computer control of materials handling systems.
- Application of group technology principles.

A flexible manufacturing system is a group of numerically controlled (NC) machines connected to an automated work part handling system (see Figure 11-9). This integrated system under computer control is capable of processing a variety of different part types simultaneously, using NC programs at various work stations. Technicians are required to carry out support functions for the operations, such as:

- Changing tools and load setting.
- Equipment maintenance and repair.
- Loading raw work parts into the system.
- Unloading finished parts from the system.
- Inputting data, changing programs, and performing other tasks related to the computer processing units.

Under this system, parts are loaded and unloaded at a central location and then automatically routed to the appropriate work stations for processing. For each different work part, the routing may be different, as may the

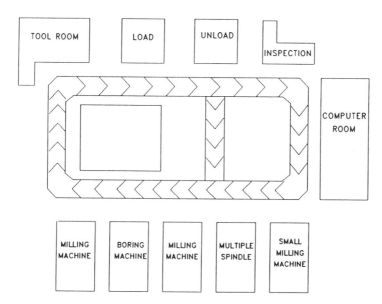

Figure 11-9. FMS layout for a typical operation.

operations and tooling required at each work station. A computer controls the parts handling and processing activities.[14]

Flexible manufacturing systems are designed for medium-volume production, or for use between high-production and low-production NC machines. High-production systems are very efficient at producing parts in large volumes at high output rates, but all parts must be identical. These highly mechanized lines are inflexible and cannot accept variations in part design. When changeovers in parts design occur, the entire line must be shut down to retool. In contrast, NC machines are ideally suited for variations in work parts. They are appropriate for job shop and small batch processing because they can be conveniently reprogrammed to deal with product changeovers and parts design changes.

In terms of manufacturing efficiency and productivity, high-production lines have volumes of over 20,000 units a year, whereas highly flexible NC machines are limited to a few hundred units a year. Flexible manufacturing systems are suited to mid-volume production of fairly complex parts, when the equipment only needs to be flexible enough to handle a limited variety of part designs.

The characteristics of a flexible manufacturing system are as follows:

- It can produce a variety of work part designs, manufacturing several different part families on the same series of machines.
- Work pieces among the part families can be introduced without downtime setup. When a certain part is introduced onto the line, it is identified to the computer control system, which then routes it to the proper machines in the system. However, each work station must be equipped with the required tooling to process the part.
- The system is designed to process a variety of parts simultaneously by using all work stations concurrently; so a mixed product manufacturing schedule should be maintained to fully utilize the system. Such a schedule permits various combinations of production rate and volumes to be established to meet specified product demands.
- Manufacturing lead times are drastically reduced by reducing the time between successive work stations on the line. Setup time, involving tooling setup and work part setup, is also minimized. The tooling setup is preset off-line by loading the tools required into a tool drum at each work station; the tool drum may be capable of holding up to 60 or more tools. The work part setups are prepared externally, generally on pallets, which are used to transport parts from station to station. The setup consists of adapting a pallet to hold a particular part and properly registering it at each work station. To hold parts in place on the pallet, fixtures are designed that can be adapted to various part configurations within a part group. This setup is performed in the load/un-

load area before the part and pallet are placed in the system. These setup features significantly reduce the processing lead time.

- Work-in-process inventory is reduced because only a limited number of parts can be loaded onto the system.
- Equipment utilization is maximized because of minimum setup times, efficient handling, and simultaneous work part processing.
- Direct and indirect labor are reduced by having one person manning several work stations.
- Management is improved through better information and control of parts moving through the system.

The components of a flexible manufacturing system include machine tools, materials handling equipment, and computers. The machine tools may belong to either dedicated or random systems. A dedicated system uses special machine tools for a limited variety of processing needs or for predetermined machinery applications. Random systems are designed to handle a greater variety of parts in random sequence, performing a wide variety of machinery operations on a variety of work parts.

The materials handling system must have the following characteristics in a flexible manufacturing system:[15]

- Random, independent movement of palletized work parts between work stations. Parts must be able to flow from any work station to any other work station independently of each other, to maximize work station utilization.
- Temporary storage of work parts at work stations for parts waiting to be processed.
- Convenient loading and unloading of work parts onto the system, which may involve manual operations.
- Automatic loading and unloading at individual processing stations.
- A computer that is compatible with the system.
- Ability to meet safety, noise, and other requirements.
- Ability to operate without obstructing the individual work stations.
- Ability to operate effectively in the presence of metal chips, oils, and so forth, that exist in a plant.

At present, a number of handling systems are available that meet these requirements, including power roller conveyors, power and free overhead conveyors, shuttle conveyors, and towline systems. The handling system moves parts between work centers and interfaces work parts in the proper sequence. To service individual work stations as well as storage, two separate handling systems may be necessary.

The operation and the control of a flexible manufacturing system require the use of a computer. The computer performs the following functions:

• Storage of parts programs for the various work stations.
• Making the parts programs available to individual machines in proper sequence.
• Production control of part mix and rate of input of the parts onto the system. These controls are based on data entered into the computer, such as production rates, parts available, number of units, machine required, and instructions.
• Control of handling system between and at work stations and coordination with the whole system.
• Status control of each work part type in the system.
• Control and monitoring of cutting tools and tool life.
• Performance of system functions and reporting on the system.

To perform these functions and prepare performance reports, the computer requires that data be contained in files. The principal data files required for a flexible manufacturing system are part file, routing file, part production file, pallet file, station tool file, and tool life file.

RELATIONSHIPS WITH MATERIALS MANAGEMENT SUBFUNCTIONS

Materials managers who are using or plan to use computers should make a thorough analysis of their complete operation, breaking it down into individual activities. For each activity, they must determine how the operations within materials management relate to each other and to other functions within the company. The form, timing, and quantity of input and output data needed for each activity must be specified. This information is needed to develop or refine the system and to create a data base for development of the computer software.

This analysis enables the materials manager to define problems and anticipate any changes required when the computer takes over control of the operation. An operational flow chart is needed for the entire system, showing how it relates to other departments throughout the company. At this time, other operations managers may need to make changes or may even be forced to computerize various activities in their own departments. A complete program can be developed that will permit operating personnel to interact through the computer.

Materials Handling

An effectively used computer offers materials management several significant advantages over manual systems, because of its ability to process huge volumes of data, especially routine, repetitive work. The primary benefit of computers to materials handling is that they make immediately available much more complete data for use in determining material requirements. Materials management can then manage by exception and be more effective in managing the flow of materials throughout the operation.

A computer-based materials handling system maintains essentially the same records as those of a manual system, but every materials manager utilizes computers in a different manner. Data inputs vary, as do desired outputs, forms, and the timing of various reports, depending upon operating needs. The materials activities that can be performed well by computers are:

- Posting of materials records.
- Computation of order quantities.
- Preparation of requisitions orders.
- Preparation of requests.
- Distribution of accounting charges.
- Preparation of purchase orders.
- Automatic preparation of follow-up memos.
- Posting of delivery and quality records.
- Auditing of requisitions.

In most companies, the computer system now used is an interactive on-time system utilizing a terminal linked to the central processing unit.

Purchasing and Inventory Control

Inventory and part records are filed and maintained in a computerized system. Such records include standard information such as maintained part number, name, descriptive data, historical usage data, current inventory balance, price data from recent purchases, and price quotations. Also recorded are suppliers' names and addresses, shipping terms, quality and delivery performance, purchase history, and open orders. Each time a store makes a withdrawal requisition, the balance on hand is compared with a predetermined reorder point figure. When the balance falls below the order point, the computer prints out a purchase requisition. It may order a predetermined quantity, or it may be programmed to compute and order the most economical quantity. The purchase requisition may also contain monthly usage data for the past year, a listing of past purchase orders and prices, and a summary for purchasing of the most recent price quotations from different vendors.

The computer cannot determine the urgency of an order except in terms of normal delivery requirements, exact shipping dates, and follow-up dates. Therefore, production and purchasing must review all purchase requisitions for control purposes, if production fluctuates and/or suppliers fail to perform under current conditions. Unique delivery dates, shipping routings, and follow-up inquiries must be handled manually, as must all purchase requisitions that are not controlled by computer.

Receiving, Inspection, and Storage

When an order is received, the receiving clerk puts conventional information directly into the computer's order record through a terminal, and the computer immediately produces the printed reports required by other company personnel. For orders requiring technical inspection, the computer periodically produces and processes reports to update the open-order file and the inventory record file.

Daily updating of records permits the preparation of numerous daily reports, such as:

- List of open purchase orders.
- List of orders or parts that are behind schedule.
- List of parts that are out of stock.
- List of orders or parts that require action because of supplier quality problems.

Such reports are important to individual managers, as they provide a summary of critical, up-to-date information about orders for inventory and production that would be impossible to obtain otherwise.

Computerization is most beneficial for operations that have a large diversified inventory, make a large number of purchases, and use a large number of suppliers. Even though large-scale operations have the greatest potential for profitable applications, small companies can also profit from a computer-based system. The first observable change in the normal routine after the introduction of such a system occurs in the generation and processing of the various reports, most of which can be prepared by the computer. Items whose inventory cannot be controlled effectively by a computer on a continuing basis are primarily those with unstable usage patterns.

Computer systems also produce changes in utilization of people. Freed from a vast amount of routine work, managers can devote more time to managerial and creative responsibilities. Because it regularly receives a large quantity of detailed, new control data, management can reduce delays in manufacturing through fewer late shipments, reduce inventories and materials costs, do a better job of planning, improve cost accounting control, and increase the speed and effectiveness of operations.[16]

An important change is the development of a new relationship between materials management and other related activities, namely, purchasing, inventory control, and production control. The computer is a common bond that draws all activities into an integrated system. The situation stimulates the development of an organization committed to a materials management philosophy. Even in more traditional forms of organization, people work more closely with their counterparts. The design of the system and the speed of the computer minimize buck-passing and cause materials problems to be viewed as company rather than departmental problems.

SUMMARY

A materials management system is an organized approach used to deal with problems involving a combination of skills from complementary disciplines, both managerial and technical, that require these skills to be expended in a unified effort. The systems approach is a group of concepts, methods, and techniques used for problem solving, decision making, analyzing organizations and processes, and evaluating performance. The systems approach entails a way of thinking that emphasizes the whole system, rather than individual parts striving to optimize a given problem or situation.

In designing a materials management system, as complete a statement of the problem as possible is required. From this, objectives are defined in specific terms that are used to describe the system. A descriptive layout of the existing situation is helpful in developing the problem and objectives. From this, the system parameters and boundaries can be defined. Development of the specific materials management system is done through a system flow chart indicating its overall structure; the flow chart serves as a foundation upon which detailed specifications are developed, concerning particular procedures, data, equipment, people, and so forth. Feedback provides a means for modification of the materials management system to improve its performance.

The development of a materials management system is a time-consuming and expensive project; the cost of putting such a system on line and satisfactorily operating and maintaining it is often comparable to the cost of bringing a new product to the market. Generally, development and implementation are carried out simultaneously. The operational testing of the system is a continuous process, but design changes should be considered only during major system changes.

A management information system (MIS) for materials management provides relevant information at the right time to appropriate individuals. The MIS helps to manage and coordinate the materials management activities. The MIS is a process that goes beyond managing by piecemeal information, intuitive guesswork, and isolated problem solving to a level of systems insight, information, high-level data processing, and problem solving.

In today's manufacturing environment, Just-In-Time and its many variations have created an increasing demand for materials management to respond immediately, which necessitates the use of computers. These changes in materials management are accelerating, requiring more and more information; so computers must be used to retrieve and evaluate information.

Recent developments in manufacturing automation have occurred in computer aided manufacturing (CAM), computerized machining centers, industrial robots, and flexible manufacturing systems (FMS), making extensive use of computers. Each of these advances has had a direct effect on materials management operations and materials management, which must perform efficiently if these innovations are to be effectively utilized.

BIBLIOGRAPHY

Allen, R. Leonard. "The Applicability of Standard Manufacturing Software to Primary Metals Processing." *APICS 23rd Annual Conference Proceedings*, 1980, pp. 85–89.

Ammer, Dean S. *Materials Management and Purchasing*. Homewood, Illinois: Richard D. Irwin, 1980.

Bond, J. B. "On the Road to CAD/CAM." *Iron Age*, Mar. 23, 1977, pp. 37–40.

Bourke, Richard W. "Selecting Software Smartly: The Early Slips." *Production and Inventory Management Review and APICS News*, May 1981, pp. 13–16.

Cook, Milton E. "How to Evaluate Software Packages." *APICS 14th Annual Conference Proceedings*, 1981, pp. 126–130.

DeSantis, Gerald F. "Implementation Considerations in System Design." *APICS 20th Annual Conference Proceedings*, 1977, pp. 210–216.

Groover, Mihell P. *Automation Production Systems and Computer-Aided Manufacturing*. Englewood Cliffs, New Jersey: Prentice-Hall, 1980.

Gunn, Thomas G. *Computer Applications in Manufacturing*. New York: Industrial Press, 1981.

Kearney and Trecher Corp. "Understanding Manufacturing Systems" (a technical paper), Vol. 1, Milwaukee, Wisconsin.

Murdick, Robert G. *MIS Concepts and Design*. Englewood Cliffs, New Jersey: Prentice-Hall, 1980.

Murdick, Robert G., Ross, Joel E., and Cloggett, James R. *Informations Systems for Modern Management*, 3rd ed. Englewood Cliffs, New Jersey: Prentice-Hall, 1984.

Optner, Stanford I. *System Analysis for Business Management*, 3rd ed. Englewood Cliffs, New Jersey: Prentice-Hall, 1975.

Pennente, Ernest, and Levy, Ted. "MRP on Microcomputers." *Production and Inventory Management Review*, May 1982, pp. 20–25.

Schaffer, G. "Computers in Manufacturing." *American Machinist*, Apr. 1978, pp. 115–122.

Smith, August W. *Management Systems: Analyses and Applications*. Hinsdale, Illinois: The Dryden Press, 1982.

Van Gigh, John P. *Applied General System Theory*, 2nd ed. New York: Harper and Row, 1978.

The robots in the 21st Century I. Asinov il Radio-Electron 58–99–101 My 87

Gerard Medioni Improving robot vision USA Today 115:10 Je 87.

NOTES

1. Optner, *System Analysis for Business Management*, p. 22.
2. Smith, *Management Systems: Analyses and Applications*, pp. 18–19.
3. Van Gigh, *Applied General System Theory*, pp. 102, 112.
4. Optner, *Systems Analysis for Business Management*, p. 96.
5. Murdick/Ross/Cloggett, *Information Systems for Modern Management*, 3/E, 1984, p. 239. Reprinted by permission of Prentice-Hall, Inc., Englewood Cliffs, New Jersey.
6. Murdick, Ross, and Cloggett, *Information Systems for Modern Management*, p. 244.
7. Optner, *System Analysis for Business Management*, pp. 56–58.
8. Murdick, *MIS Concepts and Design*, p. 11.
9. Schaffer, "Computers in Manufacturing," pp. 115–122.
10. Bond, "On the Road to CAD/CAM," pp. 37–40.
11. Groover, *Automation Production Systems and Computer-Aided Manufacturing*, pp. 253–254.
12. I Asinov, The robots in the 21st Century Radio-Electron 58–99–101 My 87
13. Gerard Medioni, Improving robot vision USA Today 115:10 Je 87.
14. Kearney and Trecher Corp., "Understanding Manufacturing Systems."
15. Groover, *Automation, Production Systems and Computer-Aided Manufacturing*, pp. 570–572.
16. Ammer, *Materials Management and Purchasing*, pp. 589–594.

12
Pitfalls, Problems, and Operation of a Total Materials Management Program

During the past decade, materials managers have made considerable progress in the coordination and integration of their activities, but many pitfalls and problems remain in the implementation of materials management programs. Uncoordinated cost reduction, for example, can be misleading; cost reductions in one area frequently appear as cost increases elsewhere. Reducing in-plant transportation equipment in order to fully utilize all of the company's forklifts would probably require inventory increases and delay production. Similarly, reductions in packaging costs can increase the costs of materials handling and customer claims.

The challenge to managers is to implement materials management systems while maintaining a clear understanding of potential problems. The problems of materials management will vary from company to company because of the unique nature of each company's operations. However, many general pitfalls and problems exist in all companies, and they are discussed in this chapter.

OPERATIONAL PROBLEMS

Operating a materials management program at times seems almost impossible. Before materials managers can effectively overcome the difficulties they face, they first must clearly understand and define them. Frequently, materials management is criticized for taking actions that seem incompatible with other company actions or the goals and objectives of the company. In such cases, materials managers usually have failed to grasp various problems that affected their decisions.

Lack of Understanding Materials Management

Even though materials management is basic to all service and manufacturing processes, it is one of the least understand areas. With its widely dispersed activity, both workers and management at all levels have difficulty understanding and comprehending its role and importance to the company. There is little publicity about, and thus little knowledge of, the role of the materials manager. Consequently, an educational program dealing with materials management processes and their role in the company's success would be valuable but this is a difficult and complex task for materials management.

There is a seemingly universal lack of education about the materials management function, even in companies that have strong training programs—a lack of awareness that includes even the personnel in materials management, plus top management and other operating functions. In general, the level of understanding of the materials management function within the company directly matches the support given to materials management, and indicates how effective materials management will be. When education about its role is inadequate, not only will the materials management function tend to suffer, but the company will be hurt as well. Even when the general level of education in the company is high, there are training needs among the various personnel of materials management. These needs are summarized in Table 12-1 for various management levels.

For materials management to be effective, concerned personnel must be well trained in the performance of their work. Such training must involve both formal education and on-the-job experience. The training must emphasize the scope and objectives of materials management, the use of equipment, and the role and future plans for materials management in the total organization. Other functional units in the firm must be educated about the role and importance of materials management. Top management of the company must be especially enlightened on the importance, concepts, and extensive responsibility of materials management. Because of the great lack of knowledge about materials management in most organizations, corporate-wide education is a major responsibility of materials management.

Lack of Commitment by Top Management to Materials Management

Despite recent interest in materials management, top management still is not committed to it in many companies. Top executives have difficulty in defining the limits and scope of materials management. Some of them consider that materials management has a minor role compared to production, sales, finance and other functions. There is a natural tendency to let today's problems in production, marketing, and finance push aside materials management's problems and needs; all too often, executives would rather be concerned with other problems that seem more important and

Table 12-1. Training Needs of Personnel for Materials Management

Top Management
- Importance of materials management.
- Role of materials management in obtaining company goals and objectives.
- Responsibility of top management to materials management.

Management (all levels)
- The role and importance of materials management in company operations.

Materials Management
- Objectives of materials management operations.
- Coordination of materials management with other functions.
- Equipment operation training.
- Managerial concepts/principles.

demanding than managing materials. However, top management will find that the solution to many of these "urgent" problems lies in a strong, effective materials management organization.

Despite the need for top management commitment to materials management, many executives give it little more than lip service, especially if it requires the expenditure of unavailable or very limited funds. Genuine commitment implies timely decisions supported by adequate funds, direct action, and a long-term obligation to the program. This kind of commitment from top management must underlie all materials management decisions. To achieve it, departmental personnel must take an active role in educating and directly involving top management in their activities. They must educate the entire company, and "sell" the importance of materials management throughout the organization.

Poor Communication by Materials Management

A major problem for the materials manager is lack of communication between materials management and its subordinates and the other managerial functions such as engineering, operations, marketing, and finance. This lack of communication is normally caused by:[1]

1. Difficulties with confused lines of authority.
2. Organizational structure being altered frequently.
3. Organization being established without proper planning.
4. Too many levels of organizational authority.
5. Wide span of control.
6. Interests of materials manager not directly related to the area.
7. Physical distance between individuals utilizing the communications system.

The initiative for communication is principally the responsibility of the materials manager, who must communicate the information needed by subordinates. It is difficult for subordinates to communicate with the materials manager; they must have a special need for information and feel confident before they can communicate effectively with the manager. Various conditions may cause subordinates to be unwilling to communicate with the materials manager:[2]

1. They are afraid that their communication will result in negative rather than positive action.
2. Subordinates feel that the materials manager is unsympathetic and not trustworthy.
3. Subordinates feel that materials managers believe they are unimportant, and that therefore their information is unimportant. The more important subordinates feel, the greater their willingness to communicate.
4. Subordinates do not have a knowledge of materials management, and thus lack interest and enthusiasm.
5. The materials manager is unavailable.
6. The materials manager shows little or no desire for information from subordinates and does not appreciate their participation.
7. Subordinates believe the materials manager has a negative attitude toward them.

Some degree of communication about the materials management function must exist at all organizational levels. Without it, trouble is inevitable, and, indirectly, the entire company's operation is affected. For example, general policies and regulations apply to all persons within the company, including materials management, and must be communicated to all materials management personnel. If communication is inadequate, and top management and other units related to materials management are misinformed about the role and function of materials management, they often set forth policies and rules that are detrimental to materials management. This lack of knowledge also creates a generally negative attitude toward materials management, which new employees adopt as they join the company.

Resistance to Changes

All managers are continuously concerned with change. There are two broad categories of change common to the company: external and internal (see Figure 12-1). External changes may differ widely, depending upon the dynamics of the operation. Some companies operate in a shifting environ-

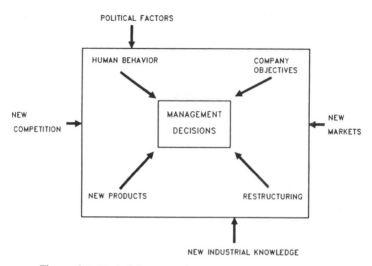

Figure 12-1. Typical forces causing external and internal changes.

ment that is altered by new knowledge and changing competitive practices, political factors, and so on. Other companies are much less dynamic but are still affected by new competition, new markets, and even new institutions.

Internal changes involve modifying company objectives, policies, location, organizational structure, product lines, management philosophies, and methods of doing business. Some of these changes are voluntary; others are forced on the company. In addition, there are changes that involve human behavior. Materials managers will frequently need to change subordinates' activities; the managers constantly will have to influence subordinates to accept change. Some subordinates will not want to change, but they must be motivated to change in the interest of efficiency.

A materials manager must overcome resistance to change, not only among employees, but in various groups involved with materials management (see Figure 12-2). People either fear or welcome change, depending on how it may affect them, and how it increases or decreases their well-being. Changes may affect their income, physical environment, status, the esteem accorded them by others, group relationships, power relationships, opportunity for self-development, and freedom of action. Because of the importance of such changes, people need to have time before committing themselves to them, to calculate their possible net advantages. During the

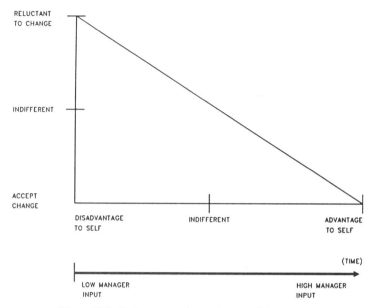

Figure 12-2. Resistance to change by materials manager.

time when commitments are being considered, materials managers have a valuable opportunity to provide positive information, sell the changes, help people overcome fears, and prepare them for change.

Materials managers must continually lead subordinates, as well as other managers in other departments of the company, in adapting to change. With zeal and confidence, the materials managers must exhibit the necessary leadership to convince doubtful and pessimistic individuals to meet new challenges. This job is never done; it is always in process because the materials management environment is constantly changing. The materials manager must deal with a dynamic environment. People within and outside the firm are not static, even in numbers, relationships, and dependency on the firm. In addition, there are promotions and transfers, hiring, labor union activities, new customers arriving and old ones leaving, and new social attitudes. These changes, plus many others, cause attitudes of employees and persons outside the firm to change as expectations change.

This is a complex problem. At times the materials manager fails to realize that changes are occurring, and sometimes they occur very quickly. At other times the materials manager recognizes change, but, not knowing their source, fails to apply the necessary and appropriate leadership techniques. Thus the materials manager may select courses of action in these situations that are inappropriate for today's environment.

Lack of Qualified and Adequate Personnel

In most companies, top management pays too little attention to providing sufficient and qualified personnel for materials management. Without proper planning and control, poor personnel choices are made, resulting in incompetent subordinates and poor group morale. Often the materials management organization is weakened. Many examples can be cited where the quality of the personnel has made the difference between success and failure. The quality and adequacy of personnel are of critical importance to materials management (see Figure 12-3).

The demand for materials managers has increased with the growth in size and importance of the materials management function in both industry and service organizations. As a result, top management sometimes fails to obtain qualified managers and fills key materials management positions with people who have training, experience, and interest in other areas, or have other major responsibilities in the company. Then their primary duties are administrating other managerial functions, and materials management does not receive adequate attention.

The failure of some top managers to develop qualified materials managers and staff shows an inability to recognize the importance of personnel. Part of this can be explained by the relatively recent emergence of materials management as a critical company function. Another reason for the lack of attention given to staffing is the slowness of top management to understand what is involved in materials management. Before top management can take action, it must identify and understand the important relationships between the materials management function and the company's other operations. If information on the duties and responsibilities of materials managers is lacking, top management may staff these positions with unqualified people.

To compound the problem, there has been little or no attention given to materials management training in some companies. Despite the recognition of its importance, there was little interest in it until recent years; and even now, top management hesitates to do anything about the development and training of materials management personnel because they are uncertain what these personnel should do. Also, they are uncertain about future staff needs. The real question becomes, how farsighted is management? Those who are concerned mainly with immediate and short-term problems are often inclined to delay attention to future personnel needs. It is costly and time-consuming to train materials management personnel. Delays, though understandable, are too frequent; top management often has dragged its feet in this area. Top management also neglects these responsibilities because many personnel leave the company after their

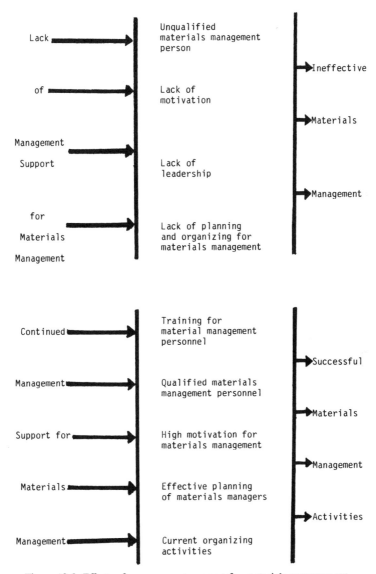

Figure 12-3. Effects of management support for materials management.

training. An added consideration is that top management is uncertain about what constitutes proper training. However, some companies have instituted good materials management training programs, and have developed qualified personnel, with consequent good results.

Improper Status of Materials Management

Lack of status can be both informal and formal. In some companies, there are significant status differentials among various activities, depending upon how individuals' peers and management rank the work. Also, status is related to the jobs people perform, and the organizational level at which their work is placed. Materials management has been at a low organizational level in most companies and accorded low status. It has been given a low position because its operations are performed by people with relatively little education, young people, and individuals who have been with the organization for short periods of time. All these factors have made materials management a low-status activity, compared to other functions such as production, marketing, and finance. In many firms, their lack of skills and experience generally has led to a lack of recognition and respect for members of the group.

In addition, materials managers have achieved inadequate status in most companies because they lack certain status symbols: proper job titles, adequate wages compared to responsibilities, adequate office space and secretarial assistance, adequate materials handling equipment, and invitations to participate in key meetings. All of these status symbols are internal and within the control of top management (see Figure 12-4).

Some of the most common problems created by lack of status are inflexibility, lack of communication, low morale, and lack of power to accomplish necessary tasks.[3] These deficiencies cause inevitable problems for materials managers, creating needless roadblocks to cooperative action.

Employees will strive for prestige, and even its various symbols; and serious problems may occur if the group lacks these symbols. A job title change is often as satisfying as a higher salary; even a change to a job of lower pay but more prestige might satisfy some people, if their pay is still sufficient.[4] A comprehensive and coordinated plan to provide appropriate

Status Symbols for Materials Management Personnel	Aid in Coordinating System For Less Materials Management Problems
■ job titles ■ adequate wages ■ decentralized operations ■ adequate space & personnel ■ adequate equipment ■ information flow to materials management people	■ flexible system ■ good communication ■ high morale ■ necessary authority

Figure 12-4. Status symbols and their effect on materials management.

status and status symbols for materials management should be implemented by upper management.

Poor Organization of Materials Management

In materials management, certain common, but avoidable, organizational failures arise in practice. A source of conflict and inflexibility, these persistent failures cause materials management to be ineffective and inefficient (see Figure 12-5). Some of the most common organizational failures, which must be particularly avoided by materials managers, are as follows:

Out-of-date Organizational Structure. It is not uncommon for materials management to continue an organizational arrangement long after its objectives, plans, equipment, product lines, and people have changed. This occurs when materials management fails to plan for a future that is significantly different from the past and the present.

Failure to Clarify and Understand Relationships. Misunderstandings about relationships engender friction and inefficiencies in materials management. The authority to do a job and the responsibility for doing it are critical; ignorance here may cause materials management personnel to be misused or ignored, or to become a cause for resentment and conflict in the company.

Mixed Lines of Authority. When lines of authority are not followed, no one is accountable or responsible in the group. When duties and relation-

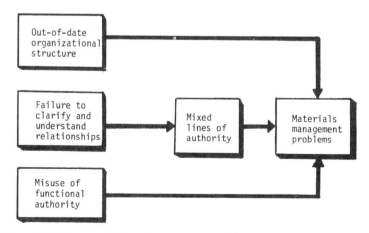

Figure 12-5. Common failures due to poor materials management organization.

ships are not specifically delineated, complaints and excessive referrals of small problems to upper management, or bottlenecks in decision making, occur regularly.

Misuse of Functional Authority. Materials management is a staff department in the company, but it generally assumes functional authority. This functional authority gives materials management control over specified processes, practices, policies, or other matters related to activities undertaken by personnel in departments other than their own. Poor organization causes the misuse of functional authority in the company, and accounts for more materials management problems than any other factor. Even more perilous is the careless application or unrestricted delegation of functional authority in the company, which creates conflict and confusion for everyone.

Lack of Established Goals and Standards

Although the materials manager is responsible for effective materials operations, in many companies appropriate goals and standards are lacking for materials management operations, especially in relation to overall company goals and standards. This is a critical problem for materials personnel who have direct relationships with many other departments. It is difficult or impossible for materials managers to be in control and take corrective action without goals and standards.

Especially serious is the inability of materials management to coordinate its actions with the other operating activities of the organization when goals and standards are lacking. Because of differences of opinion and interests among groups, materials management's efforts may not be directed toward the goals of the company. The materials group may be falsely accused of not contributing to the company's goals, being uncooperative, having an uncoordinated operation, and lacking planning, organization, and a controlled system of operation. In addition, individuals in materials management cannot see how their efforts contribute to the goals of the company in such a disorganized situation.

Lack of Adequate Facilities

Various economic and managerial factors have contributed to a lack of mechanization and automation in various materials group facilities. Automation holds the same promise for materials handling operations as for production — increasing productivity, which means greater output. But for materials management, the problem of acquiring adequate facilities is broad and not associated precisely with a given area, as it includes various activities such as receiving, stores, and physical distribution. As in many cases of automation for production facilities, there is a general trend toward acquiring increasingly special-purpose equipment, which is especially designed to handle only certain products or operations and thus has extremely limited applicability. What is gained in this special-purpose equipment through efficiency for a particular operation is often lost in flexibility; so it is difficult for materials management to adapt itself to using highly specialized equipment. A closely related consideration is the high capital investment requirements of such equipment.

As manufacturing operations rapidly are becoming automated, such as changing from batch to on-line processing, materials handling equipment needs to have special capabilities; materials management needs to have automated equipment installed to complement these automated production operations. This means moving from simple materials handling facilities to complex systems with greater capacity and efficiency, which also require greater operator skills, more maintenance, and increased capital. The major changes in manufacturing operations thus dictate to materials management major changes that it cannot control. These changes also prevent materials management from developing and obtaining necessary facilities such as warehouse space, receiving and shipping, and so on, which may be more critical to it. These conflicts occur because materials handling facilities are of vital importance to manufacturing. To complicate the problem, top management regards manufacturing operations as more important than materials management facilities.

Materials managers often lack the time and capability to provide top management with the supporting data and information needed to justify the purchase of equipment and complete systems. For new projects, materials management must provide top management with tangible information in terms of dollars, man-hours, machine-hours, units of output, rate of return on investment, or other useful quantitative units. Project features that cannot be quantified must be set forth, with the pros and cons of each provided in the proposal. In addition, the information must be accurate and the analysis error-free. All of this presentation, including data collection, requires considerable time.

For reasons already discussed and because materials management often fails to develop and present proper analysis, top management generally does not make adequate investment in materials handling facilities. As a result, materials management must cope with inefficient and out-of-date facilities that cause higher costs, management problems, and poor relationships with other operating units within the company, as well as low morale among materials management personnel.

Terminating Old Systems Too Soon

Terminating old materials management systems before new systems are developed, tested, and properly implemented in the present operation causes many problems, and materials management may have to rely on the new system before it is fully operational. More often than not, a new system will present a variety of problems when first placed into operation, and numerous corrections must be made. Materials managers sometimes fail to analyze problems by collecting and evaluating data, comparing alternative approaches, identifying equipment needs, and establishing cost justifications. Shortcuts are made that often cause parts of the system not to be implemented by materials management. Often a principal cause of this problem is that top management fails to give the new system proper support, in both time and resources.

UNDERSTANDING COMPANY POLITICS

Materials managers at all levels must be aware of the interpersonal activities in their organization, encompassing broad social, political, and ethical spectra. Social activities involve attitudes, desires, expectations, intelligence, and education, as well as the beliefs and customs of people in a given group. Political activities are primarily a combination of complex policies, rules, customs, and so forth, that affect all groups to various degrees. Ethical activities include generally accepted practices and standards of personal conduct that may or may not be codified by law but generally have the virtual force of law.[5]

Understanding the complex interweaving of these activities is an exceptionally important part of management; materials managers must be able to forecast and anticipate the political activities, expectations, and pressures that give rise to various actions of employees. Knowing the forces that normally come into play after managerial actions, management can prepare for and anticipate them and take appropriate action rather than react—that is, act in a timely manner before a crisis is at hand.[6]

Materials management personnel must be responsive to the political beliefs of particular individuals, groups, and even society. Unfortunately, attitudes and beliefs are different and constantly changing—between line and staff managers, for example, and in other groups outside the company. The variety of political beliefs within the company makes it difficult for materials managers to design an environment conducive to materials management goals and objectives, and it is even more difficult to respond to political pressures from outside the organization. Yet materials management has no choice but to consider all these factors in decision making. This requires that materials managers understand the political attitudes, beliefs, and values of the groups and individuals they interact with, and consciously respond to them in some fashion.

Political Changes

During the development of the organization, many changes, both internal and external, gradually occur, which are significant to materials managers:

- Personnel changes within the organization.
- Changes in "power" of various functions and individuals.
- Changes in the educational levels of employees.
- Changes in the logical process of the operation (more formal procedures, rules, and policies) over time, as the organization grows.
- Greater faith in science and technology; use of engineering economy concepts, engineering, and operational research techniques.
- Greater belief in the importance in finding better ways of doing things.
- Changes in local, state, and federal governments, and even in society.

These and many other changes affect the way that company managers deal with personnel. Interestingly, long-held political beliefs in many companies are modified and supplemented during crises; and there may be changes in product lines, the chief executive officer, and owners, as well as relocations. During these times, major political changes occur in the organization, whose impact materials management must evaluate. Many times this reexamination results in new company rules, policies, and procedures that are kept in place long after the change has occurred.

Political attitudes and actions also change with the ebb and flow of external events and social demands. Government affects virtually every company and every aspect of it. Its impact may be felt through the promotion of economic development programs; direct subsidies of certain industries and specific parts, such as transportation modes or raw materials; special tax advantages; support for research and development; special tariffs; or the purchase of goods and services by various governmental units.

Political activity occurs in many degrees and forms in a typical company. For example, the materials manager must provide an alternate materials handling system for a particular line in the production department. According to the company's formal policy, the materials manager would take the first action included in the following list. The other steps are not formally required and can be construed as various forms of political action.

- The materials manager submits the recommendation for approval by the production department. All of the supporting data are provided, in a formal attempt to persuade production that the recommended system is the most appropriate equipment. If unsuccessful, the materials manager would appeal to his or her superior manager, who would decide the case and issue an order. Or the materials manager could take various political steps (below).

- The materials manager attempts to get acquainted with production people on a personal basis through casual conversation, inquiries about respective backgrounds, and so forth.
- The materials manager attempts to stimulate a friendship.
- The materials manager arranges to lunch with production personnel to promote the recommended system, on a casual basis either inside or outside the plant.
- The materials manager offers to exchange favors that are possible within the regular operating rules and policies, such as special handling.
- The materials manager agrees to favors involving a slight bending of company policies.
- The materials manager agrees to a favor involving a more serious bending of company policies.

Undoubtedly, materials management could try in many other ways to persuade production to accept a recommendation. The possibilities depend upon the extent of power the two parties possess. In instances where one has control over the other, the alternatives are even more numerous and assume more importance.

Materials managers have many potential areas of political action. Numerous opportunities exist for political maneuvering with regard to promotions, budget allocations, assignment of manpower, and physical facilities. In superior/subordinate relationships, subordinates use political means to gain favors through their ability to offer or withhold their cooperation and obedience. In relationships with unions, management usually exercises a great amount of political influence. The political conflicts between line and staff members are well-known to the materials manager. Because of its specialization, with considerable areas of expertise and the ability to provide necessary services, materials management is in a position to experience some interesting conflicts and accommodations.

On the other hand, every company is encircled by a web of laws, regulations, and court decisions. Some are designed to protect workers, consumers, and communities, and others to regulate the behavior of managers and their subordinates, within the business and with other companies; many are intended to make contracts enforceable and to protect property rights. There is relatively little that a manager can do in any organization that is not in some way affected by, and often specifically controlled by, laws or regulations. Managers must respond not only to these laws and regulations, but also to social pressures; they have to foresee and deal with political pressures as well as laws that might be passed. This clearly is not an easy task.

Predicting the Political Climate

Every decision, whether it is made by materials managers or by top management, carries with it some overtones of political influence, either from within the company or from the outside. Each decision has some effect on the welfare of at least one or two specific groups, either inside or outside the organization, and many decisions affect almost all groups connected with the company. Also, a decision may be either harmful or helpful to these groups. Because decisions have such an impact, materials managers should consider outside groups as "members" of the company, like inside groups. This kind of membership is much more inclusive than the commonly used definition of company membership.[7] With such a broad constituency, materials management must evaluate the effects on all the groups whose company relationships will be changed when a decision or proposed program is put into effect.

To give their support, group members must think that they are getting what they would consider a fair deal, or better. To anticipate how various groups will respond to a proposed program, materials managers must imagine themselves as members of each group and then compare the proposed program alternatives with the program currently in effect, all from the point of view of the particular group under consideration. If the new program offers a greater amount of satisfaction than the current one, or it seems to be accompanied by fewer unwanted consequences, group members will tend to give it their support. These groups will gladly make the contribution to the company called for under the proposal, on the basis of premises set forth in the individual evaluations they receive. If groups conclude that a new program will further their own goals and objectives as well as those of the company, materials management can expect them to accept the proposal and act upon it wholeheartedly. Therefore, it is the responsibility of materials management to communicate the benefits of new proposals and make sure that each group has complete information about each one.

An analysis of constituent groups usually discloses that the groups' nonmonetary values are as important to them as monetary and material considerations. If the total benefits of a proposed program exceed those of the older plan, the materials manager can be reasonably sure that the members of the group will cooperate in its implementation. When group members anticipate decreased benefits under a proposed program, materials managers can predict that the group will make a smaller contribution in order to keep the benefits enjoyed under the proposed program equal to the benefits enjoyed under the old. It can be assumed, in fact, that in most new programs some groups will reduce their total contributions to the company. Materials management can expect some groups or group members to sever their connections and even join a competing groups that offers them greater benefits.

To avoid becoming overwhelmed by details in making decisions that affect several contributing groups, materials managers can weigh the pros and cons of these decisions; for each group, they can list the important benefits and consequences of the proposed program alternatives versus the present program. This will help them to predict with reasonable accuracy which of the alternatives the majority of the members of each group will prefer. From this analysis, materials management can predict which groups probably will oppose the proposed program and, as a consequence, make a smaller contribution to the company than their present one. The analysis also helps to ward off unrealistic thinking, forcing materials management realistically to consider political factors in addition to economic factors, or to be truthful in their thinking. Materials management has to recognize how groups and group members view nonmonetary, monetary, and material contributions. The objective of such an analysis is to increase the flow of effort to the company, or at least to diminish the concessions management must make to the constituent groups.

After the materials manager predicts the reactions of the groups whose welfare will be affected by proposed actions, the political effect on the company itself must be assessed. Some groups will welcome the new proposal, even deciding to join or support the company in some fashion; presumably, their needs will be met more fully than before. Other groups will expect the change to raise their prestige or status in the eyes of friends and other groups, or will regard it as a welcome opportunity to do some creative work; they too will embrace the change. But others will prefer the present program, rather than to make many unfamiliar, exasperating changes; members of these groups will have to change many old, familiar routines. Consequently, materials management can expect their opposition. When the program is proposed, these disaffected groups will try to find reasons why it will not work; and after the changeover, materials management can anticipate that they will consciously or unconsciously be responsible for several troublesome incidents—things that materials management should not expect to happen. Obviously, materials management must take immediate steps to gain a dissatisfied group's support; it may even be necessary to postpone the proposed change.

Because of the political nature of groups, they are specialized in various ways or have special interests; specialties exist within groups. Membership in groups gives individual members status in the eyes of friends and acquaintances—which a materials manager must not underestimate. An analytical approach to such groups can help materials managers discover useful premises for making many of their more troublesome decisions.

SELLING IDEAS

Before they can effectively present ideas and influence members of a group, materials managers first must clearly define the goals and objectives of the group's activities. Frequently, materials managers are ineffective in selling their ideas and proposals because they are unaware of the goals of the group receiving the presentation. An inappropriate proposal and ineffective communication are the most common sales mistakes; these errors guarantee that a proposal will not be accepted (see Figure 12-6). Materials

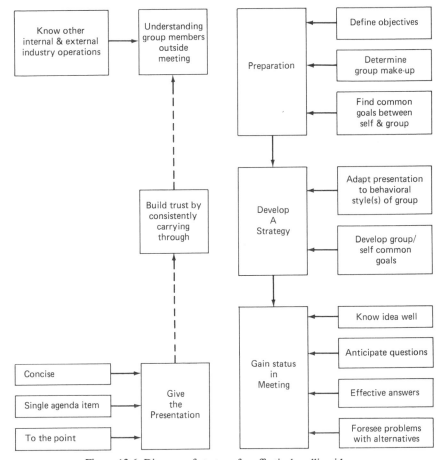

Figure 12-6. Diagram of strategy for effectively selling ideas.

managers must understand group goals and be adequately prepared before presenting proposals.

Understanding Group Members

To be effective, the materials manager must assess the group. Certain personality types are fairly easy to identify, and the materials manager can take advantage of their characteristic behavior, tailoring his or her presentation to their individual styles. There are many different styles of behavior, but some observers have grouped them into four broad classes:

- *Detailers*: These are individuals who pay close attention to details. They get involved in research and collect all the facts before reaching a decision. These people are usually conservative in their thinking. Typically they are engineers, computer scientists, and lawyers.
- *Affecters*: Affecters love everyone. They need to be involved all of the time in order to feel secure in everyday life. They always need more friends and have a strong desire to make friends. They are warm people, always on the move, and always wanting to try something new. Affecters need to be involved. One of their problems is that they cannot say no. Consequently, they usually are overcommitted and have a difficult time following through and completing a job. These people may be found in sales, social work, acting, and nursing.
- *Strangers*: These individuals are rigid in their thinking and tend to become very impatient when other people do not understand the value of their ideas. They are very imaginative and are rather impractical in their approach to everyday problems. This group includes inventors, artists, and architects.
- *Pushers*: Pushers are perhaps the most common type of people in our society. Their behavior is goal-oriented, and they are always trying to achieve these goals. Hard work and quick rewards are important to them. They give full loyalty, but demand the same. This group includes managers, athletes, and politicians.[8]

The materials manager must realize and understand human behavior, develop the ability to recognize other people's behavioral styles, and respond to these different styles in group settings. This may seem like an impossible task, but clues are everywhere. Generally, for example, pushers are unconcerned about the appearance of their office; detailers have clean, neat offices; affecters keep personal mementos and pictures in their offices; whereas strangers are erratic. When the materials manager is able to determine the individual's behavior style, the presentation can be made to fit that style. Words that tend to suit the other person's behavior style are used. The various styles bring certain ideas to mind, as the following list shows:

- *Detailer.* A cautious, specific presentation; the evaluation and analysis are astute and well-planned, following a step-by-step approach.
- *Affecter.* A presentation staged in sensitive emotional phases, stimulating involvement.
- *Stranger.* A proposal filled with futuristic ideas, creative and idealistic.
- *Pusher.* An urgent, results-now approach, for a person who is very practical, gets things done today, and must justify activity.

When the materials manager presents proposals in the language that suits the listener, success is likely. When evaluating a person's behavior style, the materials manager must always realize that individuals look at ideas and proposals differently. The presentation must be made from their perspective, not that of the presenter.

Preparation

Usually, far too little attention and time are given to preparation for a presentation. To prepare adequately, the materials manager first should define the objectives of the presentation, its ultimate purpose. For example, if the objective is to secure approval for a major equipment purchase, the immediate objective is to influence those attending the presentation to respond affirmatively. First the materials manager must determine the makeup of the group and their individual backgrounds—production, engineering, finance, accounting, and so on. In addition, each of them has specific responsibilities that have high priority and, possibly more important, personal objectives that the manager must understand and evaluate. The materials manager must determine what goals they have in common; for example, all are interested in the profitability of the company and in making their operations more attractive to top management. Now the materials manager's objective becomes specific—convince them that the proposed equipment will increase the productivity of their operation and in turn reduce the cost per unit and increase the company's profits, thereby benefiting their own specific department.[9]

The materials manager should limit any presentation to one specific topic and use the time effectively. Some materials managers believe they should use all of their allotted time and try to present too many items during a meeting, but they accomplish little because they attempt to convince the audience of too many different items at one time.

During the preparation, the materials manager must allocate adequate time to rehearsing the presentation, preferably in front of colleagues. An alternative is to make the presentation on videotape and then critique the results. In preparing for the presentation, the materials manager must carefully review the particular situation, considering the economy, the project, company objectives, and so on, and the people who will be present. This will help the manager to determine the information that is most essential and to prepare answers for anticipated questions. In determining what facts and knowledge are necessary, it is best that the scope of the goal be fully examined.

Developing a Strategy

Once the materials manager has defined the proposal in specific terms, the next step is to develop a strategy for presenting the proposal. The manager determines the group's specific interests and develops the presentation around these interests, which may include financial profitability, increased output, security, pride, or organizational position, to name a few. In analyzing group interests and the importance these interests have for the group, the manager will consider:

- Group likes and dislikes.
- Characteristics of individual members, such as education, age, and background.
- The group's position in the organizational structure.

The materials manager must use language that suits the group, at an appropriate level, and carefully chosen examples.

Gaining the Group's Confidence

Because most ideas and proposals, especially complicated ones, are not accepted strictly on their own merits, the presenter's qualifications and the respect the group members have for the individual presenting the proposal greatly influence their receptivity. Materials managers must appear competent and can strengthen their qualifications through knowledge of the proposal. There are many other ways of gaining the group's confidence. For example, presenting evidence and expertise from outside or inside the company, or demonstrating the validity of the idea, will enhance the materials manager's chances of selling it.[10]

It is important to have full knowledge of what is happening in other operations of the company and other companies in the industry. If the materials manager is proposing new systems, it is necessary to tell how they are used by others with similar operations, as well as the trends in the industry. Such knowledge of the industry is necessary for one to be convincing and thus acquire the status needed to get group acceptance of the idea. One must know the strengths and weaknesses of each alternative in a proposal. Only with such knowledge can the materials manager gain the confidence and respect of the group.

Groups frequently are unwilling to accept the materials manager's ideas because of a lack of trust and the fear that promises will not be kept. A record of not keeping promises can undermine the materials manager's credibility. The group listens to, and accepts advice from, materials managers and others who have a record of reliability.

Status in a meeting and in the company is earned in many ways. The materials manager must be able to anticipate questions from the group and answer them effectively. In addition, the materials manager is a problem solver, not a problem creator. He or she keeps everyone informed, is able to foresee possible problems that may affect achievement of the company's and other groups' goals, and plans for the human and material resources required to achieve these goals. In summary, the materials manager needs to know:

- The goals of the company and of various groups.
- How the proposal compares with the present situation, other alternatives, and proposals from the group.
- Ways the proposal will solve the problem as viewed by the group.
- How the proposal will affect other parts of the company.
- The specific advantages and benefits of the proposal.

The materials manager must learn to deal in specific facts and data. This requires not just company records but other sources outside the company that support the proposal. Gaining this type of knowledge requires a continuing effort, which involves extensive study, visiting with other units, requesting information from staff, attending conventions, visiting with salesmen and their technical people, and attending professional meetings and conferences. Developing effective sources of information to keep well informed is an important function of the materials manager, and requires a rapport with people at all levels in the organization and all possible outside groups. No group or materials manager works in isolation. No idea, project, or program can stand by itself; each will be related to, and will affect, the whole organization. In no place is this more true than in materials management, which is involved in almost all operations and departments. Therefore, the materials manager must clearly understand how a proposal will fit in with broader corporate objectives. Only in this way can the manager appeal to the biases of people who hear the proposal.[11]

Achieving Effective Presentations

Whether proposals are accepted by top management and others depends heavily on the presentations, even if the proposals are technically sound and promise attractive economic benefits. With this in mind, the manager should give considerable thought to presenting proposals clearly and concisely. Nowhere is this more important than for materials management proposals, because of the generally low status of materials management in the company.

Materials managers must realize that the audience is composed of people whose interest is not materials management. Their interest can be aroused, but it also can easily be turned off; so the materials manager must get the attention of the group quickly, at the beginning of the presentation, always speaking their language. The group's attention must be captured during the first few minutes. It is crucial to make a good first impression; there is no second chance to win the group's favor. During this time, the materials manager must establish the relationship of the group to the proposal. Next, the materials manager must generate genuine interest in the proposal, followed by a desire for the group to see it implemented. The final step is to get the group to act in support of the proposal.

In the presentation, important information should be presented in a clear, concise summary, emphasizing proposal benefits that stand out clearly and can be quickly understood with charts, graphs, sample models, and simple drawings. No point should be belabored and no unnecessary information should be presented.

The presenter should respect the time demands of the group. It is important to identify key group leaders and presell them in advance of the meeting. These individuals can be strong allies during the meeting. Then, after the proposal has been accepted by the group, the manager must assume responsibility for its success. Cooperation is generated and developed through a track record of past success, which will influence future proposals.

OPERATING AN EFFECTIVE PROGRAM

An effective materials management program is basic to all manufacturing and nonmanufacturing processes. If raw materials will be made into products, materials management must ensure that the materials are distributed to the process operations in an efficient manner. Manufacturing is constantly changing, and materials management must change with it. A number of key activities are necessary for an effective materials management program.

Developing Cooperative Relationships with Other Groups

Some materials management operations occur in almost every department of a typical manufacturing or service facility, so it is critical that materials management develop cooperative relationships with all units. The failure to form proper relationships is a primary cause of friction, lack of status, and other problems with these groups. Although the authority and the responsibility for implementation are the critical requirements for materials management, solid working relationships make the work run smoothly. This does not imply that detailed and minute job descriptions are unnecessary, or that materials management personnel cannot operate as a team—just the opposite is true. However, good relationships will prevent many common problems that could interfere with the efficiency of the materials management function.

Some statement of intergroup relationships is usual in job descriptions and the organizational chart, but generally materials management must develop informal cooperative relationships. These relationships help eliminate vague authority, inappropriate or misunderstood communications, and inefficiency, removing conflicts or at least making situations workable. As a result, materials management personnel experience increased job satisfaction.

Developing Cooperative Relationships with Outside Suppliers

Materials management should cooperate with a number of outside suppliers. Manufacturers and distributors are prime sources of information on current and future industry trends. They can furnish information on equipment selection in an effort to improve performance or reduce costs, and may suggest how a piece of standard equipment can be modified to take the place of specially designed equipment. Distributors are responsible for the installation of equipment and assuring that it performs according to the manufacturer's specifications. Consequently, it is important for materials management to know these people and formulate good working relationships with them. In addition, distributors generally provide specialized training classes and future services and parts.[12]

On special projects, the suppliers are specialized firms, used for the design, installation, and start-up of complete systems. Generally, suppliers manufacture some of the equipment used in the system and subcontract other portions. At times they may serve as the prime contractor. Engineering companies also provide a valuable relationship, as they perform engineering studies, design systems and facilities, develop project schedules, erect facilities, install equipment, and start up operations.

For outside projects to be successful and useful, all outside suppliers' groups must be familiar with the company's operation, and must be involved in the project's initial planning phase. However, materials management must be concerned with every phase of planning and installation for the system to achieve its ultimate objectives. Therefore, materials management must define and develop all requirements (reduce labor costs, meet space requirements, eliminate damage to materials) at the beginning of the project, with a master plan for the project from design to implementation and operation. It is here that materials management's relationships with suppliers will make the difference between success and failure of the project.

Motivating Others to Cooperate in Achieving Mutual Goals

Materials management must create and maintain an environment in which personnel work together in teams to accomplish the function's objectives. Therefore, managers must build motivating factors into activities, directing and leading groups and individuals in doing the work of the function. An environment conducive to work performance is designed, in which all personnel in the company contribute to achieving the materials management objectives.

One effective technique is to use a system of rewards to motivate people, such as providing status-enhancers to reflect their accomplishments, both within and outside the company. Special recognition and awards for both individuals and groups are effective rewards for outstanding performance. Awards that materials management might use include: special titles, assignment of preferred space or choice equipment, and special services. To be most effective, these prizes should be carefully graduated by accomplishment because distinction is highly correlated with scarcity.

People also like to associate with congenial colleagues; interactions in various informal groups fulfill their emotional needs. Materials management can motivate personnel to cooperate and work well together by selecting harmonious groups of co-workers, who can exchange news, ideas, plans, and confidences, and enjoy each other's companionship. Because a single group cannot satisfy all of an individual's social needs, materials management can plan many special interest groups for co-workers. Materials managers must motivate constructive groups and see that destructive groups are broken up; so the managers must monitor and work with these groups after they are organized. Any ineffective groups should be inactivated, or their members transferred. However, with proper leadership from materials managers, problems of destructive groups can be avoided.

Materials management can motivate personnel to cooperate by satisfying their need for self-esteem. By delegating authority, encouraging subordinates to contribute recommendations, and rewarding their creativity, materials managers can help fulfill the needs of workers and attain materials management objectives as well. The opportunity to participate in materials management may be fulfilling in itself. Workers throughout the company often possess valuable information that can be used to improve the materials management operation; these workers are close to the action and often have insight into materials management operations that materials managers cannot acquire. Managers can motivate them by using and considering their views, experience, and recommendations; the important thing is that they have a chance to be heard by someone with responsibility and authority. Most workers have immense reservoirs of both physical and mental capabilities that are largely untapped by their superiors; materials management can utilize these talents in a mutually fulfilling way.

With any motivational system, rewards must be immediate and well publicized to satisfy individuals' needs for status, reinforcement, and self-esteem, and their desire for recognition. The form of the reward may vary from letters of commendation to titles that are announced—or even a button denoting group membership or service. Materials management should be innovative in developing a motivational system, publicizing it, and encouraging workers to participate in it. The reward of such a system will be an active and strong materials management operation.

Accomplishing Effective Communication

Effective communication by materials managers will lead to a productive operation (see Figure 12-7); so, it is important that they understand how to communicate. The materials manager must consider such basic factors as the following:[13]

- The *background* of the people receiving the message, including family, ethnic group, religion, education, nationality, and even region of the country: An individual receiving a message interprets it within the

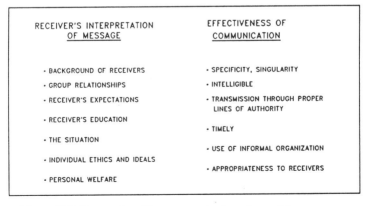

Figure 12-7. Factors that affect communication of materials managers.

framework of such cultural factors, whether consciously or not. Materials managers from different backgrounds can have difficulty in communicating; they must adapt to the culture of their colleagues. The more one has in common with other individuals, the greater the likelihood that there will be effective communication between them.

- *Group relationships*: People tend to identify with certain groups and develop loyalties and personal relationships in the group. The values and attitudes of the group tend to influence the way an individual member perceives messages from the manager. Such messages are interpreted in the light of relationships within the group.
- *Expectations*: When the materials manager sends a message, the receiver always has certain expectations or perceptions and interprets the message according to these expectations which may be based on prior experience.
- *Education*: The level of education makes a difference in the receiver's interpretation of messages, as do such other factors as the individual's expertise, use of technical data, method of analysis, and degree of sophistication.
- *The situation*, which influences the way a message will be interpreted: If an individual is always criticized when called to the materials manager's office, he or she will perceive criticism even when praise is intended. The same is true with meetings. If they are seen as a waste of time, they will be interpreted in that light even if something productive does occur.
- Standards of *individual ethics and ideals*: Ethical considerations strongly influence how a message is viewed. Varying attitudes toward honesty and thrift, for example, cause individuals to interpret messages in different ways.
- *Personal welfare*: When the materials manager's message directly pertains to the personal welfare and interest of the receiver, it is given greater attention.

When receiving messages, people tend to interpret them in the various ways described; so distortions often occur. However, by being aware of and understanding probably miscommunications, materials managers can effectively reduce them.

Effective communication may have the following general characteristics:[14]

- *Specificity*: All information should deal with a single, specific subject. People, especially engineers, require exact measurements—not vague and general statements. They expect the materials manager to be specific in communication and usually insist on receiving specific information.

• *Intelligibility*: If information is to have value, it should be expressed in writing and transmitted in a format that can be comprehended. Most materials managers are surprised to learn how poorly even the most carefully worked-out information is understood. It is the materials manager's responsibility to express messages clearly and in language familiar to the people receiving it—subordinates, peers, and superiors.

• *Proper transmission*: The transmission of information should follow organizational lines of authority and responsibility; the sender should not bypass positions in order to contact the ultimate receivers directly. Exceptions may occur when it is essential to communicate with everyone simultaneously.

• *Timeliness*: The speed and timing of communication may be most important. Efforts to obtain intelligible and specific information may have adverse effects on the organization, interrupting orderly communication processes.

• *Informal distribution*: To achieve an effective communication system, the materials manager may utilize the informal organization to complement the formal one. At times, the formal channel is inadequate and unreliable for messages. Often the materials manager will authorize a subordinate to establish contact outside the formal organization in order to ensure informal transmission of information.

• *Appropriateness*: Information should pertain to the interests and needs of the individual. Materials managers need to provide information that is warranted, such as the facts of a situation, both pleasant and unpleasant. They should always ensure that their employees are fully informed on policies, plans, and nonmanagement information.

Instituting the Proper Organization

To meet changes in the company, which may involve the acquisition of new materials handling equipment, changes in product lines, competitive influences, new production techniques, government regulatory policies, and labor policies, it may be necessary to modify the organizational structure. Good organization helps to prevent conflicts, makes assignments understandable, and defines authority and relationships. All members of the department and the company must understand the structure. A formal organization structure does not cover all relationships; it must be supplemented by informal organization. Materials management must understand the general workings of both the informal and the formal parts of the company.

Implementing Contemporary Materials Management Systems

Some of the problems of materials management can be overcome by implementing a contemporary system and employing good management practices. The establishment of objectives and orderly planning are essential to the success of the system. Without good design and planning, and the application of fundamental materials management principles, management will be based on personalities and will ignore company policies.

To reflect company goals and management philosophy, planners must consider the company's political and economic environment, its organizational structure, and authority relationships. Even with the best-laid plans and organization, continuous updating and changes are necessary. Furthermore, systems must be adapted to individual companies. A company's operations and needs must be considered; systems and procedures should be tailor-made.

Good system planning and organization can go far in making up for certain system deficiencies. This support increases materials management efficiency by establishing the details of system implementation and delineating the nature of functions, responsibilities, and the authority needed. It also will provide the materials managers future personnel, and it establishes other resource requirements and training needs. Without knowing these requirements, a materials manager cannot effectively obtain resources in a timely manner. Furthermore, duplication of effort, unclear lines of authority, long lines of communication, red tape, and obsolete management practices are avoided by good planning.

Creating a Positive Environment

Management can be defined as the planning, organizing, directing, and controlling of activities to the end that objectives are achieved with efficiency and effectiveness.[15] These management functions constitute what materials managers actually do in implementing a materials management program. The materials manager must create an environment that will favor the accomplishment of established objectives. Materials managers plan the operation of subordinates, select and train them, organize task relationships, direct employees' work, and measure actual results.

For materials management to be credible both internally and externally, an effective system — which solves problems, creates a high morale level, identifies problems, creates proper authority and responsibility, and so forth — must be achieved through good management. Not only will materials managers attack problems as they develop, but they will anticipate them and prevent their occurrence. Through effective performance of the managerial functions, these managers contribute to the accomplishments of a high-quality group effort, thereby winning a high degree of credibility. Individual materials managers must understand planning, organizing, directing, and controlling, and the relationships among them, viewing this integrated framework from the company's viewpoint rather than the narrow view of materials management. They must perform their managerial functions in a way that satisfies top management; otherwise many problems develop that soon become major obstacles for materials management personnel.

MATERIALS MANAGEMENT IN THE FUTURE

The new manufacturing technology of the future will not only change the way products are made, but will directly affect materials management methods. Unfortunately, materials managers now have no real part in strategic decision making in most U.S. companies. Most materials operations lack top management attention and understanding. This situation must change if these organizations are to obtain the benefits and opportunities inherent in the manufacturing technology of the future.

The extensive utilization of automation will change all operations, forcing the strategic focus of top management to change. The combination of such manufacturing techniques as CAD, CAM, flexible manufacturing system, robots, and so on, requires materials management and manufacturing groups to work together in a continuous process.

Role of Materials Management

The automation of manufacturing processes without the automation of an integrated materials handling system produces an unworkable system. Thus economic justification of automated manufacturing is impossible unless materials handling is included. Materials handling automation must be on an equal footing with manufacturing and computer systems in a truly automated factory. A technological revolution is occurring, which often results in fewer direct laborers, a wider variety of products, and less inventory. With machines producing the first item as rapidly and accurately as the last one, and with setup and changeover virtually immediate, manufacturers are eliminating the so-called learning curve, which traditionally shows costs decreasing as people gain more experience in making a product. The factory of the future will continue to eliminate many of time-honored materials and production management techniques. Materials management must handle small volumes of different products quickly and efficiently.

Along with these changes, sophisticated information will be available for materials management, which will allow materials managers to simulate operating conditions and compare information with predetermined equipment capacities and processes, including the movement and handling of materials. This new technology will enable materials management to explore different handling systems, using information previously unavailable, to design the most efficient systems. Materials management will be able to organize and direct huge amounts of information, providing data on such things as:

- Scheduling of materials handling sequences.
- Cost control.
- Time requirements for handling items.
- Equipment needed to handle items.
- Production schedules.
- Material procurement.
- Operating schedules for equipment.

Information will no longer be stored and conveyed in files, blueprints, routing schedules, and so forth, which make it generally inaccessible when needed; computers will store it and make it available to materials managers for decision making. In an information-intensive company, any process can be replicated easily, and the result is a system that allows materials management to change processes quickly. With multipurpose equipment, production will be able to produce more than one product and perform more than one operation; production management will be able to change the equipment's functions instantaneously, making mass production obsolete. Under these conditions, materials management must be prepared to handle very small lots for many different products and items.

Inventories will be adjustable according to production and distribution variations, and materials management will ensure the coordination of these requirements. Present materials management strategies will continue to be required, but their relative importance will be drastically altered, and additional techniques will be included in materials management. Different strategies will be emphasized as a variety of products are produced. Materials management must prepare for these changes in order for the company to take advantage of different marketing options and to be able to meet the competition of other firms with similar processes, capability, and capacity.

The increased flexibility of all phases of manufacturing will permit previously undreamed-of opportunities to make specialized products. Companies will not need large sales volumes of individual products to be profitable, as the production cost advantages of large facilities will be feasible for small units at little cost penalty. Bigger will no longer necessarily be better. At the same time, a revolution in materials management will occur to adapt to these manufacturing conditions.

Workers' Role in Materials Management

The extensive use of computers—and highly automated factories—will have a profound impact on workers. The elimination of physical labor in materials management is closely tied to the rapid utilization of automation. The elimination of workers in materials handling, receiving, shipping, and order picking will be greater than in other areas because of the extensive amount of labor presently involved. These drastic changes will create new jobs, all requiring workers with special skills and extensive training. Materials management still must be concerned with human relations, as well as many other critical responsibilities. Regardless of the eventual role or displacement of workers, materials management has no choice but to install automated equipment because of the rapid automation of manufacturing processes. It is clear that the workers' role in materials management will be drastically different from that of present materials management operators.

Materials Management Strategies

The future strategy of materials management must consider where materials will be. It will not employ traditional methods. For example, Just-In-Time requires a fast reaction to customer's needs, which depends on an effective materials management operation. It is predicted that Just-In-Time will reduce handling volumes by approximately 35 percent.[16] In addition, having full knowledge of job status and material locations through computer use can reduce time in production by 80 percent, missed deadlines by 30 percent, and scrap by 20 percent.[17]

Materials management will need to pay attention to separate handling levels for each item; just 20 percent of a company's inventory may represent 80 percent of the inventory's value, with 80 percent of the units being kept in inventory worth only 20 percent of its value. Close working relationships with suppliers will be needed for adequate supply levels to be maintained, as all items have equal importance in automated production. Thus, long-term and more mutually dependent relationships will develop between suppliers and the company, giving materials management an excellent opportunity to secure valuable relationships with outside suppliers or customers.

High quality and extreme accuracy of shipments will be essential as dependence on them increases. All purchases must arrive on time, and the company's inventory levels will be a factor in determining customer inventory levels. Materials management has a vital role in these aspects of the operation.

Regardless of how extensively Just-In-Time is used by U.S. manufacturers, those that are obligated to hold inventories because of long lead times of suppliers or competitive scheduling for shipments will continue to have inventories. In either situation, the handling, movement, and identification of materials will continue, in many cases determining the company's efficiency. Materials management will become more critical. As inventory levels are trimmed, the absolute control and handling of materials on a real-time basis will become mandatory.

To provide the level of control needed for implementing any serious stock reduction program, materials management must maintain a high level of control in receiving, quality control, stockrooms, manufacturing, finished goods, and shipping. Reliable data are needed for all materials, indicating what is available and where it is; so materials management must have information on all phases of the handling operation.

Reduction of material levels (relevant to current and past levels) through JIT of MPR will require materials management to handle materials more efficiently—not to use proportionately more people to do a job, but to find methods to automate the handling operation. Reliable and economical handling and movement are necessary to provide the speed and accuracy needed for automated manufacturing. Materials management will have to consider robotics and robotic-like devices, as well as vision systems and other sensory devices and software to coordinate these tools into high-speed handling systems.

Robots are taking much longer than expected to gain broad acceptance in materials handling.[18] This lag may be due to economic factors, as well as a lack of realistic equipment that can be utilized for materials handling. Even vision systems are only beginning to be considered economically justifiable, but eventually these systems will recognize items and direct sensitive robots to handle materials. Though still experimental, this technology is rapidly becoming feasible. Automated manufacturing will require prepackaging in unit-of-issue formats. The use of easy-to-automate picking packages will increase significantly, as manual handling is too slow and costly for fast-moving, smaller inventories. Materials managers thus must be innovators and leaders in making automation work. The rapidly changing trends in manufacturing probably will require suppliers to package materials for robotic stock issue.

Warehousing

A major segment of warehousing has yet to move out of static shelving, a principle that is over 2000 years old.[19] Shelving, manriders, carousels, and miniloads are the primary warehousing methods; and although they are the best tools for general-purpose, small-material items, they all require excessive handling, use too much energy, and still require extensive manual functions. Clearly, materials and parts selection will be an area of break-throughs, with prepackaged materials, vision systems, automatic identifi-cation, and robotic devices. To date, all these innovations are relatively expensive and have limited application, all require packaged products, and all require manual loading that usually takes longer than the automatic process.[20]

As companies reduce inventory levels, restocking will be required more often. At present, companies have a 4:1 to 10:1 ratio of issues to restock, depending on whether the items are purchased or produced in-house. This may change to a range from 1:1 to 3:1 on high-value items that are purchased, causing much higher activity.[21] In materials management, many activities now performed cannot keep pace with technological devel-opment, and must be eliminated as we know them today. For example, in the past procurement of small parts has been a major problem and usually a constant annoyance, but often accepted as a natural aspect of doing business. With stocks drastically reduced, shortages can bring manufactur-ing to a halt; so, constant control of even these items will become essential.

Quality

Quality is a more significant factor and will become even more important in the future, with materials management directly involved in quality assurance. Monitoring the quality of materials supplied by vendors will be more critical, as the quality of those materials affects the company's pro-ductivity. The utilization of robots will eliminate the quality variation introduced when humans perform certain operations. Materials manage-ment must consider current trends that may influence quality, such as changes in human resources and work teams, the use of quality-circle techniques, developments at the man–machine interface, and advances in automated offices and management information systems.

Expected Changes

There will be many opportunities for materials managers, but for those who plan for and manage change. Some changes that materials managers may expect are:

- Inventory levels will be reduced across the entire line, with suppliers' inventories considered a part of the inventory level.
- Relationships with both suppliers and customers will be permanent and will demand quality, accurate numbers, and reliable deliveries.
- Customers will demand greater flexibility in their requirements.

- Equipment controls will be used for activities currently accomplished manually.
- Lower inventory levels will require more restocking, which will decrease cycle times and increase inventory turns.
- Vision systems and robotics will be used not only in manufacturing, but in all phases of materials handling.
- Improved materials handling will be required to meet automated equipment demand, which in many cases probably will require prepackaging.
- With the increased use of small orders from suppliers, shipments will go directly to users on the production line.
- Materials management will be an essential factor in automatic production systems.
- The role of stockrooms will cease as JIT and better inventory control are initiated by management.

The impact of these expected changes on materials management is very significant. Today, materials management and storage activities account for 80 to 90 percent of the time products are in process. Inventories occupy 55 percent or more of all production space, and represent 25 percent of employee time.[22] The enormous cost of materials handling will cause most companies to devote significant resources to materials management, which has been relatively ignored in company operations. In the rush to cut or eliminate inventories, there will be enormous demands on materials management to make these changes happen.

Preparing for the Future

Materials managers can take a number of actions to prepare for some of these changes:

- They can start working with data processing in implementing flexible systems and current reports for materials management.
- They can prepare for the new role that low inventory levels will require. Lower inventories will create an intense demand for absolute control, a different relationship with suppliers, and new responsibilities for materials management.
- They can prepare to track parts and products by lot into storage and by piece through assembly. This control is necessary because every operation becomes important in automated systems.
- They can move supplies to the line without delays; so managers can begin questioning present delays and justify all.

- They can prepare for the adjustments needed as stock areas are reduced or eliminated, with the space used for manufacturing.
- They can analyze the present flow of materials to detect multiple handling operations that can be consolidated.
- They can analyze distances that materials travel between points, their weight, and the type of tote and pallet used. This analysis will reveal duplication, provide evidence justify the use of alternate methods, and show where items stop during movement.
- They can begin to use prepackaging.

A materials management revolution has just begun. The key to automation is effective, economical materials management; and automatic inventory selection and storage are especially important. Any installation, whether automated or flexible manufacturing, requires a proven, efficient materials management system. Whatever the storage method, it must involve less capacity in order to be modular and have the total flexibility to accommodate change. There will be a miniaturization of production quantity requirements. A dramatically increased level of activity will drive the design of robots, which will directly affect materials management. However, companies will apply automation piecemeal rather than waiting to build a system from the ground up. Each new segment will have to be part of a long-range plan, and advanced materials handling systems and controls will be needed to integrate the automation effort. Flexible manufacturing systems can be incorporated in old facilities, which may retain many semiautomatic operations.

Most planning has been done in response primarily to short-term goals. In the future it must be long-term. All activities, including materials management, will be integrated so that management will be able to analyze the proper way to commit capital to meet objectives. Clearly, planning must be started early by materials management if the full benefits of the materials management revolution are to be achieved. For example, future materials managers must work with manufacturing in providing custom-made products, a diverse product line, high-quality goods without higher prices, and improved customer service.

As automation becomes commonplace in manufacturing, materials management will determine the actual performance of the automated equipment and work to reduce equipment needs and investment. Handling and control of products and parts during storage and production will require that materials management take on greater tasks and contribute intelligently to the total management system. Materials management cannot be ignored in automation; manual handling of materials, incomplete bills-of-materials, and makeshift systems cannot be tolerated in the factory of the future.

SUMMARY

There are many pitfalls and problems in operating a materials management program. The most common ones are lack of education, lack of commitment by top management to materials management, inadequate communications, resistance to change, lack of qualified and adequate personnel, lack of status for materials management, poor organization of materials management, and lack of established goals and standards. Frequently, materials managers' lack of awareness of these problems produces unwanted consequences.

Interwoven in the work situation are complex political activities, expectations, and pressures from the actions of members of various groups. Materials managers must forecast and anticipate these essentially political actions and consider them in decision making. Politics occurs in many degrees and forms in a typical company. Materials managers have numerous opportunities for political maneuvering. However, others have the same opportunities but do not share materials management's objectives, causing various degrees of conflict. Materials managers must understand and interpret these behaviors, recognize group members' views, and anticipate future actions.

Materials managers must sell their ideas and proposals to others besides their superiors. This job involves effectively presenting ideas and influencing people; managers must prepare themselves adequately before presenting proposals. An effective presentation will include defining the goals and objectives of the group, understanding listeners' individual backgrounds, limiting the proposal to only one item, rehearsing the presentation, having complete knowledge of the subject as well as happenings in other operations of the company, and developing a strategy to present the proposal.

To operate an effective materials management program, managers must develop cooperative relationships with other units in the company and outside suppliers, motivate others to cooperate in achieving mutual goals, maintain effective communications practices, establish a proper organization, and use effective managerial practices. When these practices are successfully implemented by materials management, an efficient operation results.

Future technology will have a great impact on materials management operations; in particular, the extensive utilization of automation will give materials management a new and critical role. Materials management operations will have to be managed efficiently, to keep other operations such as production from having serious problems. All company activities depend on the effective operation of materials management.

For the materials manager, future opportunities will include reduced inventory levels, closer relationships with suppliers and customers, greater flexibility, greater use of vision and robotics systems, improved materials handling, smaller orders from suppliers, better inventory control, and so on. The impact of these expected changes on materials management will be substantial, but managers can prepare for them by taking a variety of actions.

BIBLIOGRAPHY

Amos, J., and Sarchet, B. *Management for Engineers.* Englewood Cliffs, New Jersey: Prentice-Hall, 1981.

Barnard, Chester I. *Organization and Management.* Cambridge, Massachusetts: Harvard University Press, 1948.

Brocker, J. "The Historical Development of the Strategic Management Concept." *Academy of Management Review,* 1985, pp. 219–224.

Cannon, Martin J. *Management: An Integrated Framework,* 2nd ed. Boston: Little Brown and Co., 1983.

Cook, Thomas M., and Russell, Robert A. *Contemporary Operations Management — Text and Cases,* 2nd ed. Englewood Cliffs, New Jersey: Prentice-Hall, 1984.

Flippo, Edwin B., and Munsinger, Gary M. *Management,* 3rd ed. Boston: Allyn & Bacon, 1975.

Galbraith, J. R. *Strategy Implementation: The Role of Structure and Process.* St. Paul, Minnesota: West Publishing Co., 1986.

Ginsberg, Michael J. *Implementation as a Process of Change: A Framework and Empirical Study.* Report CISR-13, Sloan WP 797-75. Cambridge, Massachusetts: Center for Information Systems Research, MIT.

Harlow, D., and Hankle, J. *Behavior in Organizations.* Boston: Little, Brown and Co., 1975.

Hax, A. C., Majluf, N. S., and Pendrock, M. "Diagnostic Analysis of a Production and Distribution System." *Managerial Science,* Vol. 26, No. 9 (Sept. 1980), pp. 871–889.

Jones, Manley H. *Executive Decision Making,* revised ed. Homewood, Illinois: Richard D. Irwin, 1962.

Koontz, H., O'Donnell, C., and Weihrich, H. *Management,* 7th ed. New York: McGraw-Hill Book Co., 1980.

Lowndes, Jay C. "Productivity Growth Is Key Goal." *Aviation Weekly and Space Technology,* Aug. 2, 1982, p. 44.

Mak, Paul, and Lynch, Dudly. "Easy New Way to Get Your Way." *The Reader's Digest,* Mar. 1978, pp. 105–109.

Pfiffner, John M., and Sherwood, Frank P. *Administrative Organization.* Englewood Cliffs, New Jersey: Prentice Hall, 1960.

Porter, M. E. *Competitive Strategy: Techniques for Analyzing Industries and Competitors.* New York: Free Press, 1980.

Radford, K. J. *Information Systems in Management.* Reston, Virginia: Reston Publishing Co., 1973.

Strauss, George, and Sayles, Leonard R. *Personnel: The Human Problems of Management,* 3rd ed. Englewood Cliffs, New Jersey: Prentice-Hall, 1972.

Twiss, B. C. *Managing Technological Innovation,* 2nd ed. London: Langman Group, Ltd., 1980.

Wenzel, Charles D. "Look at Foreseeable Trends in Parts Handling Offers Strategy for System Planners." *Industrial Engineer,* Mar. 1984. p. 48.

R. Edward Freeman & Daniel R. Gilbert, Jr. Corporate Strategy & the Search for Ethics P.H. Englewood Cliffs, NJ. 1988 Ch. 8.

James B. Quinn, Henry Mintzberg, Robert M. Jones, The Strategy Process, Concepts, Contests & Cases. P-H. 1988 Ch. 3, Ch. 7, Ch. 15.

NOTES

1. Jones, *Executive Decision Making*, pp. 223–230.
2. Koontz, O'Donnell, and Weihrich, *Management*, pp. 702–703.
3. Barnard, *Organization and Management*, Chapter 9.
4. Flippo and Munsinger, *Management*, p. 247.
5. Pfiffner and Sherwood, *Administrative Organization*, p. 311.
6. Flippo and Munsinger, *Management*, p. 255.
7. Flippo and Munsinger, *Management*, p. 257.
8. Mak and Lynch, "Easy New Way to Get Your Way," pp. 105–109.
9. Cannon, *Management: An Integrated Framework*, pp. 302–303.
10. Harlow and Hankle, *Behavior in Organizations*, p. 52.
11. Strauss and Sayles, *Personnel: The Human Problems of Management*, pp. 205–207.
12. Koontz, O'Donnell, and Weihrich, *Management*, pp. 490–491.
13. Amos and Sarchet, *Management for Engineers*, pp. 266–267.
14. Amos and Sarchet, *Management for Engineers*, pp. 267–268.
15. Flippo and Munsinger, *Management*, p. 23.
16. Wenzel, "Look at Foreseeable Trends in Parts Handling," p. 48.
17. Lowndes, "Productivity Growth Is Key Goal," p. 44.
18. Wenzel, "Look at Foreseeable Trends in Parts Handling," p. 47.
19. Ibid.
20. Wenzel, "Look at Foreseeable Trends in Parts Handling," p. 50.
21. Ibid.
22. Wenzel, "Look at Foreseeable Trends in Parts Handling," p. 54.

13
Control of Materials Management Functions

Companies are constantly searching for new and better ways to improve their profit structure. Programs are established and given "catchy" designations, such as productivity improvement program (PIP), quality circles (QC), and profit efficiency program (PEP). Basically each of these programs is an attempt to improve productive control of critical resources. The key word is control.

Management control is the process of ensuring that major subsystems maintain satisfactory progress to achieve strategic objectives.[1] Control is critical for achieving the goals of total materials management within every business environment. Organizational planning, direction, and accomplishment are interrelated and monitored by using control systems.

THE CONTROL CONCEPT

Measurement and control are basic to all management activities. Successful programs emanate from the chief executive officer (CEO) of the company and include all members of the organization. Measurement and control are used to monitor and improve operations of the overall company as well as individual groups, as they strive to attain common goals. Materials management uses control evaluation techniques to determine the current level of achievement and also the degree of progress over a period of time.

Need for Controls

Company goals must be established to attain the many benefits afforded by a total materials program (see Chapter 1). Maximum company profits, improve customer service, and control of resources are some of the objectives and resultant benefits. Robert Burns is often quoted as having said that "the best laid schemes o' mice an' men gang aft agley." There are various reasons why plans are not achieved, a basic one being lack of an effective control system to provide timely information to generate alarm signals and facilitate action.

It is critical that individual members of the materials organization know what the group and individual goals are. They must clearly understand what is to be achieved, and how it can be accomplished. Management must develop objectives that are realistic and attainable. Poorly defined goals result in frustrated, unhappy employees and unrealized objectives.

Control systems provide criteria for evaluating individuals, subfunctions, and the entire materials organization. Feedback data can be used to determine effectiveness and achievement, and to improve the entire materials network. For example, one objective of total materials management is to minimize all materials-related costs. This can be done by using control systems that monitor and integrate multiple activities related to the same objective (such as purchasing activities that emphasize quantity discounts, and inventory control activities that minimize carrying costs).

The Control Cycle

Control of both the overall materials organization and the individual subfunctions can be depicted as a seven-step closed loop model, illustrated in Figure 13-1. Individual segments of the overall cycle are as follows:

1. *Develop objective/standard:* Specific objectives or standards are developed and used to judge performance. These goals can be established for the overall materials management organization, each of the subfunctions, and individuals.
2. *Measure actual performance:* Information is collected regarding actual performance. Accurate feedback data is essential for good performance of the control cycle.

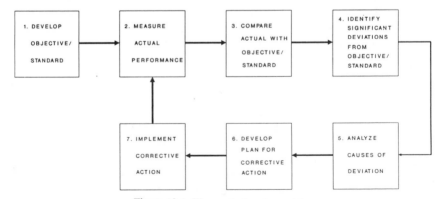

Figure 13-1. The control cycle model.

3. *Compare Actual with objective/standard:* Actual performance data are compared with the desired objective or standard. This comparison is simplified by using quantitative data, which provide an unbiased means for review.

4. *Identify significant deviations from objective/standard:* A good control system will rapidly focus attention upon individual variations from the standard that are exceptional. This reduces the time required by individuals involved in the closed loop system and provides faster resolution of problems.

5. *Analyze cause of deviation:* A myriad of alternative solutions can provide corrective action. An important step in the control process is to analyze the causes of significant deviations and determine the appropriate corrective action.

6. *Develop plan for corrective action:* A plan of action is developed to improve actual performance and achieve the desired standard. This often includes a schedule for individual actions.

7. *Implement corrective action:* The plan for corrective action is introduced, according to prior schedule, by all individuals who have been delegated responsibilities.

The control cycle is a closed loop. Data are continuously monitored to compare actual performance with the standard, and to determine if corrective action is effective. The strategy and actions are subject to change if required.

Control Measures

The materials group should have a control program that considers large variations in multifaceted operations. Both quantitative and qualitative controls are necessary. The units of measure must be structured to all personnel to relate readily to individual report items. The accuracy and validity of objectives and standards should be reviewed periodically to ensure data credibility.

Quantitative and Qualitative Controls. Materials management is concerned with the establishment and control of both quantitative and qualitative objectives. Qualitative goals and controls relate to such diverse areas as personnel recruitment and development, improvement of supplier relations, and establishment of an effective organizational structure. Quantitative goals and controls reflect specific objectives such as reducing surplus inventory, increasing order-picking productivity, and eliminating clerical errors.

Qualitative aspects of the materials program are difficult to establish and control, from the standpoint of developing worthwhile goals as well as monitoring accomplishments. Quantitative goals are based on objective data, whereas qualitative goals are subjective and depend on individual judgment. Progress related to qualitative objectives is usually slow; some long-term objectives cannot be effectively monitored over short time intervals. Quantitative objectives are measured frequently to provide information that will serve as a basis for corrective action if required. The upper management in an organization normally monitors quantitative control data frequently. Qualitative control information is reviewed less often because it does not reflect day-to-day activities.

Units of Measure. Performance can be assessed by using various units of measure. Each item should be mqnitored so as to provide useful information. For example, transportation can be measured in ton-miles and machine utilization in unit loads. The most frequently used data source is the financial accounting system, which uses dollars as a common denominator. An advantage of using dollars is that everyone in the organization can understand the term; a disadvantage is that inflation and other factors can distort the unit figures.

In some instances, the measurement of individual items should include considerations that will ensure comparability. For example, a large West Coast company has various distribution centers. Order picking was monitored using number of orders picked as a unit of measure; the company did not take into account that order size in SKU's or line items varied considerably from one distribution center to another. This inconsistency distorted the comparison data, making it impossible to compare employees accurately. The company changed the unit of measure to SKU's and improved its management control system.

Accuracy of Quantitative Standards/Objectives. Quantitative goals are easy to work with in many respects because of the simplicity of reviewing and comparing numbers. However, materials management personnel must be certain that the data have a sound base. Goals can be less precise and less meaningful than their quantitative assessment would indicate. Accurate standards and objectives are important for achieving worthwhile control of operations. The degree of accuracy required varies, depending upon the type of standard or objective. For example, a standard for warehouse operations that industrial engineers developed with work measurement techniques will be more accurate than a standard for production control developed by using historical (sometimes referred to as "hysterical") data. This does not mean that estimated or nonengineering standards cannot be useful. A valid standard of this type can effectively indicate trends of performance and operational improvement.

Evaluation Reports. Evaluation reports are an essential element in the materials management group's achievement of meaningful control. Quantitative reporting of all critical data is important for evaluation of progress, or lack or progress, and for analysis of corrective action strategies. Oral reports are useful, enabling materials management to receive information promptly. Written reports provide detailed information, develop required statistics, and can be structured to focus attention on critical areas. The frequency of reports (annual, semiannual, quarterly, monthly, or weekly) is based on their cost of preparation and value to management.[2]

Evaluation Factors

Control systems differ from one company to another, as effective systems must be specially designed to meet the needs of particular organizations. The amount of control that exists within a company determines the degree of freedom given to individuals working in it. Correct decisions as to what should be controlled and how it is to be controlled are critical to the success of a total materials management program.

System Requirements. Henry Fayol, a pioneer in management organization and control, stated: "Control consists in verifying whether everything occurs in conformity with the plan adopted, the instructions issued and principles established. It has for its object to point out weaknesses and errors in order to rectify them and prevent reoccurrence."[3] General requirements for a materials management control system are outlined below.[4]

Useful, Easily Understood Information. The key question each level of materials management must answer is, "What information do I need to control the activities within my jurisdiction?" Data collection is costly. Only information that is useful and easily understood should be obtained. A screening process can be developed to eliminate irrevelant reports and information.

Timeliness. Control should quickly report deviations. A well-designed system will be capable of identifying potential problem areas before they manifest themselves. For example, material requirements forecasts can be used to assist in planning cash and space needs. If it seems likely that a company will require additional cash, it is important to have prior notice in order to arrange sufficient financing.

Flexibility. Conditions and plans change. In the usual course of events, materials operations can become quite hectic. A system should be structured so that it is flexible enough to maintain control of operations during such events.

Economy. A control system must be worth the expense it entails. Total materials management stresses control of all operations, but it would not normally be beneficial to expend $300,000 to control $300,000 in expenditures. Also, it is often difficult to determine when the marginal costs associated with a system equal the marginal revenues (benefits) obtained from it. As a company and its materials organization grow, cost benefits can accrue from broad control systems that do not duplicate data and personnel. A smaller company, however, must rely upon simpler, less costly control systems.

Corrective Action. An effective control system must pave the way for corrective action; merely exposing deviations from the plan is not enough. The system must also locate problem areas and identify who or what is responsible for them. Deviations from the plan should be immediately pinpointed by exception alerts.

Typical Control Classifications. Materials management performance can be measured and controlled by using various classifications. Whenever possible, performance levels should be based upon objective criteria. Often, the review of one control point is insufficient to determine the full effect of a change in performance within a particular classification. For example, an increase in finished goods inventory could be a cause for concern because of high physical distribution costs. However, if other control classifications such as sales volume and marketing promotion are also reviewed, it may become evident that there is no cause for alarm.

Control classifications based upon individual needs are developed by companies to monitor various activities and operations. A few examples of typical classifications are outlined below.

Qualitative Classification:

1. Integration of total function
   * Development of goals and objectives for the overall function and individual subfunctions.
   * Establishment of meetings to promote communication and mutual understanding.
   * Development of reports.
2. Organization and training
   * Organizational structure.
   * Personnel training and rotation.

- Personnel turnover.
- Group and individual morale.
3. Policies and procedures
   - Development of policies and procedures.
   - Education of personnel regarding application of policies and procedures.
   - Monitoring application and revision requirements.
4. Profit performance
   - Establishment of profit improvement programs.
   - Integration of subfunction activities to optimize company profit objectives.
5. Innovative developments
   - Establishment of programs to promote innovative developments.
   - Monitoring effectiveness of programs.
   - Communicating and publicizing program results.

Quantitative Classifications:

1. Production control
   - Production equipment utilization.
   - Production personnel utilization.
   - Adherence to schedule.
   - Back order status.
2. Inventory control
   - Clerical accuracy.
   - Material availability.
   - Inventory turnover.
   - Inventory record accuracy.
3. Purchasing
   - Supplier quality levels.
   - Supplier delivery performance.
   - Purchase order aging.
   - Substitution of acceptable materials at lower cost.
4. Physical distribution
   - Customer service level.
   - Transportation costs (inbound and outbound).
   - On-time delivery.
   - Private vehicle fleet utilization.
5. Receiving and stores
   - Space utilization.
   - Material location accuracy.
   - Clerical accuracy.
   - Order-picking efficiency.

Question: What quantitative measures of success have you been able to attribute to the use of materials management?

PERFORMANCE MEASURE	PERCENTAGE OF RESPONDENTS USING THIS MEASURE
Inventory Improvement	38%
Dollar Savings	29%
Production Efficiency	24%
Improved Personnel Relations	3%
Improved Vendor Relations	3%
Miscellaneous	3%
	100%

Figure 13-2. Survey results—quantitative measures of materials management success. (Source: Gary J. Zenz, "Evaluating Materials Management," *Journal of Purchasing and Materials Management*, Summer 1980, p. 20.)

Survey Results. A survey conducted by Gary J. Zenz asked materials managers the question, "What quantitative measures of success have you been able to attribute to the use of materials management?" The results of the survey are given in Figure 13-2. Another survey, conducted by Miller and Gilmour, determined major performance factors used by upper management to evaluate material managers. The results of this survey are presented in Figure 13-3.

PERFORMANCE MEASURE	PERCENTAGE OF MATL. MGR.'S EVALUATED ON THIS MEASURE
Inventory Levels	87%
On-Time Deliveries	80%
Stockouts	71%
Purchased Materials Costs	69%
Transportation Costs	53%
Warehousing Costs	29%
Customer Complaints	27%
Profitability	20%
Manufacturing Costs	7%
Other	16%

Figure 13-3. Survey results—performance evaluation of materials managers (Reprinted by permission of the *Harvard Business Review*. Exhibit from "Materials Managers: Who Needs Them?" by Jeffery G. Miller and Peter Gilmour (July/August 1979). Copyright © 1979 by the President and Fellows of Harvard College; all rights reserved.)

BUDGETS

A budget is a comprehensive financial plan setting forth the expected route for achieving the financial and operational goals of an organization.[5] Budgets are the most common means of measurement and control used by materials management as well as the other groups in the organization. Even the smallest business can benefit from them. The budget is a written plan developed to monitor future operations, including all expected expenditures for a specified period of time. Normally the budget covers one year, and is divided into monthly segments. Actual expenditures are compared with budgeted goals on a monthly and year-to-date basis, and variations from the budget are reviewed.

Numerical Plan

A budget is expressed in numerical terms, which are usually monetary. However, not all budgets show dollars and cents; some are expressed in nonfinancial numerical terms. For example, a materials budget may use pounds, tons, and gallons. Personnel budgets are expressed in terms of number of employees required for various occupations and/or hours required to perform each activity. The finished goods budget can be expressed in units of completed products that will be available for customer demand. Monetary budgets at times may be misleading because they may not reflect the availability of individual items. Likewise, a budget expressed numerically in gallons may not indicate price changes. Considering the pros and cons of financial and nonfinancial budgets, a useful common denominator is generally dollars. The use of dollars data allows everyone in the organization to speak a common language.

Preparation and Application

The budgeting process normally begins with development of a sales forecast or sales budget by the marketing group. Once this budget has been approved, the materials management budget can be generated, along with budgets of other major functions such as finance, operations, quality assurance, and engineering. Typically, a budget is prepared four to six months before the fiscal year begins. Budget preparation and finalization constitute an interactive process, with many hours of effort required to develop the initial plan and subsequent revisions. The final budget for the materials groups must relate to the operating plan for the entire organization. Depending upon individual company practice, materials management may be responsible for two budgets: the materials budget and the group operating budget.

Materials Budget.   The materials budget is prepared with the sales forecast as a major input. This is true for all companies, whether manufacturing or nonmanufacturing. A manufacturing company would include inventories such as raw materials, work-in-process materials, supplies, and finished goods. The nonmanufacturing company's materials budget would consist primarily of supplies and finished goods. A materials budget may be expressed in dollars and/or units.

One might expect the development of a materials budget to be a very simple task, easily completed with the aid of a computer. The sales forecast would be fed into a computer that stored information regarding the units of material required for each product and the cost of this material, and the computer would extend and compile these costs to develop the basic framework for the materials budget. However, this description of the development of a materials budget is an oversimplification; it does not take into account many key inputs of the materials management organization.

Materials management personnel make significant contributions to the materials budget, providing input that reinforces the company's budget plans and profit objectives. The materials group is involved with materials budgeting such key matters as changes in inventory management strategies, policies that affect the material quantities (e.g., reducing finished goods inventory), and projected cost changes (e.g. purchasing negotiating a lower total cost). These functions are performed in almost all types of businesses, whereas other relationships exist only within selected organizations. For example, materials management contributes to materials budgets in manufacturing companies by developing systems that reduce work-in-process inventories (e.g., introduction of a Just-In-Time system) and by working with the engineering function to change major component specifications to reduce costs.

The development of materials budgets provides a quantitative goal for all related functions. The information in these budgets aids planning by various groups. For example, the finance department is one of the benefactors of credible data; effective materials budgets provide information that allows finance to develop realistic cash requirement schedules for each of the fiscal-year periods. Materials managers will determine objectives for the overall function and each of the subfunctions. Some of these goals are as follows:

- Reduce inventory costs by convincing suppliers to maintain the desired materials.
- Encourage purchasing personnel to negotiate lower total materials costs.
- Develop formal material cost-reduction programs, such as value analysis.

- Initiate a plan to "attack" obsolete and surplus inventories.
- Promote greater cooperation and communication between materials subdivisions and other company functions.
- Reduce total materials costs by achieving lower inbound transportation costs (e.g., through greater use of physical distribution group inputs).

Operating Budget. An operating budget establishes a general standard of performance for various expenditures related to materials group activities. It is usually developed by using the sales budget as a base input. The materials organization can improve company profits and help attain company objectives by planning and developing innovative, achievable operating budgets. These budgets provide quantitative goals against which the performance of the overall materials group, as well as individual subfunctions, departments, and personnel, can be compared.

Modern budgetary practice subscribes to the philosophy that managers should be responsible only for those costs that are within their control. Thus, an evaluation of materials operations often is concerned only with controllable costs. However, even controllable costs are sometimes affected by factors over which a manager has little influence. For example, a dramatic increase in sales volume, beyond budget forecasts, can require additional monetary expenditures by the materials organization. At this point, comparing budgeted and actual costs to measure the performance of materials management supervision becomes a meaningless exercise, unless the increased sales volume also is considered. One solution is to base performance on a flexible budget. This method produces allowable budget expenditures based upon the volume of activity actually attained; thus flexible budgets reflect current activity in comparing actual and budgeted costs.

Figure 13-4 is an example of a monthly budget report. This report includes the current month's expenditures of budget and actual costs, and provides a variance amount. It also includes information regarding year-to-date costs. It summarizes the fiscal period budget, actual, and variance data. Using exception analysis, a materials supervisor will concentrate attention on, and institute any required corrections for, items that show abnormal variations.

One of the highest operating costs for materials groups is the cost of personnel, or payroll. Budgets are effective in controlling personnel costs, but managers must make many subjective judgments about the number of personnel required. Having too few employees in a group such as purchasing or inventory control can mean the loss of much more money than is saved in payroll costs. Increases in materials management operating costs

Month: March 1989   Dept.:   Materials Management

ACCOUNT DESCRIPTION	CURRENT MONTH			YEAR-TO-DATE		
	BUDGET	ACTUAL	VARIANCE	BUDGET	ACTUAL	VARIANCE
Payroll	$11,954	$10,987	$ 967	$35,862	$32,961	$2,901
Travel Costs	1,275	605	670	3,825	1,051	2,774
Telephone	165	122	43	495	272	223
Entertainment	150	0	150	450	293	157
Dues and Subscriptions	45	0	45	140	0	140
Outside Services	300	0	300	1,000	0	1,000
Data Processing (External)	0	0	0	0	0	0
Stationery & Supplies	200	200	0	600	700	(100)
Want Ads	200	0	200	600	0	600
Educational Assistance	700	575	125	700	575	125
TOTALS	$14,989	$12,489	$2,500	$43,672	$35,852	$7,820

Figure 13-4. Jabe System Company monthly operating budget report.

often result in lower materials costs, and reductions in operating costs for other firm functions.

Nonsalary costs are often more difficult to control than costs related to personnel. Once salaries and wages are finalized in a budget, there is normally no variation, as long as the number of personnel and salary/wage increases do not exceed the budgeted amounts. However, there can be many reasons for variations in nonsalary costs. For example, travel and telephone costs can increase dramatically if unexpected problems occur, such as strikes by suppliers' employees, receipt of poor-quality materials, and shipment delays.

WORK STANDARDS

One effective way to measure and control materials management activities is to use work standards, also known as engineering standards or simply standards, which are useful for many of the materials jobs performed in offices, factories, distribution centers, and so forth. A standard represents the amount of time it takes for an employee to perform a single unit of work. It may be expressed as minutes per unit of output, units of output per hour, or some other ratio of time to work.[6] Standards are used for many purposes, including scheduling labor requirements, identifying and correcting bottlenecks and productivity problems, and identifying areas that need improved systems.

Work measurement is the process of calculating or defining the amount of worker time required to perform one unit of output and thereby establishing a work standard. Some tasks are more difficult to measure than others, and the complexity of a job will affect the suitability of work standards. For example, it would be much more difficult to develop work standards for all activities of a master scheduler working in production control than for an order picker working in a distribution center. Some basic criteria may be used to judge the applicability of work measurement:

1. The work must be done in a repetitive, reasonably uniform manner.
2. The work must be homogeneous in content over a period of time so that it is consistent from one period to another.
3. The work must be countable; that is, it should be describable in precise, quantitative terms (e.g., so many cases, forms, letters).
4. There must be a sufficient volume of work, done in a routine manner, to make it worthwhile to count and maintain records.[7]

Work Measurement Techniques

Work standards have been applied in various businesses, including manufacturing, hospitals, government, and transportation. The most common techniques for developing standards are historical derivation, work sampling, time study, and predetermined time methods. Each has some application for materials activities.

Historical Derivation. Possibly the simplest method for developing a labor work standard is to use historical records. In some respects the term standard is not applicable because past performance may not have been normal. This technique is less expensive and time-consuming than most others, but because of its inherent weaknesses it is used only for activities that are not critical and in situations where precise standards are not required. Historical standards have been applied for materials management activities in small companies that do not require refined systems. A more precise system employing historical data involves the use of quantitative techniques to refine the data. Quantitative techniques such as trend line and regression analysis can be effective in selecting "best" (in a statistical sense) data.

Work Sampling. Work sampling develops a standard based upon random samples of employees' activities over a period of time. It also can be effectively used to study the causes of delays (ratio-delay studies). Using the technique, an observer makes random visits to work areas for a predetermined number of times during the day. The observer records what is occurring at the instant of each visit and rates employee performance. The percentage distribution of the various work elements, as they occurred during the random observations, tends to equal the actual percentage of the time that is devoted to these activities. Work sampling can be applied to materials management activities that are not highly repetitive, as can be observed in some office workplaces.

Time Study. Since its development by Frederich Taylor before the end of the nineteenth century, stopwatch time has been widely applied. This technique is performed by timing a worker with a stopwatch as a job is performed. Times for all necessary job elements are summarized, adjustments are made for abnormal work paces (often referred to as performance rating), and allowances are added for personal conditions.[8] The adjusted time can be expressed as a work standard. Time study has been applied to both office and factory materials management activities; a key requirement is that the work must be fairly repetitive. Examples of time study applications in the workplace include receiving and stores activities and office clerical jobs. Common complaints about time studies include their inconsistency due to the subjectiveness of the work-rating activity and their use for study of nonstandard work methods. An example of the development of a work standard is presented in Figure 13-5.

Predetermined Time. Predetermined time standard systems utilize data developed for basic body movements, elements of operations, and entire operations. All motions and/or activities of a job are determined and recorded; then the appropriate amount of time for each work element is obtained from a catalog or book, and a standard is developed for the job. Predetermined time systems also can be used to develop standards for future activities. This technique can be helpful for comparing alternative

Standard Description: Order Picking

ELEMENT DESCRIPTION	CONSTANT(C) VARIABLE(V) ELEMENT	STANDARD TIME (MINUTES)
1. Obtain order from desk.	c	0.0969
2. Remove label & place on control sheet.	c	0.1548
3. Initial control sheet.	c	0.1307
4. Review order & obtain cart.	c	0.5869
5. Travel from order desk to 1st pick bin.	c	0.7114
6. Pick 20 SKU items to tote boxes.	v	35.2574
7. Write department number on tote boxes.	c	0.0048
8. Rearrange items in tote boxes.	c	0.0744
9. Identify shipping quantities on tote boxes.	c	0.2989
10. Place tote boxes on conveyor (to shipping).	c	1.0414
11. Sign out on control sheet.	c	0.1307
12. Travel back to order desk.	c	0.2784
Total		38.7667 Minutes

Note: Element number 6 considers variable factors such as travel distance, weight of item, number of pieces picked, cube size, and location of item in bin. Allowances for personal conditions, fatigue, and delay are included in elemental times.

Figure 13-5. Development of a work standard.

work activities, improving work methods, and estimating labor cost. Materials management standards based upon predetermined time systems are more consistent than those using time study. Two of the better-known predetermined time systems are the Work Factor and Methods-Time Measurement (MTM) systems.

Application Examples

Work standards have been successfully applied to various types of jobs in a wide range of industries. The following examples will provide insight into the use of work standards for materials management activities.

Pfizer, Inc.[9]. This New York City pharmaceutical and chemical manufacturer instituted a comprehensive productivity evaluation system for both office and warehouse operations. Its management developed performance-based standards by collecting and analyzing data for the various functions performed in the central office and warehouse. Trend line and regression analysis was used to establish the work standards. Company officials made sure that standards were reasonable. All standards are reviewed annually, and adjustments are made to reflect changes in equipment and techniques. It is important that output rates are not increased arbitrarily.

Two monthly reports are used to monitor operational efficiency. One measures office activities and the other warehouse operations. Pfizer recognizes facilities as well as individual employees for outstanding performance. A mounted sterling silver "Number One" is awarded to the most productive distribution center, and gifts are provided for each employee in that facility. The standards program has benefited Pfizer by improving worker efficiency and reducing operating costs. Pfizer's performance ratings are a day-to-day management tool, and they play an integral role in long-range planning and budgeting as well.

Certified Grocers, Ltd. of California.[10]. A unique incentive program was developed and implemented by this California company, with the basic premise that workers who have jobs that require physical handling are not motivated by salary increases. The Certified Grocers incentive plan provides employees with extra pay when the work effort exceeds requirements. As a result of this standards program, employee output has increased 15 to 20 percent, and absenteeism has declined. Management, the union, and employees all endorse the program. The union has found that the program establishes reasonable standards, provides job security for workers, and introduces a negotiable feature in the contract. Employees have the opportunity to decide whether or not they want to do extra work and receive additional rewards.

The incentive plan is based upon engineering standards established by a consulting company, which used time study techniques. Each activity was studied, and data were developed, taking into account a variety of factors that affect work content. For example, walking at a working pace was measured and converted to a minutes-per-foot standard. A computer was used to develop work standards and individual employee data.

EFFICIENCY INDICES

Productivity efficiency has served as a basic means for measuring and controlling business activities for many years, and efficiency indices have been used as a principal technique for monitoring productivity. This technique is very popular because the required computations are easily understood, and it affords a great deal of flexibility for a wide range of materials management applications.

Definition and Use

Efficiency indices are calculated as ratios,[11] which can be used for day-to-day and short-range control as well as long-range planning. Efficiency indices are a practical means for measuring and controlling operations. They are easy to develop and apply. A computer is not required, as the calculations can be performed manually; but computers normally are used to generate indices because they offer time and cost advantages. (Examples of the calculations are given below.)

The initial development of efficiency indices came in response to the inability of management to determine which activities or operations were causing problems, and to what degree a problem existed. Data are often available to compute an index. When appropriate data are not available, a comparison of estimated data collection costs in relation to potential benefits will indicate whether or not it is worthwhile to obtain new or additional data.

An efficiency index is normally expressed as percentage, which is accomplished by multiplying the ratio by 100.

Typical Control Indices

Efficiency indices are used to monitor activities and operations in an effort to eliminate a variety of problems. Some typical applications of these indices in materials group subfunctions follow.

Production Control. Typical problems are:

1. Poor customer delivery.
2. Excess shop overtime.
3. Ineffective use of employees.
4. Ineffective use of equipment.

Efficiency indices used to monitor these problems are as follows:

• Schedule effectiveness:

$$\frac{\text{Number of items produced on schedule}}{\text{Total number of scheduled items}}$$

• Shop overtime:

$$\frac{\text{Overtime hours}}{\text{Total hours}}$$

• Employee utilization:

$$\frac{\text{Scheduled hours}}{\text{Available hours}}$$

• Machine utilization:

$$\frac{\text{Scheduled machine hours}}{\text{Available machine hours}}$$

Inventory Control.   Typical problems are:

1. Excessive inventory.
2. Clerical staff errors.
3. Infrequent inventory turns.
4. Inaccurate inventory records.

Efficiency indices used to monitor these problems are as follows:

• Control of total inventory:

$$\frac{\text{Actual inventory value}}{\text{Planned inventory value}}$$

• Clerical accuracy:

$$\frac{\text{Number of clerical hours}}{\text{Number of clerical tasks performed}}$$

- Material turnovers:

$$\frac{\text{Cost of goods sold (year)}}{\text{Average monthly inventory cost}}$$

- Inventory record accuracy:

$$\frac{\text{Number of inventory items within } \pm\, x\% \text{ of physical count}}{\text{Total number of inventory items}}$$

Purchasing. Typical problems are:

1. High administration cost.
2. High operating cost.
3. Excessive supplier quality rejects.
4. Late delivery of purchased materials.

A study was made by Michigan State University of purchasing performance measurement and control in both private and public organizations.[12] Some of the efficiency indices that were being used by respondent companies are indicated below:

- Administration:

$$\frac{\text{Actual monthly purchasing administrative expense}}{\text{Monthly direct material input (dollars)}}$$

- Labor:

$$\frac{\text{Actual monthly expense} - \text{Monthly budget}}{\text{Monthly budget}}$$

- Supplier quality cost:

$$\frac{\text{total purchase value per item} + \text{quality problem cost}}{\text{Total purchase value per item}}$$

- Late delivery:

$$\frac{\text{Number shipments late}}{\text{Number shipments scheduled/Time period}}$$

Physical Distribution. Typical problems are:

1. Excessive truck fuel costs.
2. High outside (noncompany vehicle) transportation costs.

3. High order picking labor costs.
4. High shipping labor costs.

A study was made by A. T. Kearney, Inc. of physical distribution productivity measurement.[13] Some of the following efficiency indices were used by respondent companies:

• Trucking energy consumption:

$$\frac{\text{Ton-miles transported}}{\text{Line-haul fuel use (gallons)}}$$

• Outside transportation:

$$\frac{\text{Total ton-miles transported}}{\text{Total actual outside transportation costs}}$$

• Order selection labor utilization:

$$\frac{\text{Dollar value selected}}{\text{Labor hours}}$$

• Shipping labor utilization:

$$\frac{\text{Weight shipped}}{\text{Labor hours}}$$

Receiving and Stores. Typical problems are:

1. High receiving labor cost.
2. Excessive receipts of nonordered material.
3. Poor storage space utilization.
4. Frequent order picking errors.

Efficiency indices used to monitor these problems are as follows:

• Vehicle unloading:

$$\frac{\text{Weight unloaded}}{\text{Labor hours}}$$

• Control of nonordered materials:

$$\frac{\text{Nonordered materials detected (number of dollars)}}{\text{Total orders (number of dollars)}}$$

• Storage space utilization:

$$\frac{\text{Number storage slots occupied}}{\text{Number storage slots available}}$$

• Order picking accuracy:

$$\frac{\text{Number of order picking errors}}{\text{Actual orders (SKU or number)}}$$

Materials Handling. Typical problems are:

1. High materials handling labor cost.
2. Excessive equipment.
3. Poor materials handling accident record.
4. Excessive materials movement.

Efficiency indices used to monitor these problems are as follows:

• Materials handling labor utilization:

$$\frac{\text{Total hours} - \text{Materials handling labor}}{\text{Total labor hours}}$$

• Equipment utilization:

$$\frac{\text{Equipment meter hours}}{\text{Total available equipment hours}}$$

• Materials handling safety:

$$\frac{\text{Lost time hours due to material handling accidents}}{\text{Total hours (all employees)}}$$

• Materials movement:

$$\frac{\text{Number of moves}}{\text{Number of operations or activities}}$$

MANAGEMENT BY OBJECTIVES

Management by objectives (MBO) is one of the performance evaluation systems currently being used by major company functions, including materials management. This technique was first advocated by Peter Drucker.[14] George S. Odiorne, who popularized the technique, described it as follows:

A process whereby the superior and subordinate managers of an organization jointly identify its common goals, define each individual's major areas of responsibility in terms of the results expected of him, and use these measures as guides for operating the unit and assessing the contribution of each of its members.[15]

Basic System

Management by objectives (MBO) has been implemented by many materials organizations. Its widespread use is supported by an A. T. Kearney, Inc. survey of a broad section of physical distribution management. Fifty-nine percent of the 600 respondents indicated that they utilize an MBO program.[16]

MBO systems maximize personal involvement in the pursuit of work-related goals by allowing employees to generate their own objectives. In this respect MBO can be called a "bottom-up" approach to establishing goals (see Figure 13-6).

Anthony P. Raia has developed an eight-step MBO program (see Figure 13-7), which is outlined below.[17]

Step 1 — *Formulate long-range goals and strategic plans.* This represents a critical review and analysis by upper management of the fundamental purpose of the business. A clear, concise statement of the central purpose of the enterprise is determined.

Step 2 — *Develop specific overall organization objectives.* Specific objectives to be achieved within a time period are determined. These are related to overall company performance and should be in the form of a specific quantitative goal, such as "to reduce inventory levels by $600,000.00" and "increase product quality — having a maximum of 1 percent rejects at final inspection." Normally these objectives are defined by the company's chief executive officer.

Step 3 — *Establish departmental objectives.* Each major department manager develops specific quantitative objectives for his or her department. This action is taken by all groups, including materials management, finance, and engineering. Subunit supervisors also do this for their activities. These objectives are refined versions of those set in Step 2. Materials management may have as a goal to "reduce total inventories by $500,000.000." An individual supervisor may state his or her objective as to "reduce surplus and obsolete inventory by $88,000.00."

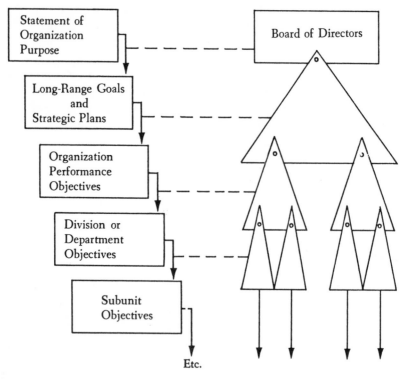

Figure 13-6. Goal-setting flow. (From *Managing by Objectives* by Anthony P. Raia, p. 30. Copyright © 1974 by Scott, Foresman and Company. Reprinted by permission.)

Step 4 — *Set individual job objectives.* Realistic, challenging, and specific quantitative objectives are set by all members of the organization. The goals developed by each individual relate to those established in Step 3. Each individual develops a general description of actions required to achieve planned objectives. In actual practice, the specific goals are modified and finalized after discussions between the supervisor and the employee. The goal is stated in specific quantitative terms such as "identify surplus and obsolete inventory in stockroom #2 and reduce inventory by $42,000."

Step 5 — *Formulate action plans.* Detailed action plans are formulated to achieve individual objectives. Milestones, or time goals related to individual tasks, are important for future follow-up.

Step 6 — *Implement and carry out corrective action.* A logical continuation of Step 5 is to implement the plans. This requires effort to be made on an individual basis, as well as the coordination of tasks with the plans of others. When required, corrective action is taken based upon criteria

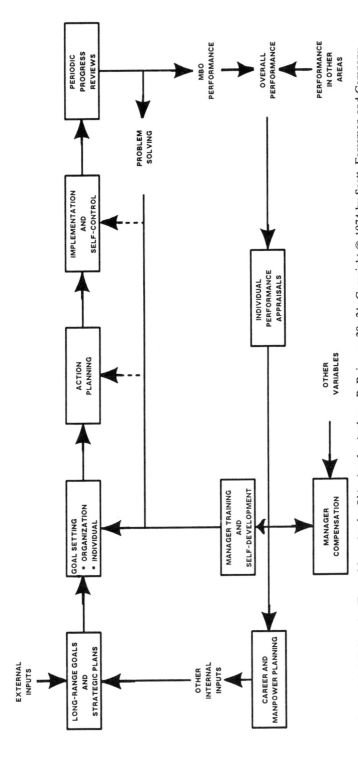

Figure 13-7. MBO cycle. (From *Managing by Objectives* by Anthony P. Raia, pp. 20–21. Copyright © 1974 by Scott, Foresman and Company. Reprinted by permission.)

and standards against which performance is measured, along with a relevant data base and feedback reports.

Step 7 — *Review progress toward objectives.* Periodic, systematic reviews to measure progress toward objectives are a key element in every MBO program. Problems are identified and resolved. At times objectives and priorities may be revised on the basis of new information.

Step 8 — *Appraise overall performance, reinforce behavior, and strengthen motivation.* A critical part of a successful MBO program is continued appraisal by upper management of overall performance and support in areas such as management training and self-development, employee compensation, and career and personnel planning.

Like any other good system, to be successful MBO must have a proper introduction. The program should be maintained with improvements and continued participant interest. Upper management should provide ongoing and genuine support for all activities. In practice, it resembles the old nursery rhyme, "When she is good, she is very, very good, and when she is bad, she is horrid."

Oliver Wight made the logical point that although MBO is a sound program, many authors addressing this subject do not recognize that without a valid planning system there is no way to measure MBO performance.[18] For example, it is impossible to measure the performance of a purchasing manager if the schedule is not valid. How can a production supervisor's performance be accurately measured if the majority of items on a past-due parts list are unnecessary at the same time that the supervisor's list of required parts is incomplete?

Application Example

Jabe Systems Company had a problem with late customer deliveries. It so concerned the CEO that it was selected as the major MBO objective for the year. The overall goal established by the company was "ship on time 95 percent." Incidentally, the goal for the preceding year was "reduce overall inventories by 10 percent." All of the major company groups developed objectives related to the new overall objective. Some examples of materials management departmental objectives are given below:

- *Production and inventory control:*
  1. Schedule accuracy: fabrication, subassembly, and final assembly to start and finish on time—95 percent.
  2. Engineering change orders: processed within 24 hours—90 percent.
  3. Interplant orders: shipment of all orders according to schedule dates—90 percent.

- *Purchasing:*
  1. Supplier shipments received by schedule date—95 percent.
  2. Disposition and shipment of rejected material to be achieved within two weeks—95 percent.
  3. Quality of purchased materials not to exceed preceding year's established goals as follows:

Material Code	Reject Goal
A	8%
B	4%
C	7%
D	8%

- *Stores:*
  1. Stockroom count accuracy—98 percent.
  2. Cycle counts to be maintained for full coverage—98 percent.
  3. Process obsolete material for return and/or scrap; develop priorities and maintain schedule—80 percent.

- *Physical distribution:*
  1. Orders received on customer premises within five days of promised shipment—95 percent.
  2. Maximum aging (arrangement for shipment) to be one week—95 percent.
  3. Customer orders to be picked within five days of order receipt—95 percent.

As discussed in Raia's MBO cycle, Step 7, an integral part of this control system is periodic review of the progress made toward individual goals, which is accomplished by meetings of all concerned employees. Data are reviewed to determine whether there is any need for corrective action. Charts can be very useful for monitoring progress. Figures 13-8, 13-9, and 13-10 are examples of charts used to control timely delivery progress in the Jabe Systems Company.

Figure 13-11 is a control chart that illustrates efforts made by the production and inventory departments in the preceding year to reduce surplus and obsolete inventory at the Jabe Systems Company. Note that statistics regarding individual monthly activities are included on the right side of the control chart. Observers can determine goal status at a glance. The specific data are available if desired.

SUMMARY

Materials management, like all other major groups within a business organization, is responsible for instituting effective control programs. Total materials management should provide criteria for evaluating the entire group as well as all subfunctions and individuals. The basic control cycle

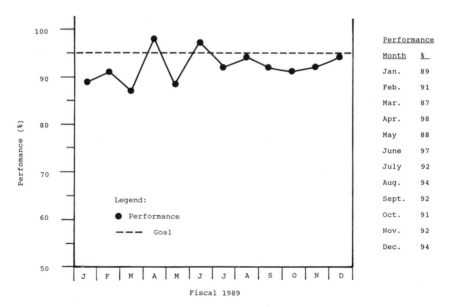

Figure 13-8. Jabe Systems Company. Production control. Year's performance versus goal. Subassembly schedule accuracy.

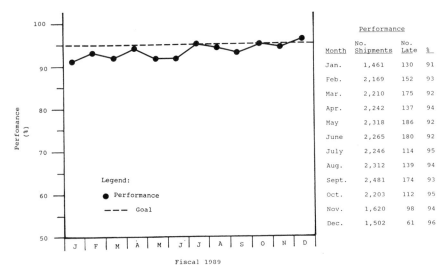

Figure 13-9. Jabe Systems Company. Purchasing. Year's performance versus goal. Purchased material schedule accuracy.

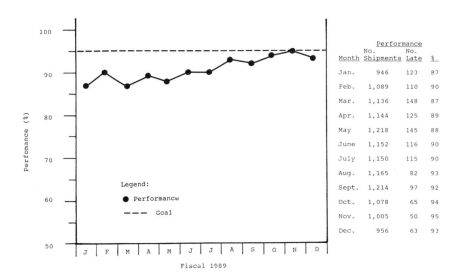

Figure 13-10. Jabe Systems Company. Physical distribution. Year's performance versus goal. Customer delivery accuracy.

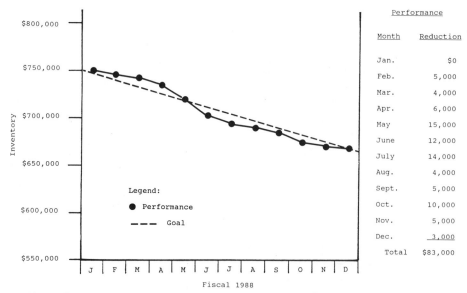

Figure 13-11. Jabe Systems Company. Production and inventory control. Year's performance versus goal. Surplus/obsolete inventory reduction. Goal $82,000.

provides a mechanism for control activities. Materials operating programs should include both quantitative objectives and controls.

A budget is the most widely used technique for measurement and control. Materials management is responsible for two budgets: materials and operating budgets, the materials budget normally having the higher total costs. Materials groups can significantly aid the effort to minimize budget costs. Salaries commonly comprise the highest portion of an operating budget. Nonsalary costs are often more difficult to control than salaries.

Work standards may be used to control materials management activities. Work measurement techniques vary considerably in terms of development cost, consistency, and applicability. Historical standards can be effective for noncritical activities. A more precise historical standard makes use of trend line, regression analysis. Work sampling standards are based upon random sampling of work activities. Time study makes use of stopwatch observations to establish an engineering work standard. Predetermined time standard systems provide objective, consistent results using data developed for various work movements.

Efficiency indices can be designed to monitor the many problems of materials operations. This measurement technique provides a means for instituting controls using easily obtainable data. Management by objectives (MBO) is a performance evaluation technique applied to all major groups within a business, and at all organization levels. One of MBO's benefits is that it contributes to "bottom-up" goal setting.

NOTES

1. Higgins, *Organizational Policy and Strategic Management*, p. 207.
2. Colton and Rohrs, *Industrial Purchasing and Effective Materials Management*, p. 255
3. Fayol, *General and Industrial Management*, p. 107.
4. Hodgetts, *Management: Theory, Process and Practice*, pp. 166–167.
5. Meigs and Meigs, *Accounting; The Basis for Business Decisions*, p. 980.
6. Dilworth, *Production and Operations Management*, p. 558.
7. Grillo and Berg, *Work Measurement in the Office*, p. 10.
8. Gaither, *Production and Operations Management*, p. 676.
9. Harrington, "New Work Measurement Techniques Can Mean Big Savings," pp. 48–49.
10. "An Incentive Plan That Works," pp. 48–51.
11. Here the popular dictionary definition of ratio is applicable: "the quotient of one quantity divided by another of the same kind; usually expressed as a fraction." David B. Guralnik, editor-in-chief, *Webster's New World Dictionary* (New York: New World Dictionaries/Simon and Schuster, 1984), p. 1179.
12. Carter and Hoagland, *Purchasing Performance: Measurement and Control*, pp. 124, 139, 202, 220.
13. A. T. Kearney, Inc., *Measuring Productivity in Physical Distribution*, pp. 56, 74, 112, 120.
14. Hodgetts, *Management: Theory, Process, and Practice*, p. 379.
15. Odiorne, *Management by Objectives*, pp. 55–56.
16. A. T. Kearney, Inc., *Measuring Productivity in Physical Distribution*, p. 23.
17. Raia, *Managing by Objectives*, pp. 18–22.
18. Wight, "Materials Management in Focus," p. 15.

BIBLIOGRAPHY

"An Incentive Plan That Works." *Modern Materials Handling*, Oct. 6, 1981.

Colton, Raymond R., and Rohrs, Walter F. *Industrial Purchasing and Effective Material Management.* Reston, Virginia: Reston Publishing Co., 1985

Dilworth, James B. *Production and Operations Management.* New York: Random House, 1983.

Fayol, Henry. *General and Industrial Management*, Trans. Constance Storrs. London: Pitman Publishing, 1949.

Gaither, Norman. *Production and Operations Management.* Hinsdale, Illinois: The Dryden Press, 1987.

Gannon, M. J., and Smith, K. G., "The Ten Commandments of Management In Effective Firms," *Business*, Apr-May-June, 1988, pp. 41–44.

Grillo, Elmer V., and Berg, Charles J., Jr. *Work Measurement in the Office.* New York: McGraw-Hill Book Co., 1965.

Harrington, Lisa H. "New Work Measurement Techniques Can Mean Big Savings.," *Traffic Management*, Sept. 1982.

Higgins, James M., and Vincze, Julian W. *Strategic Management and Organizational Policy.* Hinsdale, Illinois: The Dryden Press, 1986.

Hodgetts, Richard M. *Management: Theory, Process and Practice.* Hinsdale, Illinois: The Dryden Press, 1982.

Kearney, A. T., Inc. *Measuring Productivity in Physical Distribution.* Chicago: National Council of Physical Distribution Management, 1978.

Meigs, Walter B., and Meigs, Robert F. *Accounting: The Basis for Business Decisions.* New York: McGraw-Hill Book Co., 1984.

"Managing in The 90's," *Industry Week*, Apr. 18, 1988, pp. 17–68.

Monczka, Robert M., Carter, Phillip L., and Hoagland, John H. *Purchasing Performance: Measurement and Control.* East Lansing: Michigan State University, 1979.

Odiorne, George S. *Management by Objectives.* New York: Pitman Publishing, 1965.

Raia, Anthony P. *Managing by Objectives.* Glenview, Illinois: Scott, Foresman and Co., 1974.

Wight, Oliver W. "Materials Management in Focus." *Modern Materials Handling*, Mar. 7, 1983, p. 15.

14
Financial Considerations Related to Materials Management

Financial management is the study and practice of monetary decision making within a company. Financial managers are members of a management team responsible for assessing the financial implications of any decision made by the firm.[1] There are many stages during the growth or the contraction of a company where financial decisions determine its success or failure. For example, expansion funds can be obtained from many sources, such as the sale of stocks or bonds, bank loans, and capital equipment leasing. Input into each financial decision comes from members of the management team, which includes groups such as materials management, engineering, and marketing. However, the financial management group makes the final decision in choosing the best alternative, evaluating the present and future impact of the decision.

Materials management makes significant contributions to the control of vital business resources, the quality of its contribution greatly impacting the company's financial condition. Materials management personnel must understand the basic principles of financial management and have the ability to communicate intelligently with financial personnel, in order to maximize the effectiveness of their function.

ROLE OF FINANCIAL OFFICER

The role of the financial officer has changed significantly through the years. During the early 1900s emphasis was primarily on the legal aspects of company operations. Industrialization in the United States brought another set of requirements, related to the procurement of expansion funds. The depression of the 1930s caused financial personnel to concentrate on reorganization and bankruptcy. Since that time emphasis has been on integrating the financial function and putting it at the center of the decision-making process.

Primary Functions

On a broad scale, the financial function of a company can affect the national economy, in terms of both domestic and international activities. Although some of the larger firms, such as General Motors or Westinghouse, have an obvious national impact, each U.S. company, large or small, has an effect. A review of the financial manager's primary functions (see Figure 14-1) provides some insight into various relationships, both internal and external.

Weston and Brigham delineated the financial functions in the following manner, as they relate to planning for, obtaining, and using funds to maximize the value of a firm:[2]

Planning and Forecasting. the financial manager must be a central resource and prime mover to accomplish overall company planning and forecasting. This individual should interact with all other executives who are responsible for general activities within the firm.

Investment and Financial Decisions. Company growth normally requires the support of increased investment by the firm. Financial managers must guide the company's growth rate. During the course of this movement, many financial decisions must be made. Some of these include selection of

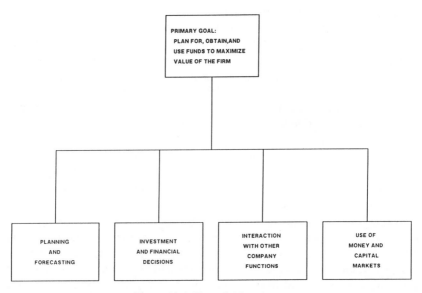

Figure 14-1. Financial functions.

internal or external funds, and long-term or short-term funding sources, and use of debt versus owners' equity.

Interaction with Other Company Functions. Finance interacts with all company functions. The financial executive must communicate with all segments of the firm to help them to operate efficiently. Because all business decisions relate in some manner to financial considerations, the finance group is centrally involved in this process.

Use of Money and Capital Markets. The central responsibilities of financial managers relate to decisions on investments and how they are financed. These key decisions have a direct bearing upon the value of the firm.

Organization Structure

Finance is often divided into two major areas, which fall under the responsibility of the controller and the treasurer (see Figure 14-2). The number of personnel required to perform the activities within these areas depends upon company size. The treasurer, who reports to a finance executive, typically is responsible for contacting banks to obtain loans, and for working with investment bankers to obtain funds through the sale of stocks or bonds to the public. The treasurer is responsible for reporting critical information regarding cash and working capital, develop cash budgets, and monitor credit management. Obtaining advantageous credit terms and collecting accounts receivable monies promptly are critical aspects of maintaining the company's financial position. Other responsibilities of the treasurer include insurance, pension fund management, and review of capital expenditure justifications.

The controller, who also reports to the finance executive, is responsible for developing and maintaining all financial reports. These duties include the preparation of budgets, financial statements, and ratio analyses. It is the controller's responsibility to correct any discrepancies in the budget. Another activity is general and cost accounting. Secretarial, reproduction, and mail services are examples of some general office activities. Other duties of the controller include payroll, taxes, and internal auditing.

Relationship between the Finance Manager and Materials Manager

Both the finance executive and the materials management executive will ideally report to the chief executive officer, as discussed in Chapter 2. Their relationship will provide a basis for cooperation and clear communication.

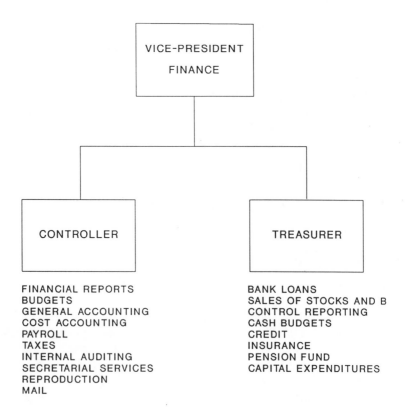

Figure 14-2. Financial organization structure.

The finance manager interacts with the materials manager when performing activities such as reviewing and approving capital expenditures, conducting internal audits of materials operations, and compiling analysis and decision-making data. Conversely, the materials manager interacts with the finance manager in activities such as developing information for planning long-range resource requirements, developing cost reduction programs, and ensuring adherence to budget constraints.

The objectives for both finance and materials management should be the same. Their objectives relate to the entire firm and include minimizing costs, maximizing profits, and maximizing the value of the company. At times, the two managers may have different interpretations of what is best for the business. For example, the finance manager attempts to balance both liquidity and profitability in the use of company funds. Although the impact of a given decision on liquidity can be readily determined, it is often difficult to assess the corresponding affect on profitability.[3] Reducing inventory may appear to be a viable way to improve the company's cash position. However, inventories might be so reduced that there is a negative effect on profits, and programs such as marketing are endangered. Materials management input is critical for this type of decision.

Financial personnel may decide to increase the payment period for accounts payable in order to conserve cash. This sometimes arbitrary decision can have a negative effect upon other company activities. It is important for materials management to evaluate how a change in payment policy will affect supplier relationships, and to what extent it will impact upon business. Unfortunately, although a change in payment periods can increase cash reserves and interest income, it is difficult to develop a quantitative figure that reflects possible future losses associated with deteriorating supplier relationships. Computation of such losses is often an after-the-fact activity, based upon such factors as late deliveries, poor product quality, or increased prices.

The finance group can provide valuable assistance to materials personnel in evaluating the financial condition of present and potential suppliers. This works as a screening procedure to reduce the risk of supplier difficulties. For example, purchasers of computer systems from U.S. manufacturers have been suddenly surprised to learn of their suppliers' bankruptcy. Proper financial analysis would have revealed this possibility in advance of the purchase.[4]

A major source of conflict between finance and materials management concerns the type and scope of accounting. The accounting system is frequently oriented toward the general financial information required for upper management, stockholders, or the Internal Revenue Service. Finance is reluctant to develop other information, but the materials group needs specific data to control its individual activities. Managerial accounting data must reflect changes in costs due to operational changes, the true cost variance between different methods and systems, and the impact of changes in volume.[5] Materials supervision cannot evaluate trade-off costs or make knowledgeable decisions without complete and accurate managerial accounting figures. Another problem is the tendency for accounting personnel to group many specific costs into overhead. Materials management can overcome these accounting difficulties by teaching financial management the importance of segregating costs and by justifying more detailed methods of data collection and reporting.

BASIC FINANCIAL STATEMENTS

When discussing financial statements, we can use the practice of scorekeeping at sporting events as an analogy. During each game it is necessary to keep accurate scores and records, and a similar kind of "scorekeeping" is a necessity in the business world. Monetary measurements are a common measure of profitability for an enterprise. However, many different aspects of the business need to be measured. Financial transactions and statements provide a bird's-eye/general account view of what is occurring within the firm. The basic financial statements are the balance sheet and the income statement.

Balance Sheet

The balance sheet represents the financial condition of the company at one point in time, such as at the end of a fiscal year. It is often referred to as a "snapshot" of the firm's position at a given date. The balance sheet contains all of the information included in the basic accounting formula:

$$\text{Assets} = \text{Liabilities} + \text{Net worth}$$

Another way of expressing this equation is to say that total assets are equal to the claims of creditors plus the claims of owners.

Figure 14-3 presents a balance sheet for the Jabe Systems Company. Here the firm's assets of $4,016,000 balance its liabilities of $1,950,000, plus its net worth of $2,066,000.

Current assets include cash, accounts receivable, inventories, and prepaid expenses. Fixed assets include property/land, buildings, and equipment required to conduct the company business, which will not be disposed of within a one-year period. Depreciation on buildings and equipment is deducted from the fixed assets to provide a net fixed assets amount. The assets on this balance sheet are abbreviated. Assets for a larger firm could also include marketable securities, patents, and construction in progress.

The debts or liabilities of the company are shown in the right-hand column. These include its current liabilities, such as accounts payable, notes payable, and federal taxes payable, and its long-term liabilities, including mortgages and notes payable. Liabilities for a larger company could also include dividends payable, customer deposits, and accrued royalties.

The owners' equity is referred to as net worth, proprietorship, or capital. It includes the stated value (par value) of outstanding shares of stock and retained earnings that have not been distributed to the owners in the form of dividends. Net losses in excess of retained earnings are deductions from the owners' equity, and are referred to as a deficit. The owners' equity indicates the amount that assets can shrink before the creditors' position is jeopardized.[6] Net worth can also include additional monies contributed by the owners beyond the original investment.

ASSETS

Current Assets:		
Cash	$ 230,000	
Accounts receivable	1,100,000	
Inventories	640,000	
Prepaid expenses	46,000	
TOTAL CURRENT ASSETS		$2,016,000
Fixed Assets:		
Gross plant, building and equipment	3,000,000	
Less: Depreciation	1,000,000	
NET FIXED ASSETS		2,000,000
TOTAL ASSETS		$4,016,000

LIABILITIES

Current Liabilities:		
Accounts payable	$1,000,000	
Notes payable	300,000	
Provision federal taxes	100,000	
TOTAL CURRENT LIABILITIES		$1,400,000
Long-Term Liabilities:		
Mortgage	500,000	
Notes payable	50,000	
TOTAL LONG-TERM LIABILITIES		550,000
TOTAL LIABILITIES		$1,950,000
NET WORTH		
Stock	1,500,000	
Retained earnings	566,000	
TOTAL NET WORTH		$2,066,000
TOTAL LIABILITIES AND NET WORTH		$4,016,000

Figure 14-3. Jabe Systems Company. Balance sheet, December 31, 1989.

Materials management activities have a vital impact upon the balance sheet. For example, inventory purchases immediately increase current liabilities. Later, after a supplies payment, there is a decrease in cash and in current liabilities, and an increase in inventory. Investments, such as for an automated storage retrieval system, will result in an increase in fixed assets and long-term liabilities. The disposal of obsolete and surplus materials will increase the cash assets.

Income Statement

Income statements are commonly referred to as a profit and loss or P and L statements. They summarize the operations of a company during a specific period of time, usually a fiscal period. Note that the income statement is based on a flow that shows what has occurred between two points in time, whereas the balance sheet is a snapshot of the firm's position on a specific date. The basic formula for an income statement is as follows:

$$\text{Revenue} - \text{Expenses} = \text{Profit}$$

Figure 14-4 presents an income statement for the Jabe Systems Company. Here the primary source of revenue is sales. There are often deduc-

		%		%
Sales			$4,680,000	
Cost of Goods Sold:				
Material	$2,480,000	(53.0)		
Direct labor	680,000	(14.5)		
Plant overhead	230,000	(4.9)	3,390,000	(72.4)
Gross Margin			$1,290,000	(27.6)
Operating Expense:				
Selling	490,000	(10.5)		
Research & development	200,000	(4.3)		
Administrative	118,000	(2.5)	808,000	(17.3)
Net Income before Interest & Taxes			482,000	(10.3)
Interest Expense			171,000	(3.7)
Net Income before Taxes			311,000	(6.6)
Federal Income Tax			60,000	(1.3)
NET INCOME			251,000	(5.4)

Figure 14-4. Jabe Systems Company. Income statement for year ending December 31, 1989.

tions from sales due to returned merchandise, discounts, or allowances. The remainder is referred to as net sales. The cost of goods sold is composed of all costs directly related to manufacturing products. A primary expense related to the materials management group is for materials; it includes all materials required to produce company finished goods. For Jabe Systems, there are electronic instrument materials, including metal, wire, glass, and so on. Some products, such as automobiles, are more complicated and are composed of numerous types, shapes, and quantities of material. Normally materials represent a very high percentage of sales. The 53.0 shown in parentheses beside the material cost of $2,480,000 (see Figure 14-4) indicates that material expense outlays controlled by materials management represent 53 percent of total revenue.

Direct labor includes all personnel costs directly related to production of a product. This routinely includes performance of various tasks such as shearing, fabricating, welding, subassembly, painting, and final assembly. Companies do not all use one uniform system to segregate their costs. For example, some companies include inspection or materials handling personnel who service an assembly line as part of their direct labor. Other companies account for these employees as indirect labor and include the associated costs as plant overhead.

Plant overhead normally includes the costs incurred in operating a manufacturing facility that cannot be isolated and charged to production of a particular product. These costs include numerous accounts. Some of them are related to building expenses such as rent, maintenance, heat, and electricity. Overhead costs are also associated with plant operations such as equipment maintenance, materials handling, warehousing, and inspection. Other costs include salaries for plant management, production supervision, personnel management, clerical employees, purchasing, and inventory control. Insurance, taxes, safety supplies, oil, and grease are also included. Frequently, overhead cost is allocated directly to a product, for computing actual product cost or estimating the cost of a new product.

Gross margin represents profit after the cost of goods sold is deducted from sales. The next major business cost included in the income statement is operating expense. It is normally composed of selling, research and development, and administrative expenses. Selling costs are marketing expenses; they include all costs associated with a complete marketing program, including sales, market research, and advertising.

Research and development costs include monies spent for personnel, facilities, and operations. Some of these expenses include the costs incurred for engineering personnel, laboratories, research equipment, secretarial personnel, patents and trademarks, and licenses. Administrative costs include the expense of overall management of a firm. In the case of a large company with multiple facilities, administrative costs include the entire corporate group and all associated costs, such as salaries of officers and staff, public relations budgets, and legal fees.

Net income before interest and taxes is computed by deducting operating expenses from gross margin. This represents the company's profits prior to satisfying interest and tax obligations. Interest expense is subtracted to yield net income before taxes. Net profit, commonly referred to as *the bottom line*, is the result of subtracting federal income taxes from the net income before taxes. Unfortunately for some firms, the bottom line is a negative amount, which indicates a net loss.

Figure 14-4 shows the results of computing the ratio of each income statement item with respect to sales, expressed as a percentage. The advantage of this type of analysis is that it allows the user to make a faster and more effective comparison than would be possible using discrete dollar amounts. Knowing that selling expenses have increased from 8.5 percent to 10.5 percent may be more revealing than knowing that they increased from $442,000 to $490,000. Percentages also can be an effective financial analysis tool for comparison of company expenses with industry data.

Impact of Materials Management on Financial Statements

Because the materials group can significantly affect the firm's ability to control its resources, its activities have a major impact upon finance. Peter Scifres indicates that policy/decision variables in the materials management area affect both major financial statements—the balance sheet and income statement. Some of these materials group decisions and their effects are summarized below:[7]

Increase Customer Service:

Statement	Direct Impact(s) by Materials Management Activities
Balance sheet	None direct.
Income statement	Increase in unit sales, resulting in higher sales revenue and cost of goods sold. Net income will increase if added revenue is higher than additional cost of goods sold.

Increase Inventory Turnover:

Statement	Direct Impact(s) by Materials Management Activities
Balance sheet	Decrease in inventory. Increase in cash and/or decrease in accounts payable.
Income statement	None direct.

Decrease Purchasing Total Costs:

Statement	Direct Impact(s) by Materials Management Activities
Balance sheet	None direct.
Income statement	Decrease in cost of goods sold by the amount of reduced purchased materials cost. This will increase the net income.

Decrease Transportation Costs:

Statement	Direct Impact(s) by Materials Management Activities
Balance sheet	None direct.
Income statement	Decrease in cost of goods sold by the amount of reduced transportation costs. This will increase net income.

Increase Data Integrity:

Statement	Direct Impact(s) by Materials Management Activities
Balance sheet	Increase or decrease in inventory, depending upon whether this account was previously over or understated.
Income statement	Decrease in cost of goods sold by savings generated from improved efficiency of operations. Net income will increase.

FINANCIAL RATIO ANALYSIS

Financial planning is a key responsibility of the finance manager. Normally, the success of a company depends upon its ability to forecast future events and monetary needs. A fundamental method used by financial personnel to evaluate current conditions, develop forecasts, and establish future objectives is ratio analysis, where the ratios express relationships between different quantities of significant accounting information.

Within the company, financial ratios are based upon data obtained from the balance sheet and the income statement. Ratios also may be used to compare the company with other firms. Information regarding other companies is available through services such as Dun & Bradstreet. *Dun's Review*, *Fortune*, and *Business Week* periodically report ratios for selected companies. The four main types of ratios measure liquidity, activity, leverage, and profitability.[8]

Liquidity Ratios

Normally, one of the first concerns of a financial manager is liquidity. Liquidity ratios measure a company's ability to pay short-term commitments. They compare the assets available to pay current bills with the level of those obligations. Two commonly used liquidity ratios are discussed below.

Current Ratio. The current ratio measures the company's ability to satisfy its creditors with regard to short-term debts and liabilities. This is the most frequently used liquidity ratio. The basic ratio, as calculated for Jabe Systems (see Figure 14-3), is:

$$\text{Current ratio} = \frac{\text{Current assets}}{\text{Current liabilities}} = \frac{\$2,016,000}{\$1,400,000} = 1.4$$

The ratio for Jabe Systems is quite low; most companies consider 2.0 or higher to be appropriate. This ratio varies by company and type of industry. Jabe Systems' current low ratio could be raised by such transactions as increasing cash by retaining earnings, using long-term debts as a means of borrowing money, or paying current liabilities. High current ratios provide protection against such problems as noncollectible accounts receivable and unsalable inventories. If a banker were reviewing a loan application, or if a creditor were planning a credit allowance for purchases, he or she might be negatively affected by the low current ratio for Jabe Systems.

Quick Ratio or Acid Test. The quick ratio or acid test ratio is essentially the same as the current ratio except that the numerator, current assets, is decreased by the amount of inventories. This ratio is often viewed as a more accurate indicator of a firm's liquidity than the current ratio because inventories are typically the least liquid of current assets and are often subject to liquidation loss. This ratio, for Jabe Systems, is:

$$\text{Quick ratio} =$$
$$\frac{\text{Current assets} - \text{Inventory}}{\text{Current liabilities}} = \frac{\$2,016,000 - \$640,000}{\$1,400,000} = 0.98$$

Jabe Systems has a 0.98 ratio of truly liquid assets for every dollar of current liabilities. Generally a ratio of 1.0 or higher is typical, but, again, this depends upon the company and the industry. Companies in industries with highly profitable cash receipts can sometimes maintain lower liquidity and thus have lower quick ratios.

Activity Ratios

Activity ratios measure how effectively a company is using its resources. The ratios all involve comparisons of information from the balance sheet and income statement. Four commonly used activity ratios are discussed below.

Inventory Turnover. This is a frequently used indicator of how many times per year a firm has been able to sell its inventory. It is one of the important ratios used by materials management to monitor its effectiveness in controlling inventories. The basic ratio for Jabe Systems (see Figures 14-3 and 14-4) follows, assuming an average inventory of $600,000:

$$\text{Inventory turnover} = \frac{\text{Cost of goods sold}}{\text{Average inventory}} = \frac{\$3,390,000}{600,000} = 5.6$$

The inventory turnover ratio for Jabe Systems appears to be low. The company may be carrying obsolete and/or surplus inventories. Financial statistics compilers such as Dun & Bradstreet substitute total year sales in the numerator of the above equation. If you want to compare your company ratio to data published by companies like D & B, it is necessary to use the following equation, which contains figures for Jabe Systems:

$$\text{Inventory turnover} = \frac{\text{Sales}}{\text{inventory}} = \frac{\$4,680,000}{640,000} = 7.3$$

Average Collection Period. This ratio measures the average number of days it takes a firm to collect its accounts receivable monies. The two steps in this computation are to first calculate the number of sales per day, and then determine the average number of days in a collection period. The basic ratios for Jabe Systems appear in the following illustration:

$$\text{Sales per day} = \frac{\text{Sales}}{360} = \frac{\$4,680,000}{360} = \$13,000$$

Average collection period =

$$\frac{\text{Accounts receivable}}{\text{Sales per day}} = \frac{\$1,100,000}{13,000} = 85 \text{ days}$$

The average collection period is compared with the firm's credit terms to determine whether or not customers are paying their invoices on time. Invoices that are allowed to age without proper follow-up result in bad (unpaid) debt. Assuming that Jabe Systems has credit terms of 30 days net payment, then the 85-day average collection period indicates that they are considerably behind in collections. This situation contributes to many problems, including poor cash flow.

Total Assets Turnover. This ratio is similar to inventory turnover in that it measures turnover of all the firm's resources. It provides an indication as to how effectively the company utilizes its total assets. The basic ratio, illustrated for Jabe Systems, is as follows:

$$\text{Total assets turnover} = \frac{\text{Sales}}{\text{Total assets}} = \frac{\$4,680,000}{4,016,000} = 1.2$$

Total assets turnover for Jabe Systems can be compared with previous company data and objectives as well as with other companies in the industry. Assuming that 1.2 turns is low for the industry, Jabe's management should review its operations to ascertain whether it has too many assets or too great a resource capacity for present sales. Another possibility that must be considered when reviewing company efficiency is that Jabe Systems is at a temporary low point in sales, and there may be no real cause for concern.

Fixed Assets Turnover. This ratio measures turnover or utilization efficiency of fixed assets. The basic ratio, with illustration for Jabe System, is:

$$\text{Fixed assets turnover} = \frac{\text{Sales}}{\text{Fixed assets}} = \frac{\$4,680,000}{2,000,000} = 2.3$$

Jabe Systems should compare the 2.3 with past performance and industry data. Again, if the ratio indicates that the company's plant and equipment are not operating efficiently, Jabe must evaluate whether its fixed assets are too great, and/or it needs to improve productivity. The 2.3 indicates that Jabe Systems generates $2.30 in sales for each dollar of fixed assets.

Leverage Ratios

In the financial management of a company, leverage may be defined as the use of outside money to operate the business. Ratios can be used to determine the degree to which leverage is being employed. Debt financing requires interest payments, whereas owners' capital contributions do not. There are two major strategy considerations in the use of leverage. One involves the risk of not being able to repay debts that are leveraged to a high degree. The second consideration is that low leverage means the firm is not using investors' money to finance its growth. The two commonly used leverage ratios are discussed below.

Debt to Total Assets. The debt to total assets ratio, or simply debt ratio, measures the degree to which creditor funds are being employed. A business owner who uses high leverage may prefer to minimize capital investment by outsiders to prevent dilution of control. Conversely, if debt is very high, creditors may become concerned with potential losses, which could result in the event of bankruptcy. The basic ratio (normally shown as a percentage), using figures for Jabe Systems, is:

$$\text{Debt to total assets} = \frac{\text{Total debt}}{\text{Total assets}} \times 100 = \frac{\$1,950,000}{4,016,000} \times 100 = 49\%$$

This calculation indicates that creditors have provided almost one-half of the company's financing. Forty-nine percent may be a high figure; it could mean that further borrowing or increased creditor debt may be difficult to negotiate. Owners, on the other hand, may interpret the 49 percent as an indication that any increases in earnings will yield a substantial percentage return.

Times Interest Earned. This ratio measures the firm's ability to meet annual interest payments, as the failure to pay interest owed to creditors can result in legal action. The net income before taxes is used in this computation, as interest charges affect tax liability because they are tax-deductible. The basic ratio, calculated for Jabe Systems, is as follows:

$$\text{Times interest earned} =$$
$$\frac{\text{Profit before interest and taxes}}{\text{Interest charges}} = \frac{\$482,000}{171,000} = 2.8$$

The above calculation indicates that interest is satisfied by the profit before interest and taxes 2.8 times. Like previous ratios, the times interest earned figure for Jabe Systems is low for the industry. It is reasonable to conclude that this company may have difficulty borrowing money.

Profitability Ratios

A company's profitability ratio provides a good measure of the net result of its overall business management. Profits are an integral part of the business cycle. It is in the best interest of owners, creditors, and employees for a firm to make the largest possible profit. The three commonly used profitability ratios, usually expressed as percentages, are discussed below.

Profit Margin on Sales. This ratio measures the company's profitability in relationship to total sales revenue. Profits earned by U.S. companies normally average less than 5 percent of sales.[9] The profit margin on sales ratio, calculated for Jabe Systems, is:

$$\text{Profit margin on sales} = \frac{\text{Net profit after taxes}}{\text{Sales}} \times 100 = \frac{251{,}000}{\$4{,}680{,}000} \times 100 = 5.4\%$$

Jabe's 5.4 percent profit margin is average for a U.S. industry. Normally company management reviews profitability by comparing current ratios to previous periods as well as to other companies in the same industry.

Return on Total Assets. This percentage measures the earning ability of a company. Often referred to as return on investment (ROI), it shows the firm's rate of return for monies invested in assets. The basic ratio, calculated for Jabe Systems, is:

$$\text{Return on total assets} = \frac{\text{Net profit after taxes}}{\text{Total assets}} \times 100 = \frac{251{,}000}{\$4{,}016{,}000} \times 100 = 6.3\%$$

The return on investment for Jabe Systems is slightly low, perhaps because of a low percentage of profit on sales and/or a low asset turnover.

Return on Net Worth. This ratio measures the owner's earnings with respect to investment. It is sometimes referred to as return on equity. The ratio, calculated for Jabe Systems, is:

$$\text{Return on net worth} = \frac{\text{Net profit after taxes}}{\text{Net worth}} \times 100 = \frac{251{,}000}{\$2{,}066{,}000} \times 100 = 12.1\%$$

Jabe Systems' 12.5 percent return on net worth appears to be low, depending upon the history of the company and how it compares with other companies in the industry.

All of these financial ratios are summarized in Figure 14-5. Company management can use these ratios to help determine the strengths and weaknesses of Jabe Systems. The company's major functions (materials management, marketing, engineering, operations, etc.) will work toward improving its financial condition. The finance group will take the lead in developing strategies and implementing plans.

CASH FLOW

One of the finance manager's key responsibilities is to review and control the flow of funds through the organization. He or she analyzes cash flow over the short term and plans for future periods as well.

In every business there is a continuing cycle of events that may increase or decrease the cash balance. Figure 14-6 illustrates various elements that affect a company's overall cash flow. Some basic cash outflows include payments for purchases of materials and equipment. Inflows occur with various transactions, such as receipt of monies from accounts payable and sale of assets.

Sources of Cash

Just as the human body requires blood to sustain life, a business needs cash to maintain solvency. Many seemingly healthy businesses have become insolvent because they lacked sufficient cash to meet their obligations. Cash management should not be an occasional exercise, nor should it be practiced only by big business. Rather, it must be recognized and used as a vital management tool, and practiced on a daily basis by every business, regardless of size.[10] The planning, forecasting, and development of company cash resources are as critical to a business as the generation of new blood is to the human body.

Income. All firms, regardless of industry or their structure as profit or nonprofit organizations, must have a primary source of income. Most companies collect cash at the time of a sale and/or accounts receivable funds from previous sales of goods or services. Forecasts are made to predict the amount of time that will pass between the date when an invoice is issued and the date when payment is received.

Depreciation. The standard accounting procedure is to treat depreciation as an annual charge against income that reflects the cost of buildings and equipment used in operations. This amount is deducted from sales revenue in the income statement. Because depreciation is a paper transaction rather than an actual cash outlay, it represents available cash.

Sales of Assets. A source of funds that involves materials management is liquidation of company assets such as inventory, buildings, and equipment. There can be various reasons for using this alternative. Inventory, a prime source of cash, can include obsolete and surplus materials. Buildings

RATIO	FORMULA FOR CALCULATION	CALCULATION (USING JABE SYSTEM DATA)	
Liquidity			
•Current ratio	$\dfrac{\text{Current assets}}{\text{Current liabilities}}$	$\dfrac{\$2,016,000}{\$1,400,000}$	=1.4 times
•Quick ratio or acid test	$\dfrac{\text{Current assets} - \text{Inventory}}{\text{Current liabilities}}$	$\dfrac{\$2,016,000 - \$640,000}{\$1,400,000}$	=0.98 times
Activity			
•Inventory turnover	$\dfrac{\text{Cost of goods sold}}{\text{Average inventory}}$	$\dfrac{\$3,390,000}{600,000}$	=5.6 times
•Average collection period	$(1)\ \dfrac{\text{Sales}}{360}$	$\dfrac{\$4,680,000}{360}$	=\$13,000/day
	$(2)\ \dfrac{\text{Accounts receivable}}{\text{Sales per day}}$	$\dfrac{\$1,100,000}{\$13,000}$	=85 days
•Total assets turnover	$\dfrac{\text{Sales}}{\text{Total assets}}$	$\dfrac{\$4,680,000}{\$4,016,000}$	=1.2 times
•Fixed assets turnover	$\dfrac{\text{Sales}}{\text{Fixed assets}}$	$\dfrac{\$4,680,000}{\$2,000,000}$	=2.3 times
Leverage			
•Debt to total assets	$\dfrac{\text{Total debt}}{\text{Total assets}} \times 100$	$\dfrac{\$1,950,000}{\$4,016,000} \times 100$	=49%
•Times interest earned	$\dfrac{\text{Profit before interest \& taxes}}{\text{Interest charges}}$	$\dfrac{\$482,000}{\$171,000}$	=2.8 times
Profitability			
•Profit margin on sales	$\dfrac{\text{Net profit after taxes}}{\text{Sales}} \times 100$	$\dfrac{\$251,000}{\$4,680,000} \times 100$	=5.4%
•Return on total assets	$\dfrac{\text{Net profit after taxes}}{\text{Total assets} \times 100}$	$\dfrac{\$251,000}{\$4,016,000} \times 100$	=6.3%
•Return on net worth	$\dfrac{\text{Net profit after taxes}}{\text{Net worth}} \times 100$	$\dfrac{\$251,000}{\$2,016,000} \times 100$	=12.5%

Figure 14-5. Summary of financial ratio analysis.

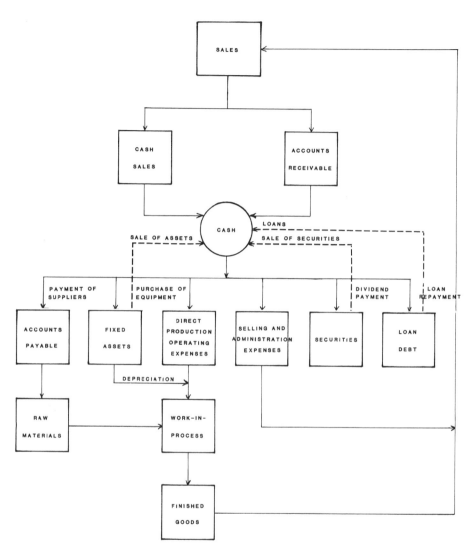

Figure 14-6. Overall cash flow cycle.

and equipment may be sold because they are obsolete, inefficient, or underused. At times, desirable assets are liquidated because of immediate cash needs. An important consideration in the sale of assets is the fact that actual market value often differs from book value. In recent years, the values of existing equipment and buildings have generally appreciated because of the increased cost of new facilities.

Sale of Securities. A firm may decide to appropriate funds by selling stocks or bonds to the public. This is an involved and time-consuming process, however, so it is not feasible for companies that require immediate cash. First, an investment banker may be selected who can underwrite the sale. Then, Securities and Exchange Commission (SEC) registration and approval must be secured prior to the sale. Finally, the investment banker pays cash based upon the security value less commission. Another consideration relative to the viability of this option is that the public is not always interested in purchasing stocks or bonds.

Borrowing Funds. A common source of capital, loans are financed by various institutions on a short-term or long-term basis. Financing of cash requirements plays a key role in the growth of a business. The two basic types of loans are the secured loan and the unsecured loan.

Secured loans. Unsecured loans provide the greatest flexibility to a firm, but there are times when a bank requests some security as collateral to protect itself against possible default. Many types of security can be used to collateralize a loan, some of the more common forms of collateral being marketable securities, inventory, accounts receivable, and facilities.

Unsecured loans. Unsecured loans are primarily available for short-term financing. It is common for companies to obtain such financing when funds are not sufficient to meet cash outflow demands. A line of credit is a temporary informal borrowing arrangement in which a firm can obtain funds up to a stipulated maximum amount upon request. Another unsecured loan is a revolving credit agreement; this is an agreement between a company and a bank where the bank is legally bound to provide credit to the borrower up to a fixed amount. The firm pays a commitment fee for any unused funds.

Uses of Cash

Both day-to-day activities and continued growth generate tremendous demands upon a firm for funds; so the financial executive attempts to balance cash flow by developing realistic forecasts of cash inputs and outputs. The following review of some of the needs and uses of cash provides insight into the many problems of a finance manager.

Supplier Expenses. Timely payment of monies due to suppliers is necessary to sustain company operations; it represents the major category of expenditures. Most suppliers will not continue shipment of materials after a specified period of nonpayment by the customer, and when materials are not adequate to meet customer demand, sales revenues go down. Delayed payment of suppliers also can disrupt vendor–user relationships, which are important to purchasing and other materials management subfunctions. An additional consideration is that timely payments allow firms to take advantage of discounts given for payment within fixed periods of time. Figure 14-7 contains a formula and sample calculation for computing the cost of not taking a cash discount.

Capital Investment. The growth of every company is related to the acquisition of fixed assets. These cash outlays often account for a significant percentage of total expenditures. New equipment is required for production, warehousing, materials handling, office operations, and many other areas. Land and buildings for manufacturing, distribution, and business offices require sizable cash expenditures. Capital investment requirements sometimes can be forecast by assessing the need to replace out-of-date facilities and predicting expected growth in capacity requirements. However, at other times capital investment funds must be allocated unexpectedly. For example, the materials management group of Company X decides to implement a Just-In-Time system and informs Company Y that in order to continue as a supplier it must now have a facility within five miles of Company X's plant. Company Y is faced with the choice of constructing a new plant/warehouse or losing the business revenues from Company X.

The formula for calculating the cost of not taking a cash discount is as follows:

$$\text{Cost of not taking cash discount (percentage)} = \frac{\text{Discount \%}}{\text{Net cost}} \times \frac{360 \text{ (days in year)}}{\text{Net days (difference)}} \times 100$$

Example. Assume terms of sale are 2/10 Net 30 for a $100 purchase. The firm has the use of $98.00 for 20 days, and the computation of cost of not taking a discount would be as follows:

$$\frac{2}{\$98.00} \times \frac{360}{20} \times 100 = 36.7\%$$

If the cost of not taking a discount is greater than the cost of funds, then the company should take the discount. Other factors such as the firm's liquidity position must also be considered.

Figure 14-7. Calculation of cost of foregoing cash discounts.

Selling and Administrative Expenses. Selling expenses involve the entire marketing function, but traditional accounting terminology still uses the word "selling." Frequently, the word "general" is added to make this category "selling, general, and administrative expenses." Many different types of expenses are included in this cost classification. Typical selling expenses include salaries for sales personnel, advertising expenditures, entertainment costs, travel expenses, telephone, postage, and outbound transportation fees. Some administration expenses are salaries for administrative and office personnel, rent, property taxes, legal expenses, uncollectible accounts, stationery, printing, and telephone.[11]

Dividends. Payment of cash dividends to stockholders is controlled by the company's board of directors. Some companies disburse neither cash nor stock dividends; they retain all earnings for company growth and operations. A firm with relatively stable earnings is more likely to pay dividends than one whose earnings fluctuate. The tax situations of stockholders also influence the payment of dividends. For example, a corporation with a limited number of high-income stockholders may pay a low dividend in order to minimize stockholders' tax payments. Figure 14-8 illustrates the relationship between corporate profits before taxes, taxes,

CORPORATE PROFITS

SEASONALLY ADJUSTED ANNUAL RATES, QUARTERLY

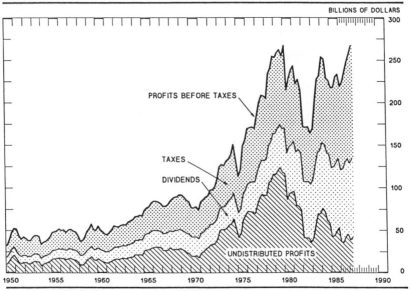

Figure 14-8. Corporate profits, dividends, and undistributed profits. (Source: Board of Governors, Federal Reserve System, *1987 Historical Chart Book*, Washington, D.C., 1987, p. 60)

dividends, and undistributed profits between 1950 and 1988. It shows that cash dividends were more stable than either corporate income or undistributed earnings during that period.

Payment of Loans. Commercial banks and other lending institutions periodically provide loans to companies for various reasons, such as short-term cash and growth requirements. Loan payments vary, depending upon how the cash is used. Prompt repayment of loans helps to establish and maintain a firm's credit rating. In addition to interest charges, some banks require a borrower to maintain a minimum checking account balance, generally equal to 15 to 20 percent of the loan amount. Called a compensating balance, this is a cost for the company because interest is not earned on the money. Consequently, it raises the effective rate of interest on bank loans.

LONG-TERM INVESTMENT DECISIONS

The materials management and the finance manager frequently collaborate in making decisions about long-term investments. Many of these relate to large capital investments for buildings or equipment. Capital investments involve some degree of risk, partly because of the long periods of time required to achieve repayment of expenditures. Also, the need for particular equipment or buildings can be affected by variables such as the economy, product demand, and product design. The fact that each company has a limited amount of capital should be taken into account in planning long-term investment. Because of the many potential problems involved, finance managers have to analyze capital investments firmly and objectively. They may ask the materials manager to consider alternatives that either do not require capital expenditures or are less costly.

Make or Buy

Companies periodically must decide whether they should buy a part, subassembly, or product, or make it themselves. Another variation of this question is whether a company should buy transportation services from others or provide its own trucks, maintenance services, and drivers. Materials management is an important contributor to this decision. The finance manager analyzes the various trade-offs involved, a key factor being the firm's liquidity position. Sometimes a well-justified plan to expand facilities in order to increase manufacturing capacity is denied because the current ratio is precarious, and the firm is not sufficiently liquid.

Profitability ratio analysis is also a consideration in make-or-buy decisions. Return on investment (the ROI) is a key ratio. The finance manager sometimes establishes a minimum ROI for projects that will be reviewed. This figure provides guidelines that the materials management group can use to determine the financial acceptability of justification analyses. There are exceptions to these minimums, but each exception would have to be examined and approved by financial personnel.

Lease or Own

Many financial implications are involved in a decision to rent, lease, or own land, buildings, and equipment. Leases are commonly used by companies to acquire many types of properties. Short-term equipment such as automobiles, computers, duplication equipment, and materials handling equipment leased routinely. Long-term leases are utilized for facilities such as warehouses, major production equipment, and office buildings. Some lease contracts include an option to purchase the item within a specified period of time.

There are many financial advantages to leasing rather than owning property. A lease enables a company to avoid large cash outlays and long-term investments in low-yielding capital assets, allowing the firm to reserve its funds for working capital. Because lease payments are an expense of doing business, they are tax-deductible. Another benefit is that equipment leases can be promptly terminated if the equipment becomes obsolete in the fast-changing environment of high technology. The finance manager sometimes takes advantage of a lease situation by using it to distort the company's true debt condition when reporting financial information to the public. Lease agreements either are not disclosed in public financial statements or are included only in statement footnotes. Consequently, the firm's debt picture may appear considerably more favorable than it would had the property been purchased.[12] One advantage of the leasing alternative for materials management as well as other company groups is that a lease can be used to obtain assets while circumventing the capital budgeting justification process.

There are also disadvantages to leasing. Property ownership provides a depreciation deduction for tax purposes, whereas property leasing does not. This deduction is even more advantageous if accelerated depreciation is allowed. Also, lease payments normally are higher than mortgage and other ownership costs. Other aspects of ownership can be beneficial. The property owner may obtain increases in value due to appreciation from conditions such as inflation. Also, if the lessee improves the property in any way, such as carpeting offices or adding a new parking lot, the added value accrues to the owner when the lease terminates.

Risk and Uncertainty

The finance manager considers return on investment when ranking various proposals made by materials management and other company functions. However, projects above a particular ROI level do not all obtain automatic approval; other factors must be considered, such as the risk and uncertainty associated with capital budget items. A materials management executive would make a serious error by neglecting to estimate the risk factor for each recommended project.

The risk associated with any proposed project is defined in terms of the degree of variability expected in future returns on the project. For example, anyone buying a 90-day U.S. government treasury bill at a fixed interest rate can accurately forecast the return on that security and be assured of a risk-free investment. However, if the same monies are used to buy stock in a company that plans to drill for oil in waters off the coast of Africa, then the probability of a risk-free investment is drastically reduced. If expected future returns on an investment are highly variable, the risk factor is great.

When financial analysts develop probability distribution of expected returns for a project, their degree of precision can vary considerably. Statistical techniques can be used to closely measure probability distribution if a project is similar to one performed in the past; the best assurance of accurate risk estimates is to use good data. Unfortunately, data and/or previous experience is not always available. When planning a project, the materials manager is faced with the trade-offs of risk and return. For a large number of projects with multiple measures of risk and return, the decision-making process becomes complex.

Another factor is the human element. Some materials managers are prepared to take greater risks than others. The decision maker who assigns probability and trade-off considerations is the ultimate arbiter. Different managers will assign different trade-off estimates to identical alternatives for a variety of reasons. For example, many managers are more willing to take risks when spending company funds than they are when they spend personal monies. Figure 14-9 illustrates risk preferences that people exhibit in their personal lives. When the stakes are low, most individuals tend to be more willing to gamble than are when large amounts of money are involved. For example, Richard M. Hodgetts asked businessmen if they would be more willing to accept an outright gift of $5.00 than they would be to gamble on winning $15.00 or nothing with the correct call on the flip of a coin. Most respondents were willing to gamble for $15 or nothing. Conversely, when the stakes are raised to $50,000 and $150,000 respectively, most managers choose the safe choice of a certain $50,000.[13]

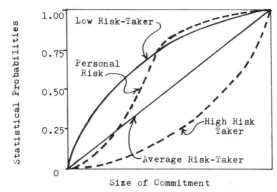

Figure 14-9. Risk-preference curves. (From *Management: Theory, Process, and Practice*, 3/e, by Richard M. Hodgetts. Copyright © 1982 by CBS College Publishing. Reprinted by permission of CBS College Publishing.)

Economic Justification

Countless long-term investment decisions are made every day. The increased interest in mechanized and automated plants, warehouses, and offices expressed by materials management personnel has led to huge monetary investments. In most cases finance managers depend upon others to justify their individual departmental proposals. An examination of the methods used to justify projects would reveal that some serious errors are made, some of which tend to encourage poor investments. Others prevent investments in projects that could be profitable.

Considering the current economic conditions of limited capital resources and worldwide competition, it is not surprising that company management demands clear and valid justification of long-term capital expenditures. Any economic justification recommended by materials management must include a review of all plausible alternatives. Potential benefits as well as negative aspects of each alternative should be discussed. Omitting legitimate alternatives from an analysis will lead to questions later on in the approval process, which can cause delays and threaten credibility.

Methods for comparing alternatives and justifying a project were briefly discussed and illustrated in Chapter 9. Payback, return on investment, and discounted cash flow are three of the common techniques. Norman L. Nadish, in an article on how to gain approval for projects, discussed pertinent points that all materials management personnel should consider as they develop their justifications.[14] Briefly, Nadish advised that:

1. Executives are busy and sometimes do not look beyond the first page. Summarize and sell the project on page 1.

2. Prepare your justification as if you had to hand-carry the proposal to the bank and convince them to lend you money.
3. Avoid technical jargon and keep the text simple and clear. Most reviewers do not have the same background and experience as the author.
4. Realize that you have something new and vital to sell. However, no matter how good it appears to you, it must be sold to the others. Do not oversell! A few well-chosen facts are more convincing than glamorous assurances that are vague and indefinite.
6. Carefully evaluate high-cost areas such as labor, floor space, materials, inventory, and waste, and provide a thorough justification.
7. Quantify specific values accrued through increased productivity and throughput, improved inventory turnover, simplified safety and environmental requirements, and a reduction in rejects and rework, accidents and compensation costs, and personnel turnover.
8. Before submitting the final proposal, allow associates to review it and give you their comments. Listen carefully to what they have to say. Redraft the proposal to incorporate suggestions that will strengthen its chances for approval.

TERMINOLOGY

To ensure good communication between finance and materials management, each group must understand the terminology and technical terms used by the other party. Finance personnel should increase their knowledge of materials-related systems, concepts, and terminology, and vice versa. In recent years, a greater number of finance personnel have attended college courses, seminars, and professional society meetings concerned with materials management. Their added knowledge of the subject will enable members of the finance group to understand and communicate with the materials function.

Similarly, it is critical that materials management personnel understand financial terminology. Some keys terms are defined below:

Auditor: An independent accounting firm retained by the company to verify the correctness of financial records.

Blue sky laws: State laws that regulate security transactions occurring within the state.

Cash flow: The flow of company funds, which occurs in a continual cycle. It is composed of many inputs and outputs that involve both internal and external groups.

Commercial paper: Unsecured promissory notes, normally sold by large companies, that reach maturity in less than nine months.

Cost of capital: The minimum rate of return that can be accepted on new investments while maintaining the company's cash value.

Current assets: Assets that can be converted into cash within a one-year period. Normally these include cash, marketable securities, accounts receivable monies, and inventory.

Current liabilities: Liabilities that must be paid within a one-year period. Normally this includes notes payable, accounts payable, taxes payable, and accrued wages.

Depreciation: An accounting practice that provides for the gradual reduction in value of an asset over its useful life. This represents an expense and is not a cash outlay.

Factor: A financial institution that purchases and takes responsibility for a company's accounts receivable.

Fixed assets: The capital assets of a company that produce the goods and/or services it sells to generate revenues. Normally this includes plants, business office facilities, warehouses, and equipment.

Gross profit margin: Often called gross margin, this measures the difference between net sales and the cost of goods sold.

Intangible assets: Company assets that are not of a physical nature, but increase its profit potential. Normally these include trademarks, patents, licenses, and goodwill.

Investment bankers: Firms that purchase new issues of stocks and bonds from a company and sell these securities to the public.

Letter of credit: A document issued by a bank that extends a stipulated amount of credit to a company for a specific period of time and for a specified purpose.

Line of credit: An informal borrowing arrangement between a company and a bank that provides the business with funds up to a maximum amount, usually within a defined time period. A *revolving line of credit* legally obligates the bank to lend the money to the company.

Long-term debt: Debts that have a maturity date of more than one year from the date of a financial statement. Normally these include long-term bank notes, mortgage loans, bonds, and other purchase obligations.

Net worth: The owner or stockholder equity in the company; composed of the stated value of the stock (par value), contributed monies in excess of par, and retained earnings. Other terms used for net worth include *proprietorship* and *capital.*

Overhead: Costs that are not directly related to individual production items. These costs include fixed costs such as management salaries and real estate taxes, as well as variable costs such as heat and electricity.

Prime rate: The rate of interest charged by commercial banks to customers with the highest credit ratings.

Pro forma statement: Income statement or balance sheet that is projected into future periods based upon forecasts and assumptions.

Prospectus: Detailed information about a company that is provided to potential investors and is required by the Securities and Exchange Commission (SEC).

Retained earnings: Income derived from the company's operations that has not been paid out to the stockholder or owner.

Syndicate: A group of lenders who jointly assume responsibility for making a large loan or purchasing a block of securities for resale.

Working capital: An amount of capital that is related to the company's production cycle; it is defined as follows:

$$\text{Working capital} = \text{Current assets} - \text{Current Liabilities}$$

SUMMARY

It is important that materials management personnel understand the basics of financial management and communicate intelligently with finance personnel, in order to maximize the effectiveness of the materials management function. The role of the finance officer must be understood from the standpoint of primary functions, organizational structure, and relationship with materials management.

Just as "keeping the score" is important for sports events, business must also keep score. Two basic financial statements are used by companies to measure and control operations. The balance sheet depicts the firm's financial condition at a point in time; it reflects the basic accounting formula: Assets = Liabilities + Net worth. The income statement, commonly referred to as the profit and loss (P & L) statement, is a summary of the company's operations over a period of time; the bottom line of this statement indicates the net income or loss for that period of time. Because materials management plays a key role in controlling company resources, it has a major impact upon the figures that appear in the financial statements.

Ratio analysis is used by financial personnel to evaluate current conditions, develop forecasts, and establish future objectives. The four major types of ratios measure liquidity, activity, leverage, and profitability. Liquidity ratios include current ratio and quick ratio. Activity ratios consist of inventory turnover, average collection period, total assets turnover, and fixed assets turnover. Leverage ratios include debt to total assets and times interest earned. The profitability ratios are profit margin on sales, return on total assets (the ROA), and return on net worth.

The lifeblood of a business enterprise is cash. it is critical that financial management review and control the flow of funds throughout the organization. In order to manage cash flow, the finance manager must constantly monitor the sources of cash, such as income, sale of assets, and sale of securities, and also the use of cash for supplier expenses, capital investment, and dividends.

Materials managers must cooperate with finance in monitoring a sound relationship between inventory purchases and cash flow. They must maintain the organization's flexibility and responsiveness to opportunities in the marketplace.

The finance manager frequently evaluates long-term investment plans. One reason for this constant monitoring is the firm's limited amount of available cash for long-term investment. Some business considerations that relate to capital expenditures are: make or buy; lease or own; risk and uncertainty; and economic justification.

Good communication requires that materials personnel understand basic terminology and technical terms used in financial management, such as cash flow, working capital, depreciation, retained earnings, investment banker, factor, line of credit, and pro forma statement.

NOTES

1. Henderson, Trennepohl, and Wert, *An Introduction to Financial Management*, p. 5.
2. Weston and Brigham, *Essentials of Managerial Finance*, p. 3.
3. Conti, "How to get Finance Off Your Back and On Your Side," p. 294.
4. Leenders, Fearon, and England, *Purchasing and Materials Management*, p. 522.
5. Cavinato, *Finance for Transportation and Logistics Managers*, pp. 107–110.
6. Amos and Sarchet, *Management for Engineers*, p. 247.
7. Scifres, "Materials Management: Impact on Financial Statements," pp. 315–318.
8. Engler, *Business Financial Management*, pp. 41–53.
9. Koontz and Fulmer, *A Practical Introduction to Business*, p. 50
10. "Cash Flow Forecasting," p. 21.
11. Matz and Usay, *Cost Accounting Planning and Control*, p. 19.
12. Dobler, Burt, *Purchasing and Materials Management*, p. 356.
13. Hodgetts, *Management: Theory, Process, and Practice*, pp. 200–201.
14. Nadish, "Justifying Assembly Automation," pp. 46–49.

BIBLIOGRAPHY

Amos, John M., and Sarchet, Bernard R. *Management for Engineers*. Englewood Cliffs, New Jersey: Prentice-Hall, 1981.

"Cash Flow Forecasting." *Small Business Report*, June 1983.

Cavinato, Joseph L. *Finance for Transportation and Logistics Managers*. Washington, D.C.: The Traffic Service Corporation, 1977.

Conti, Robert F. "How to Get Finance Off Your Back and On Your Side." *1980 Conference Proceedings*, American Production and Inventory Control Society.

Dobler, Donald W., Lee, Lamar, Jr., and Burt, David N. *Purchasing and Materials Management*. New York: McGraw-Hill Book Co., 1984.

Drucker, Peter F. *The Frontiers of Management: Where Tomorrow's Decisions Are Being Shaped Today*. New York: E. P. Dutton, 1986.

Engler, George, N. *Business Financial Management*. Dallas, Texas: Business Publications, 1975.

Henderson, Jr., Glenn V., Trennepohl, Gary L., and Wert, James E. *An Introduction to Financial Management*. Reading, Massachusetts: Addison-Wesley Publishing Co., 1984.

Hodgetts, Richard M. *Management: Theory, Process, and Practice*. Hinsdale, Illinois: The Dryden Press, 1982.

Koontz, Harold, and Fulmer, Robert M. *A Practical Introduction to Business*. Homewood, Illinois: Richard D. Irwin, 1984.

Leenders, Michael R., Fearon, Harold E., and England, Wilbur, B. *Purchasing and Materials Management*. Homewood, Illinois: Richard D. Irwin, 1985.

Levinson, Harry, and Rosenthal, Stuart. *CEO: Corporate Leadership in Action*. New York: Basic Books, 1984.

Matz, Adolph, and Usay, Milton F. *Cost Accounting Planning and Control*. Cincinnati, Ohio: South-Western Publishing Co., 1984.

Nadish, Norman L. "Justifying Assembly Automation." *Assembly Engineering*, Apr. 1982.

Ray, Michael L., and Myers, Rochelle. *Creativity in Business*. New York: Doubleday and Co., 1986.

Scifres, Peter N. "Materials Management: Impact on Financial Statements." *1980 Conference Proceedings*, American Production and Inventory Control Society.

Weston, J. Fred, and Brigham, Eugene F. *Essentials of Managerial Finance*. Hinsdale, Illinois: The Dryden Press, 1987.

Index